The Bewitched World of Capital

Historical Materialism Book Series

The Historical Materialism Book Series is a major publishing initiative of the radical left. The capitalist crisis of the twenty-first century has been met by a resurgence of interest in critical Marxist theory. At the same time, the publishing institutions committed to Marxism have contracted markedly since the high point of the 1970s. The Historical Materialism Book Series is dedicated to addressing this situation by making available important works of Marxist theory. The aim of the series is to publish important theoretical contributions as the basis for vigorous intellectual debate and exchange on the left.

The peer-reviewed series publishes original monographs, translated texts, and reprints of classics across the bounds of academic disciplinary agendas and across the divisions of the left. The series is particularly concerned to encourage the internationalization of Marxist debate and aims to translate significant studies from beyond the English-speaking world.

For a full list of titles in the Historical Materialism Book Series available in paperback from Haymarket Books, visit: www.haymarketbooks.org/series_collections/1-historical-materialism.

The Bewitched World of Capital

Economic Crisis and the Metamorphosis of the Political

Giacomo Marramao

Edited and translated by
Matteo Mandarini

Haymarket Books
Chicago, IL

First published in 2023 by Brill Academic Publishers, The Netherlands
© 2023 Koninklijke Brill NV, Leiden, The Netherlands

Published in paperback in 2024 by
Haymarket Books
P.O. Box 180165
Chicago, IL 60618
773-583-7884
www.haymarketbooks.org

ISBN: 978-1-64259-991-6

Distributed to the trade in the US through Consortium Book Sales and Distribution (www.cbsd.com) and internationally through Ingram Publisher Services International (www.ingramcontent.com).

This book was published with the generous support of Lannan Foundation, Wallace Action Fund, and the Marguerite Casey Foundation.

Special discounts are available for bulk purchases by organizations and institutions. Please call 773-583-7884 or email info@haymarketbooks.org for more information.

Cover art and design by David Mabb. Cover art is a detail from *Construct 67, William Morris, Fruit/Kazimir Malevich, Square,* acrylic on wallpaper (2012).

Library of Congress Cataloging-in-Publication data is available.

Contents

The Marxism of Crisis and the Political Morphology of Capital 1
  Matteo Mandarini

Note on the Translations 29

1 Introduction 30

2 Councils and State in Weimar Germany (with Guido De Masi) 78

3 The Theories of Breakdown and Organised Capitalism in the Debates of 'Historical Extremism' 121

4 'Theory of the Crisis and the Problem of Constitution: In the Margin to the *Konstitutionsproblematik*' 161

5 Korsch in Italy 191

6 Gramsci's Marxism and the Theory of Transition 206

7 Corporate Pluralism, Mass Democracy and Authoritarian State 215

8 From the Crisis of the 'Self-Organised Market' to the 'Authoritarian State': Notes on the Relationship between Political Economy and *Critical Theory* 233

9 Political System, Rationalisation and 'Social Brain' 263

Bibliography 275
Index 295

The Marxism of Crisis and the Political Morphology of Capital

Matteo Mandarini

Giacomo Marramao's writings of the 1970s, some of which are collected here, were part of a broader reflection by a number of Italian Marxists on some of the most important of the workers' and the communist movements' engagements with the state and with the cultures of crisis to which those movements responded in the first half of the twentieth century. Much of his focus at this time was on:

> the precocious reception, within the 'young Viennese Marxist school',[1] of that culture of crisis that expresses at the highest level the complexity of a capitalism that transforms itself by incorporating the elements of 'science' and 'organisation', and the more properly 'structural' aspect constituted by the process of crisis and disaggregation of the Habsburg State...
> MARRAMAO 1980: 260

This crises of bourgeois society and culture forms the backdrop for the rethinking of Marxism in the period discussed in these writings, but – as we shall see – it will be taken up again within the specific conjuncture in which the Italian workers' movement and its organisations find themselves in the 1970s as well.[2] Indeed, Marramao's work can be said to be characteristic of what Anto-

---

1 But also on the Social Democratic Party in the inter-war period as well as on the early work of the Frankfurt School.
2 The expression the 'culture of crisis' refers to the bourgeois culture of the turn of the nineteenth century in particular, from Nietzsche through the inter-war period in central Europe, including figures as diverse as Mahler, Schoenberg, Weber, Schmitt, Rathenau, Klimt, Dix, Schiele, Spengler, Hofmannsthal, Rilke, Musil, Roth, Kraus, as well as Freud, Wittgenstein, Einstein (the list could be extended much further of course). Perhaps we can summarise most effectively what caught the attention of Marramao and others in this period with the following words from Alberto Asor Rosa: 'Of the great contemporary bourgeois culture and the extraordinary artistic experience of the early 1900s we note: that they are born and develop as the symptoms of an objective *incompleteness* of the bourgeois system and they represent it, not in the way of praise or denunciation, but as a reflection that is matured and transfigured in the rebellion of languages and methodologies' (Asor Rosa 1964: 221–2). So by the culture of crisis, we refer to that historical moment that led from 1848 to the

nio De Martinis and Alessandro Piazzi describe as the attempt to turn the famous 'crises of Marxism' into a *'Marxism of crisis'* (De Martinis and Piazzi 1980: xxii).

After a brief political biographical sketch, I shall turn to a discussion of the theoretical context within which Marramao developed his work on Austro-Marxism, Council Communism, Weimar Social Democracy, and the 'Frankfurt School'. I shall briefly discuss the Italian historiographical and political analysis of this historical period, which took place in the 1970s, before trying to situate his analyses in relation to other important philosophers of the Italian Communist Party (PCI). Arguably, one of the most significant contributions of his work of this period – other than the reappraisal of the workers' movement of the inter-war period and of its intellectuals – is his development of theoretical tools to understand the changing forms, or what he terms the 'morphology', of capitalism in the twentieth century.[3]

Marramao's political and intellectual development took place during an extraordinarily rich period for communist and Marxist thought and practice in Italy. Traversing some of the most important experiences of *Operaismo* (Workerism) as well as the powerful influence, intellectual and political, of the Italian Communist Party and some of its leading intellectuals, even prior to his joining the party in the mid-1970s, Marramao's writings are marked by a focus on the ambiguities of Left-communism's political radicalism and the inescapability of a relation to the bourgeois state.

'recasting of bourgeois Europe' (Maier 1975); a period when the certainties of the earlier structures and ideologies of bourgeois rule began to be undermined by the economic crisis of the final quarter of the century, which introduced new actors onto the stage: the mammoth industrial firm and cartels that put in question the supposed transparency of the market; the growing threat of an urban-based mass working class, and the emerging conflicts between the imperial powers following the late but fast advancing capitalist development of a now unified Germany, the result of which was to be the horrors of the First World War – bringing together industrial slaughter of the conscripted mass of workers, the end of the largest European continental empire, and the emergence of a new model of social and economic development in the east to rival that of the bourgeois epoch. The self-consciousness of the period took the form so admirably summarised by Asor Rosa above in terms of the 'objective *incompleteness* of the bourgeois system'. It is this that forms the backdrop for the attempt to bring together the highest moments of bourgeois reflection on the new capitalist social relations, with those theoretical and practical advances brought about by the workers' movement within this period of crisis of bourgeois order. For a fascinating discussion of this period, in English, focussing in particular on Vienna and the collapse of the Austro-Hungarian Empire, see Janik and Toulmin 1973.

3   Marramao draws this notion of 'morphology' from the 'genetic method' developed by Antonio Labriola (cf, Labriola 1902, pp. 1169–70).

His own political trajectory began in the heady atmosphere of the extra-parliamentary Left and the intellectual current to the left of the Italian Communist Party, *Operaismo*, in the second half of the 1960s.[4] Marramao's first political experiences were formed in the Potere operaiso pisano (Workers' Power of Pisa), the Centro Francovich in Florence and, eventually, between 1969–71 with the largest and most established of the extra-parliamentary Left groups, Lotta continua. Despite their differences, more or less pronounced, these organisations took seriously the Workerist injunction, summarised in Tronti's words from this transcript from an editorial board meeting of *Quaderni rossi* from 1963:

> probably Marx's thesis according to which capital explains everything that lies behind it is no longer true because clearly today there is something that explains capital and which alone can explain capital; that is the working class itself. (Tronti 1963: 291)

It was, therefore, during the period of his militancy with Potere operaio pisano, in particular, that Marramao had formative first experiences of militancy in going to the factory gates to establish relations with workers. This injunction was both political – taking up a position in many ways largely vacated by the PCI within the factory – and intellectual, it was only by understanding the workers that one would understand capital.

At the same time as militating in various formations of the extra-parliamentary Left, establishing long-standing political and intellectual friendships with figures such as Lapo Berti, Claudio Greppi, Adriano Sofri and Guido De Masi, Marramao graduated in Philosophy in 1969 under the supervision of the enormously influential historians and philosopher, Eugenio Garin. Garin would go on to supervise his doctoral thesis, *Marxismo e revisionismo in Italia* (Marramao 1971), which was examined by the Marxist historian (and member

---

4 The more political Workerism that attracted Marramao can be said to emerge from a split within the founding journal of Workerism, *Quaderni rossi*, edited by a socialist, Raniero Panzieri, and communist, Mario Tronti. A number of other figures played an important role in the journal and would go on to be central figures in post-war Marxist and communist thought: most notably Asor Rosa, Rita di Leo, Edoarda Masi, Antonio Negri, Vittorio Rieser, Romano Alquati. In the course of 1963 a split instigated by Tronti took place that would lead to the founding journal of 'political' Workerism, *Classe operaia*. Tronti decided to bring this experience to a close in early 1967, when he came to believe that the breadth and depth of the struggle demanded more than small vanguard organisations (or *'gruppuscoli'*), and that only the Italian Communist Party had sufficient organisational capacity and was sufficiently embedded within the working class to hope to organise the struggle.

of the PCI central committee) Ernesto Ragionieri as well as the philosopher Mario Rossi. During this time, the influence of another Marxist philosopher, Cesare Luporini, would prove equally intellectually fruitful. After completing his thesis in 1971, Marramao left Italy for a period of study in Frankfurt, not returning to Italy until 1975. It was only then that he would become a member of the PCI, remaining within it until the 'svolta della Bolognina' (turn) of 1989.[5]

Marxismo e revisionismo in Italia, Marramao's first book, took up a left critique of Gramsci, following some of the indications in Tronti's early (Della Volpean inspired) critique of the Sardinian Marxist (Tronti 1959). In the course of the 1970s, his writings developed in a continuous – sometimes unspoken – dialogue with the work of a number of those who had traversed the experience of Workerism: some, such as Guido De Masi, who had remained within the extra-parliamentary Left,[6] but also many of those who – in contrast to those such as Negri, Romano Alquati, Sergio Bologna, and others – decided to make a not entirely comfortable home for themselves within the PCI.[7] These were, once again, Tronti, Asor Rosa and, perhaps most importantly for Marramao, Cacciari, a close friend and fellow philosopher. The closeness with Cacciari was no doubt in part due to their generational closeness (Marramao is two years Cacciari's junior, whereas Asor Rosa and Tronti are both more than ten years their seniors),[8] but it ran much deeper to the point that each came – in the course of the 1970s, through their own labours, through different paths and many different theoretical reference points to complementary – though by no means identical – theoretical conclusions.[9]

---

5   Marramao, along with fellow philosopher Massimo Cacciari, were both in favour of the *svolta*, which was first publicly announced in 1989 by the then Secretary of the Partito comunista italiano, Achille Occhetto. He called for a change in the party name so as to declare a new course, no longer wedded to the history of Soviet communism, following the fall of the Berlin Wall. Unlike Cacciari, however, Marramao never joined the *Partito democratico della sinistra* (Democratic Party of the Left) that resulted, arguing that a chance had been missed. Occhetto, he argued, should have worked with Pietro Ingrao, the historic leader of the left of the PCI, to propose a party that should be more open to social movements, trade unions and the different forces of the progressive left in society at large. This opening would, he argues, have prevented the bureaucratisation and particularly the self-referentialism of the political sphere.

6   A significant article written with De Masi appears as Chapter 3 below: 'Councils and State in Weimar Germany'.

7   Adapting the well-worn phrase of Tronti's, we can say that these 'PCI Workerists' operated 'within and against' the PCI.

8   Tronti was born in 1931, Asor Rosa in 1933, Cacciari in 1944 and Marramao in 1946.

9   These complementary philosophical positions would increasingly diverge again in the course of the 1980s and beyond. It will not be the aim of this brief introduction to trace the individual

In the following pages I shall aim to shed light on the underlying reasons for the engagement with German social democracy, Council communism, and Austro-Marxism, all of which – as we shall see – were anything but mere archival investigations aiming to clarify this or that aspect of the workers' movement. The engagement was driven by extremely concrete and immediate, even pressing problems with which the PCI, and its intellectuals and activists, were confronted in this pivotal decade for the Italian workers' movement.[10]

The problem is explicitly defined in an apparent aside in the introduction to a collection of writings of Austro-Marxists and Left socialists that Marramao assembled in 1977. In a section on the debate between Otto Bauer and Hans Kelsen, he states that there is nothing 'scandalous' in drawing an 'analogy' between the terms of that debate and those taking place at the time in Italy if:

> one bears in mind that in both cases the debate on these themes, far from being a merely academic matter, is born of a political conjuncture that puts at the order of the day the relationship between the workers' movement with the problem of the leadership of the state.
> MARRAMAO 1977: 73

This problem, of how the workers' movement or the Party as the representative of the workers' movement should relate to or engage with the bourgeois state, would form the focus of the work of a number of PCI intellectuals; but specifically, and arguably most acutely, it would become a central motif for those thinkers and militants who passed through the experience of *Operaismo* to join (and in some cases re-join) the PCI.

While the PCI can be said in many ways to have already been through a process of adaptation to the demands of the bourgeois state, as a consequence of Palmiro Togliatti's patient and consummate political manoeuvring (and his appropriation of Antonio Gramsci's thinking as the theorist of the 'national-popular' revolution), for many of the *Operaisti* it was precisely this aspect of its practice and ideological commitments that they had subjected to the most savage and withering attacks in the course of the 1960s.[11] It was, therefore, not

---

paths, with their convergences and divergences, but instead to situate Marramao's work in the historical and – principally – theoretical context of the period.

10   The engagement with some Frankfurt School theorists, on the other hand, usefully traces their roots to their engagement with Weimar communist thought and practice.

11   One of the highpoints here is most certainly Asor Rosa's *Scrittori e popolo* (Asor Rosa 1966; my translation of this seminal text, *The Writer and the People*, appeared in 2020 for Seagull

a path that was open to them. For them, the engagement with the bourgeois state, which was the inevitable consequence of their decision to become active in the PCI, was a problem that required a wholesale rethinking of the theory and practice of the workers' movement. This problem was, of course, by no means new and could be traced back to the origins of the politically organised workers' movement in the German Social Democratic Party (SDP).[12] It would be subject to further intense reflection by Austro-Marxists in the inter-war period. The Austro-Marxists, who had specific roles within the government of important regions of Austria itself, most famously in the period of Red Vienna, became the object of Marramao's interest in the mid-1970s, as Enrico Berlinguer's Eurocommunist middle course between social democracy and 'actually existing socialism' was being charted in Italy. Marramao's work of collation and analysis of these writings (translated by his wife and long-time collaborator, Gabriella Bonacchi) during the 1970s, would serve as a critical tool charting the parallels between Eurocommunism and the 'Marxist centre' (Marramao 1980: 242) proposed by Otto Bauer, between social democracy and Bolshevism.[13] The diagnosis of Austro-Marxism's limits and failures would prove to be a warning to the PCI for the course taken.

The exploration of the problem of the relationship of the workers' movement and the state at this time took a number of different forms. Some thinkers, such as Tronti, explored the problem through a reappraisal of the New Deal and social democracy, through a rethinking of the relation between bourgeois state and capital (resulting in the famous – or infamous – lecture on the 'Autonomy of the Political'), or even through a rethinking of the origins and nature of the bourgeois state itself (in his texts on the 'political' Hegel, on Cromwell, and in the anthology of texts on 'power' from the sixteenth to the eighteenth century).[14] Others, such as Rita di Leo, focussed on the concrete problems of state (trans-)formation, the development of industry and worker representation in the course of Soviet development.[15] Even here the focus remained on how the working class (and its representatives) confronted the state and eco-

---

Books). But one should not forget Marramao's own doctoral thesis, which contained substantial critiques of (Togliatti's) Gramsci (Marramao 1971). For a somewhat critical take on this appropriation of Gramsci, cf. Liguori 2012.

12   Although ultimately it can be taken back even further to the influence of Ferdinand Lassalle.

13   'I wrote [the book] *Austromarxismo* in the form of a tragedy [...] It was the best part of social democracy because it remained tied to Marxism' (Marramao in a personal communication, June 2013).

14   Cf. Tronti 1971, 1977a, 1977b, and 1979–82.

15   Cf. R. Di Leo 1970.

nomic development, even if this was (putatively) under socialist conditions. This was also the theme of some important texts by Cacciari and Paolo Perulli on the NEP. Asor Rosa, Manfredo Tafuri, also contributed important work on a number of these themes.

It is not possible here to explore the enormous wealth – and complexity – of theoretical and historical material that this disparate group of thinkers developed in these years. Instead, I wish to focus on some specific aspects of that 'culture of crisis' that we opened with, which form the object and backdrop for Marramao's thinking during this period. These can be summarised under the headings of 'Negative Thought', the 'morphology of capital' and 'the Political'. Aspects that reveal themselves in the cultures of crisis that illuminate the theory of the state, of Party and class relations that are the objects of the Political as the field of intervention, and of its 'morphology'. We shall, therefore, set aside Marramao's thought for a moment and start with a discussion of negative thought before turning to how this intersected with a reconfiguration of the question of the Political that plays such an important role in Marramao's thinking during the period of the writings in this collection. We shall conclude by attempting to draw out some general consequences of his reading of the 'Political and its transformations' (as per the title of one of Marramao's most important books of the period, from which a number of the chapters of the present volume are drawn).

1   Negative Thought

'Sulla genesi del pensiero negativo' (Cacciari 1969) is an example of non-reductivist ideology critique understood as the 'critique of the self-presentation of bourgeois thought inasmuch as it is a constitutive determination of capitalist social relations' (Bertoletti 2008: 13). That is, Cacciari turns to 'negative thought' as the self-consciousness of bourgeois critical thought as it grasps its own structuring by capitalist social relations; a *critique* of the values of synthesis and pacific reconciliation characteristic of dominant bourgeois thought. The critique that it mobilises is – he argues – able to grasp the processes of disenchantment and rationalisation of capitalism that typically are occluded in the fantasy of 'Freedom, Equality, Property and Bentham' (Marx 1990: 280 – the Weberian terms recur repeatedly in all the thinkers we shall be considering).

Negative thought is perhaps best understood in relation to the critique of the Hegelian dialectic of the mid-to-latter half of the nineteenth century most closely identified with the work of Schopenhauer, Kierkegaard and Nietzsche (Cacciari 1969). In Cacciari's challenging and controversial text, which would be followed by numerous others in the course of the 1970s, he argues that negative thought refuses the resolution of conflict, of contradiction that – he maintains – characterises the Hegelian synthesis.[16] On the one hand, he argued, the dialectic was 'isomorphic to the bourgeois form of capitalist development' (Bertoletti 2008: 14); as he writes in 'Pensiero negativo e razionalizzazione':

> The dialectical system is *Wille zur Ohnmacht* [Will to Powerlessness] precisely because it develops forms of overcoming of conflict – because it proposes equilibria-syntheses.
> CACCIARI 1977b: 46

That is, rather than confronting conflict and its systemic causes in the operations of capital, it neutralises them in visions of beatific order, of founding syntheses in which everything has its place. This is well represented in the language of political economy and the 'Eden of the rights of man' (Marx 1990: 280), where rent flows to the landlord as an eternal right, to the capitalist flows profit, and to the worker wages. On the other hand, the dialectic provides a figure for the dialectical reversal – evident in the passage from the expropriation of the proletariat to the point when the 'expropriators are expropriated'. In other words, the dialectic makes contradiction a moment of development of the system, but it also permits the manoeuvre of reversal where the negative moment posits itself as the rationality of development, where not-capital becomes the synthetic moment, the highest *Ratio*, where subject-object become one in – for instance – communist planning. Negative thought, in contrast, is a tradition of, paradoxically, anti-bourgeois bourgeois thought that refuses any promised solace (whether in the dream of the invisible hand of the market that reconciles all differences, or in utopian communism as the transparency of human relationships), recognising instead the centrality of conflict, its permanence, and the necessity of the management of that conflict for capitalist development. Rather than diluting the capital / worker dichotomy with the consoling uto-

---

16   We do not have the space in this introduction to consider whether or not this account of Hegel is legitimate – there are numerous readings of Hegel, from Adorno to Zizek, for which synthesis and pacification fail to adequately encapsulate the extraordinary torsions and acrobatics of speculative philosophy that Hegel's thought permits. Whether or not Cacciari's account of Hegel is legitimate, however, is beside the point. What Cacciari wants to do in his critique, is to elucidate the self-consciousness of capital and the tools that are thereby provided for the workers' movement. In other words, the core of the issue is the diagnosis of synthetic bourgeois utopias and their critique within the self-reflection of capital.

pias of national unity, and other such reactionary nostalgias (characteristic both of left and right, as Asor Rosa argues in his acerbic critique of Togliattian Gramscianism),[17] it looked instead at the realities of nineteenth century development, recognising them as relying upon the increasing expansion of an ever more dense concentration of workers on the one hand, and an ever greater expansion, concentration and consolidation of capital on the other. Negative thought was the attempt to confront without dissimulation the complex conflicts this expansion and concentration produced in the morphology of modernity, observing with disenchanted eyes the relentless drive of capital and technology to consume the human and non-human world, dismantling organic and inorganic life, recombining elements and forms in a juxtaposition that might easily be viewed as chaos by those schooled in nostalgic visions of community, but which to the disenchanted eyes of those schooled in 'rationalised' human society assumed very different formal and material features.[18]

Negative thought stands, therefore, in radical contrast to the bourgeois utopias of pacific totalisation (at home in both much Right and Left thinking), to its attempts to absorb all eccentricity into the system and its development, and

---

17 Cf. Asor Rosa 2020 (1965).
18 Consider the extraordinary description of the coming of the railway to Camden Town in the opening of chapter 6 of Charles Dickens' *Dombey and Son*: 'The first shock of a great earthquake had, just at that period, rent the whole neighbourhood to its centre. Traces of its course were visible on every side. Houses were knocked down; streets broken through and stopped; deep pits and trenches dug in the ground; enormous heaps of earth and clay thrown up; buildings that were undermined and shaking, propped by great beams of wood. Here, a chaos of carts, overthrown and jumbled together, lay topsy-turvy at the bottom of a steep unnatural hill; there, confused treasures of iron soaked and rusted in something that had accidentally become a pond. Everywhere were bridges that led nowhere; thoroughfares that were wholly impassable; Babel towers of chimneys, wanting half their height; temporary wooden houses and enclosures, in the most unlikely situations; carcases of ragged tenements, and fragments of unfinished walls and arches, and piles of scaffolding, and wildernesses of bricks, and giant forms of cranes, and tripods straddling above nothing. There were a hundred thousand shapes and substances of incompleteness, wildly mingled out of their places, upside down, burrowing in the earth, aspiring in the air, mouldering in the water, and unintelligible as any dream. Hot springs and fiery eruptions, the usual attendants upon earthquakes, lent their contributions of confusion to the scene. Boiling water hissed and heaved within dilapidated walls; whence, also, the glare and roar of flames came issuing forth; and mounds of ashes blocked up rights of way, and wholly changed the law and custom of the neighbourhood. In short, the yet unfinished and unopened Railroad was in progress; and, from the very core of all this dire disorder, trailed smoothly away, upon its mighty course of civilisation and improvement'.

to its conception of the rational only as the whole to which all particularity is reduced as elements whose meaning is only given by that whole. Thus, we see, for example, in Hoffman the 'I' not only

> 'breaking' with the other, but with itself and in itself: it projects itself and divides in an infinity of reflections, the synthesis of which [...] is explicitly declared unrealisable [...]. The split [*scissione*] is *present* in every moment [...].
>
> CACCIARI 1969: 136

For Schopenhauer, on the other hand, the dialectic is unable to 'grasp the Grund' (Cacciari 1969: 138), in that the thing-in-itself must remain outside time and un-subsumable under any concrete temporally determined concept – outside of understanding. It is, therefore, an element that cannot be made to function within the system; it remains without, irrevocably severed from it.

> Crisis is revealed precisely by the making absolute of the opposition [*contrasto*]: between the dialectic and the in-itself, between system and subject.
>
> ibid.

This 'glorification of conflict [*contrasto*]' is necessary so as to find 'a language that is not mediated by the needs of the system'; that is 'not submitted to the ends of bourgeois society' (Cacciari 1969: 139 – i.e. to the system as the whole = the rational). It seeks then the 'unmediated, the un-schematised' so as to find the substantive contradictions, real conflicts that underlie modernity. This lucidity, this attempt to shed all illusions of a possible synthetic pacification of conflict, this trans-valuation of all values, beyond good and evil, was what was prized in these thinkers,[19] in which it would be a case then of 'rationalising the world and not ... pointlessly defining for it a *Ratio*' (Cantarano 1998: 326). But at the same time, Cacciari points out that we can see how this vision, though disenchanted, could easily operate as an ideological function of the system itself – this was the ideological block within negative thought itself. For this clarity in refusing contradiction as that which is to be overcome, as a

---

19 To the later triptych of Schopenhauer, Kierkegaard, Nietzsche, Cacciari's later contributions to this reflection on negative thought would add analyses of Heidegger, Hofmannsthal, Lenin, Loos, Rathenau, Weber, Wittgenstein, as well as Schumpeter amongst others (see the essays collected in Cacciari 1977d).

pretext for synthesis, leaves one with a negative understood as the permanence of non-resolution and, therefore, as the permanence of conflict – including class conflict – which can then at best only be *better organised, better managed*, ameliorated.[20] What we are left with is yes, the possibility of restructuring, but a restructuring of the same, a *systemic* restructuring. If the conflicts of the system could be overcome, we would be back with bourgeois consolation, synthesis, the world re-enchanted; but to refuse it, is to re-affirm the system: *amor fati*, and the will to power remains an immanent practice of rationalisation, manipulation, of change within the strictures of the conflicts that compose it.[21]

Weber's and Lenin's reflections on rationalisation combine to supplement the recognition of the inescapability of conflict, thereby directly linking negative thought to the history of the increasing integration and coordination of all social relations of production:

> The system *cannot* maintain itself in dialectical form; the system is, must be and can be, will to power, to which all elements, all parts, all 'resistances' are subordinated. [...] [T]he 'very body' of this will is the contemporary capitalist system.
> CACCIARI 1969: 195, 196

The conclusion of this critique of bourgeois values of synthesis and, more specifically, of the dialectic, was the realisation by bourgeois thinkers that there could be no easy resolution to the conflicts that they encountered. That the massive technological, economic and social transformations of the century would not be overcome from within capitalism. Put differently: not only would the working class have to bear the diremption from its conditions of existence, but the bourgeoisie would have to live with conflict as well – however dominant their class might remain. Moreover, unlike the working class, the bourgeoisie could not even work to overcome conflict by bringing the capital relation to an end, at least not without annihilating itself and its privilege. One might resort to reactionary nostalgias of nationhood, community, and race – symbolic attractors that are always a temptation in the search for stability – but to

---

20   Hence the strong focus on German Social Democracy, Austro-Marxism, etc., that often involves what is at times a celebration of their anti-romantic anti-utopianism, combined with an awareness of their political paucity.

21   We shall return to this idea when we discuss Marramao's discussion of the particular contribution of Austro-Marxism, what we might see as having been a Left appropriation of negative thought.

those bourgeois who wanted to remain with their eyes open to the conflicts of the age, the path chosen would be that mapped most acutely by the 'bourgeois Marx', Max Weber.[22]

The privileged locale, or *topos* for many of those trying to think the new *forms* of rationality and the practices for managing it in the twentieth century, was Weimar Germany. The extensive engagement with this period by historians and militant intellectuals was a return to the crucible of the twentieth century. Not only a crucible in that Weimar's collapse led to the horrors of the second world war, but in the sense that Weimar acted like a vessel of experimentation with the forms of social conflict and order.[23] By turning to some of these analyses, we will see how the pivotal questions of negative thought, the Political and the morphology of capital become coordinates for Marramao's original theoretical contributions.

---

[22] The characterisation of Weber as a Marx for the bourgeoisie is from Albert Salomon (see Mommsen 1974, 47). Some decades later, Tronti would add, 'not the Marx of the bourgeoisie, the Lenin of the bourgeoisie' (interview with Marramao at the Fondazione Basso, on the 19 September 2013). For an extraordinarily rich account of this Weber-Lenin 'axis' in terms of the question of rationalisation-bureaucratisation and the inescapability of conflict, which rather than being supressed (dialectically or otherwise), would need to be *governed*, see Cacciari 1977c, and in particular pp. 120–40. As Cacciari writes: 'It was the political problem of organisation of the *class*-party that came to the fore for both Weber and Lenin. And it did so in analogous manner: party *for power*, within development, synthesis of strategy and tactics, founded on the effective result – the new party. [...] Bureaucracy and the Political presuppose one another. There can no longer be any "pure" Political – and "pure" Bureaucracy would also mean impotence. Bureaucracy and the Political: once again the two guiding concepts of the principle of the organisation of development' (1977c, 131, 133). For a critical but extremely useful account of Tronti's Weberianism, see Farris 2011.

[23] Equally important was so-called Red Vienna. On the back of the significant work of historians such as Enzo Collotti, Gian Enrico Rusconi and Lucio Villari (see as an example the essays collected in Villari 1978), Weimar and Vienna would form favoured spaces of reflection for Marramao (as well as Cacciari, Asor Rosa, Manfredo Tafuri, and others) throughout the 1970s. The similarity, or otherwise, of the conjuncture between Italy in the 1970s and the experience of Weimer and Vienna half a century earlier – a workers' party on the edge of power, a global economic crisis, shifts in the production process bringing about transformations in the composition of the working class, political extremism on the streets – gave this period an unexpected urgency for thinkers and militants in Italy. This fascination would not end in this period. Indeed, Marramao was still contributing important work on Red Vienna over twenty years later (in *Dopo il Leviatano*), to which he would dedicate a substantial chapter: 'La Vienna di Wittgenstein e la Vienna di Bauer', pp. 183–245.

2   The Morphology of Capital

In 'Razionalizzazione capitalistica nella Repubblica di Weimar',[24] Villari argues that the process of rationalisation of Germany's productive system during the Weimar years spread beyond the 'scientific organisation of production and of work' characteristic of Taylorism, to encompass all the productive forces, so that 'from the capitalist producers to the proletariat and to culture [...] they all perceived all manner of possible *concordances* between the instruments of Taylorism and traditional German "rationality"' (Villari 1978: 73 – emphasis added). This extended to the arts, the applied arts (think, for instance, of Bauhaus), literature, music, etc., all of which reflect back the new, 'rationalised' social relations. But of course, if such 'concordances' come about through a historical conjunction, they must remain as unstable and unsettled, and 'German rationality' is as perturbed by these formal transformations, this shifting *morphology* of capital, as bourgeois social relations are themselves.

At the heart of the processes Villari discusses, and that would be discussed by Cacciari and Marramao as well, were the massive German *Konzerne* (cartels) that resulted from Germany's late nineteenth and early twentieth century exponential economic expansion. This was the 'oligopolistic form' (Cacciari 1979: 10) at the heart of the first round of rationalisation that Rathenau theorised in the years preceding the First World War. The processes of rationalisation that he analysed in the final years of the nineteenth century were, in Villari's words, 'exceptional' forms, still at the stage of technico-productive 'experimentation' (Villari 1976: 41). The process that he would then oversee as one of the chief executives of the behemoth AEG and in his role in raw material provisioning and supply for industry throughout the war years, through till his assassination in 1922, was instead the moment when we move from experimentation to rationalisation as an 'organic element of industrial development' (ibid.).[25]

The importance of Rathenau's analyses becomes apparent when contrasted with the processes of a 'rationalisation' characterising the activities of the

---

24   The aim of Villari's paper, which he gave at a conference held in Bologna in 1977 called *Weimar. Lotte sociali e sistema democratico nella Germania degli anni '20*, was to show how the collapse of Weimar stemmed from a loss of confidence in the political institutions to either, on the side of capital, further the free development of capital, and, on the workers' side, to open the path to socialist development. We have already said a little about the first path, Marramao will say a good deal more about the paths chosen for the latter.

25   The extent of this process of rationalisation or socialisation of productive relations in the post-war years will be something to which we return when examining De Masi and Marramao's discussion of council communism ('Councils and State in Weimer Germany').

Dawes Committee, which – as we shall see – is thought of in terms of the 'natural laws' of market exchange.[26] As head of AEG, as senior figure in the ministry for Raw Materials during the war, then in charge of the Commission for Socialisation (1920),[27] and later as Minister for Reconstruction, Rathenau oversaw a process that began to 'dismantle' (Villari 1978: 78) the 'principle of autonomy' of German capitalism from social and political concerns. Cacciari says that Rathenau recognised the *'necessity* [...] of overcoming the form and the conception of the capitalist relations of production characteristic of the "age of liberalism"' (Cacciari 1977a: 347). It is worth quoting in full from Villari's account. Rathenau's work:

> from the opening salvos of the war till his death, was two-sided and convergent: using the technical planning experience accumulated by the large firms to transfer it to all to the productive apparatuses of the nation, expelling any parasitic structures; to use the force of political state rule, further augmented by the needs of war, in order to control the economic, social and cultural development of the nation and subordinating to the collective interests those of individuals and thereby spreading the progressive advances of the technical programming of capitalism for all.
> VILLARI 1976: 49

In contrast, that overseen by the American financier Charles Dawes began by giving the *Reichsbank* autonomy to direct credit provided independently by private investors overseas *only* to those firms with the 'highest productive potential' (Villari 1978: 81). The different ways of financing the German productive base stemmed of course from very different historical and conjunctural causes. However, there were two very different conceptions of development at work here. On the one hand, the idea that the market left to its own devices – with a few tweaks from the *Reichsbank* – would operate as a

---

26 The Dawes Committee was instrumental in raising international funds (from the US, United Kingdom, France) to invest in the German *Konzern*: 'Between 1924 and 1930 the Dawes Plan would make available to German capitalism around ten billion dollars. This was not aid but public and private *loans* for investment or investments *tout court* above all by American companies, but also English, French, Swiss, who found in the German cartels that fertile ground that no other capitalist country was able to make available to the great capacity of United States' finance' (Villari 1978, 82).

27 Cf. Maier 1975, 216–18.

principal of order, as an immanent *ratio*, systemic-synthetic (or what Cacciari had previously called a dialectical moment of 'equlibria-synthesis') that would pacify conflict within the whole.[28] On the other hand, as Cacciari again argues, Rathenau's concern emerges very much from the specificities of the ongoing German debate on the effect on the *political form* of the emerging monopoly or cartel form (*Konzern*), of these 'new collective socio-economic figures and "subjects"' (see 'Introduction' below) that involved both an ever tighter integration of production and circulation – a bourgeois 'socialisation' – and at the same time produced a conflict between these new subjects (between fragments of capital, *Konzern*, and unions). While there was an awareness that such an effect was inevitable, the form that it would take remained undecided, the one certainty being that the effect would not be linear. As Marramao writes, these

> new 'subjects' [constantly unsettled] the established equilibriums, [and] dissolved *in practice* the illusion of an evolutionary coming-together of *socialisation* and *democratisation*.
> ('Introduction', see p. 62)

He goes on to point out how in the 1930s, the state changes both in terms of function but also of structure in order to form and direct development. It does so because it cannot evade the plurality of collective 'subjects' (the *Konzern*, unions, mass parties, etc.) that emerge, each with their own interests and that thereby constitute a terrain of 'permanent conflict' which required a 'political compromise' between these subjects:

> But precisely because it is the fruit of a compromise, economic policy is not *planned* on the basis of *one* single interest (even the 'common' interest) but rather is the result that on each occasion emerges from the conflict between the various 'autonomies' into which the political system is 'constitutionally' divided.
> ('Introduction', see p. 74)

---

28 Or in more common parlance, that would – through the proverbial 'shakeout' of underperforming, inefficient firms – determine which industries should grow and which should 'go to the wall'. This position would, of course, come under severe pressure following the Great Crash and would remain a minority one (some might have thought terminally) until the 1970s, when a combination of elements would come together to revive its fortunes – the results of which can be seen today.

The task was then to understand this as a *political morphology*, the task of which is to map and to manage those 'autonomies', to intervene and structure them, to *form* them and govern them.

The war would give a fundamental impetus to the process of integration and necessary coordination of production and, hence, to the increasingly central role of the state in economic and industrial planning.[29] One of the implications of this shift was that the decisions taken at the level of an increasingly socialised production, circulation and distribution ended up being *political* decisions. While Rathenau was determined to make sure that this new role for the state would not be one to place it in the position of competitor with monopoly capitalism (Cacciari 1977a: 352), according to Cacciari he was unable, even in theory, to resolve the potential sources of conflict between them. So, unable to provide a satisfactory answer to the form that the '"new State", "equal" to the new [socialised] organisation of economic life' (Cacciari 1977a: 359) should take, nevertheless the question he poses is derived from a 'cold and disenchanted analysis of the new form of the relations of production. The centrality of the Political, in the concreteness of its institutions and functions, is an integral part of it' (Cacciari 1977a: 360). It is this role that Marramao is particularly interested in exploring at this time through his reflections on Austro-Marxism and on Council Communism, which emerged in the Weimar period, both of which can be understood as a Left appropriation of negative thought, and as the attempt to open capitalist planning of production to a more proper *socialisation of production*, which would include the political participation of the working class.[30] The reason for doing so was not, as I have already stated, for archival reasons, but for specific, conjunctural reasons linked to the attempt, in the mid-70s, by West-European communist parties to chart a way between social democratic reformist and Soviet-style revolutionary paths to socialism.[31] At the heart of this question was a rethinking of the relationship of the party to

---

29 This was something that Lenin 'celebrated' on his return to Russia in 1917 as the birth of 'state monopoly capitalism', the necessary building block for socialism at the heart of the most advanced of capitalist economies.

30 In contrast to the Kautskyian, and generally Second Internationalist position, which saw the working class as immediately expressing such socialisation, and hence that the very process of development would lead quite naturally, inevitably to socialism, much of left social democracy and Austro-Marxism argued instead that this ignored the central role of the state in the process of socialisation. For this reason, the question of the political control of the levers of bourgeois state power, and hence of the specific relation of the party, as organisation of the working class, to that state, could not be ignored. See Clarke 1991, 308–11 for a brief discussion.

31 Berlinguer held a number of meetings with heads of the French and Spanish communist parties to chart this new course in the middle of the 1970s. This was precisely the time

the institutions of bourgeois democracy. Where better then to look for lessons than to Weimar Germany and Red Vienna? Indeed, a few years later Marramao would call the Viennese inter-war experience the period of the 'most intense reflection on the problem of the relation of the State to democracy' as well as it being the period of Austro-Marxism's 'most widespread influence within the workers' movement' (Marramao 1980: 271). But equally important for Marramao was the Weimar experience of the Council Communists, specifically in terms of a Left alternative to the state-centred plans for socialisation – and as an example of a path different and antagonistic to the state-centred one of social democracy. In order to examine this, I shall briefly contrast the readings of the Councilists given by Cacciari to that of Marramao (and De Masi).

In 1972, Cacciari edited a collection of Lukács' writings from 1920–1, to which he wrote a substantial introduction.[32] In this introduction, Cacciari argued that the council communists:

> failed *objectively* to the extent that they were the expression of class strata, and hence also of outlooks and needs, that are *retarded* with respect to the processes of *Rationalisierung*.
> CACCIARI 1977C: 88

In essence, their analysis was based upon a class of skilled, professional workers and hence a class fraction that was due to be liquidated in the de-skilling process of the new forces of production (those of Taylorism and the assembly line). The process of capitalist restructuring in the course of the large-scale rationalisation of production was to have dramatic effects on the class composition of skilled workers. 'The privileged position, within the cycle as a whole, of the skilled, professional worker, is systematically dismantled' via the process of rationalisation, which acts as

> a plan to increase the *potential* of industry while at the same time defeating any reassertion of the workers' 'control' – incentivising the reproduction of *ungelernte* [unskilled] class strata, opposing them to the traditional 'privileges' of the professional workers, and founding upon them the new processes of production.
> CACCIARI 1977C: 86–7

---

when Marramao was exploring the 'centre Marxism' of Austro-Marxism and when he decided to join the PCI.

32   This introduction was then reprinted in a collection of Cacciari's writings of the period, which is the one referenced here (see Cacciari 1977c).

Only the SDP majority 'attempted to gauge the processes of massification of the relations of production' (Cacciari 1997c: 88), while capital would use it against all attempts bolshevisation, breaking up any vanguard formations and restructuring the process of production to remove any remaining labour hierarchies and differentiations that could interfere with the 'programming and rationalising of production' (Cacciari 1977c: 92). Cacciari goes so far as to speak of capital 'choosing [...] social-democratic organisation so as to realise a "synthesis" between the path of development and the processes of class recomposition' (Cacciari 1997c: 89).

Shortly after Cacciari's intervention, Marramao, writing with long-standing friend and comrade De Masi, took issue with Cacciari's interpretation. Focussing on the 'retarded' development of the class that the Council Communists purportedly privileged, De Masi and Marramao argue that the great processes of capitalist rationalisation and socialisation had already came to an end with the war. Defeat in the war and the onerous reparations agreed at Versailles meant that large-scale German business could only find overseas buyers, 'labour-productivity was the only immediate material resource' ('Councils and State in Weimar Germany'). The result of this was that German capital – *pace* Cacciari, *pace* Rathenau – returned to its pre-war 'heterogeneity'. In short, Cacciari rather 'too enthusiastically accepts capital's ideology' of the ever-forward march of rationalisation, standardisation, homogenisation. The failure of the socialisation commission as early as 1919, after the government neglected to support the socialisation of the mines, showed instead social democracy's '*hegemonic incapacity*'; the result being that processes of rationalisation continued, but were limited to individual firms. Moreover, the leading sectors of the economy *after* the war were not those that had undergone the most intense processes of rationalisation – quite the opposite. It was not, therefore, some purported derivation of Council Communism from a dependence on a retrograde, obsolete level of class composition that was at issue,[33] but rather the failure of social democracy's socialisation strategy, which led theoreticians and militants of the Workers' Councils, and leading representatives of the old social democracy (such as Max Adler), to re-examine the concept of socialisation dropped by the SDP; for it was understood that, through a correct socialisation policy, one could begin to adequately move from the control of production to the control of the territory. Reflections on the Councils highlighted how they were specifically designed to bring together

---

33 A reading that also demonstrates a degree of economism in the relation between economic development, class composition, organisational and political form.

social, economic, organisational and political forms and practices. Hence, in contrast to Cacciari, De Masi and Marramao maintain that in the course of their practical and theoretical struggle, the Council Communist workers:

> expressed their real conditions of existence and their own objective political possibilities (in the absence of an alternative mass organisation able to connect the 'political' to the 'social' level); not the professional stratifications already eliminated by capital's initiative.

We will not outline the nuanced accounts that De Masi and Marramao provide of the thinking and practice of the left social democrats and left-communists (most notably perhaps Adler and Korsch), but we can say that all are concerned with the means to integrate the social and political by means of the 'conscious and organised *intervention* of subjectivity'[34] ('Councils and State in Weimar Germany', p. 88); all are convinced of the decisive need, at a 'determinate moment in the development of the productive forces [...] for the working class to manage the process' ('Councils and State in Weimar Germany', p. 95). That is, they are focused on the:

> will of the working class to take up the rationalisation and planning of the productive process so as to emerge from it as the hegemonic class over other social groups. [...] To transform this need into a science of politics and into a theory of organisation [...].

Alongside the concrete, material difficulty of 'the direction of the party and of the relationship with the [bourgeois] state' (Marramao 1979: 167), we find here also a specific transformation of the *theory* of conflict – which is no longer to be understood as a mediated moment of development (synthesis) that it was for much Second International Marxism[35] – and hence of rationalisation. This new *theory* of crisis subtracts crisis from being a specific moment of an automatic dialectical development, while the new *theory* of the political no longer con-

---

34 Another aspect that increasingly differentiates Marramao from Cacciari is this question of subjectivity in relation to the Political. It is not possible to go into details about this here, but suffice it to say that the 'Subject' was increasingly removed from the rethinking of the Political that Cacciari would develop via Heidegger's critique of humanism (Heidegger 1998); whereas for Marramao the Political would continue to be a terrain that operated *between* collective social subjects (and with reference to them) *and* in relation to the formal levers of the state.

35 Marramao puts the weakness of second international Marxism down to its 'inability to grasp the *determinate* and *profound* meaning of the great transformations of capitalism' (Marramao 1979, 171). It was to this lack that Austromarxism attempted to respond.

ceives of it as an immanent moment[36] whose role is to synthesise and coordinate the conflicts that emerge on the socio-economic plane. Instead, the renewal of the critique of political economy – inflected with negative thought – renders the political a (relatively) autonomous moment of 'translation' between different rationalities, different 'technologies and "specialisms"' ('Introduction', p. 70). We are left with a new 'science of the political' alongside a renewal of the Marxist critique of political economy. What this amounts to is a new approach to the political morphology of capital, of practices and mentalities, in terms of the real interaction of economy and politics, class struggle and institutions, that can never be synthesised, but which exists in permanent conflict, to be managed, coordinated, directed.

3   The Political

In the 1960s, Tronti's 'Copernican Revolution' in Marxism was one that combined Marx with Nietzsche, to which he added the combination of Lenin and Weber (and Marramao would add Carl Schmitt), arguing both for a perspectivism that placed the standpoint of the working class as the privileged one from which the capitalist totality could be understood (rather than starting from capital to explain the working class); and for working class practice as will-to-power, force against force, that was the dynamic, ontological core of social transformation (including the force of capitalist innovation and restructuring itself).

In 1972, Mario Tronti, as ever showing himself to think from extremes,[37] took up yet another heretical stance, arguing for the *autonomy of the Political* from the class relation. By 1967, Tronti's assessment of the level of the class struggle was that the highpoint of the movement of workers (and to an extent students) of the 'Hot Autumn' of 1969 was over, and that the risk was now of the class being isolated. His bold claim, following from this assessment, was that in order that the working class not be confined to the factory, to the space within which it can most effectively and immediately be managed, where its weapons can be most easily captured and contained, the Party (by which he meant the PCI) should operate at a distance from it, independent from it and capture the

---

36   As it was for Rudolf Hilferding for instance (see Marramao 1979, 153–60).

37   'It is well known: I like to think from extremes. To think from extremes is the only way to produce theoretical discoveries. Strong thought in a hard reality. The plane of action is quite another thing. The error is [...] to act from extremes' (Tronti 2009, 64).

highest rungs of the state – a sort of revolution from above – because only the state had shown itself able to intervene in the operations of capital as a whole. On the basis of this political assessment, and a rethinking of the history of capital that consciously contrasted with the classical Marxist account, Tronti argued that instead of a single history of capital, one should think of a 'process of distinction and separation' of capital and State.

> We find ourselves before capital and its state, almost as if they were two parallel histories. *Two parallel histories* that do not always coincide and sometimes even come into conflict.
> TRONTI 1972a: 16

Capital and State, each with its own rules, techniques, machineries that the workers' movement would need to learn to operate through its organisations: party and union. Arguably, the implication of Tronti's position was that not only was the Party autonomous from the class and its interests (although operating *for* the class),[38] but since the tactics of struggle of the working class within the spaces of production were necessarily different from those of the Party within the institutions of the state, then work-place organisations such as unions should be allowed to find their own tactical tools for struggle on the socio-economic terrain.[39] In short, what Tronti was noting, on the basis of both a re-reading of the history of capital and through a conjunctural assessment (these two never far from one another in his work), is that what we

---

[38] The exact nature of an autonomy (usually theorised through shifts in the location of tactics and strategy) that is not yet a complete disconnect remains unclarified in Tronti; it might well be a reason why he would eventually row back from it, given the perhaps practically unpalatable and theoretically irresolvable consequences of retaining too rigid a separation between Party and Class.

[39] It is certainly true that any autonomy of union tactics would be relative, in that *only* the state operates – and has been shown in the past to operate – at a sufficient level of generality to be able to intervene in the operations of capital as a whole (hence the greater autonomy of the political); nevertheless, the emergent differentiation, irreducibility of state to capital, implies strongly that there would need to be a substantial degree of operational autonomy for the union as well. Once again, a reflection of the NEP and the relation of unions to Party and state contained important and suggestive lessons (Perulli 1975, 157–67). That Tronti held back from making this explicit needs interpreting. Did he fear the reaction of his party, or was it rather the extreme point from which he wanted to take his reflection, his epistemo-political standpoint, 'bending the stick', not as Lenin wanted to straighten it (Lih 2006, 25–7), but rather to *produce* precisely the operational autonomy and flexibility he was calling for from the organisations of the workers' organisations?

have is the development of a set of autonomies, which Cacciari and Marramao would rethink through the Wittgensteinian notion of 'language games' (or via the idea of 'technologies' and 'specialisms'), the logics of which are irreducible to one another and, hence, whose autonomy can place the one in conflict with the other as the exigencies of each clash between different language games. Thus, the thinking of Tronti, Cacciari and Marramao followed parallel and intersecting paths over this period. While Tronti's 'autonomies' followed largely from the 'process of separation' – of the distinction between state and capital that he read as emerging most clearly with the culture of crisis of which we have spoken – Cacciari and Marramao focus on the culture of crisis as the period of the separation marked the period of a separation of technologies, disciplinary languages, literary, musical and visual forms, etc. from any natural or artificial unity. The loss of synthesis meant there was no *Ur-grund*, no primal scene encompassing all conflicts of faculties, but, in contrast to Tronti's notion of 'autonomy', for Marramao it was important that in each case the *morphology* of the differing relations should be mapped and managed, both consciously and politically.

As we have seen, then, there were points of contrast between the positions taken by these thinkers (some merely of emphasis, some more substantive). We have outlined one such contrast in the discussion around the Council communists. There is another between Marramao and Tronti, where the former *qualifies* the idea of the autonomy of the Political by stating at the abovementioned Bologna conference on Weimar that Otto Bauer's account of the state had overlooked the '*specific functions* of the Political, of relative autonomy (or better: of the modes of "autonomisation") of its area of action with respect to the dynamic economy–social class' (Marramao 1979: 173). That is to say, the state and the economy could not be understood as purely and simply *autonomous from one another*, but should be understood as *morphologically interwoven*; so that *processes* of autonomisation should be grasped as an *internal transformation*, and

> strategic and organisational problems [should be grasped] setting out from the specific modality in which capitalist transformation and the new morphology of the economy-politics nexus are interwoven with class composition and dynamic as a whole [...].
> MARRAMAO 1979: 188–9

What these processes of autonomisation might be, how they might be related to the changing morphology of capital – to the immanent transformation of capitalist social relations, class composition, organisational forms, mentalities and epistemologies – which may then be registered in the institutions of the state and its administration, cannot be given once and for all, but are always conjunctural. It is always the specific conjuncture that specifies and circumscribes the possible forms of morphological transformation – which would be the central topic of *Il politico e le trasformazioni* (see Chapters 2, 3, 4 and 8 below). And it is this that also sheds light on the specificity of Marramao's Marxism in this period. Marx's critique of political economy was – Marramao argues – concerned with undermining the self-consciousness of capital, its synthetic presentation of its immanent order. If the 'synthetic' presentation provided by political economy were to be allowed to stand, then there would be no need of will, power, the political. Instead, an ordering *Ratio* would reveal itself as – say – an 'invisible hand' leading self-interested rational subjects to the best of all possible worlds.

> *Capital* unveiled and threw into crisis the 'neutralizing' function of the abstraction of exchange, showing the emergence of the 'political', the class antithesis of what the epoch's true 'science of power', Political Economy, had represented as 'non-political': namely, the 'neutrality' of the exchange between capital and labour power.
> (see 'Introduction', p. 40).

More recently, Marramao has stated his differences with the Tronti of this period as being that:

> There is a *specificity* to politics but not an *autonomy*, because politics is always within a *morphē*, a form, a morphology, and hence any political intervention is always within a conjuncture.[40]

A final, crucial point, where the reflections and the political practice of these thinkers come together, is around the role that the Party should play in relation to the bourgeois state. The state must be reconceived as one of those logics (or language games), a tool able to intervene – also through its administrative apparatuses – across the territory; its role is to be able to intervene, to intersect and provide the instrumentation to manage the different logics it encounters:

---

40 Interview with Marramao, 13th June 2013, at the Fondazione Basso Rome.

the logics of class, logics of race and gender, of culture, of science, etc. The role for the Party, on the other hand, is conceived as the true space of the Political within the morphology of twentieth century capitalism, the aim of which is to take command of the state and / or its administrative institutions; to be the *agent* of intervention in these multiple logics, irreducible to any ordering *Ratio*, so as to manipulate, coordinate them, appropriating them in the '*sectarian*' service of the development Party hegemony – hegemonic because most capable of 'translating', that is, aligning, the different language games in such a way as to escape their disaggregation and their subordination to any singular, ideological, synthetic logic (such as that of capital: the market, or that of the State: bureaucracy).[41] As Cacciari explains this reconceived role for the party as the element of the Political:

> The Political prevents an 'autonomy', a specific form of production [from being able to] establish itself as Law. For if it were to do so, it would block the process of trans-formation [...]. For this reason, the Political is not neutral, but is a specific activity, a specific technique, functional to the continual mutation of the reciprocal boundaries, so that such a dynamic is not interrupted by the pre-dominance of any one game.
> CACCIARI 1978a: 133–4[42]

The state wants to be the neutral space of coordination of the different languages, but is only one language amongst multiple others, whose only privilege is that it is extensive enough to intervene in them all.[43] The Party, however, was to be the tool, the 'specific technology' whose task is to both block any one regional logic from dominating, while at the same time appropriating the space of intervention for itself. Between the state and the regional powers distributed across the social body there is a 'reciprocal influence'; it is in the gap between the two that a '*positive and productive* practice of crisis as a new space of "*constitution*" should be sought out and trialled' ('Introduction' p. 75); the party is the agent of that practice.

---

41   'As a consequence, the problem of hegemony came to coincide – for the capitalist class no less than for the working class – with the question of *construction* (and continual redefinition) of a necessarily composite ruling bloc' ('Introduction' p. 74).

42   For a further, extremely dense but stimulating account of the relation between autonomy, state, and decision, See Cacciari 1978b, specifically pp. 54–61.

43   It should not be conceived of as different in kind: the 'state-form is, in fact, nothing other than the "codification" of a plurality of power relations disseminated across the various segments of the "social brain", from institutions to "specialised" spheres' ('Introduction' p. 75).

4   Conclusion

In conclusion, what can we say today about this model of competing autonomies, specialisms, technologies and the Political as the space of intervention, of their '*sectarian*' coordination, preventing the rise to dominance of any one?

Two things: on the one hand, yes, autonomies remain and are even extended; no predetermined coordination, no automatic virtuosity to conflict (whether for capital or for antagonistic classes) as exists in certain readings of the dialectic; they persist but as increasingly fragmented – a fragmentation that hampers capital too, since it is only through the struggles of its enemy that even capital knows itself.[44] On the other hand, the space of the Political has been vacated, evacuated, with even the Left, in many of its most radical guises, preferring a space of immanent, (socio-cultural) struggle where the space of the Political increasingly resembles that of civil society, Hegel's 'system of needs', against the relation to the 'transcendent', to that relation to the state, to the only form of (failed) 'totality' – other than the structurally always incomplete one of capital – that we know. Thanks to this evacuation, one of the autonomies, of the Ratios, of those language games has come to predominance, turning the 'games into paradigms' (Cacciari 1978a: 134): that is the game of free-market capitalism, a game that has, like all games, 'one-law-of-its-own and *only* this one' (Cacciari 1978a: 126); but in its case it has been more effective than most in trying to reduce the irreducible heterogeneity of all the others to its one law. This is an endless task but one for which it appears to have endless patience.

Whether or not the Party remains *the* form of the Political is as yet unclear, but that language game, that technology, that *form*, that morphological force able to straddle, to translate, to coordinate the different autonomies is sorely lacking – and what is perhaps worse, the very the awareness that it is missing is lacking. With that we are without the initial impulse required to produce the form of the Political, of its tools for action and change; we lack that urgency to produce 'the catastrophe in the sense of the radical subversion of form, the mutation of form'.[45] Perhaps not all is lost, however. As Tronti writes in one of his recent collections of interviews and essays: 'He who hopes, waits; she who despairs, acts' (Tronti 2011: 55). Marramao's writings of the 1970s were not a counsel of despair, and yet, in turning a suitably disenchanted gaze on the first substantive engagement of the workers' movement with the bourgeois state

---

44   'Workers' struggles are an irreplaceable instrument of capital's self-consciousness; without them, it cannot see, cannot recognise its adversary, and so does not know itself' (Tronti 1971, 284–5).

45   Interview with Marramao at the Fondazione Basso in Rome, the 13th of June 2013.

and the first attempts to chart a middle course between reform and revolution, between social democracy and bolshevism, he was able to underline that, despite the failure of that attempt, there was no univocity in the relationship of socialisation and democratisation. Instead, one would need to 'to plan the forms of a possible convergence between political *participation* and *decision-making*, and to do so outside of any abstract exercise in institutional modelling' ('Introduction' p. 63).

Bibliography

Asor Rosa, A. 1964, 'La fine della battaglia culturale', in G. Vacca, *Politica e teoria nel marxismo italiano 1959–1969*, De Donato, Bari 1972.
Asor Rosa, A., 1966, *Scrittori e popolo*, Samonà e Savelli, Rome.
Asor Rosa, A., 2020, *The Writer and the People*, Seagull, London / Kolkota.
Bertoletti, I. 2008, *Massimo Cacciari. Filosofia come a-Teismo*, Edizioni ETS, Pisa.
Cacciari, M. 1969, 'Sulla genesi del pensiero negativo', *Contropiano*, 1969, 1.
Cacciari, M. 1977a, 'La Nuova Economia di Walter Rathenau', *Democrazia e diritto*, XVII: 347–60.
Cacciari, M. 1977b, 'Pensiero negativo e razionalizzazione. Problemi e funzione della critica al sistema dialettico', in *Pensiero negativo e razionalizzazione*, M. Cacciari, Marsilio Editori, Venice.
Cacciari, M. 1977c, 'Sul problema dell'organiszazione. Germania 1917–21', in *Pensiero negativo e razionalizzazione*, M. Cacciari, Marsilio Editori, Venice.
Cacciari, M. 1977d, *Pensiero negativo e razionalizzazione*, M. Cacciari, Marsilio Editori, Venice.
Cacciari, M. 1978a, 'Critica della "Autonomia" e problema del politico', in *Crisi del sapere e nuova razionalità*, ed. V.F. Ghisi, De Donato, Bari.
Cacciari, M. 1978b, 'Trasformazione dello Stato e progetto politico', *Critica Marxista*, 5: 27–61.
Cacciari, M. 1979, *Walter Rathenau e il suo ambiente*, De Donato, Bari.
Cacciari, M. and P. Perulli, 1975, *Piano economico e composizione di classe. Il dibattito sull'industrializzazione e lo scontro politico durante la NEP*, Feltrinelli, Milan.
Cantarano, G. 1998, *Immagini del nulla. La filosofia italiana contemporanea*, Bruno Mondadori, Milan.
Clarke, S. 1991, *Marx, Marginalism and Modern Sociology*, MacMillan, London.
Collotti, E. 1978, 'Italia e Weimar: aspetti di una polemica e limiti di certe analogie', *Italia Contemporanea*, 2: 5–18.
De Martinis, A., A. Piazzi, 1980, 'Alle origini dell'autonomia del politico', in *Soggetti Crisi Potere*, M. Tronti, Capelli Editore, Bologna.

De Masi, G and G. Marramao 1976, 'Consigli e Stato nella Germania di Weimar. Note storiche per una riflessione teorica', in *Problemi del Socialismo*, 4th series, a. XVII, n. 2, April–June.

D. 1970, *Operai e sistema sovietico*, Laterza: Bari.

Farris, S. 2011, 'Workerism's Inimical Incursions: on Tronti's Weberianism', *Historical Materialism*, 19.3: 29–62.

Heidegger, M. 1998, 'Letter on Humanism' in *Pathmarks*, W. McNeill (ed.), Cambridge University Press, Cambridge.

Janik, A. and S. Toulmin, *Wittgenstein's Vienna*, Touchstone Books, New York.

Labriola, A. 2014, 'In memoria del *Manifesto* dei comunisti' (1902), in *Tutti gli scritti folosofici e di teoria dell'educazione*, edited by L. Basile, Bompiani: Milan.

Liguori, G. 2012, *Gramsci conteso. Interpretazioni, dibattiti e polemiche 1922–2012*, Editori Riuniti, Rome.

Lih, L. 2006, *Lenin Rediscovered: What is to be Done? in Context*, Haymarket Books, Chicago.

Maier, C.S. 1975, *Recasting Bourgeois Europe: Stabilization in France, Germany, and Italy in the Decade after World War I*, Princeton University Press, New Jersey.

Marramao, G. 1971, *Marxismo e revisionismo in Italia. Dalla 'Critica sociale' al dibattito sul leninismo*, De Donato, Bari.

Marramao, G. 1977a, 'Saggio introduttivo', in *Austromarxismo e socialismo di sinistra fra le due guerre*, La Pietra, Milan.

Marramao, G. 1977b, 'Democrazia industriale e "rivoluzionamento del diritto" in Korsch', *Democrazia e diritto*, XVII: 361–72.

Marramao, G., 1979, *Il Politico e le trasformazioni*, De Donato, Bari.

Marramao, G., 1980, 'Tra bolscevismo e socialdemocrazia: Otto Bauer e la cultura politica dell'austro-marxismo', in *Storia del marxismo*, Vol. 3.1, Einaudi editore, Turin.

Mommsen, W.J. 1974, *The Age of Bureaucracy: Perspectives on the Political Sociology of Max Weber*, Basil Blackwell, Oxford.

Rusconi, G.E. 1975, 'Weimar: un modello di crisi per l'Italia degli anni settanta?', *Quaderni di Sociologia*, 1–2: 5–54.

Tronti, M., 1963, 'Tronti, la rivoluzione copernicana' in *L'operaismo degli anni sessanta. Da Quaderni rossi a Classe operaia*, edited by G. Trotta and F. Milana, Derive Approdi, Rome 2008.

Tronti, M. 1959, 'Alcune questioni intorno al marxismo di Gramsci', in *Studi Gramsciani*: 305–21.

Tronti, M. 1971, *Operai e capitale*, Einaudi editore, Turin.

Tronti, M. 1977a, *Sull'autonomia del politico*, Feltrinelli, Milan.

Tronti, M. 1977b, *Stato e rivoluzione in Inghilterra*, Feltrinelli, Milan.

Tronti, M. 1979–1982, *Il Politico*, vol. 1 & 2, Feltrinelli, Milan.

Tronti, M. 2009, 'Politica e cultura' in *Non si può accettare*, ed. P. Serra, Ediesse, Rome.

Valiani, L. 1970, 'La sinistra socialista nella crisi finale della Repubblica di Weimar', *Rivista Storica Italiana*, 82, 3: 704–13.

Villari, L., 1976, 'Crisi del capitalismo e autocritica borghese: Walter Rathenau', *Studi storici*, 17.1.

Villari, L. 1978, 'La razionalizzazione capitalistica nella Repubblica di Weimar', in *Weimar. Lotte sociali e sistema democratico nella Germania degli anni '20*, ed. L. Villari, Il Mulino, Bologna.

Villari, L. (ed.) 1978, in *Weimar. Lotte sociali e sistema democratico nella Germania degli anni '20*, ed. L. Villari, Il Mulino, Bologna.

Note on the Translations

This collection brings together a number of writings from the 1970s and early 1980s by the Italian philosopher Giacomo Marramao, relating to Council Communism, Austro-Marxism and early Critical Theory. Some of these were initially translated for the journal *Telos*, although these have all been revised for the current volume. Three other pieces are published here for the first time and translated by David Broder with Matteo Mandarini.

The pieces have not been arranged in accord with the chronology of their composition, but according to the broad historical chronology of their objects of study.

CHAPTER 1

Introduction

'Capitalism', Schumpeter wrote in 1928, was in 'so obvious a process of transformation into something else, that it is not the fact, but only the interpretation of this fact, about which it is possible to disagree'.*,1 The aim of this book is to critically document the degree, intensity and characteristics of this 'disagreement' within the Marxist field. The immediate rationale behind the studies gathered together here,2 which were composed over the last six years, springs from the general assumption that the passage from the 1920s to the 1930s highlighted a critical point, an incandescent laboratory from which conflicts burst forth and tendencies took shape whose offshoots and consequences seem all the more relevant to the current crisis. Obviously, this goes for *theory* no less than for *praxis*, for the ideas of 'planning', 'development' and 'transformation' no less than for the experiences that *social actors* actually accomplished.

All the essays – while revealing differences of emphasis, self-corrections and internal revisions – bring into focus, from different angles, the terms in which the various versions of Marxism (or, more simply, 'Marxisms', as in the now widely-established usage) confronted the relationship between the forms (mutations of form) of politics and the transformations of capitalism. For this reason, we believe these texts make for something more than a mere collection of essays and instead can be said to represent the balance-sheet of a series of investigations and debates. We have preferred, then, to organise them historico-thematically, rather than according to the chronological order of their first appearance. That no definitive proposal springs from this balance-sheet – they but outline future hypotheses and problems to be worked on – will be clear enough from a simple consideration of the rhapsodic character of the study

---

* [From *Il Politico e le trasformazioni. Critica del capitalismo e ideologie della crisi tra anni Venti e anni Trenta*, Bari 1979 – editor's note.]
1 Schumpeter 1928, p. 385.
2 [Three other chapters from this book are translated here: 'The Theories of Collapse and Organised Capitalism in the Debates of "Historical Extremism"' (originally chapter one part one); 'Theory of Crisis of the Problem of Constitution' (part one chapter two); and 'From the Crisis of the "Self-Regulated Market" to the Authoritarian State. Notes on the Relationship Between Political Economy and "Critical Theory"' (chapter one part two). Much of what Marramao says regarding the essays in *Il Politico* is true of all the essays translated in this collection – editor's note.]

and the intentional self-limitation of the themes (by transversal or sectional 'cuts') from which the various essays proceed.

Another of the principal reasons for gathering these studies together was rooted in the conviction that if – on the one hand – Norberto Bobbio's exhortation to put the question of the 'political theory of Marxism' *radically* in discussion has a liberatory rather than academic character,[3] it could – on the other hand – receive an adequate response only on the terrain of the confrontation of the workers' movement with the great processes of capitalist transformation and of the impact of the Political *in* and *on* these processes. Here, we need to be specific about two points of 'method'.

First, one must decisively reject the tendency – ever more commonplace in Italian commentaries in recent years – to treat the terms 'Marxism' and 'workers' movement' as if they were synonyms. Typical of this tendency is the method of 'reduction to a system' that homogenises – through an arbitrary act of violence against both history and theory – the multiple expressions of a political-cultural phenomenon to an undifferentiated unity. To this operation of 'reduction to a system' corresponds a particularly rigid univocal representation of the relationship between theory (Marxism) and praxis (workers' movement – with its experiences of struggle and its 'institutional outcomes'): the workers' movement as the faithful (and thus the only possible) realisation of Marxism. It is clear that this procedure left intact – simply turning on its head – the justificatory schema sedimented in the 'self-consciousness' of the vulgate that was hegemonic in the Second and then the Third International: theory turned into a tool of tactics, Marxism petrified into a 'science of legitimation'.[4] In fact, already at the beginning of the twentieth century, the mass workers' movements in the West were clearly not a homogeneous bloc but rather a complex agglomeration of socio-cultural factors. At the same time, during the rise of the Second International there was a pluralisation of Marxism and, consequently, a multiplication of the points of intersection between 'revisionism' and 'bourgeois' social science. In the first part of this volume we sought to bring to light the extent to which these phenomena formed a context interacting with the new tendencies of capitalist development taking shape already in the Great Depression years of 1873–96, and the intensity with which this complicates the diagram of relations between Marxist intellectuals' theoretical elaborations and the practical choices of the workers' parties.

---

3   I am referring, of course, to the now famous articles with which Bobbio opened the debate in *Mondoperaio* in 1975, later republished in full in the volume *Il marxismo e lo Stato*.
4   The expression is from Oskar Negt: see Negt 1969.

Second, it is necessary to free ourselves from the 'philosophy of history' implied in both the interpretative and prescriptive schema of the 'crisis-expansiveness of Marxism', according to which, through some miraculous cyclical motion, every time that Marxism goes into crisis it is possible to overcome this crisis by drawing Marxism back to its original source and developing its original impulses. As I have argued elsewhere,[5] this optimistically expansive vision of the 'Marxist cycle' risks playing a consolatory function – a scientifically and politically defensive one – that drastically simplifies, despite its claim to being 'dialectical', a far more complex and multi-faceted series of events. The now centennial itinerary of Marxism has not been only a matter of crises and developments-realisations by way of various 'returns to Marx'; it has also been marked by irrevocable *falls* and the *persistence* of those achievements that have been 'internalised', as true and proper points of no return by the most advanced and perceptive part of 'bourgeois' thinking, to the extent of becoming the heritage of the contemporary world (and of common sense).

Similarly inadequate is the linear schema – substantially univocal – that underpins the interpretative polarisation (the 'official' and the 'heretical' versions) that reduces the relations between Marx and Marxism to the categories of 'development' or 'deformation'. Again, the real picture of these relations is rather more discontinuous and diverse than would appear from these ideological assumptions, although it is true that one part of Marxism (or some 'Marxisms') has in many respects deformed Marx, it is likewise true that there have been many Marxist theorists who did not merely 'return to Marx' (this itself being a way – perhaps a more sophisticated and elegant one, but no less baleful for that – of 'deforming' Marx); rather, they tried to redefine his theoretical postulates, following the impetus given to political research by the processes of transformation of scientific thinking in the course of this century.

These preliminary points should have clarified the perspective from which the following essays will try to shed light on certain moments of theoretical elaboration, emblematically expressing the directions that set off from the various points of contact and intersection between Marxism (understood in a broad sense, including its 'critical' variants such as the Frankfurt School) and the developments in the socio-political sciences upon which Central European culture drew. We must now, even if only schematically, reflect on the value of the analyses developed here and on the not-insubstantial modifications to the frameworks that sustained them.

---

5   See the final essay of this collection, 'Political System, Rationalisation, and "Social Brain"'.

1 Methodological and Political Aspects of the 'Crisis of Marxism'

In the first chapter of the second part and in the second chapter of the first part (the oldest essays in this collection, drafted between late 1972 and 1974, and in part in the opening study of this volume),[6] I strongly highlight the efforts of such Marxist theorists as Henryk Grossman, Paul Mattick and Michal Kalecki, who sought to 'reactivate' the categorial framework of the critique of political economy, developing its *dynamic* aspect. Although I am still convinced of the central importance of this aspect, today I would substantially revisit my evaluation of the first two authors, both in terms of their methodological premises and how far their models have 'held firm' faced with the novelties emerging from the 'great transformation'[7] – and thus in terms of their capacity to establish, even if indirectly, an effective connection with analysis of the *political forms* of the crisis. In any case, the reasons behind this partial rectification of my evaluation lie upstream of my historical-critical judgment on Grossman and Mattick's contributions. They depend, that is, on a substantial further examination and revision of my previous position concerning the 'expansive' potentials of a critique of political economy (in the orthodox Marxist understanding of the term), the theoretical key adequate to understanding the new 'structural' and 'phenomenological' configurations of contemporary capitalism.

Here, I must, however, note that my now changed standpoint (which is especially evident in the theoretical framework underlying the final chapter, on Alfred Sohn-Rethel and the political-historiographical debate on the nature of National Socialism [not translated for this volume – Editor's addition]) only in a minimal degree concerns the problems of 'reconstructing' Marx's scientific model. These latter problems can be considered largely exhausted after the numerous post-WWII contributions and debates on the logic of *Capital*: it is today impossible to think of further development on this terrain, except in terms of critical-textual integration and philological precision. Rather, this difference of standpoint mainly concerns historical-epistemological position and, thus, the vexed question – to which we shall repeatedly return – of the relationship between the critique of political economy and the critique of politics.

In this regard, I should say in advance that I have always considered the obsessive search for a 'derivation' (*Ableitung*) of the state-form from the logico-categorial apparatus of the critique of political economy, which made its ap-

---

6 [Chapter 1, part 2: cf. below 'Political Economy and Critical Theory'; for chapter 2, part 1: cf. 'Theory of the Crisis of Problem of the Problem of Constitution'; cf. also 'The Theories of Collapse and Organised Capitalism in the Debates of "Historical Extremism"' – editor's note.]
7 Polanyi 1944.

pearance in the West German debate of the early 1970s, to be sterile – a mark of that political subalternity that mistakes the search for theoretical autonomy with self-isolation in a ghetto cut off from the most advanced circuits of contemporary scientific and cultural debate.[8] Already in the above mentioned essays, which were situated within these debates and polemicised against post-Frankfurt-school tendencies (diametrically opposed to the *Ableitung* hypothesis) to reduce the analysis of political forms to classically empiricist terms, I took a stance against the flattening of the critique of politics onto the critique of political economy. I emphasised instead that in the mature Marx, the dialectic far from operating as a general law of history was critically restricted to *Darstellungswiese*, to a 'method of presentation'. The relationship between categorial metamorphosis and the critique of politics could not then be formulated in the mechanistic terms of linear dependence-derivation, but rather in the constructive-projective ones of 'constitution'. This is not to deny that my position at that time conceived the two moments as being *absolutely concomitant with one another*, establishing a sort of bilateral correspondence between them. That is to say, there could be no historically and morphologically determinate science of politics without a development or reactivation of the categorial framework of the critique of political economy. The former was thus ultimately, if not a direct emanation of the latter (as within the 'technicians' of the *Ableitung*), then closely interdependent with the latter's potential to explain the morphology of capitalism. I then had no doubts as to this potential, and thus established a sort of one-to-one relationship between the 'morphological moment' and the level of the critique of political economy. This type of position continued to characterise the Italian Marxist debate until recent years, when, in the late 1970s, a substantial break took place between Historicism and Della Volpism, and through a clear theoretico-political turn it adopted the problematic of the social formation as its object.[9]

What has now gone into crisis is this very one-to-one relationship: the certainty that the critique of political economy is intrinsically able to function as an *explanans* of the morphology of contemporary capitalism. The rapid evolution of the debate in recent years, under the pressure of real problems, today poses as a priority the task of relativising the scientific project advanced in *Capital* and *Theories of Surplus Value* from the Marxist standpoint as well. I too am of the view that this can only take place by way of an epistemologically updated engagement. I do not believe, however, that we can easily 'settle

---

8 These issues can be found discussed in the journals *Das Argument, Probleme des Klassenkampfs* and *Die Gesellschaft*.

9 For a critical discussion of this turn, see my essay 'Dialettica della forma e scienza della politica' in *Critica Marxista*, 6, 1975.

accounts with Marx' through a critique that starts out from an equivalence between the themes of 'fetishism' and of 'alienation' (which correspond to different phases of Marx's development, which are not necessarily opposed, as Althusser would have it, but in any case, very contextually determinate). Still less do I believe that we can claim to have finished the discussion on the logic of *Capital* once and for all just by reproaching Marx for a presumed failure to distinguish between 'dialectical contradiction' and 'real opposition'.[10] This is certainly not the place to once again take up these problems. For me it suffices to recall that the current of studies going from Otto Morf and Roman Rosdolsky to the more recent research by Helmut Reichelt and Hans-Georg Backhaus has rigorously delimited the meaning and the role of the 'dialectic' in the critique of political economy: a meaning and role that play out only *within* the dynamic structure of the 'method of presentation'. The dialectical form of 'representation' is, for the mature Marx, *the only one* adequate to its object – the 'essential' preserves of the capitalist mode of production – and expresses a transformation process marked by discontinuities and internal ruptures – the metamorphoses of categories – through which is constituted the reign of the value-form, from the level of direct production to the overarching social level of the system's reproduction.

At this point, one might legitimately raise the question of the historically conditioned nature of the 'essentialist' epistemological framework to which Marx's programme makes reference. But to avoid any linguistic confusion, we need here to get to grips with the specific modalities in which this paradigm is presented and operates within the categorial scaffolding of Marx's *science*.

Marx's 'essentialism' should not be flattened onto a humanistic and romantic-communitarian conception of alienation. The outcome of the *Enthüllung*, Marx's unveiling of the world of commodities, does not coincide with the 'rediscovery, beneath the mask of fetishized objectivity, of the alienated human subject' – as Colletti argued in 1968,[11] in only apparent paradoxical convergence with the young Lukács's analysis of reification. On the contrary, it coincides with the denunciation of a *real separation inherent to the capitalist mode of production* (in its historically determinate, transient character) and to its fundamental law of movement: from the circular movement of decomposition-subsumption (under the rule of exchange value) to the cyclical dynamic and the (irrepressible) tendency to crisis. I do not exclude the possibility of retra-

---

10   Cf. L. Colletti, 'Marxism and the Dialectic', in *New Left Review*, I, 93, September–October 1975.
11   Colletti 1969, p. 89.

cing (and documenting) the presence in Marx of nostalgia for the organic unity of the *Gemeinschaft* (*à la* Tönnies), which would indeed explain the utopian reverberations of his ideas of the extinction of the state and the self-government of the producers. The persistence of such 'nostalgia' could, however, only be discovered through a complex analysis of the socio-cultural habitat within which Marx lived and operated, and it seems absolutely inadmissible to try to 'deduce' it from a 'logical flaw' underpinning his system.

It is no less misleading to interpret the essentialist paradigm as a generic 'substantialism' or 'naturalism', the manifestation within the capitalist formation of a 'natural law' that exists independently of the historical mode of production.[12] This thesis, just like the discourse on the erroneous character of dialectical logic, runs the risk of ignoring the *dynamic aspect* of Marx's theory of capitalist development, understood as an asymmetrical and discontinuous process of valorisation-transformation. The question that really needs to be posed is: what are the epistemological limits conditioning Marx's great innovation-idea of 'critique' as the dissolution of political economy's pretence to scientific-natural objectivity and as 'disenchantment' of the supposed natural-eternal character of the capitalist mode of production?

The complexity of the problem lies entirely in the fact that it is impossible to separate the 'metaphysical' from the 'scientific', the 'critical' from the 'analytical'. Marx's 'essentialism' is at one with his theory of the capitalist process as *permanent contradictoriness and production of crises*, as a cyclical chain of ruptures-transformations, as a 'connection of crises' (*Krisenzusammenhang*).[13] The aporia in Marx's approach is to be found, rather, in the *deductive character* of the process by which he gradually gets to grips with the commodity form. My position is much closer to those who recognise the historical limit of Marx's efforts to be that of the 'classical' epistemological framework to which his theory of capitalist development as a dynamic of crisis-transformation continues to refer.[14] The impact of his theoretical innovation is thus smothered by a classical (Galilean-Newtonian) idea of science, in which the examination of the

---

12 See Lippi 1979.
13 I contend that my reconstruction of certain passages of the critique of political economy in the essay appearing here as 'Theory of Crisis and the Problem of Constitution', is still an accurate one. Today [1979], however, I would, emphasise much less the potential implications of critique of politics.
14 On this specific point see Veca 1977 and, more generally, the important contributions to the epistemological debate of recent years in Gargani 1975, G. Giorello (particularly Giorello 1976), Mondadori 1978, and Santambrogio 1978. For a first balance sheet of this debate, see Curi (ed.) 1978.

'laws of movement' – which objectively represent the historically transitory nature of the mode of production founded on the exchange of commodities (the law of the tendency of the rate of profit to fall) – is rooted in the traditional distinction between the 'essential core' and 'outward appearances' of things: 'all science would be superfluous if the form of appearance directly coincided with their essence'.[15]

But what consequences follow for understanding the capitalist transformations actually taking place and for the role the Political plays within them? It is again necessary to proceed by making precise distinctions, casting aside the inevitable risks of schematicism.

The limits of Marx's 'essentialism' were already criticised, as is well-known, by Marginalist theorists in the last years of his own century.[16] The fact that this attack coincided with the phase of capitalist reorganisation following the 1873–96 Great Depression and the explosion of the controversy over revisionism is, without doubt, of crucial significance and condemns to rapid obsolescence any attempt to locate the key to these disputes in the separate field of the history of ideas. Equally remarkable, however, is the fact that Bernstein – negatively conditioned by Kautsky's vulgarisation of historical materialism – too hastily attributed the predictive shortcomings of Marx's theory to the pitfalls of the dialectic. In this sense, the Histomat of the Second International appears as the direct antecedent of the Third International's Diamat. Its retarding influence was such as to bridle for a long time the liberatory potential implicit within the revisionist polemic: it would be necessary to wait for the 'second generation of Marxists' before the complex problems inherent to 'Marx's system' could be addressed with politico-cultural openness and more adequate methodological tools.

The neoclassical critique of Marx, though on the one hand presenting the undoubted advantage of posing the question of the epistemological *Hintergrund* of *Capital* (thus indirectly bringing out the deterministic naivety of the Cunowian and Kautskyian vulgarisation), has its own limitations in the rigid symmetry it establishes between classical physics and 'Marxist science' under the banner of the 'crisis of foundations'. As such, it loses what I above called the *dynamic side* of Marx's theory: the 'representation' of capitalist development as a cyclical process of alteration-transformation of the plane on which the simple reproduction of the system is organised (it is no coincidence that many years afterwards, a 'bourgeois' scholar of the standing of Schumpeter felt the need to

---

15   From Marx 1981, p. 956.
16   See Cacciari 1976, pp. 11–29.

recover this aspect of Marx – precisely as he polemicised against the neoclassicists – as being the 'one great attempt' to produce an endogenous theory of development, based upon the analysis of factors internal to that change).[17]

Nevertheless, every transformation can and must – according to Marx – become the object of a *causal explanation* through recourse to the 'essence' of the mode of production. Hence the relation of perfect adequacy that he establishes between the *critique of political economy* and the scientific explanation of the *morphology of capitalism*. In this schema – which *derives* the 'laws of motion' from the 'essential core' and then, from these, the system's fundamental tendency towards breakdown – political crisis is presented as a dependent variable of the crisis of the relations of production, precisely insofar as the critique of politics is considered a direct emanation of the critique of political economy. The political moment is thus configured as concentrated violence and an instrument of class rule (the complex of apparatuses of repression), or as the linear expression of a relation of force already established in the economic-productive sphere – but this only in transitory situations of equilibrium, characterised by the executive's 'momentarily becoming autonomous'.[18] The absence, in Marx, of any theory or positive analysis of the institutional forms and functions of the Political does not therefore point to something missing or a 'lacuna' in his overarching system, but is, instead, the consequence of the particular modalities by which this system itself was 'constructed'.

In this context, worthy of particular attention is the interpretative hypothesis that finds in *Capital* the decisive critique of a 'specialism' – political economy – whose internal contradiction it brings to light.[19] The reliability of this hypothesis could be indirectly strengthened by Carl Schmitt's claim – made in his 1929 talk 'Das Zeitalter der Neutralisierungen und Entpolitisierungen' – that the economic is the nineteenth century's specific field of 'neutralisation' (just as the Theological, the Metaphysical and the Moral were for the previous centuries).

Schmitt's reconstruction is not supposed to be a new philosophy of universal history, but rather a consideration limited to the dynamic of the *Abendland*, that relatively homogeneous area of Western *Kultur* from which the modern concept of the Political developed. The succession of fields or 'central spheres'

---

17 See Schumpeter 1911. A rich and insightful essay on Schumpeter's theory appears in Giva 1977.

18 A particular scenario described by Marx, as is well-known, in his historico-political writings like *The Eighteenth Brumaire* and the *The Class Struggles in France*.

19 I am thinking above all of the last works of B. de Giovanni: Giovanni 1978a; 1978b; and 1978c.

(*Zentralgebiete*) thus delineated is not meant to amount to any sort of teleological perspective: it does not designate a rising path but merely demonstrates the points at which the 'pluralist' dynamic of the Western 'spiritual sphere' has crystallised, the presuppositions of this latter being existential and not normative.[20] Moreover, because *Zentralgebiete* is nothing to do with a new doctrine of 'stages', the *Zentralgebiete* do not in themselves resolve the multiplicity of phenomena of each 'age', but instead only locate the terrain within which the 'neutralization' and control of conflictual tensions take place. The succession of *Zentralgebiete* does not proceed in the dialectical form of 'sublation' (where the final level comprises all those that preceded it), but rather in terms of the shift from one domain to the next:

> The succession of stages – from the theological, over the metaphysical and the moral to the economic – simultaneously signifies a series of progressive neutralizations of domains whose centers have shifted.[21]

For Schmitt, this shift takes place each time that the growth of the contradiction and struggle between opposed forces makes a *Zentralgebiete* de facto ungovernable. But with the shifting of the centre of reference, far from there being some definitive 'neutralisation', a *new terrain of struggle* is constituted:

> In the new sphere, at first considered neutral, the antitheses of men and interests unfold with a new intensity and become increasingly sharper. Europeans always have wandered from a conflictual to a neutral domain, and always the newly won neutral sphere has become immediately another arena of struggle, once again necessitating the search for a new neutral sphere. Scientific thinking was also unable to achieve peace. The religious wars evolved into the still cultural yet already economically determined national wars of the nineteenth century and, finally, into economic wars.[22]

Leaving aside the many objections that could be raised at the level of historical reconstruction, Schmitt's suggestive portrayal appears particularly penetrating in its identification of the *political significance* of the crucial moment of the neutralisation process represented by the crisis of state 'sovereignty'. In this

---

20   Schmitt 1993, p. 132.
21   Schmitt 1993, p. 137.
22   Schmitt 1993, p. 138.

sense, it indirectly casts light on the effective historical function of Marx's critique. While it is indeed true that it is 'in the liberal doctrines of the *pouvoir neutre* and the *stato neutrale* in which the process of neutralization finds its classical formula because it also has grasped what is most decisive: political power',[23] what follows is that the *epochemachend* contribution of Marx lies in his political – in the strong sense of the word – character: his immanent critique of economic 'science' demolished the nineteenth century's 'central sphere' and brought to light the antagonistic character of its constitutive relations. *Capital* unveiled and threw into crisis the 'neutralizing' function of the abstraction of exchange, showing the emergence of the 'political', the class antithesis of what the epoch's true 'science of power', Political Economy, had represented as 'non-political': namely, the 'neutrality' of the exchange between capital and labour power.[24]

There can be no doubt that putting into crisis the neutralising mechanism of classical economics represents a point of no return for contemporary social analysis (not only for Marxism but even for any consciously conservative outlook that does not want to feed on nostalgias). And yet it was precisely the historical 'centrality' assumed by the Economic in the nineteenth century that conditioned Marx's theoretical project, leaving the enormous possibilities for developing this 'discovery' tangled in its web. Believing an internal critique of the 'economic' to be the axis on which the entire morphology of capitalism turned, Marx elliptically projects what pertains to this sector onto the totality of social relations and their historical transformation. Given these premises, it follows that although the discovery of the 'politicality' of the 'non-political' irrupts from Marx's problematic, what is lost, even when compared to Hegel – not, let us repeat, as a symptom of a simple analytical 'lacuna' in his 'system' (that might perhaps to be remedied by the barely-begun text on classes, or the never-written one on the state ...) – is the wealth of inter-relations connecting the political to the politico-institutional, the social subjects to the state sphere with all its multiple articulations and complex dimension of 'legitimation'.[25]

---

23   Ibid.
24   Cf. B. De Giovanni 1978b. Although my argument makes use of different theoretical tools, in many aspects it overlaps with that set out by De Giovanni.
25   On this cf. Cacciari 1978. The complexity of the 'Hegel problem' was already at the centre of previous readings, albeit in a different form: cf. De Giovanni 1970; Bodei 1975 [2014]; and Tronti 1975.

2 'Rationalisation' in Weber and Schumpeter and the 'Neoclassical' Revisionism of 1920s Social Democracy

Marxism ossified further the various planes of this totalising outlook, mechanically flattening Marx's analysis of the dynamics of capitalism into a theorem of breakdown and immiseration, whose sociological corollary is represented by the well-known dichotomous vision of the social structure. If, however, the main currents of Marxism – from Histomat to Diamat – did crudely reduce Marx to a system, transforming his (logico-)dialectical representation into an elephantine choreography of history, then there was also a Marxism whose course of development tended to meet, or at least intersect with, the high points of the research carried out in the field of political and social science. I am not alluding so much to the 'heretical' Marxisms as to those currents that played a politically important (at times even leadership) role in the great Central European social democracies.

As demonstrated by the trends running from the *Bernstein-Debatte* to the creation of the Austro-Marxist tendency around *Marx-Studien* and *Der Kampf*, the pluralisation of Marxism had already begun during the rise of the Second International. Our study[26] is focused above all, however, on the post-WWI period, when the tendencies of this 'revised' Marxism entered into a not only theoretical but also practical relation (albeit obviously not unequivocally) with the policies – antithetical in tactics, symmetrical in results – within the social democracies of Austria and the Weimar Republic. In this context, we consider to be decisive turning points the assumption of leadership of the Austrian Social-Democratic Party by the 'Austro-Marxist Left' after the fall of the Habsburg Empire, as well as the German Social Democrats' theoretico-political leadership's passage from Kautsky's 'social-naturalist' conception to Hilferding's 'social-technological' one during the stabilisation period.

The importance of this moment lies, without a shadow of a doubt, in the fact that this provoked the Central European workers' movement to engage in a close, lasting engagement with the problem of constructing a positive theory of the state, from the perspective of using-reforming it as a means of 'social technology' [*Sozialtechnik*] even before 'the seizure of power'. That said, the reconsideration – without summary judgment and condemnation – of the wealth and complexity of the political (and governmental) experiences of interwar social democracy can today be of real use only if it is not limited to a generic, in

---

26 [This is true also of all the chapters contained in this edited collection as well – editor's note.]

the last instance rhetorical, analysis 'rehabilitating' its ideological statements and strategic platforms. Instead, it must translate into a truly *critical* analysis, one that is capable of discerning – by way of a recognition of the correspondences and differences between the theoretico-political elaboration and the *actual economic-institutional dynamics of 1920s capitalism* – the deeper reasons for the defeat from the incidental ones.

We have also tried to take account of these complex inter-relations – the consideration of which would alone require an *ad hoc* work – in our reconstruction of some of Weimar and Austro-Marxist social democracies' internal debates on the question of the state in 'organised capitalism'. Our analysis concludes, on this point, by underlining a limitation common to the two hypotheses that appear as the two 'horns' of the dilemma posed by Central European social democracies' internal debate on the Political in the 1920s: (i) the 'social-technocratic' position of Hilferding (with a significant 'twin' in Renner's 'statist-legalist' stance) and (ii) the position of the Austro-Marxist Left (Bauer and, in part, Max Adler) seeing the democratic state as a parallelogram, or a functional representation of the relation of class forces, captured in their own historically determinate period (the 'equilibrium' phase).

We could define this limitation as of a *neoclassical* type, meaning by this, on the one hand, the break with the mechanistic 'paradigm' of Second International Histomat and substantial convergence with the problematic of 'rationalisation' advanced by Max Weber and later developed by Joseph A. Schumpeter; and, on the other hand, the considerable evolutionist flattening of Weber and Schumpeter's discourse onto a substantially static vision of the democratic form, as a system of equilibrium between those factors susceptible to being oriented towards socialism through progressive adjustments: the gradual withering of the coercive aspects of the state in favour of the expansion of its technical functions of control of social conflict, etc.

It should not be forgotten, however, that this crucial theme is not a purely theoretical one: the mass social democracy of the 1920s was not limited to theorising, but also *practising* a *post-liberal* type of capitalism, one whose socio-institutional physiognomy seemed to have been profoundly changed by the complex political implications of the rationalisation process (or *processes*). Its evolutionist (or, in any case, non-problematising) vision of *Rationalisierung* had specific consequences on the terrain of the tactical-strategic choices that led it to defeat (as we will see in the final part of this introduction). For the moment, we ought to hold its two aspects apart (purely for reasons of exposition) and focus on an examination, even if in a very brief and summary way, of the analogies and differences between Weber and Schumpeter's notion of 'rationalisation' and that of the 'revised Marxism' of 1920s social democracy.

The concept of *Rationalisierung*, which was introduced by Weber and later developed by Schumpeter, distinguished itself sharply from both the *Historische Schule* tradition – which from List to the early Sombart was founded on the notions of *Wirtschaftsstufe* [economic stage] and *Wirtschaftssystem* [economic system] – and from the *Soziologie* of Tönnies and Simmel.[27] The historicist framework, conditioned by the weight of romantic organicism, would in the 1920s converge with – or better, short-circuit – the problematic expressed in Tönnies's dichotomy between *Gemeinschaft* (the 'natural-organic' community) and *Gesellschaft* ('unnatural-artificial', 'mechanical' society). This antithesis – underlying which was a metaphysical-pessimistic interpretation of industrialised society – tended in the Weimar debate on the *Mechanisierung* of 'modern rationalisation', to be identified with Spengler's pairing of *Kultur-Zivilisation*.[28]

Weber's problematic constantly diverged from this tradition. His concept of 'rationalisation' was constructed as an open break with any nostalgia for the organic recomposition of the social body. The becoming-autonomous of 'formal rationality' from 'substantive rationality' was not resolved by a simple calculating break-down of the productive process into its constituent parts (as was claimed by a reductive interpretation that was so influential among Marxists), but rather implied a veritable segmentation of what Marx had called the 'general intellect'. This same 'calculation', the prerogative of entrepreneurial activity, appeared in the specifics of modern capitalism (characterised by the *disciplining* and not the anarchy of profit) together with an unequivocal *political* expression, which profoundly altered the 'equilibrating' criterion of marginal utility.[29]

The 'rationality' of the firm was thus indissolubly interlinked with the processes of *socialisation* and expansion of the bureaucratic-administrative sphere. 'Sociologically speaking', Weber wrote in his greatest work, composed in a crucial period of the transformation process, that 'the modern state is an "enterprise" (*Betrieb*) just like a factory'.[30] This, indeed, represented its 'historically specific character': the advance of the rationalisation process not only dissolved the 'relative independence' of artisanal labour, domestic industry, the free seigniorial peasant and the *commenda* – which was based on the fact that all of these social figures were in possession of the tools and monetary means of production – substituting for this a relation of 'hierarchical dependence' upon

---

27 For the analysis of these currents of German thought, the best reconstruction remains that of Rossi 1971.
28 Cf., in this regard, Maldonado 2002.
29 Cf. Weber 1978, vol. 1, p. 108.
30 Weber 1978, vol. 2, p. 1394.

the entrepreneur, but also simultaneously laid the basis for the concentration of political power itself. The constitutive economic foundation of 'modern capitalism' – 'the "separation" of the worker from the material means of production' thus proved to be 'the common basis of the modern state ... and of the private capitalist economy'.[31]

The 'rationality' of the system's mechanisms thus lay, for Weber as for Marx, in the structural nexus between *separation* and *formalisation*.[32] However, for Weber unlike Marx, the immanent development of 'economic' categories did not suffice to explain the morphology of this progressive formalisation, since *Sozialisierung* had now come directly to concern the political-state sphere: 'Increasing public ownership [...] today unavoidably means increased bureaucratization'.[33] This difference cannot be explained only in light of their different theoretical presuppositions; it also clearly reflects a change in historical 'period'. The ambivalence of moments of transition did, however, ultimately affect Weber's problematic. Indeed, Weber does not seem to go beyond delineating the nexus of rigorous consequentiality that link the two moments – the Political and the Economic – to the *continuum* of rationalisation: 'The "progress" towards the bureaucratic state, adjudicating and administering according to rationally established law and regulation, is nowadays very closely related to modern capitalist development. The modern capitalist enterprise rests primarily on *calculation*'.[34]

The modern Political was thus posited as the highest expression and fulfilment of *Rationalisierung*, as a moment governing the complexity of society through 'specialist' disaggregation. As I have noted elsewhere,[35] the whole secret of Weber's proud statement that 'science is the party of the bourgeoisie' lies in this reciprocity-symmetry of the 'political' and the 'economic'. Behind this statement stood the lucid awareness that the capitalist state was undergoing a decisive change of form, which entailed the dual effect of (i) a dissolution of the traditional boundaries of civil society (of the 'private' sphere mirroring the *pouvoir neutre* of competitive capitalism) and (ii) the concentration-autonomisation of the political sphere (political-statehood) in the strict sense: the more the state inserted itself into 'civil society', thus weaving in what Gramsci in his *Notebooks* called, following Hegel, its '"private" fabric',[36] the more

---

31 Ibid.
32 On this, cf. De Giovanni 1976, pp. 125–39.
33 Weber 1978, vol. 2, p. 1394.
34 Ibid.
35 Marramao 1977, no. 2.
36 Gramsci 1992, p. 153.

autonomous became its moments of decision-making and control over the social dynamic. With the realisation of the rationalisation process, politics too became a 'specialism': 'politics as a vocation'. Indeed, in his famous 1918 lecture 'Politik als Beruf', Weber stated that the formation of the modern state is everywhere 'initiated through the action of the prince. He paves the way for the expropriation of the autonomous and "private" bearers of executive power who stand beside him, of those who in their own right possess the means of administration, warfare, and financial organisation, as well as politically usable goods of all sorts'.[37] This process – which brought together 'under a single head' the set of means necessary for political organisation – was 'a complete parallel to the development of the capitalist enterprise through gradual expropriation of the independent producers'.[38] We will later have opportunity to see in what sense this parallel negatively conditioned his capacity to understand both the 'part' actually played by the Political in the dynamic of transformation and the inherently antagonistic character of rationalisation itself. What we must underline here is the essential place Weber attributed to the concept of *separation*, in the conclusion to his argument, in specifying the characteristics of the modern capitalist state:

> In the contemporary 'state' [and this is essential for the concept of state] the 'separation' of the administrative staff, of the administrative officials, and of the workers from the material means of administrative organisation is completed.[39]

It would be farcical here to attempt to separate these consequences of the formalism of reason from the problem of 'Caesarism', thus separating out the 'scientist' Weber from the 'political' Weber. Although this is not the right place to question the criteria that informed the various historico-political judgements on Weber's *oeuvre*, I believe that it is not entirely unhelpful to briefly raise two considerations.

1.) I do not consider it legitimate (nor, given the documentary evidence, possible) to use the label 'theorist of imperialism' to solve the matter of how to frame Weber historically. Such a 'hyper-political' reductive interpretation risks dissolving the methodological novelty that underpins the whole of Weber's analysis of capitalism, as expressed in his conception of the 'ideal type', in a ritual 'ideology critique' of the Lukácsian-Third International-type. However

---

37 Weber 2009, p. 82.
38 Ibid.
39 Ibid.

one wishes to evaluate it (and the concrete practico-ideological use that Weber himself makes of it), the ground-breaking significance of this concept – which represents the culmination of the long controversy on method that began in 1883 with Dilthey's famous *Einleitung* – lies in the fact that it forcefully introduced into the social sciences the dimension of *planning*. This methodological 'innovation' cannot be understood outside its historical context, characterised by the crisis of the 'spontaneous' market mechanisms that had up until the 1873–96 Great Depression regulated capitalist development. It dealt a fatal blow to the teleological 'paradigm' which had constituted the organic expression of this development on the historical and social science terrain (the idea of an objective process endowed with an immanent meaning, directed towards an End), and it openly called for a *science-as-project that constitutes its own object*, as against the traditional dimension of science-as-reflection, limited to recording how the automatic processes of society played out (from which the majority tendency of Second International Marxism never separated itself).[40]

2.) One must distinguish between the complex problematic that underlies the phenomena of the concentration of state power in Weber's analysis and the way that they were grasped by social-democratic theorists. While it was clear to Weber – as we saw above – that this 'autonomisation-effect' accompanied the rationalisation of the economic process and the governance of potential social conflict through 'specialist' disaggregation, the workers' movement was dazzled by it and thus lost sight of the web of morphological interrelations within which this increased autonomy was inextricably inserted. I discuss this in terms of a 'bad' autonomy of the political in relation to the tendency unfolding already before World War I in Bernstein and immediately afterwards in Hilferding and Renner.[41]

While the leading intellectuals of 1920s social democracy adopted a concept of rationalisation that was but a pale imitation of Weber's problematic, the debate that they developed on 'organised capitalism' still represents an important attempt to map new ways in which the relationship of politics to economics was configured in a post-liberal framework, redefining the tasks of the workers' movement within it. In this regard, I believe it worth underlining the points of contact between Hilferding's analyses of the 1920s, which I focus upon partic-

---

40 On the Weberian notion of the 'ideal type', see M. Rossi, 'Introduzione' in Max Weber, *Il metodo delle scienze storico sociali*, Turin 1958, pp. 24–5.
41 Cf. Zarone 1978. On the 'political Weber', cf. Mommsen 1984, which remains a work of fundamental importance. [Marramao references chapter three of *Il Politico e le trasformazioni* which has not been translated for this volume – editor's note.]

ularly in the third chapter of the first part,[42] and some themes to be found in Schumpeter's reflections on the metamorphoses of capitalism induced by the rationalisation process.

Schumpeter developed the category *Rationalisierung* further and gave it a more pronounced character, so that it came to function not only as a criterion for the determination of the specific traits of a given social formation (Weber's question as to the 'historical identity' of capitalism, which found its most complete formulation in *Wirtschaft und Gesellschaft* [*Economy and Society*]) but also as a key to reading *the dynamic of capitalism*. The kernel of this 'reading' was the recognition of the growing incompatibility between the set of 'rationalising' behaviours and the social order that supported them.

This motif overthrew – even more radically than in Weber – the neoclassical postulate that confined economic analysis to the examination of a stationary configuration. The 'essentially discontinuous character' of the capitalist process, we read in the 1928 essay 'The Instability of Capitalism', 'does not lend itself to description in terms of a theory of equilibrium'.[43] In Schumpeter's theory of rationalisation, the categories of 'entrepreneur' and 'innovation' play a central role. They identify the dynamic factors that constantly set the previous order of equilibrium in crisis:

> we see that there is, indeed, one element in the capitalist process, embodied in the type and function of the entrepreneur, which will, *by its mere working and from within* – in the absence of all outside influences and disturbances and even of 'growth' – destroy any equilibrium that may have established itself.[44]

Entrepreneurial activity, introducing continual innovation into the productive process, constantly alters the stationary situations that resulted from the previous round of 'innovation'. Schumpeter's conception of *Rationalisierung* thus overthrew the generally accepted causal nexus: the 'primary change' does not *follow* industrial development, but rather *created* it; the innovative restructuring of the 'functions of production' was not an *ex post* intervention to confront the 'critical' destabilising of the previous equilibriums, but instead stood at the origin of this instability – *it was not an effect or 'result' of the crisis, but rather the 'factor' that produced it*.[45]

---

42 [The reference is once again to chapter 3 of *Il politico e le trasformazioni*, which has not be translated for this volume – editor's note].
43 Schumpeter 1928, p. 378.
44 Ibid. p. 383.
45 Ibid. p. 377.

Moreover, for Schumpeter the very advance of the rationalisation process inexorably undermines the 'social function' of the bourgeoisie, progressively depriving entrepreneurial activity of all individualist characteristics. It was in 'The Instability of Capitalism' that Schumpeter introduced the theme – that would become central to the 'political' Schumpeter – of the 'transition to socialism'. The link was the identification of the present phase as the transition from 'competitive' capitalism to 'organised' or 'monopolistic' capitalism: the *Stabilisierungsperiode* was the tip of the iceberg whose basis was constituted by a profound metamorphosis of the innovation process.[46] In the new period that was taking shape, innovation activity tended not to be incorporated in new enterprises (as in 'competitive capitalism') and developed increasingly within the framework of the 'big units now existing' (trusts and cartels), independently of individual volition. This was wholly in tune with the internal logic of rationalisation, since innovation now encountered much less friction and resistance (the failure of individual entrepreneurs thus becomes less significant, entails less danger), and 'tends to be carried out as a matter of course on the advice of specialists'.[47] For Schumpeter, the phenomenon of property coexisting with relatively stable prices, as seen between 1923 and 1926, demonstrated the tendency for fluctuations to soften in capitalism of an organised type. The reason behind this lay in the fact that, in this new order now being formed, 'Progress becomes "automatised", increasingly impersonal and decreasingly a matter of leadership and individual initiative'.[48]

The significance of this 'fundamental change' went, however, 'far out of the sphere of things economic'.[49] It meant, indeed, 'the passing out of existence of a system of selection of leaders ... [whereby] success in *rising* to a position and success in *filling* it were essentially the same thing – as were success of the firm and success of the man in charge'.[50] This had been replaced by a different system which, basing itself on the principle of appointment or election, operated a drastic 'divorce [of the] success of the concern from success of the man'.[51] It was at this point that Schumpeter made his prognosis, as 'a more ambitious diagnostic adventure' than one limited to purely economic facts, – and without *making absolutely any value judgement* – of the inevitable advent of socialism

---

46   Ibid., pp. 384–5.
47   Ibid., p. 384.
48   Ibid., p. 385.
49   Ibid.
50   Ibid.
51   Ibid.

as the logical consequence of the very process of rationalisation. 'Capitalism, whilst economically stable, and even gaining in stability, creates, by rationalising the human mind, a mentality and a style of life incompatible with its own fundamental conditions, motives and social institutions, and will be changed, although not by economic necessity and probably even at some sacrifice of economic welfare, into an order of things which it will be merely [a] matter of taste and terminology to call Socialism or not'.[52]

Schumpeter had thus already traced the guidelines of the analysis that he would only complete many years later in *Capitalism, Socialism and Democracy*. He seemed to draw not only on the 'dynamic' Marx, the 'theorist of development', but also Marx as 'theorist of breakdown'. But if Schumpeter's conclusion appeared identical to Marx's, the reasoning that underlay it contrasted with it completely: his prediction as to the progressive dissolution of the social bases of capitalism and their *Hineinwachsen* in 'socialism', which began in organised capitalism with the change in the entrepreneurial function, was not based on economic causes (as Marx saw things) but rather on moral ones. Yet the point that is most important to stress in the overall economy of our argument, is that the 'transition' to socialism in Schumpeter, although indissolubly linked to the social effects of the rationalisation process – which uprooted the entrepreneurial function – *did not, as such, entail a change in the system's forms of rationality* (and it is in *this* respect that the 'correspondences' with the Weimarian Hilferding appear truly surprising).[53]

For Schumpeter, there was an 'essential sameness' between the logic of socialist and capitalist systems.[54] Socialism represented only an incremental step, not a qualitative leap and change of form with respect to the rationale of capitalism: even if 'it is undeniable that the socialist blueprint is drawn at a higher level of rationality'[55] (insofar as the centralised organisation of production would 'eliminate the cause of the cyclical ups and downs whereas in the capitalist order it is only possible to mitigate them'),[56] this did not make it 'a case of rationality versus irrationality'.[57] Socialism is posited, rather, as the completion of the *same* process of rationalisation-socialisation that modern capitalism had initiated: the 'socialist course' represented a step beyond big business on the road this latter had set out; it might prove to be superior to

---

52 Ibid, pp. 385–6.
53 [The reference is once again to chapter 3 of *Il poltiico e le trasformazioni*, which has not be translated for this volume – editor's note.]
54 Schumpeter 1974, p. 183.
55 Ibid, p. 196.
56 Ibid, p. 195.
57 Ibid, p. 196.

'big-business capitalism' as the latter had proven superior to 'the kind of competitive capitalism of which the English industry of a hundred years ago was the prototype'.[58]

Hilferding and Renner, for their part, presented the impulse towards rationalisation (which for Schumpeter had an 'endogenous' character absolutely intrinsic to the 'capitalist process') as the effect of a countertendency set in motion by the workers' movement. For 1920s social-democratic Marxism, 'revised' in the light of the great lesson of Weber and Kelsen, countertendencies no longer represented simple brakes or obstacles slowing the pace of the *fundamental law*'s onward march (as in the 'classical' understanding), but were instead new variables and *socio-cultural* imperatives that profoundly affected the form of development. Thus, at least theoretically, there is an overcoming of mechanistic determinism together with the substitution of the category of 'necessity' with that of 'possibility'. An analogy with Schumpeter's conception of 'critical factors'[59] of development can be glimpsed in the break from the 'classical' Second International vision of mechanical dependency which linked social demands to the relations of production. Moreover, Hilferding's thesis (expressed from 1915 onwards) that the process of the rationalisation-functionalisation of entrepreneurial activity as a substantial factor for *Sozialisierung* and the breaking up of crystallised hierarchical-authoritarian structures was also reinforced.

However, the analogy remains at this level of extreme generality. While for Schumpeter 'critical' and 'cultural' factors were simultaneously *dynamic factors in the production of crisis* – such that there is an indissoluble link between *critique* and *crisis* – these appear in Hilferding and in Renner as functions of the evolutionary adaptation and equilibration of the social system. In the 'reformist' wing of social democracy, the neo-classical limitation took the form of the equation *Sozialisierung = Demokratisierung* and of a hyper-institutional solution in which the state emerges as the only true subject of the transition to socialism. In the Austro-Marxist Left (in particular in Bauer and Friedrich Adler), this limitation took the form of an attempted *refoundation* of political theory's 'classical' vision of the state machine as a complex of functional relations, as a parallelogram of relations of force between classes that explicitly invoked Mach's critique of mechanism.[60] Indeed, in the third chapter of the

---

58   Ibid.
59   See Giva 1977, pp. 52 ff.
60   Mach's influence on the terrain of political theory (and, indeed, on that of economic theory) was of course an indirect one, but no less significant for that. If we were to overlook his critique of mechanism, we would be unable to understand the *Neuorientierung* of

INTRODUCTION

first part[61] we seek to bring to light the salient aspects of this 'critical' (anti-substantialist) redefinition of Marxism – which merely substituted *Funktionsbegriff* for *Ursachenbegriff* – and the implications of the aporia rooted therein. From the above, then, it should be clear in what sense and to what degree all these efforts *failed to go beyond* the understanding of the morphological changes in capitalist society expressed in Weber or Schumpeter's problematics.

3   The 1930s Turn and the Metamorphoses of the Political. The Frankfurt Tradition and the New Theorists of the 'Late Capitalist State'

Before considering the practico-political consequences of this inadequacy on the theoretical plane, to avoid losing the thread of our argument it would be opportune to dive into the 'years of high theory',[62] so as to explain the critique levelled against the type of answer that the Frankfurt School gave to the question of the changing relations between politics and economics during the passage from competitive capitalism to organised capitalism.

I maintain that the approach laid out in 'Political Economy and Critical Theory', composed between late 1972 and early 1973,[63] is still valid *in general terms*. In the case of the Frankfurt school, as in that of the post-WWI 'Marxisms', my approach shows that the only fertile testing ground for *Kritische Theorie* and its variants and derivations (I am thinking above all of the significant developments of it in the work of Jürgen Habermas) is that of a point-by-point study of the categorial framework and analytical implications through which – already in the first years of the Institut für Sozialforschung – it engaged with the great crisis and the processes of the economic-institutional reconstruction of 1930s capitalism.

---

the Central European social sciences or of Austro-Marxism itself. See E. Kauder, 'Austromarxism vs. Austromarginalism', *History of Political Economy*, IV, 4, 1972.
61   [Which does not appear in this volume – editor's note].
62   Shackle 1967.
63   Before, that is, the appearance of the important work by Martin Jay, *The Dialectical Imagination* (Jay 1973), which is by far the best historical reconstruction of the Frankfurt school currently available. I later had the opportunity to discuss at length with the author, finding significant points of convergence on a series of aspects of Critical Theory. My essay can be considered in all aspects complementary to Jay's reconstruction, on account of its sweep, critically documenting the work of the Frankfurt School from the specific angle of their analyses of the nexus between crisis and capitalist reorganisation in the 1930s.

Any critical study of the thematics of the Frankfurt School would need to show an awareness of its fundamental stages and theoretical 'indices', which was made easier by the now substantial Italian literature on this question.[64] Moreover, for me the historical significance of its central problematics and analyses of mass society – that draw upon a rigorous and complex interdisciplinary toolkit – was beyond question. For this reason, I considered it more useful to shed light on its limitations and internal dissonances, at the same time strongly distinguishing my method and the merit of my critique from the usual Marxist ones that were inspired by an 'orthodoxy' more backward than their 'target'.

From Horkheimer and Pollock's rich reflections on the characteristics of the crisis – which also clarified the need to integrate the 'classical-Marxist' paradigm with other 'competing theories' – there emerged in the early 1930s the hypothesis of the 'authoritarian state' (with a state-capitalist foundation) as the possible outcome of an as yet unresolved conflictual dialectic. This hypothesis (which began to take shape around the middle of the decade, given the violent impact that US society and the Stalinist turn in the USSR had on the intellectuals grouped around the *Zeitschrift für Sozialforschung*), was systematised as a model in Horkheimer's *Autoritärer Staat* and Pollock's *State Capitalism*. Notwithstanding the need for a radical refoundation of theory seeking to fit the Marxist conceptual framework to the morphology of the 'new order', in this model it was possible to see a fundamental aporetic aspect: Marxist essentialism and its doctrine of the 'laws of natural-social movement' were never really put into question. The *fundamental character* of the tendency towards breakdown continued to permeate these works, though there now also emerged an 'epochal' countertendency to it, namely the 'authoritarian state', whose strength lay in its *de facto* capacity to block this tendency, *fixing*, so to say, its social results in a de-historicised dimension. The opening words of *Autoritärer Staat* were emblematic: 'The historical predictions about the fate of bourgeois society have been confirmed'.[65] But where did this 'frozen orthodoxy' (which formed the backdrop to the majority current of the Institut für Sozialforschung and which continued to operate also in Adorno's post-WWII reflections) come from?

Its aporia should be sought, in my view, in the equation of capitalism and 'the exchange abstraction' [*Tauschabstraktion*] – in the idea that the formal *ratio*

---

64   The first systematic analysis in Italy of the Frankfurt school was given in Rusconi 1968. Also fundamental were the essays in Rusconi and Schmidt 1972.
65   Horkheimer 1978, p. 95.

of value is the only adequate marker of the 'essential core' of capitalist society inasmuch as it is founded on the production of commodities. The countless 'phenomenal' variations of this foundation do not dissolve the 'essential core', even if they are capable of hindering its effects by means of the countertendential cement of institutionalised violence.

The context created by the 'latent' trend to catastrophe and of the continual rationalisation-autonomisation of institutional control constituted a 'single mechanism' that suppressed any degree of autonomy for the 'civil' and the 'private', the prerogative of the individual emancipation of the bourgeois subject. It also reproduced itself by way of a form of domination that *pre-emptively depoliticised* the masses, guaranteeing their loyalty to the imperatives of accumulation and valorisation with the help of the mass media and techniques of manipulation. More than an increase in the factor of integration of 'state' and 'civil society', the new authoritarian order represented a veritable expropriation of civil society, depriving it of its power. But what this one-dimensional schema presents *prima facie* as the autonomy of the state, in reality *functions* as *absolute dependence* on a 'law of social nature' [*gesellschaftliches Naturgesetz*] whose convulsions the state must inexorably address, a law which springs from the very 'substance' of social relations.

Sohn-Rethel and Habermas's theories, though representing important variations on the Horkheimer-Pollock-Adorno line (in that the pair broke from the orthodox postulate on the theory of value, to which this 'line' continued to hold firm despite everything),[66] did not distance themselves from its theoretical starting point. Though Sohn-Rethel did, on the one hand, have the indisputable merit of placing the accent on an aspect too often overlooked in the Frankfurt School's analyses – the novelties in capitalist morphology brought about by the subcutaneous processes of rationalisation and socialisation of the labour process, which irreversibly threw into crisis exchange-value as a function of 'social synthesis' – on the other hand he drastically reduced the role of the Political to a merely external sticking plaster to the fundamental fracture that risked paralysing the late-capitalist formation for good. More precisely, the fracture was one between the 'production economy' (which responded to the logic of 'socialisation', which Schumpeter had liberated from 'rationalisation' and the 'market economy' (which continued to follow the more properly capitalist logic of valorisation).

---

66 Symptomatic in this regard was Adorno's well-known intervention at the May 1968 Unesco symposium on 'The role of Karl Marx in the development of contemporary scientific thought', published by De Gruyter.

Habermas's 'variant' presents a more complex physiognomy. He proposed to analyse the changes in the form of the state in organised capitalism within the context of a reconstruction of the new morphology of crisis. In this way, he attempted to identify the specific role played by the political system and the ways through which it contributed to determining the dimension of social conflict and the functioning of economic mechanisms, that were different from those of the period of competitive, free-trade capitalism. In *Legitimationsprobleme im Spätkapitalismus*, we find a rather important observation: 'During the course of capitalist development, the political system shifts its boundaries not only into the economic system but also into the socio-cultural system'.[67] The effect of this shift lies in the fact that 'rationality crisis [...] takes the place of economic crisis' and as a consequence 'the logic of problems of capital realization is not merely reflected in another steering medium, that of legitimate power; rather, the crisis logic is itself altered by the displacement of the contradictory steering imperatives from market commerce into the administrative system'.[68]

The incontrovertible novelty thus lay in the fact that he stressed the change in form and logic of crisis. However, for Habermas this occurs as a *dislocation* movement which *nonetheless* still has its point of departure in the *crisis of the Economic*: the state is *constrained* by the 'logic of its means of control' to 'admit more and more foreign elements into the system', insofar as it 'compensates for the weaknesses of a self-blocking economic system and takes over tasks complementary to the market'.[69] The fundamental activity of the late-capitalist state thus bifurcates into the distinct yet symmetrical functions of *accumulation* and *legitimation*, while the political system 'shifting its boundaries' has the specific 'epochal' effect of *repoliticising the relations of production*. The key to understanding the significance of this outcome (and this definition) lies – in this case as well – in the equivalence drawn between capitalism and the exchange abstraction. For Habermas – operating within the theoretical tension between Marx and Weber – the historical peculiarity of capitalism lies in the breakdown of 'traditional' (or precapitalist) societies' relation of homology between the juridical form and the relations of production. Whereas in the feudal system, where there reigned a form of legal inequality that *replicated* real inequalities, the relations of production had an *immediately* political character, in capitalism they were *de*politicised, since power was no longer exercised in

---

67   Habermas 1976, p. 47.
68   Ibid.
69   Ibid.

the form of direct political dependency but rather through the mediation of exchange value and its specular image, the form of 'equal law'.

> In liberal bourgeois society the legitimation of power is derived from the legitimation of the market, that is from the 'justice' of the exchange of equivalents inherent in exchange relations.[70]

Habermas thus also *historically legitimised* Marx's *deduction* of the theory of crisis and the critique of politics from the mirror reflection of juridical form and the commodity form. Marx, we read in the essay 'Technology and Science as Ideology', 'carried out the critique of bourgeois ideology in the form of political economy. His labour theory of value destroyed the semblance of freedom, by means of which the legal institution of the free labour contract had made unrecognizable the relationship of social force that underlay the wage-labour relationship'.[71] And in *Knowledge and Human Interests* Habermas returned to this theme with yet greater clarity:

> Marx, confronted with contemporary capitalism, analyses a social form that no longer institutionalises class antagonism in the form of immediate political domination and social force; instead, it stabilises it in the legal institution of the free labour contract, which congeals productive activity into the commodity form. This commodity form is objective illusion, because it makes the object of conflict unrecognisable for both parties, capitalists as well as wage labourers, and restricts their communication. The commodity form of labour is ideology, because it simultaneously conceals and expresses the suppression of an unconstrained dialogic relation.[72]

With the crisis of market automatisms, the legitimation of bourgeois authority mediated by *Naturwüchsigkeit* – the 'almost-natural' spontaneity of the exchange relation – begins to crack and a new form of legitimation is constituted in its place, based on *Ersatzprogrammematik*, the 'compensatory programme'.[73] So, for Habermas as for Sohn-Rethel the transition from competitive capitalism to organised capitalism heralded the crisis of exchange

---

70 'The Idea of the Theory of Knowledge as Social Theory', in Habermas 1971.
71 Habermas 1989, p. 250.
72 Habermas 1971, p. 59.
73 Habermas 1970, pp. 30–1.

value's function of 'social synthesis', as an abstract *medium* of *Vergesellschaftung*. However, for Habermas, unlike for Sohn-Rethel, it was impossible to produce a theory of 'late capitalism' without analysing the modalities by which the political-institutional level emerged as a factor substituting for the 'spontaneous' nexus of socialisation and valorisation. Yet it is precisely here that the classic Frankfurt aporia (as explained above) reappears: the state continues to be subordinate to the 'fundamental law' of exchange, even though *in a different way*; it no longer appears in the role of universal-abstract guarantor of a 'self-governing' process of market valorisation, but instead as a factor that is continually forced to intervene to rectify the 'malfunctioning' of the mechanism of competition. The emergence of the 'interventionist state' is thus presented as a mere *consequence*, as a *response dependent* on crisis of the market and of the form of legitimation proper to the classic bourgeois state.

Thus also in Habermas we see the apparent contradiction between emphasis on the political character of late-capitalist crisis – in which the legitimation mechanism seems to have restricted the Economic to a simple 'subsystem' – and the purely 'negative' definition of the state's role. The outlines of the original aporia are clearly demarcated in his interpretation of the change in the form of the crisis as a linear shift of its centre (and of its fundamental axis of development) from the economic to the political and socio-cultural sphere. (As we shall see, this is not only a matter of a diachronically diluted and 'misunderstood philosophy of historical materialism',[74] but also an inadequate conceptualisation of the real history of the relations between the state and the market in the capitalist social formation).

Analogous problems spring up in Offe, whose analysis in many ways overlaps with Habermas's (though it is not identical with it).[75] Important here, as in Habermas, is the extension of his reflections to problematics and phenomena that are usually overlooked by the Marxist tradition and which he accesses through the simultaneous, interlinked use of different 'linguistic codes' which underlie a number of categorial constellations: namely, those of the critique of political economy, of the sociological tradition (of the Weberian in type), as well as functionalist (Parsons) and systemic (Luhmann) theories.

Let us start by underlining Offe's definition of 'capitalism': the characteristic element of a capitalist structure is not the *juridical power over the disposal* of property, but rather the 'concrete and typical *mode* of disposal', which in contemporary social formations also includes the *institutionalised programme*

---

74 Cacciari 1978.
75 In the exposition that follows I will implicitly be making reference to Offe 1972; Offe 1973; and Offe and Ronge 1978.

concerning the dominant strategic criteria. The concept of 'capitalism' does not, therefore, represent only the general, descriptive index of a given social structure, but rather the *endogenous logic of a specific development model*.

This starting point allows us to draw a sharp line of demarcation between the two visions of the state that are to this day dominant in the opposed 'Marxisms': the 'instrumental' theory of the state, which is today emblematically expressed in the various versions of *Stamokaptheorie*, and the theory of the state as an 'ideal collective capitalist'.

a) The first case affirms a rigidly *instrumental* relation between the state apparatus and the socio-economically dominant classes (or fractions of classes). By 'instrumentality' we do not mean the relation of means and ends (in this sense – unless we are to take a 'statolatrous'[76] position – the state can only ever be an instrument and not an 'end in itself'); we intend instead to designate the establishment of a mechanical dependency between the political sphere and the dominant class or group in society. All of the more or less explicitly 'statist' strategies of the transition to socialism are based on this 'paradigm'. *Stamokaptheorie* (the theory of 'state monopoly capitalism') is emblematic in this regard, bringing its fundamental assumption up to date in the form of the 'fusion of monopolies and the state' (the contradiction here tending to be posed as the antagonism between the 'public functions of the state' and its being instrumentalised for 'private' or 'corporatist' ends by the 'most powerful monopolistic groups').

b) In the second case, we proceed from the late Engels's famous definition and read this century's transformations of capitalism in terms of the progressive decline of conflictual competition between single capitals and the increasing expansion of state-regulated exploitation. Typical of this 'paradigm' – common to many versions of the 'planner-state'[77] – is a *univocal* connotation of the processes of rationalisation-socialisation (under the one-dimensional banner of social planning) that leads to the complex set of state activities being defined as just so many functions of the valorisation process.

Clearly setting himself apart from both these theories, Offe maintained that, on the one hand, the 'capitalist state' protects and gives institutional form to the capitalist production relation and to the complex set of social relations that are articulated around it. On the other hand, it does not carry out this task in terms of the sectarian or 'corporatist' defence of this or that socio-economic

---

76   [Marramao is warning against an 'idolotrous' relation to the state – editor's note.]
77   Negri 1977, for example. [A number of essays from this book are contained in Hardt and Negri, 1994. On the 'planner state' cf. Negri 2005 – editor's note.]

group but rather by adopting the role of protector and guarantor of the 'common interests' of all members of a 'capitalist class society'. The task that every state strategy of a capitalist character is called upon to fulfil is that of creating the conditions for *every 'citizen' to be included in the exchange relation.*

But because the capitalist state's Archimedian point of equilibrium is to be found in the commodity form, its loadbearing structure historically began to give at the moment when, with the crisis of the self-regulating market, the mechanisms connecting the single units of value to one another through the medium of the exchange abstraction break down. In order to address the disaggregating and delegitimising effects of the crisis in the classic 'automatisms', the post-1929 state could no longer merely guarantee and protect, it *had* to *directly* pose itself the task of *universalising the commodity* form, since this was the single condition of stability of the two *Teilstrukturen* or fundamental components of capitalist society: 'politics' and 'economy'.

The transition to the 'interventionist' state was thus necessitated by 'the enduring tendency, which emerges openly on the historical plane as well as on the empirical one of the dynamic of capitalist development, to paralysis of the "marketability" of value and hence to the interruption of the exchange relation'.[78] Offe rightly insists that the theories that 'neo-Marxism' elaborated to explain the equilibration mechanism's loss of functionality were both varied and controversial. Think of the Baran-Sweezy thesis, which looks to the market's incapacity to absorb the flow of profits following monopolistic concentration; or of Sohn-Rethel's that, starting out from the process of the socialisation of production, explains the crisis in the 'rebalancing' function played by exchange in terms of the growing division of labour between the various branches (and within large-scale industry itself), resulting – on account of the increased quota of fixed capital invested in production – in an increasing specialisation and an ever lesser degree of flexibility and capacity to adapt.

Whatever interpretation we embrace, for Offe one fact remains incontrovertible: the Great Crash undermined, even 'in the bourgeois camp', the traditional confidence in the effectiveness of automatic market self-regulation, to the extent that not even the most orthodox liberals were prepared to give credence to hopes that the value units that had been forced out would 'spontaneously' be reintegrated. The state's task is thus to *maximise both capital's and labour power's* probability of entering into the sphere of exchange. Consequently the politics of capitalist states today is 'methodically purified of residual feudal notions as well as of the ideological restrictions contained in

---

[78] Offe and Ronge 1978, p. 39.

INTRODUCTION 59

liberal programmes and recipes'.⁷⁹ The 'new course' does not, however, eliminate the dysfunctions of exchange, but rather makes them organic. How, then, is the state to respond to the structural problem of the paralysis of the mechanisms of exchange? If we discard the neo-free-marketeer hypothesis of the restoration of rebalancing mechanisms (these already having proven irredeemably 'antiquated' and 'ineffective'), the only alternative is to use subsidies to support those value units who would not otherwise be able to remain within the exchange relation. Hence the use of state 'assistance' to resolve the problem of 'decommodified' value units. In this regard, Offe and Ronge note the emergence of what they define as 'administrative recommodification', which they understand as a third solution differing from both 'laissez faire' and 'protectionist policies of welfare states'. Such a strategy involves not only passively 'restoring' those sectors of the economy that are unable to remain within the sphere of exchange but more generally 'the establishment of the conditions of survival of the mechanism of exchange between different juridical subjects, that is, between different economic subjects'.⁸⁰

Nonetheless, having set out to universalise the commodity form, this type of state intervention results in a 'partial expropriation' of the owners of capital, which in turn threatens the exchange relations between owners of commodities. Reformist measures thus do not result in a 'rationalisation' of the state as a function of valorisation (as claimed by those who uphold the thesis of an 'ideal collective capitalist' or certain theorists of the 'planner-state'); that is, they do not make it a tool of the dominant socio-economic groups (as maintained by the classical-Marxist standpoint and its 'stamokapist' [State Monopoly Capitalist] variant). Instead they enter into contradiction with the interests of the capitalist class, as demonstrated by 'the vigorous resistance [to these policies] that is not uncommon by the political organisations of this class'.⁸¹

But where is the mechanism generating this new level of contradiction? According to Offe, as for Habermas, in the fact that 'the state's attempts to maintain and universalise the commodity form requires organisations whose operations *overstep* the limits of the commodity form'.⁸²

The complex theory of 'late capitalist' crisis elaborated in these important developments of the Frankfurt tradition thus resulted in a 'reformulation' of the classical-Marxist paradigm of a fundamental contradiction between the productive forces and relations of production, as an 'antinomy between the

---

79 Ibid., p. 42.
80 Ibid., p. 44.
81 Ibid., p. 47.
82 Ibid., p. 48.

enduring logic of capitalist production, "anarchically" directed toward the production of "abstract" exchange values, and the "rationalising" logic of state intervention, this latter being called upon not in order directly to produce exchange values, but to promote them and sustain their production through regulatory and planning services corresponding to the production of "concrete" use values'.[83] But – and for us, this is the decisive point – such a reformulation does not break with the 'classical' schema of the dependence (no longer expressed in mechanistic terms but, as with the 1920s social-democratic theorists, in functional ones) of the Political on the 'regularities' (movements of equilibrium and disequilibrium) of the Economic, precisely insofar as it does not go beyond the 'paradigm' of the *foundational quality* of the contradiction, instead limiting itself to *refounding it* with the aid of *Systemtheorie*.[84] Thus we see again in these analyses – which had the great merit of sweeping the stage of so many of the paleo-Marxist prejudices while opening themselves to the most advanced contributions of the social and political sciences – the old philosophical idea of capitalism-as-alienation. It follows directly that the traditional split between the *objective side* (crisis) and the *subjective side* (critique) reappears here:

> The structural weakening of the moral fibre of a capitalist commodity society, which is to say the normative-moral foundation of exchange society – rooted in the very attempts to stabilise and universalise the commodity form through policy measures – does not imply any automatic tendency toward crises or the 'breakdown' of capitalism. And yet, this structural contradiction can certainly become, on the ideological plane, the nexus of social conflicts and political struggles, and the starting-point for overcoming the commodity-form as principle of organisation of social reproduction.[85]

As we said before with regard to Habermas, where this split is clear in his 'critical-discursive rationality' of *Oeffentlichkeit*, whose only operational possibility is that of exploiting interstices of communication that are still *herrschaftsfrei* ('free of domination'), we not only need to re-emerge from an old theoretical aporia, but also, and above all, from an inadequate and deforming

---

83 Zolo 1977, p. 8.
84 For a critique of Offe's analyses as 'subordinated' to Luhmann's systemic paradigm, see Krämer-Badoni 1978. Krämer-Badoni does, however, seem rather too nostalgic for 'totality' to bring this critique to its full potential.
85 Offe and Ronge 1978, p. 51.

historical framing of the transition from 'competitive capitalism' to 'organised capitalism' or 'late capitalism' (*Spätkapitalismus*). This is conceptualised as the transition from a generic 'self-regulating market' system to an equally generic 'interventionist state'. The degree of indeterminacy in this interpretative schema is so wide as to mystify its practical-analytical effects – and little does it matter whether an accurate rendering of empirical observations is provided. In this respect, the theoretical limit of the Frankfurt School identification of capitalism as a 'depoliticised' market system also appears as a historico-political analytical limit. The capitalist market, in fact, has never been 'invertebrate' or been an 'impolitical order' in the true sense (as Habermas claims in *Technik und Wissenschaft als Ideologie*),[86] precisely because it represents the form of 'neutralisation' proper to a determinate phase of bourgeois hegemony. As a consequence, the market is always configured as the *result of determinate power relations* between different subjects who, in their reciprocal conflictual stance, give a political intent to abstract relations of exchange. It is a matter of no little significance, then, that in the last decades of the previous century, during the Great Depression (1873–96), new collective socio-economic figures and 'subjects' (*Konzern*, monopolies, trade unions) appeared within the market system of almost all capitalist countries. These conditioned and, to a significant degree altered and transformed the previous symmetries and 'rules of the game'. To document the 'morphological' effects of this phenomenon, we need not trouble the now substantial output of German and Anglophone social history. For, already in Weber, there was notable attention given to the changes produced in the market system by the newly socialised subjects.[87] This aspect of Weber's thought was utterly overlooked by the dominant current of critical theory. If Habermas's Weber was the Weber of 'legitimation', Horkheimer and Adorno's Weber was the Weber of *ratio* as an all-pervasive dimension, a 'negative totality' of capitalist *Herrschaft*. The 'Frankfurters', following in the wake of Lukács's *Geschichte und Klassenbewusstsein* [History and Class Consciousness], produced a purely philosophical reconstruction of the rationality-domination nexus, and thus *did not pose themselves the question of the historical factors of power that underlay calculative disaggregation*. They saw in this nexus only the mark of capitalist alienation: the effect of the *in-human essence* of the mode of production founded on the exchange of commodities. As such they denied themselves even the possibility of grasping the *political* significance of the rationalisation process, whose immediate effect was the crisis of the previ-

---

86 Habermas 1989.
87 Cf. the essays collected in Mommsen 1989.

ous equilibria (and thus also any hypothesis of 'neutralisation' oriented to the 'axiom of parallels', that is, the criterion of 'perfect competition'),[88] and whose long-term result was the 'pluralisation' of the ruling class itself.

In the early 1920s, Schumpeter glimpsed the general tendency of this process perhaps even more clearly than did Weber: the new 'subjects', constantly unsettling the established equilibriums, dissolved *in practice* the illusion of an evolutionary coming-together of *socialisation* and *democratisation*. Weimar Social Democracy fell victim to this latter illusion and, failing to grasp the pluralistic-conflictual structure produced by rationalisation, did not see that it was precisely the driving forces of 'organised capitalism' that threw the precarious political equilibria into crisis and, together with these, the very 'representativeness' of the parliamentary-democratic form (telling was the clash between the various sectors of German industry which developed through 'transversal' alliances between different powerful economic groups, social strata and institutional bodies that Sohn-Rethel brought to light in his analysis of the transition to National Socialism). The laceration of the Republic in its final years, with the breaking-up of its 'constitutive pacts' and the drastic shrinkage of institutional space, was but the extreme consequence of the intimate contradictoriness of the processes of 'socialisation' themselves. Not by chance, it was precisely in these years that the sharpest and most far-sighted political scientists of the Social-Democratic Left (Franz Neumann, Ernst Fraenkel and Otto Kirchheimer, who collaboured on *Die Gesellschaft*) reflected on the fragility of the 'political compromise' that underpinned Weimar democracy, and its limited efficacy as a 'neutralising state', one that was faced with an ever less governable 'corporatist pluralism', ever less possible to reconcile with a 'general interest', and thus arrived at an identification of the crisis of 'legitimacy' in the parliamentary-democratic form.

In the final decisive moment of this crisis (which was of absolutely unprecedented economic-institutional complexity), the limits of the two great Central European mass workers' movements came to light. On the one hand, in Weimar Germany there was the schism between the Social-Democratic strategy which, by identifying 'legality' with 'legitimacy', ended up fetishising the 'democratic state' form and addressing the social-economic 'powers' and new 'collective subjects' of socialisation as malfunctions or 'corporatist regurgitations' that could be overcome through the neutral mechanism of the *Demokratisierung* of tasks; and the Communist strategy which, from 1928 onwards, emphasised 'the primacy of economics', posing itself as the representative of social insub-

---

88 See Keynes 1936.

ordination against the state. Whereas, on the other hand, in Austria Otto Bauer developed the strategy of a veritable 'third way' between a democracy 'without qualities' of the Weimar SPD and the Leninist 'soviet model'; but he thus managed only to draw from the theory of the state as a parallelogram of reciprocal power relations between classes only the weak corollary of entrenching the autonomy of the working class *in the social*, to the point of organising armed self-defence (with the creation of the *Schutzbund* paramilitary organisation).

The fundamental aporias of social-democratic policy can be schematically summarised under three main headings:

1) the contradiction between recognition of the 'social complexity' of organised capitalism (as well as – as we saw in the previous paragraph – the need for a theory adequate to this new phase) and the rigidity of the 'worker-industrialist' assumption,[89] which social democracy continued to *de facto* adopt in its practical decision-making. This prevented it from having any access to the forms of consciousness of the *Mittlestand*, that 'intermediate layer' whose political shifts played a *determining role* during the period of the Weimar Republic's dissolution. (However, the *strategic* engagement with this issue demanded a break with all linear or functional images of this contradiction and an understanding of the structural asymmetry of the process of capitalism's formation, which Ernst Bloch had summarised in masterly fashion in the concept of the 'contemporaneity of the non-contemporaneous').[90]

2) An 'exogenous' vision of the crisis and hostility towards anti-conjunctural policies: for Hilferding, the state could only organise from outside the 'materials' which the economic process delivered it 'good and ready', and it could never interfere in this process by disturbing its 'social-technological' equilibria. Emblematic in this regard was his rejection of the anti-conjunctural plan advanced by Woytinksy, Tarnow and Baade in the famous 'WTB plan', the source of the SPD's 1931–2 conflict with the ADGB.[91]

3) Inattention to the asymmetry between the phenomena of diffusion of power (and the growing complexity of society) and the process of concentration-simplification of political and decision-making mechanisms. This dyscrasia between *participation* and *decision-making* – as Kirchheimer had already noted in 1930[92] – was based on the tendency, organic in all

---

89   See Rusconi 1977.
90   See Bloch 1991.
91   Woytinsky 1961, pp. 464 ff. [The *Allgemeiner Deutsche Gewerkschaftsbund* was a confederation of German trade unions of the Weimar era – editor's note.]
92   See Kirchheimer 1964. A significant anthology of Kirchheimer's works on this period is

forms of organised capitalism, towards the progressive weakening of the centrality of Parliament and the hollowing-out of its functions.

The points we have just summarised, taking Weimar as our example, can be found in most European countries at the turn of the 1920s and 1930s, notwithstanding the notable peculiarities of different national cases. It is symptomatic that the US social historian Charles S. Maier modelled his important study of the 'architecture' of stabilisation in post-WWI Europe primarily on the 'German case'.[93] Weimar represents for us today, as it did then for the intellectuals most alert to the new processes taking place, a laboratory of concentrated and traumatic experiences as well as a testing ground for our analysis, operating beyond the traditional ideological schemas that have previously been deployed.

It is telling in this regard that the historiographical debate has still not managed to provide a satisfactory reply to the question of the transition from Weimar to National Socialism. Indeed, a full engagement with the points cited above brings out the inadequacy (and above all the partiality) of those reconstructions that see the key to understanding this 'transition' in the continuity of the Prussian *Obrigkeitsstaat*, characterised (from Bismarck to Hitler and beyond) by a constant authoritarian vocation, as well as the inadequacy of those that believe it can be seen as the inexorable underground river of rationalisation imposing its own directives to the detriment of the political-institutional shell that seeks to impose itself at each point.[94] It should be easy enough to evince from what we have so far said that in our view things are rather more intricate and segmented than these reconstructions would have it, and that – what matters more – we will struggle to understand them unless we go beyond monocausal explanatory schemas and the mistaken dilemma between 'the primacy of politics' and 'the primacy of economics'. The very historical significance of the rationalisation process and of the transformations it induced in the structure of the capitalist economy is, in our view, literally inconceivable in isolation from its relation to the functions of authority and the specific subjects that prevail in the relation of force in each given moment. And it is in *this* constellation, not in separation from the state-form, that we must seek the key to understand the transformations of the Political themselves.

---

currently being produced, edited by Angelo Bolaffi. For a framing of the debate in these years, see Racinaro's 'Introduzione' in Kelsen 1978.

93 Maier 1975. On the questions we here address, see in particular pp. 356–86 and his conclusion.

94 For a lucid and very well documented balance-sheet of the historiographical debate on the 'German case', see Collotti 1978.

This is all the more relevant in relation to the 'turn' of the 1930s. The difficulty of shedding light on the specific characteristics of this 'turn' coincides with the difficulty of discerning the complex, asymmetrical inter-relations that link the changes in political form to the processes by which the masses were institutionally integrated into the contradictory dynamic of capitalist socialisation and the *impasse* that latter had reached by the late 1920s.[95] Here, too, we need to go beyond the – opposed yet equally totalising – views that have hitherto dominated the field of Marxist interpretations: namely, that which sees the birth of a planner-state emerging from the 1929 rupture, and that which instead sees coercive-authoritarian state intervention as the most extreme, and at the same time emblematic expression of the 'general crisis' of capitalism. (These two variants, as we know, were simultaneously present – and often short-circuited – in the analysis of the Communist International between 1928 and 1934). In order to go beyond this ideological and 'spectral' vision of this problem, it is worth starting out again from an analysis of the 'consequences' of rationalisation.

The lengthy debate begun by the Verein für Sozialpolitik already brought to light the manner in which the emergence of oligopolistic 'powers' produced not only a profound restructuring of the market, but also a new level of conflict, inasmuch as the new subjects proved capable of producing specific 'effects of sovereignty' (which were thus also centrifugal with respect to the sovereignty of the 'state-shell'), gathering composite social strata around themselves.[96] At the beginning of the *Stabilisierungsperiode* it was already apparent to the more clear-sighted observers of Weimar events that the ever-more *mass* and *organised* dimension of social conflict necessitated a new state-form, a new level of political mediation adequate to the contradictions induced by this same dynamic of 'socialisation'. But there was less clarity as to *how* this state-form should be configured and *what* framework its relations with the pluralistic dialectic of the new 'collective entities' should assume, except in a disenchanted 'reactionary' *Beobachter* like Carl Schmitt, whose capacity for 'ideology critique' seems much stronger and more intense than that offered by liberals and enlightened conservatives, to say nothing of the social democrats.

---

95   See Fano 1978.
96   See, in this regard, the *Verein für Sozialpolitik*'s long series of 'Schriften', and, on the same theme, Böse 1939. Significant contributions were also published in the *Archiv für Sozialwissenschaft und Sozialpolitik*, in which Schumpeter's important article 'Sozialistische Möglichkeiten von heute' (later republished in Schumpeter 1952) also appeared in the 1920s. R. Racinaro, 'Introduzione', in Kelsen 1978, aptly draws attention to latter.

Even Walther Rathenau did not seem, on this point, to go beyond identifying (albeit in a very acute manner) the crisis of 'political Politics' and the increased distribution of power among a dangerously dispersed multiplicity of 'ideal states'.[97] Instead it was Keynes who, starting out from a similar reading of the situation, made a decisive step forward. His famous 1926 essay 'The End of Laissez-Faire', set out from what he defined as '[o]ne of the most interesting and unnoticed developments of recent decades'[98] – the process of socialisation of the large-scale enterprise and the separation of capital ownership from management – and goes on to throw a light on the tendency of the new organisms of stockholder capital 'to approximate to the status of public corporations rather than that of individualistic private enterprise'. For Keynes, a new order was taking shape that threw into crisis the old equilibriums and the 'contractual' framework which was their direct expression; an order for which 'the ideal size for the unit of control and organisation' would lie 'somewhere between the individual and the modern State'.[99] Faced with this new constellation of relations, the only possible programme consisted in 'the growth and the recognition of semi-autonomous bodies within the State'. Having anticipated accusations of 'corporatism' and of proposing 'a return to medieval conceptions of separate autonomies', Keynes here made a forceful effort to emphasise the impossibility of rebuilding an effective political leadership without a mentality that was 'flexible regarding the forms of this semi-socialism':[100]

> We must take full advantage of the natural tendencies of the day, and we must probably prefer semi-autonomous corporations to organs of the central government for which ministers of State are directly responsible.[101]

For Keynes, the state-form adequate to the new processes of dissemination-pluralisation of power would have to leave behind the 'cordial discord' between free-trade individualism and the socialist planner-state, ideologies which were equally incapable of grasping the meaning of the processes now underway

---

97 Rathenau 1925, p. 269. See, R. Racinaro 'Introduzione', in Kelsen 1978, and Cacciari's essay on Rathenau, soon to be published with De Donato. [This came out in the same year: Cacciari 1979 – editor's note.]
98 'The End of Laissez-Faire' (1926), in Keynes 2010, p. 289.
99 Ibid., p. 288.
100 Ibid., p. 290.
101 Ibid.

because both were rooted in a classical (nineteenth-century) paradigm of science and development:

> I criticise doctrinaire State Socialism, not because it seeks to engage men's altruistic impulses in the service of society, or because it departs from *laissez-faire*, or because it takes away from man's natural liberty to make a million, or because it has courage for bold experiments. All these things I applaud. I criticise it because it misses the significance of what is actually happening; because it is, in fact, little better than a dusty survival of a plan to meet the problems of fifty years ago, based on a misunderstanding of what someone said a hundred years ago. Nineteenth-century State Socialism sprang from Bentham, free competition, etc., and is in some respects a clearer, in some respects a more muddled version of just the same philosophy as underlies nineteenth-century individualism.[102]

Despite his rather different political and cultural context, Keynes's framing of the question identified the two fundamental movements of the transition period that we earlier picked out in the 'Weimar case': the pluralisation of power, and the phenomenon – closely intertwined with this – of the progressive 'publicisation' of activities and subjects that had previously operated within the 'private' sphere. Here, we can again observe that Keynes, the Anglo-Saxon, did not equally far-sightedly capture a later, but no less fundamental consequence of this tendency: the dislocation of the functions proper to the political system from the Parliament-government axis to that of the government and public corporations.[103] The institutional model to which Keynes aspired would, in any case, be composed of

> bodies whose criterion of action within their own field is solely the public good as they understand it, and from whose deliberations motives of private advantage are excluded, though some place it may still be necessary to leave, until the ambit of men's altruism grows wider, to the separate advantage of particular groups, classes, or faculties – bodies which in the ordinary course of affairs are mainly autonomous within their prescribed limitations, but are subject in the last resort to the sovereignty of the democracy expressed through Parliament.[104]

---

102   Ibid., pp. 290–1.
103   See the interesting contribution Cavazzuti 1978.
104   'The End of Laissez-Faire', in Keynes 2010, pp. 288–9.

In this framework of consensual harmony, the intensity of the aforementioned shift tended to become blurred. After all, the latter is an element in contradiction to the state's 'sovereign power'. However, if in the 'organised capitalism' of the 1920s this contradiction could still assume – as Polanyi highlighted[105] – the form of a sovereignty 'divided' between a parliamentary-democratic state controlled or in any case conditioned by the constant pressure of a mass workers' movement, and the extra-institutional powers created by 'socialisation'; then, after the 1929 crisis, with the public recognition of new subjects, the contradiction forcefully entered into the heart of the 'political system' itself.

Franz Neumann brought this crucial node to light in the wonderful introductory chapter to his *Behemoth* dedicated to 'The Fall of the Weimar Republic'. Drawing a close link between 'pluralism' and the crisis of the sovereignty of a state founded on the contractual principle, he emphasised the contradictory character of the pretence of reducing the pluralistic-corporatist order of organised capitalism to the classic parliamentary-democratic model. If we recognise the irreversibility of the processes of socialisation, then once

> the state is reduced to just another social agency and deprived of its supreme coercive power, only a compact among the dominant independent social bodies within the community will be able to offer concrete satisfaction to the common interests. For such agreements to be made and honored, there must be some fundamental basis of understanding among the social groups involved, in short, the society must be basically harmonious. However, since the fact is that society is antagonistic, the pluralist doctrine will break down sooner or later.[106]

From Neumann's analysis there emerges an aspect of decisive importance for understanding the real characteristics of the 1930s turn: the state-form under the rationalisation-socialisation process could never 'plan' the multiplicity of dispersed powers, boxing them into a harmonious institutional framework. Indeed, not even its most extreme and repressive forms (as the example of the Nazi regime demonstrates) succeeded in translating 'pluralist' corporatism into an 'absolute' corporatism *unrelated* to the conflictual reality of the powers that had emerged. Here we see a truly qualitative leap compared to the period analysed in masterly fashion by Max Weber, in whose analysis it was still possible to conceive the relation between rationalisation of the eco-

---

105 Polanyi 1944.
106 Neumann 1943, pp. 19.

nomic sphere and rationalisation of the political sphere in terms of a 'perfect parallel' which excluded the possibility of any *internal* complications in the institutional system. But we also see a dynamic whose results escaped even the acute eyes of Schumpeter, who in seeking to demonstrate the constant divergence between capitalist rationalisation and imperialism, attributed the conflict among powerful groups within the political system to a malfunction reducible to the residual presence, within the ruling elite, of fractions of pre-capitalist origin that were 'external' to the endogenous-rational logic of the system.[107] It escaped Schumpeter that this contradiction within the political system in reality represented an effect of this same rationalisation process, precisely in the sense that the 'new state' did not suppress but on the contrary internalised the conflictual order inherited from the mass society of the 1920s.

In this sense, it is no coincidence that National Socialism soon freed itself of the reactionary-corporatist utopias of Othmar Spann and directly attacked – through the mouthpiece of its 'philosophical oracle' Alfred Rosenberg – the very idea of a 'totalitarian state', in the 9 January 1934 *Völkischer Beobachter* (an attack that fully conformed to the ideas that Rosenberg had espoused in his *The Myth of the Twentieth Century*). On the other hand, even though Italian Fascism adopted 'corporatism' as its doctrine and programme, there was an abyssal divide between this ideology and the reality. This does not mean that there is not a politico-institutional turn of enormous significance, but merely that this turn should be located not so much in the birth of a total, planned form of organisation, but rather in the fact that a) the state's actions and 'interventions' produce new variables in the socio-economic dynamic, which profoundly affect the functioning of the system as a whole; and b) the political system takes on extended dimensions and a 'pluralist' structure, and is configured as a complex not only of apparatuses but also of multiple institutions. From this perspective, the 'corporatist state'[108] born in Italy under Fascism does not represent an 'exception' or an anomaly reducible to that country's mere backwardness (although backwardness did play an undeniable role in conditioning

---

107 See Schumpeter 1991. See also the lucid balance-sheet on the question of 'imperialism' offered by Guido Carandini, 'Introversione del imperialismo', *Rinascita–Il Contemporaneo*, 48, November 1978, from his contribution to the Istituto Gramsci's November 1978 seminar on 'The State and the Transformations of Capitalism in the 1930s'.

108 On this question, see the fundamental works of Sabino Cassese, in particular Cassese 1974. Also of importance is 'La "Restaurazione antifascista liberista". Ristagno e sviluppo economico durante il fascismo', in Fano 1974. For a reframing of the analysis of the Italian state, which seeks to marry the re-elaboration of history with the updating of theory, see Barcellona 1977.

certain of the regime's basic choices). Rather, it is situated on the path of 'organised capitalism's' historical tendency, as outlined in general terms above.

At this level of the problem, it is natural and legitimate to demand that we define the whole range of modalities through which the politics-economy nexus functions in this new phase. However, it would be mistaken, indeed dangerous, to try to resolve the problem of its definition through a rhetorical insistence on the (albeit incontrovertible) mass characteristics that politics assumed in the 1930s, such as the role played by the 'bourgeois party-state' in the transmission-perpetuation of new forms of social reproduction, and so on. The limitation of these formulas – aside from their inexcusably generic nature – lies in the fact that they constantly run the risk of falling back into what is once again a totalising and, so to speak, 'holistic' vision of the relationship between the economy and politics; or of representing the relationship between 'the change in the form of the state' and 'bourgeois hegemony' in substantially *functional* terms. This schema risks being unable to bear fruit precisely on the terrain that it seeks to emphasise – the political one – if it fails to see that the 1930s shift in the nature of the political was *in itself* an expression of this crisis of 'synthesis' that was the object of reflection and analysis of 'bourgeois' high culture in the twentieth century. That is, if it fails to grasp that it is precisely because of the definitive dissolution of the separate, self-sufficient character of the state that there opens up the possibility for politics to access the universe of technologies and 'specialisms',[109] whereas this possibility would be lost if politics goes back to presenting itself (even if in the form of 'new hegemony') as a totalising language.

To maintain that the shift represented by the 1930s did not suppress but rather 'internalised' the conflictual-pluralist order inherited from the mass society that had been produced by the great processes of rationalisation-socialisation, does not mean stopping at the descriptive polarisation of 'corporative-pluralism'/'total state'. It means, rather, posing the question of the complex status that this 'contradiction' assumes in contemporary capitalism and of the *specific modalities* by which it takes shape *within* the political system, thus basing the discussion of the 'practicability' of the institutional terrain on this *analysis* and not on abstract appeals to principle.

Viewed from this perspective, Habermas and Offe's analyses appear sterile, despite being in many respects important and innovative. An aporetic aspect,

---

[109] See, on this, the final part of Racinaro's 'Introduzione' in Kelsen 1978. I have developed these themes that I have here only been able to mention in my paper 'Corporative Pluralism, Mass Democracy, Authoritarian State', delivered at the aforementioned Istituto Gramsci seminar on 'The State and the Transformations of Capitalism in the 1930s'. [This appears as Chapter 7 of this volume – editor's note.]

which we earlier found in the 1920s 'neo-classical' revision of social-democratic Marxism, seems to reappear – in a much more complex and refined conceptual constellation – within their theories of the contemporary politico-institutional system. That is to say, the simultaneous presence of a 'bad' autonomy of the Political and of a structural-functionalist vision of the relationship between the state and the economy. This aporia reveals itself particularly clearly in the definition of the political system as an institutional 'filter' that picks between the demands and tendencies of social conflict *as a function* of the overall interests of capitalism. There comes into view here the dual, simultaneous risk of making the sphere of legitimising structures appear autonomous and setting it in an interdependent relationship with the 'needs of valorisation' and the imperatives of social reproduction. This is also the case when the need to maintain equilibrium and social control *compel* the state into adopting measures that seem to work in the exactly inverse sense, as in the case of regulatory services that produce 'use values'. The fact that the state operates opposed registers to *react* to the same *mechanism* confirms its dependence on the 'laws' of the exchange relation and their *malfunctions*. If it is the latter that compel the regulating intervention of political administration, then the contradiction does not lie *in the state* but *only* in the exchange relation. The autonomy of the Political and its absolute dependence thus paradoxically come to coincide, representing the two sides of a single aporia (and the recourse to 'the complexity of society' thus remains an empirical concern, completely unstuck from the theoretical form of the subject).[110]

The question that Habermas and Offe's analyses do not manage to provide any answer to is the following: how can political mediation filter 'the market of pluralist interests' without itself being caught in the conflict between 'corporations'? The theory that sees the contemporary, industrialised state as being the sphere of 'political exchange' (the leading representative of such an analysis in Italy is Alessandro Pizzorno)[111] raises similar questions. This thesis does have the advantage, over those of Habermas and Offe, of drawing on much more extensive empirical evidence and recognising the composite and 'pluralistic' character – thus not homogenised – of the political system. It still has its own 'axiom of closure', however, in the translatability of all potentially antagonistic interests into contractable interests. On the 'political market' every solution is a transaction: all interests must be 'exchangeable', and in order to be exchangeable they must remain 'particular'. Transferred from the economic terrain to the

---

110   See Krämer-Badoni 1978, pp. 59 ff.
111   Cf. Pizzorno 1977.

institutional one, the notion of the market risks again functioning as a 'neutralising' mechanism. Even in this case, however, it might justifiably contended that behind the 'market', behind the political exchange relation, there are always subjects operating who express relations and projections of conflictual powers, for whom the meaning of this thesis could be directly overturned: the fact that there are only transactional solutions to social conflict, which are thus temporary and impossible to plan for, far from only being interpretable in terms of 'integration', is the manifest sign that the contradiction has fully and irreversibly entered into the political system itself.

Expunging the moment of contradiction (and the concrete subjects that are its bearers), the theories of 'selective institutional filter' and of 'political exchange' risk limiting themselves to a purely representation of the contemporary state-form as a mere reflection of a self-sufficient social conflict that it simply registers. In this way it reduces its own role to the simple administrative and/or coercive control of this conflict. They risk, that is, falling short of Keynes's critique of 'Say's law' and silently restoring a negative-unproductive vision of the Political.

Thus, while opposing Habermas and Offe's analyses to the paleo-Marxist orthodoxy may have a certain legitimacy, it risks being only a rearguard action. I think that the more relevant question today is instead that of working to find out to what degree the 'Frankfurt' current is inconsequential heresy, or better, whether it reproduced – in the language of systems theory – the limit that we see in any neo-classical refoundation of Marxist postulates.

In their vision of the state as an instance of the administration and control of potential social conflict – a vision that expressly referred to Niklas Luhmann's *Systemtheorie* – one loses the dynamic-transformative aspect that had been at the basis of Keynes's 'epistemological break' from the 'axiom of parallels' that the neo-classical paradigm had stopped at.[112] The intervention of the Political responded functionally (and here lies the general limit of the Systems perspective, despite its notable cultural updating of European social scientific debates) to the demands of the mere 'governmentality' of the various 'subsystems'. It absolutely did not have the effect of producing new social links and figures, nor throw into crisis – as Keynes and Schumpeter would have it – the prior equilibriums and the plane of 'governmentality' on which the liberal order was established.

Here lies the fundamental difference between the theoretical framework opened up by the Keynesian revolution and the attempts, old and new, to

---

112 See Keynes 1936.

refound Marxism on a neo-classical or functionalist-systemic basis. In these 'revised' Marxist doctrines, the state always intervened *ex post* to repair the imbalances and malfunctions autonomously produced by the crisis of the exchange mechanism, and intervened *ex ante* only in a 'negative' function in order to dissolve the possibility of 'generalisable' interests forming. Conversely, the Keynesian epistemological caesura identified the space for a change in the *function* and *structure* of the capitalist state with a clarity and incisiveness greater than any other theorist of the 'revolution of the 1930s', Schumpeter included. Keynes's theory had a prescriptive-political aspect absent from Schumpeter's problematic, where the governance of crisis was presented as a moment internal to the 'normality' of the crisis itself, and its readjustment as being of an absolutely endogenous character that could not be influenced by public intervention. For Schumpeter, the political governance of the crisis could not even be relatively autonomous; the only autonomy was that of the cycle. Not by chance, in Schumpeter there emerges a sort of 'cross-section of a critical programme',[113] represented by the logico-historical *continuum* of economic activity in general, in which a sphere of operation (even if a limited one) was carved out also for the neo-classical paradigm.

Augusto Graziani has adeptly brought into relief the deep fracture that divided Keynes from Schumpeter, behind 'the apparent uniformity of their views'.[114] However, he also noted that Schumpeter proved more far-sighted than did Keynes in his prognoses. For Schumpeter was the author who, with Michal Kalecki, proved able to grasp most acutely the political effects of the Keynesian model – the entrepreneurial class's *political* countertendencies to full employment – which marked the historic transition from the economic cycle to the 'political cycle', and dislocated the axis of contradiction onto the relation between full employment and social stability (control).[115] The discussion thus goes back from the structural polarity of state and economy to the critical subjects and factors that, through their conflicting intentions, determine the contradictory dynamic of the transformation process. The crisis of 'Keynesian policies' today marks the conclusion of a whole historical epoch of the capitalist state. In the course of this phase, the state underwent a profound change not only in its *function* but also in its *structure*. From the 1930s onward, the political system became the framework that gave form and direction to economic development (in a certain sense constituting its presupposition).

---

113   Giva 1977, p. 90.
114   A. Graziani, 'Introduzione' in Schumpeter 1977, p. 24.
115   On this topic, cf. D'Antonio 1978 and Mario Tronti's paper at the Istituto Gramsci's seminar on the 1930s, which bore the title 'Lo Stato del capitalismo organizzato'.

At the same time, however, expanding to the point of taking in institutions and sectors that had until then belonged to the 'private sphere', the political system was transformed into a terrain of contradiction and permanent conflict, and, *therefore*, was also the natural site of alliances and compromises. The 'political compromise' between the various 'powers' under institutional pluralism, and the collective subjects that conditioned it through their organised pressure (trade unions), thus became the prerequisite of any anti-crisis intervention by the state.[116] But precisely because it is the fruit of a compromise, economic policy is not *planned* on the basis of *one* single interest (even the 'common' interest) but rather is the result that on each occasion emerges from the conflict between the various 'autonomies' into which the political system is 'constitutionally' divided.

The rupturing of the functional relation that, with the increasing burden of 'social complexity' had already in the 1920s thrown into crisis the theory and praxis of the 'class-nomenklatura' party, was thus displaced 'upwards', now also embroiling – and irreversibly so – the relationship between the state and the ruling class. The institutional terrain was no longer the *exclusive* prerogative of the economically dominant class (which, instead – as the far from one-dimensional New Deal experience demonstrated – often entered into conflict with state-interventionist policies). As a consequence, the problem of hegemony came to coincide for the capitalist class no less than for the working class, with the question of *construction* (and continual redefinition) of a necessarily composite ruling bloc.

The historical significance of the current crisis of 'Keynesian policies' mines the very foundations not only of the social basis but also the form of the 'compact' established in capitalist countries after 1929. In this sense, it seems appropriate to define this as a 'paradigm' crisis.[117] The Keynesian recipe presupposes a framework of *consensual equilibrium* among the components of society, which cracks as soon as the impossibility of determining in advance its contractual and conflictual variables becomes visible.[118] It is precisely these variables that induce and produce the crisis of this 'paradigm'.

The discussion of the historical parabola of the state-form born of the events of the 1930s thus returns once more to the subjects who, through their action and self-organisation, give shape to the social system, determining the asymmetries, bottlenecks and shifts of the dynamic of transformation. If it is right

---

116   Cf. De Brunhoff 1978.
117   See Tarantelli 1978.
118   See Cacciari 1978b and 1978d.

to say that the *morphology* of the crisis today forms a single whole with its integrally *political* character, we should however add that such a definition runs the risk of remaining at a purely contemplative level, thus an analytically and politically sterile one, if we understand this morphology in totalising terms and we do not disaggregate the 'single mechanism' through a sort of 'new anatomy'. If we are truly looking to produce a theory that is also capable of having a real 'impact on our project' then first of all we must clearly enunciate where lie the difficulties and the still-tangled knots of the relation today existing between the Political (in the strict sense) and the regional instances produced by the processes of social politicisation. This relation in fact comprises two fundamental questions, that concerning the *politics-specialisms* relation and that concerning the *Politics-new subjects* relation.

I think that it is impossible to understand these critical points without first making a distinction, of a substantive rather than methodological character (to the point that it has proven indispensable to our analysis of the rationalisation process). That is to say, we have to distinguish between the *state* and *power*. In this regard, there is much value in Foucault's warning that we cannot resolve the sphere of the exercise and functioning of power through a theory – however 'extended' – of state apparatuses alone.[119] The state-form is, in fact, nothing other than the 'codification' of a plurality of power relations disseminated across the various segments of the 'social brain', from institutions to 'specialised' spheres. If we lose sight of this multiplicity of determinations and interconnections, we will be left with only a pale and partial image of contemporary capitalism's morphology, and we will grasp little of the novelties being produced in the current crisis. In the same way, a state-form that fails to take account of this 'pluralist' texture will be nothing more than an empty shell or a naked apparatus of force unable to control a dynamic that is increasingly homogenised by centrifugal and delegitimising forces.

Between the two moments there is not, however, only a relation of otherness (or, as Foucault seems to maintain, a dependence of the diagram of institutional relations upon diffuse 'power-knowledges'), but rather a field of forces and reciprocal influences. It is precisely in this 'intermediate' camp – which is not a generic 'limbo' between them, but the place in which conflicts tend to escape from their particularist ghettoes and interact 'horizontally' – that a *positive and productive* practice of crisis as a new space of '*constitution*' should be sought out and trialled. It would be utopian indeed to delude ourselves as to the possibility of 'planning' a new state-form without starting out from *this*

---

119   See Foucault 1977.

pluralist-conflictual reality, which can no longer be reduced to 'the centrality of the working class' in the traditional, 'Ptolemaic' sense of the term. Thus, there can be no real 'determinacy in the planning' of the *political intentionalities* that emerge from the 'sectional' contradictions of social power (and knowledge). There arises again the need for a 'problematic of constitution' capable of going beyond the point where political theory traditionally stops, allowing philosophy or ethics to continue alone. That is, the need to *analyse the status of the contradiction in the context of the 'forms of consciousness' of the subjects who live and produce it* reappears in all its practical and theoretical urgency. Beyond the falling off of this planner drive, empty 'old adages' inevitably return – namely, the separation and opposition of 'life' (the 'everyday' and concrete needs) and 'forms' (politics reduced to a specific profession or instrumental technique).

The difficulties that this theoretico-political programme must overcome today are owed to the fact that the 'constitution' of new subjectivities does not result from the solid structural scaffolding of forms, but rather – to use a drastically abbreviated form of words – from *form in crisis*: from the power relations shot through by contradictions and segmented by caesuras that it would be a vain illusion to think of attributing, in linear or functional manner, to a 'single mechanism' of social reproduction. But the fact that all guarantees to a 'totality' as reference-point have broken down should not lead us uncritically to prefer the 'outlook' of subjects as if this were the only alternative.[120] Rather, taking the 'separation' as given, it is a case of constructing and planning new forms of practicability that are productive of the crisis.

This same 'problematic of constitution' must, therefore, begin by clearing the field of the ambiguous elements that nestle in the weak and linear vision of the spread of politics which, after chasing evolutionism out of the door (stressing the historical turn resulting from the extension of the state and its change in form), wants to let it back in again through the window; as if politics were 'socialised' (and the constitution of specific subjectivities into political subjects takes place) without passing through the ruptures and 'disarticulations' that have irreversibly cracked this 'form's' capacity for recomposition. On the properly politico-institutional level of the project of transformation, such a consideration must, if it is developed coherently, entail the overcoming of the 'participationist' ideology that – failing to note the deep asymmetry between the 'socialisation of politics' and the process of transforming decision-making

---

120   Cf., in this regard, the acute observations in Asor Rosa 1978. As for the complex set of problems that I can here only touch on, I refer the reader to the important essay Donolo 1978.

mechanisms – holds that the question of power is spontaneously resolved through a progressive expansion of representative institutions, following an evolutionary logic that via successive degrees must lead from political democracy to 'social democracy'. If we really want to abandon this 'Say's law of politics' – this axiom that 'socialisation' and 'democratisation' are perfectly parallel, which even in the 1920s manifestly showed its fatal inability to address the strictures and contradictions resulting from this same process of the dissemination of power – then it is necessary to plan the forms of a possible convergence between political *participation* and *decision-making*, and to do so outside of any abstract exercise in institutional modelling. However, such an operation presupposes full awareness of the historical transitions that have, in recent decades, been consummated in a geometrical progression: categories like 'state' and 'economy' today designate (after the Keynesian revolution, after the variables introduced into the relations of production by public expenditure) ambits that are *morphologically different* from not only nineteenth-century capitalism but also the 'organised capitalism' of the 1920s. Similarly, concepts like 'political' and 'social', though they are today structurally 'interdependent' and 'interactive' with a much greater degree of intensity than was true in the past, can display completely separate or even opposed languages, to the extent of being posed in the current crisis as *two different logics* that relate to one another in variable forms and senses, absolutely impossible to translate into a univocal code.

Finally, if the novelty of today's crisis concerns qualitative aspects (and not only quantitative displacements) of the transformation process, it follows that it no longer makes sense to theorise and act politically on the basis of categories like 'anarchy' and 'planning', 'spontaneity' and 'leadership', 'corporatist interests' and 'general interests'; that it is no longer possible, as it was in the past, to reason in terms of 'structural reforms' (which was also a profoundly innovative concept) and 'alliances'; and, above all, that what is required of us today in order to develop a theoretico-political project adequate to our present is to *redefine* politics, beyond the old 'monist' postulate, and relating it to the needs, political demands and forms of 'constitution' of the new subjects.

CHAPTER 2

Councils and State in Weimar Germany (with Guido De Masi)

1   Crisis of the Socialisation Programme and the Economic-Institutional Consequences*

Even before the implementation of the Weimar Constitution, Rudolf Wissel, finance minister of the first social-democratic government in German history, pointed out with bitter disappointment to the Party Congress of June, 1919 that:

> By building the edifice of *formal* political democracy, we have done nothing but pursue the programme already begun by the imperial government of Prince Max von Baden. We have completed the constitution *without a profound popular participation* and we have not been able to placate the masses' tacit resentment because we did not have an adequate programme ... We have failed to influence the revolution so that Germany would have been animated by a new spirit. The very essence of our culture and of our social life seems to have changed very little – and often not for the better. People think that the revolution's conquests have an exclusively negative character, that an individual's military and bureaucratic domination has been substituted by another kind, and that the criteria of government are not substantially different from those of the old regime ... I think that history will harshly judge both the National Assembly as well as the government.[1]

This sharp and unequivocal declaration of the bankruptcy of the socialisation programme tended to underscore the *political* reason for this failure: the lack of active mass participation in the governing of institutions. Social democracy's self-criticism focused here on the crux of the problem: the fundamental *eco-*

---

*   [This article appeared first in *Problemi del socialismo*, XVII, 2, April–June 1976, pp. 7–54. It was first translated by *Telos*, 28, 1976 and revised for this volume – editor's note].
1   SPD-*Parteitag zu Weimar, Juni 1919. Diskussionsprotokoll*, p. 363; the passage is also cited by Rosenberg 1972, p. 94. For a general account, see *Illustrierte Geschichte der deutschen Revolution* (Berlin, 1929), reprinted by Verlag Neue Kritik (Frankfurt a. M., 1970); and Abendroth 1969, pp. 51–67.

nomism of the party and the fatal obliteration of the mass base, of the socialised dimension, of politics understood as the specific dynamic form of the relation between the 'political' and the 'social' and, at the same time, as the working class's ability to run in the first person the transition phases by hegemonically recomposing – in so far as it was the main productive force – the segments of the 'general intellect'. The failure of a vast and ambitious programme of economic reconstruction by the SPD also put an end to the various attempts by the members of the 'Socialisation Commission' led by Kautsky, Wilbrandt, Hermann, etc.,[2] to reconcile planning and workers' councils (*Arbeiterräte*), socialisation, and 'industrial democracy'.

Wissel's reference to the last imperial government was very pertinent. In fact, for several decades the German workers' movement had adapted its organisation and struggles to the structure of the Bismarckian state,[3] and after the November revolution the new constitution based itself on the model of prewar union structure. The June 1919 Nuremberg union congress, for instance, fully ratified the agreements of the November Convention.[4] Indeed, it went further by promoting studies and projects for a type of 'labour community' (*Arbeitsgemeinschaft*) in which the relative functions of unions and employers would be regulated according to the new political course. The resolution of the Nuremberg Congress assigned to workers' councils the task of carrying out and controlling the socialisation programme gradually decided upon by the council of peoples' commissars and proposed by the socialisation commission.

The timing was particularly inappropriate for this union and social-democratic project of parallel control of the economy and of the councils.[5] Its failure on the eve of the implementation of the constitution ushered in a phase of rethinking for all components of the workers' movement. Between the Novem-

---

2   On the failure and the progressive demobilisation of the *Sozialisierung-Kommission*, cf. von Oertzen 1954, pp. 249–69; also Ritter and Miller 1975, pp. 259–76, and Schneider and Kuda 1969, pp. 88–115.
3   On the relation between social democracy, unions, and the Bismarckian State, cf. Roth 1971; and Dawson 1890.
4   The 'Stinnes-Legien Agreement', ratified by the November Convention, established that all the mobilised workers had the right to return to their old workplace. Furthermore, for the first time, German employers recognised the right to a collective labour contract for firms with more than 50 workers. In addition to the introduction of an eight-hour workday, there were also provisions for the constitution of 'arbitration committees' and 'conciliation councils' with equal representation of blue collar workers, clerks, and employers for mediating all contractual matters and labour conflicts in the spirit of the *Arbeitsgemeinschaft*. On this, see Abendroth 1955, pp. 22–4; and Giaccaro 1940, pp. 259–60.
5   On the union project of parallel control of the economy and of the councils, see von Oertzen 1954, pp. 153–96; and Tormin 1954.

ber revolution and the January repression a particular type of state developed in which it was difficult to recognise any class imprint.[6] As the direct expression of the November movement, the councils ended up caught between the new state, which was the product of the very labour organisations hegemonised by the 'social doctrine' of the majority of social democracy, and individual employers now free to move within this new type of 'labour community' (*Arbeitsgemeischaft*) which they opposed, but which they temporarily accepted while waiting to take over management and control of the social relations of production.

Between November and December of 1919, the social democrats had done everything in order to exorcise the spectre of the 'anarchic-bolshevik' model – expressed in the slogan 'All Power to the Councils' – by largely retreating behind the directives of the old Erfurt Programme.[7] The failure of the socialisation commission[8] opens a cycle of theoretical and practical re-evaluation of both the Second International socialdemocratic tradition and the Leninist theoretical and organisational model. The reasons for this must be sought in the peculiar form of Weimar Germany's political and economic structure more than in the international economic and political situation (to which workers' movement historiography usually refers in order to explain this complex phase).[9]

For too long, the SPD had derived political categories from the features of a specific socio-productive structure (that of Wilhelminian Germany). During the first weeks of government, it was convinced that a unity of party, union, and councils (excluding some extremist fringes) could breathe life into that sophisticated whole of bourgeois juridical norms which, elaborated by Hugo

---

6   Cf. Paul Levi's important observations in Levi 1920, pp. 114–25.
7   In the 31 December 1918 speech concerning the programme at the founding Congress of the German Communist party (The Spartacus League), Luxemburg pointed out that: 'Up to its collapse of on 4th August, German social-democracy adhered to the Erfurt Programme in which the so-called immediate minimal tasks were at the forefront, and socialism was allowed to spark only as a far-away falling star, as an ultimate goal' (Luxemburg 1919). Up to the *Junius Pamphlet*, Berlin 1816, the Spartacist Left accused social democracy of having betrayed the Erfurt programme. Only in the 'Rede zum Programm' did Luxemburg reject as completely obsolete the 1891 social democratic programme. For the appropriate documentation, see Weber (ed.) 1993.
8   The Socialisation Commission resigned 3 February 1919, after the government had rejected the proposal to socialise the mines (15 January 1919). Although it withdrew the resignation on request of the minister R. Wissel, it actually did not propose any more concrete socialisation proposals, only research projects. Cf. Ritter and Miller 1975, pp. 282–301.
9   A late example of this 'internationalist' tendency is Mandel 1970.

Preuss, became the Weimar Constitution.[10] But the failure of the socialisation project undermined the unity of the three organising parts of the workers' movement, and only the legislative apparatus of the young republic was left standing. It was certainly not very easy for social democrats to operate with a constitution which did not vindicate the tradition of the well-being and happiness of all citizens, but which accorded 'to every social category the right to take part in political life on the basis of equality, to participate in the regulation of working conditions and of retributions, along with all of the economic development of the nation's productive forces'.[11] The Weberian constitutional scheme prevented workers' councils from expressing themselves in the state hegemonically, since they were counterbalanced by other elements in a complex representative framework. Consequently, it ruled out the creation of any stable alliance between the various classes and social stratifications. In fact, the Weimar constitution was a complex of non-hierarchical representative organisms within a consolidation of power relations based on proportional representation only capable of temporary and precarious alliances, which were soon replaced by other even more precarious ones. Thus a full state forum could not arise.

The objective need for a politics of alliances able to weld the labour struggle (with its high level of consciousness) with other strata of the 'labouring population', especially the peasants, was weakened by immediate tactical concerns and tacit compromises among individuals who proclaimed themselves spokesmen for the various class sectors. It was therefore no accident that the army, the parliamentary group of the SPD, and the general commission of unions agreed to put an end to the 'council anarchy' into which the Reich had collapsed. Only a swift agreement between the social democratic majority (SPD), the independent social democrats (USPD), and the councils on 6 December 1918, prevented the first military *coup* against the executive committee of the workers' council of greater Berlin.[12] Subsequently, Groemer and Noske would play their macabre roles in the Spartakus revolt of January 1919.[13]

---

10 On Hugo Preuss and the Weimar Constitution, see Eyck 1962, pp. 64–79. Cf. also Ziegler 1932.
11 Article 165 of the Weimar Constitution.
12 In agreement with General Lequis, a regiment guided by Captain Spiro was to arrest the executive committee of the councils of greater Berlin and the peoples' commissars supporting the USPD (Haase, Dittman, and Barth), and elect Ebert as President of the Republic. Cf. Ryder 1967, pp. 188–93.
13 On the relations between the military and some social democratic leaders, cf. Elben 1965; and Ritter 1969–73, pp. 7 ff.

The failure of the Kapp putsch on 12 March 1920, due to massive union mobilisation, the relaunching of the council movement and the electoral collapse of the SPD on 6 June 1920, closed this initial phase of the republic and thus threw light onto the specificity of class relations in Germany. The practical objectives and organisational requirements of the revolutionary process were only slightly controlled by the movement's vanguard, rarely understood by party theoreticians and only partly satisfied by political leaders.

As stated above, despite its juridical formalism, the Weimar constitution reiterated the deliberations of the June 1919 Nuremberg union council: in a state with no hegemonic class, the union tends to integrate its functions. Thus, the Army and the union emerged as the protagonists of the initial events and continued a power confrontation that had arisen during the war under the regime of special laws concerning labour regulations and war production.[14] The union's success in blocking the Army leaders' counter-revolutionary offensive revealed both strengths and weaknesses in the movement. At any rate, it is an important development in the history of the republic during a period of intense political and theoretical debate concerning relations among party, union and councils, while the army began to appear as the principal bourgeois force.[15]

While on the eve of the Kapp putsch a republican court would even sacrifice the Centre Party leader Erzberger, the only 'non-militarised' representative of the bourgeoisie in the days of the November revolution, to the *Dolchstoss-Legende* (the knife-in-the-back theory),[16] personalities such as Stresemann (ex-nationalist and leader of the *Volkspartei*) and Wirth (Centre Party) were growing politically by adjusting to the new social reality. They appeared as lucid representatives of a capital which already felt able to collaborate and to compete on an equal footing with the SPD and, eventually, to replace it in the governing of the state. Thus, a dialectic of compromises (rather than of alliances)

---

14 Legien, the president of the union, had made an agreement with the minister of interior for banning strikes during the war. On this, see Abendroth 1969, p. 19.

15 Actually, rather than stepping aside from political life, the army chose to keep the Weimar Constitution's institutional framework with the aim of hegemonising the more intransigent sectors of the nationalist right (judiciary, bureaucracy and the press). Big capital was absent from this 'nationalist bloc' for the entire first half of the 1920s. Instead, it sought an 'alternative use' of the social democratic *Arbeitsgemeinschaft*. During this period, the nationalist satire against 'capitalist sharks' as war profiteers and traitors of the German people, was not very different from that of Grosz' caricatures. Cf. Nolte 1968.

16 Erzberger had sued Helfferich, a deputy of the German Nationalists, for 'continued and aggravated calumny'. Helfferich then accused Erzberger of treason for having signed the armistice, and incompetence. On 12 May, the court for all practical purposes sided with the nationalist deputy, although it did give him a token fine.

began, in which the determining element was social democracy's *hegemonic incapacity*. The main points of the tacit agreement, never officially endorsed, for a stable institutionalised arrangement after the putsch attempt included: (1) the social democratic and union control of labour power within the productive process; (2) capitalist and monopolist control of the economy and finances; (3) abandonment (according to the SPD, only 'suspension') of all socialisation programmes in view of the rapid and rational relaunching of the development of the productive forces; and (4) army intervention in public life only in cases where labour pressure in the factories exploded outside.

It is incorrect to contend that at this point a linear plan of 'rationalisation' of the economy began.[17] It is a symptomatic error of recent scholarship to believe that the simple adding of the majority organisation of the working class to the sectors (even the most advanced) of financial and industrial capital should lead to the rationalisation of production. The reality of German capitalism in the spring of 1920 was much less rosy – unless one confuses the figure of Hugo Stinnes[18] and the complex of factories, mines, hotels and financial institutions that he operated with a new cycle of development. Even the social democrats understood the difference between concentration and cycle.

The chronic inability of German capitalism to carry out an efficient restructuring of the productive apparatus boiled down to the bothersome problem of

---

17   For example, Cacciari, in the introduction to an anthology of writings by the young Lukács, 'Sul problema dell'organizzazione. Germania 1917–1921' (in Lukács 1972), in order to show the ideological 'backwardness' of the council movement with respect to corresponding levels of class composition, too enthusiastically accepts capital's ideology. Germany's portion of world industrial production in 1913 had fallen to 15% compared to 17% in 1900, notwithstanding the very great increase in military contracts. Cf. Bettelheim 1971, pp. 16–34 and Arndt 2015, pp. 25–30. The defeat unsettled the entire pre-war productive framework and, naturally, the class composition as well. But, contrary to what is usually believed, the leading industries in the immediate post-war period were not those that had introduced substantial innovations in the productive process and into the composition of the class, but rather, precisely the technologically more backward ones. At the same time, on the level of subjective-political behaviour, 'productivism' and the so-called 'labour ideology' were not restricted to 'craft workers' and to remnants of 'professionalised' strata which had escaped capital's restructuring violence; it appeared in even stronger forms in workers employed in factories which were technologically the most advanced. Thus, the ideology of rationalisation ran through a political and economic reality much more complex and differentiated than indicated by recent interpretations of the European council movement.

18   Stinnes' empire would collapse in 1924 following Schacht's ruthless deflationary policy. Unable to deal with inflation, in the years 1920–3 German capital was carried away by the flux.

war credits.[19] The military policy of Kaiser Wilhelm II had succeeded in unifying the multitude of small and medium high-precision mechanical industries[20] with the naval and heavy industry. Having survived the war and the confiscation by the Entente, the industrial apparatus re-emerged at this point in its full heterogeneity. Exportation was the only outlet for factories able to survive and labour-productivity was the only immediate material resource. To accept an alliance with this type of capital, without attempting a radical transformation, meant that the party and the union would lose control over very large sectors of the class, and not only over the 'professionalised' labour sectors already on the way to extinction and thus susceptible to council ideology.[21]

Thus we find ourselves at some distance from an organic programme of *Rationalisierung*. Given the impossibility of re-establishing pre-war economic levels and methods,[22] the inability of social democracy and capital to rationalise meant the loss of a historic opportunity to test out a new field of confrontation and struggle. For the respective classes, through a forced coexistence, had acquired a higher reciprocal consciousness and, at the same time, a general vision of economic and social processes with their relative political and institutional *forms*. New meanings and locations had developed for economic categories such as reconversion, planning, money, credit, rent, etc. However, reduced to a mere sociology of the empirical (as in the doctrinaire version of the Second International), the critique of political economy was not only unable to produce a science of politics and a subsequent revolutionary organising project, but is even incapable of renovating the old political economy.[23]

---

[19] For an analysis of war credits as the determining cause of inflation in Germany, see Keynes 1919, pp. 187–208; and Schumpeter 1939, Vol. II, p. 719.

[20] Cf. Bologna 1972, pp. 3–27.

[21] We may well ask whether this thesis of 'professionalism' in Cacciari is not a new reformulation of the old thesis of 'labour aristocracy'. This is, in fact, the expression used by Perulli in a criticism of the 'council ideology' altogether analogous to Cacciari's. Cf. Perulli 1970, p. 366.

[22] Wissel, who was the stoutest defender of the parallelism of rationalisation/socialisation, was also a victim of this illusion. This is how Rosenberg summarised his 'singular monetary theory': 'Wissel stressed that he was not disposed to a socialisation whereby "today I give the entrepreneur a means of payment whose low value, we hope, in three, five, or ten years will be doubled or tripled". Thus, he really believed that the devaluation of the Mark was merely a transitory matter and that in the space of a few years the paper Mark would gain parity with the gold Mark. So little did he understand the German economic situation after the last war'. Cf. Rosenberg 1972, pp. 35–6.

[23] The situation is different in the Soviet Union, where the debate concerning accumulation

The elections of June 1920 clearly registered this general political and even *historical impasse* within the workers' movement: from 11,509,000 votes in January 1919, the SPD went to 6,104,000, while the USPD rose from 2,317,000 to 5,047,000 votes. The two parties were now almost equal. At this point, the concept of socialisation, rejected by the SPD, was appropriated and reexamined by the theoreticians and the militants of the workers' councils, as well as by leading representatives of the old social democracy such as Max Adler who had trouble identifying with the choices made by their party.

2   Socialisation and Councils

In this historical-political context, two phases of the council movement (*Rätebewegung*) can be distinguished: the first from the November 1918 revolution to February 1920, and the second one ending with the defeat of the labour uprising of 1923 which marked the movement's collapse.[24]

The development of these phases was marked by two moments in the theoretical reflection on the councils. This is clear in the writings of two major intellectuals of the mittel-European workers' movement: Karl Korsch and Max Adler. Despite the different evaluations of the October revolution, Korsch's and Adler's strategic models and political-theoretical proposals appeared at first as 'critical revolutionary variants' of the 'Leninist-bolshevik conception' rather than as alternatives to it.[25] Actually, both were exponents of the left current of the socialist movement from 1919–20: Korsch as the 'organic intellectual' of the *Rätebewegung* (council movement wing) led by members of the Berlin USPD such as Däumic and Müller; Adler as the leading theoretician of the left-wing of Austrian social democracy.[26]

It is not by chance the the topic that forms the common object of the reflection of Korsch and Adler is that of socialisation, and it does so under two aspects: the politico-organisational aspect (the problem of the organs of socialisation) and the theoretico-political aspect (the relation between mass movement and direction, the constitution of the mass movement as the historical subject; the dialectic of the class movement and institutions; and the problem of the state).

---

and industrialisation moments of originality in the critique of political economy. Cf. Bucharin and Preobashenski 1969. Cf. also R. Di Leo 1970.
24   Cf. von Oertzen 1954; Torwin, *op.cit.*
25   Cf. U. Cerroni 1973, pp. 75 ff.
26   Leser 1968, pp. 511–59.

Korsch's writings on socialisation (1919–20)[27] express both the tragic greatness and the fatal limitations of the movement. Strongly influenced by the theme of industrial democracy (which, in many respects, connects him to Bernstein) and by the anarcho-syndicalist ideology of direct action, Korsch poses the council system and its intrinsically liberatory connotations as the only alternative to the mere administrative management of power as theorised and practised by the social democrats. The only practical instruments for the realisation of this alternative are the councils whose functions must include the contrasting requirements of central planning and democratic self-management of the enterprise. This synthesis is expressed by Korsch with the formula of 'industrial autonomy':

> Industrial autonomy exists when in every industry ('industry' is used here in the broad sense of any planned activity including agriculture), the representatives of the workers participating in production step in as executives controlling the production process, in place of the previous private owner or controlling manager. At the same time the limitations already forced upon capitalist private ownership of the means of production by state 'social policy' are further developed to become an effective public property of the whole.[28]

The contradictoriness of Korsch's position is apparent. It would however be equally unjust to exalt the (presumed) adjustment to the practical needs of the movement or to condemn its 'radical-utopian' aspect (to use Rosenberg's famous expression), i.e. its anti-bureaucratic and anti-statist imprint. In its specific historical context, Korsch's council theme was an unsuccessful theoretical attempt to overcome the movement's practical impasse. Although his model is no longer viable, his writings expressed the dramatic complexity of the problem of the relation between ideology and class struggle, theory and politics. Following the displacement of revolutionary strategy from the state-political domain to that of economics ('industrial autonomy'), the concept of the double nature and function of the councils, which would immediately overcome the hiatus between politics and economics and the party-union duo (typical of the social democratic tradition), ended up as a pragmatic-syndicalist

---

27 Korsch 1975, pp. 60–81. On this topic, see the works of Rusconi 1969, pp. 767–7, 1974, pp. 1197–1230 (part of this article has been translated into English as 'Introduction to "What Is Socialisation?"' in *New German Critique*, 6, Fall, 1975, pp. 48–59), and 1976, pp. 61–78.

28 Korsch 1975, p. 75.

narrowing of the theme of *Sozialisierung*.[29] This does not mean that Korsch's analysis was irrelevant. Some of his points remain fundamental, such as the new identity of socialisation and nationalisation,[30] and the necessity to generalise the council system (*Rätesystem*) by transcending the corporatist-entrepreneurial limitations imposed by the socialdemocratic leadership.

And yet, Korsch's attempts to define the concrete outcomes of his proposals never went beyond outlining a mediation (which, translated into political terms, sounds like a compromise) between 'control from above', by an undefined 'collectivity', and 'control from below,' by those directly participating in production. This formal solution, which was characterised by the 'bad' utopianism typical of the juridical ideology in which Korsch's intellectual formation had its roots, was a result of an oversimplified view of the complex relation between state and *bürgerliche Gesellschaft* [civil society]. In this sense, the immediacy of the anti-state position was a mirror reflection, on the ideological level, of a non-materialist conception of revolutionary politics and, therefore, of a still reductive and partial reception of the theme of 'constitution'. The obfuscation of the process of the working class' self-constitution into a 'class for-itself' led Korsch to underestimate the specific weight of that 'objective factor which is subjectivity,'[31] and to avoid the problem of the forms of its emergence from the articulated complex of the historical present.

Just as his anti-statist position was the other side of the absence of a Marxist concept of the state, the *undifferentiated* unity of politics and economics in the council reflected the elision of the *Konstitutionsproleblatik* (problem of constitution) as the specific problem of the materialist analysis of the forms of consciousness and of the (subsequent) scientific foundation of the field of politics. Thus, his strategic conception of 1919–20 ended up expressing – at a high level – a theoretical antinomy of European Marxism and, at the same time, the political backwardness of the workers' movement as a whole.

Unlike Korsch, Max Adler seemed to grasp the critical point of the political way out of the 'council strategy'. Indeed, he was the only one who attempted to thematise the relation between councils and the state; this makes him, even more than Korsch and despite his repeated critiques of the 'bolshevik model',

---

29 This reduction indicates an even more serious shortcoming if one considers the role that the state was destined to play after the 1929 crisis.
30 Korsch 1975, p. 70.
31 On this, see zur Lippe 1974, pp. 1–35. For Korsch's intellectual formation, see Buckmiller 1973, pp. 15–85. For a criticism of Korsch's positions, see Negt 1975–6, pp. 120–42.

an interlocutor with Leninism.[32] His awareness of the complexity of this relation made Adler wary of the *immediate* resolution of the problem of the revolution suggested by the slogan: 'All power to the councils'. Such a slogan could resolve the problems of the strategy for gaining power only by presupposing as accomplished a process that was only beginning and which could be brought to completion only by the *conscious* and organised *intervention* of subjectivity: socialisation. The mere radicalisation of the economic and self-managerial moment actually moved in a direction opposed to *Sozialisierung*. In his important pamphlet of 1919, *Demokratie und Rätesystem*, Adler wrote that: 'there is a risk that the system of workers' councils might cease to be the instrument for the overturning of capitalist society and turns into an institution for the defense of the interests of this very same society'.[33] In order for the *Rätesystem* to become a '*true organ of socialisation*', it needed to critically confront the theme of the state and institutions. It had to accept the politico-strategic challenge of Leninism, which Kautsky had rejected with doctrinaire disdain.

Adler grasped the *political problematic* of the revolution in Europe: the dialectic between mass movement (and demands of the autonomous organisation of the masses) and institutions. This relation had, as its point of departure and goal, a process of socialisation which, managed by the councils, came to constitute the continuity between *before* and *after* the gaining of power: an element of continuity substantiated, in turn, by a progressive development of proletarian consciousness in a socialist and revolutionary sense. Yet, when it came to indicating the practical means to meet this need, Adler proposed a compromise as formal as that of Korsch. On the level of the democratic-institutional framework, he proposed a combination of councils and National Assembly and, on the level of socialisation and mass politicisation, 'revolutionary socialist propaganda,'[34] which would overcome labour corporativism as the presupposition of a 'real general will'.

> This, however, presupposes that all immediate economic interests (whose defense is usually at the center of party parliamentary struggles), each of which is engaged in deriving the maximum profit from the bourgeois

---

32   Cf. Adler 1924, pp. 81–9 and, later, the discussion with T. Dan over the Soviet Union, 'Zur Diskussion über Sowjetrussland', in *Der Kampf*, XXV, 1932, pp. 215–24 and 301–11. Cf. also his pamphlet 'Linkssozialismus. Notwendige Betrachtungen über Reformismus und revolutionären Sozialismus' (1933), now reprinted in Adler 1970, pp. 206–60.
33   Adler 1919, p. 76.
34   Adler 1919, p. 85.

state apparatus, are clearly relegated to the background behind the *common interest of social transformation* which can lead to the overcoming of the present conditions of state and society, i.e., beyond class divisions.[35]

Thus, we find in both Korsch and Adler a dichotomy between the analytic level of material working-class struggles (and of their corresponding autonomous organisational forms) and the level of the politico-theoretical perspective and general strategy. In Korsch this dichotomy shows itself in the hiatus (and subsequent juxtaposition) between the economic level of self-management and the anti-state political solution, and in Adler in the gap between the 'sociological' (empirico-economic) analysis of the concrete historical forms of the class struggle (both in relation to the problem of the state and in relation to the peasant question), on the one hand, and universalist-transcendental solutions, on the other.[36] Thus, both lacked a hinge to connect the analytic with the dialectico-organisational component of the account; which is to say, the analysis of the nexus of production and class struggle which could allow the deduction, on both the historical and theoretical level, of the genesis of the 'forms of consciousness' (*Bewußtseinsformen*) from the structural (and, for the individuals of which the class is composed, also experiential) context defined by the social relations of production.[37] Adler approached the 'problem of constitution' more than Korsch, not only because he posed the problem of the state in complex and problematic terms (by advancing against the doctrinaire underpinnings of the structure-superstructure dichotomy, the notion of

---

35 Adler 1919, p. 91. On this, see Cerroni 1973, pp. 80–3.
36 As we have seen, unlike other contemporary theoreticians, Adler is aware of the latent risks of the council system if the terms of its political outcome are not defined. Thus, it cannot be said that the blind alleys in which he runs are the natural result of a naïve or altogether idealistic conception of organisations. These blind alleys, which should be analysed in the context of Adler's philosophical discourse, have meta-theoretical roots that condition and limit the use of certain categories. The fact that a theoretico-practical uncertainty remains, which is evident in the use of the concepts of politics and organisation, must be related to a – more or less conscious – influence of Lassalle's organisational model, which is juxtaposed to the 'rational kernel' of the need for a materialist deduction of forms of consciousness and for the introduction of the theme of subjectivity. The concept of class *Selbsttätigkeit* (self-activity) consequently tends to become fixed into an abstract postulate and, symmetrically, politics evaporates into a mere ethico-transcendental dimension (proletarian universalism, humanism, etc.).
37 On the relation between the constitutive process of class consciousness and of experience, see the historical and sociological analysis by Vester 1970. On the same theme, see Negt and Kluge 2016.

'sociological unity of state and society'),[38] but also because he connected the concept of the councils to the concept of 'the socialisation of consciousness' (*Vergesellschaftung des Beußtseins*).

This leads to the question of neo-Kantianism in the European workers' movement and the various ways in which neo-Kantian themes have been appropriated and utilised within the context of socialdemocracy's internal political battles. Not even the more intelligent approaches to this problem have avoided the dangers of a reductive schematism ultimately resulting from the assumptions of a particular political and historiographic tradition. In this sense, the criticisms brought against the council movement are not meant to resolve all of its complexity and wealth, but rather, are meant to stimulate specific analyses of the details and internal differentiations on the ideological level as well.

Cacciari has pointed out how in the left socialist Kurt Eisner (the famous hero of the Bavarian revolution, killed in February 1919), the defence of the councils was 'closely linked to his interpretation of neo-Kantian ideology at the beginning of the century'.[39] In effect, on the ideological level, the translation of Wilhelminian *Lebensphilosophie* themes into the debates within the workers' movement came to be interwoven not only with Eisner's neo-Kantian discourse (and that of other intellectuals such as Vorländer and Max Adler as well), but also with Friedrich Adler's Machism, and certain sociological elaborations of Robert Michels as well as the development of Luxemburgian critiques of the principles of the dominant forms of social democracy. As Cacciari noted [of Eisener's explicit link of Kant-Marx]:

> In addition to social democratic empiricism, Marx leads us back to Kant's transcendental project. The idealist myth of socialism as 'tactic' is born here, in this context, although it will become 'official' only within the the left-wing of the Third International. But born here too is Marxism as 'cultural tradition', as Philosophie – Marxism as ethical norm, which takes up the enlightenment-Kantian ratio so as to 'realise' it on the historical plane: that is, Marxism as historicism. What is still in Kant (and in liberal ideology) a formal Individualität, becomes Humanität in Marx

---

38 Adler 1922, pp. 29 ff. For Adler, base and superstructure – which scholastic and schematic Marxism hold rigidly distinct – are actually united 'in the same identical character and, more precisely, in a spiritual character' (p. 88). On Adler's concept of the state, see Sultan 1973, pp. 100 ff.

39 Cacciari 1972, p. 38. Cacciari refers to Kurt Eisner's work on Kant (1904), now reprinted in *Die Halbe macht den Räten* (Cologne, 1969). On the problem of neo-Kantianism in the mittel-European workers' movement, cf. Zanardo 1974.

and in the socialist conception. Sozlialismus is a *community* of subjects – redemption of the great utopia of 'classical [German] philosophy' from its 'bourgeois' interpretation. The act of this Humanitätsideal, the subject of its histroical trajectory: the working class. [...] Sozialismus speaks only the language of the *totality* of its end. This concept of 'totality' – of Marxism as ideology of totality *against* the specialisation-bureaucratisation of bourgeois science, *against* social democratic 'politics', will become ever more central in the development of Linkskommunismus, until it achieves it definitive systematisation in Lukács *History and Class Consciousness*.[40]

Neo-Kantian socialism saw itself as the potential saviour of the totality of human experience from capitalist fragmentation and alienation [this sentence, which appears in the *Telos*, translation, does not appear in the Italian original – ed.].

However, apart from this correct uncovering of the cultural sources of the ideology of socialism as *Sollen*, Cacciari reaches no pertinent conclusions. The problem cannot be resolved by an *a posteriori* emphasis on the subjective and theoretical backwardness undoubtedly present in the left socialist and communist components of the council movement, of which the neo-Kantian ideology was the philosophical source. This ideology did not arise as an ideal-typical expression of social democracy, but rather as the effect and reaction to this crisis – a political and 'spiritual' crisis of the party which does not begin with World War I, but is already present in the *Bernstein-Debatte*. It is no coincidence that Bernstein aimed to introduce Kantianism into the the SPD as an antibody: it was a political operation (dictated by the objective need to adjust the general conception and party's work-style to ongoing capitalist transformations) whose actual meaning is difficult to grasp if one merely seeks to extrapolate – with a gesture typical of *Kulturgeshichte* – the 'antibody' from the context of its influence and valence within the debate on the nature and function of the party, only to then liquidate it as an altogether 'bourgeois' element. The risk in Cacciari (and in those holding similar positions), is that of recycling – *mutatis mutandis* – conclusions not so different from the *topoi* of the Third International; a historiography that has frequently posed as a tradition in contrast to our alleged political 'false consciousness'.

The political meaning of the anti-determinist battle has been lost in Stalinist and post-Stalinist historiography. The attribution of anti-reformist connotations to the 'subjectivist-activist' reception of Marxism was not peculiar to theoreticians who in the 1920s lined up decisively on the side of the Bolshev-

---

40   Cacciari 1972, pp. 38–9.

iks, such as Lukács and Korsch, but also to militant intellectuals who, although critical of Leninism and of the October Revolution, tried to find a strategic alternative to the involution of social democracy, able to produce not merely an insurrectional outcome, but a 'revolutionary';[41] one which would recover *in its entirety* the unitary potential of struggle present in the European working class. Thus, even the struggle against 'revisionism' and its 'anti-materialist ideology' cannot be dogmatically understood as a struggle between a 'correct line' (Marxist-Leninist), and both opportunistic and/or extremist left or right deviationist tendencies.[42] Understood in terms of its political class roots, and measured in terms of the real 1920 level of struggle, this 'orthodoxy' was nothing more than one of the many elements in the complex theoretical and political frameworks behind the events of the European workers' movement. Furthermore, this is an element that appeared only in the late phase of the Weimar Republic, during the phase of the 'Bolshevization' of the German Communist Party, which was *subsequent* to the theoretical and organisational disintegration of the movement. In other words, 'Bolshevization' took place in Europe not in the attack-wave, but in the defensive retreat and practical defeat of labour struggles.[43]

This is not the place to discuss theoretical-political questions of the young Lukács. In this context, it is relevant to point out parallels between certain philosophical themes of Max Adler's Austro-Marxism and Lukács: the neo-Kantian dichotomy between necessity (*Müssen*) and duty (*Sollen*) – capitalist objectivity and ethical-transcendental ideal of socialism – corresponded in Lukács to the contraposition between the quantitative objectivity of the world of commodities (*Verdinglichung*, reification) and the subversive explosion of the qualitative dimension (*Klassenbewußtein*, class consciousness: subjectivity which is both of labour and generically human).[44] If in the neo-Kantian Austro-Marxists the immanence of the relation was altogether absent, in Lukács it was simply *posited* – advanced as a need – but not *resolved*: the negative dialectic

---

41 An excellent account of this is to be found in 'Von der Revolte zur Massenorganisation', in Jenssen 1930, pp. 9–30.
42 This trivial and sterile interpretation is recycled in the 'Introduction' to Sandkühler and de la Vega 1970b. Equally banal are the pages of Sandkühler and de la Vega's preface to the collection of theoretical texts around 'neo-Kantian socialism' between 1896–1911 (1970a).
43 Cf. Weber 1969. See also Flechtheim 1969, pp. 248ff.; and edited with commentary by H. Weber in Weber 1963.
44 See Tafuri 1971, pp. 261–4. On Lukács, see P. Ludz's introduction to G. Lukács' *Schriften zur Ideologie und Politik* (Lukács 1973), especially pp. xxiff (on the relation between neo-Kantianism and syndicalism in the young Lukács' conception of political ethics), in addition to Dutschke 1974, pp. 144–53, and 240–6.

from which class consciousness emerges has a purely declaratory immanence since Lukács failed to ground it in the *specificity of the object*, that is, he failed to explain its genesis starting from the ('historically specified') terrain of the social relations of production and from the determinate levels of class composition. To break the ultimately technistic vision of the 'world of commodities' as mere quantity, to catch the qualitative-dialectical element inherent in it as an abstract expression of a determinate relation of production, means to lay the groundwork for a welding of the analysis of capitalist objectivity and the genesis of subjectivity, between the critique of the economy and the theory of class organisation.

3 Party, Union, and Councils

The historical process of the constitution of the proletariat as a 'class for itself' had already experienced the temporary co-existence of a mass party and a vanguard (the Bolshevik experience), but the presence of two mass parties (SPD and USPD) represented an absolutely new situation. If 'the real center of capitalist initiative lay in the connection between the new organisation of labour, the socialisation programme, and the institutional order',[45] it had already largely failed by the spring of 1920. The collapse of the socialisation programme[46] and the failure of institutional stabilisation (necessitating union mobilisation against a series of military putsches), led to the reemergence of the problem of the restructuring of labour and the related questions of political organisation. In practice, the union had shown itself more adept in the defence of the constitution than in the control of the planning of labour within financially shaky factories. This was to be expected, considering that the 'free unions' tied to the General German Union Association (ADGB) were structured and divided by categories already obsolete in 1913.[47] Thus, in the left-wing of the USPD and KPD, the theory of the councils reappeared as the only project able to provide a positive political outcome to the plan of the restructuring of class composition, not within an already given productive process (the socialdemocratic project), but within a developmental model to be defined along with the workers' political gains.

According to Däumig, the leading theoretician of this project, the class could control the key point of labour productivity. The workers' council, however,

---

45 Cacciari 1972, p. 20.
46 Cf. Ritter and Miller 1975, pp. 282–302.
47 This is the basis for the council theorists' project of 'revolutionising' the union structure.

would also have had to take over those roles that the union was no longer able to fulfill: the contracting of wages and the redefinition of functions and categories. Organisationally subdivided into economic and political councils, the workers' councils (*Arbeiterrat*) had to transform into class unity and political mobility the professional de-qualification that the reordering of the economy would have required – a reordering, of course, not based on principles of planning from above, but measured in terms of the needs of the 'community': 'Naturally, by socialisation I do not mean a monopolisation or the creation of a "constitutional factory", as some are suggesting to the workers. Experiments of this type have already been made many times, but how have they ended up for the workers?'[48] It was not the factory that had to adjust itself to the state's laws, but the state which had to accept the workers' self-organised power.

> We must involve in the council system all the discontent of the masses against the parliamentary system [...]. If the Weimar authorities intend to grant themselves a life-long appointment, let them do it. In fact, in so doing they serve our cause very well [...]. Kautsky claims that the councils have their justification only during the transition period and that is all! But doesn't Kautsky himself claim that the revolution is a long process of transition?[49]

Only the *Rätesystem* could bring about the unification of the whole proletariat and initiate the phase of transition to socialism with direct mass participation.

> I am not adamant about the expression 'council system'; it is the only means to move closer as rapidly as possible to socialism and, furthermore, also for realising it fully and conserving it.[50]
>
> I have always claimed that the revolution also disperses party boundaries [...] that is to say that here it is not the question of the party that has to be considered first of all; what is important is to show with facts that we want to energetically realise socialism [...]. The slower we do this, the earlier capitalism sinks its roots and large numbers of workers not politically active slowly become used once again to the old capitalist organisms. Proletarians have no wish to wait so long [...]. In this way, proletarians

---

48 'Die Rätesystem' in Daumig 1969, p. 22.
49 Daumig 1969, pp. 21–4.
50 Daumig 1969, p. 25.

become confused, even more lost in their desperation and are carried into undertakings none of us approve of.[51]

Däumig's hypothesis of a class recomposition entirely within the industrial sector gains more credence when we recall that the period between the January Berlin insurrection and the proclamation of the 'Munich Soviet Republic' (March 1919) was full of strikes, street demonstrations, and insurrectional attempts, followed by the Army's harsh repression in Bremen, Düsseldorf, Westphalia, Brunswick, Halle, etc. It was not a matter of 'revolutionary gymnastics', as was claimed by the German Communist Workers' Party (KAPD) leaders (along with the left-wing of the KPD), but rather of a liquidation of the most revolutionary workers as soon as they extended their action beyond the factory gates.[52] Thus, socialisation and councils represented the base of a new organisational process within which the party and the union progressively tended to change their functions in a constantly evolving politico-economic structure.

R. Müller, defined by the Spartacists as 'the most mystical of the council theoreticians',[53] drew a clear parallel between socialisation and the council system: in the same way that the councils introduced the first phase of the communist society while they still had not created communism (still relying on bourgeois juridical norms), so socialisation was not yet socialism and much less communism. 'Socialisation means depriving capitalist society of economic power; but this is possible only by means of a political struggle'.[54] There is a determinate moment in the development of productive forces when it is decisive for the working class to politically manage the process. The *Arbeiterrat* or workers' council must, then, politically *anticipate* a social form which does not yet exist at the economic level (communism), where socialisation can, at most, substitute a form of production organised for the satisfaction of the needs of consumers (represented in the district councils) in place of the anarchy of capitalist production.

Schematic thinking and late-Proudhonian naïveté broadly compromised Müller's argument. Yet, a conception of workers' councils emerged which did not 'subordinate the class to the productive process'.[55] The *Arbeiterrat* ap-

---

51 Daumig 1969, p. 21.
52 Daumig 1969, p. 26.
53 This was E. Ludwig's description at the KPD Congress of April, 1920.
54 Müller 1918, p. 10.
55 The question of 'Proudhonism' and 'productivism' in the council strategy had been strongly debated even in Italy in the columns of *Ordine nuovo*. Cf. the polemic between Gramsci

peared as the general political organism of a phase of transition characterised by the politico-subjective organisation of the proletariat, which posits proletarian consciousness – over and above the awareness of being the object of exploitation by capital – as the protagonist of a historical and (reproductive) social process in which the power relation between capital and labour was shifting decisively in favor of the latter. Economics was no longer seen as a set of objective laws that the economic operator mechanically applied, but as a *social relation* – historically changeable, and therefore capable of being politically controlled – between the struggling classes. Thus, the historical reason for Müller's pointedly anti-parliamentary position, so close to Korsch's anti-statism, becomes understandable. The contrast with Haase (the leader of the USPD) on the possible co-existence between councils and parliament, was not purely political, but was generated by different theoretical presuppositions and by the conviction that the parliamentary juridical system and capitalist production, were inextricably bound together – just as tightly, if not more so, than socialisation was bound to the representative council system.

> A socialisation applied from above, as was attempted during the period of the socialisation commission, does nothing but preserve the capitalist mode of production. In the best of cases, next to the owner of the means of production, the state itself appears as a beneficiary of labour power, and both divide-up the surplus value created by labour.[56]

In Müller's 'pure' theory of the councils, party and union tend to disappear as class institutions insofar as they belong to a socio-economic formation en route to extinction.

> When, in July 1916, 55,000 Berlin workers suddenly went on strike, not in order to better their economic position, but for political reasons, bourgeois society, and even more, the leaders of social democracy and of unions, were absolutely unable to understand this unheard of state of affairs which completely overturned the experiences of the workers' movement [...]. Here arose the first attempts for a third organisation, that of workers' councils. The large factories constituted the nerve-centre of the movement. This brief exposition of their development shows us that the coun-

---

and Tasca in *Ordine nuovo*, June 5, 1920, p. 26; June 12, 1920, pp. 39–40; June 19, 1920, pp. 47–8; July 3, 1920, pp. 63–4.
56   Müller 1918, p. 10.

cil idea is not a specifically Russian phenomenon and that, rather, it has been articulated as a new organisational form of the working class from the very development of economic and political relations.[57]

As in Korsch, however, the problematic feature of Müller's argument was that it resulted in a political impasse. Since the organisations of the workers' movement were burdened with an economistic and subaltern practice (from time to time transfigured from a formalistic and rarefied concept of 'politics' understood as a mere parliamentary schematism or interbureaucratic tacticism), the need for a revolutionary-political praxis was initially expressed in the rejection of official 'politics' and in the rigid polarisation of theoretical attention upon autonomous working-class organisations, which were extrapolated and disconnected from the whole texture of social relations of production to which they logically and historically belonged. Thus, these expressions of the theory of the councils were a step further than the conceptual framework of the Second International, but still considerably short of the needs of the movement as a whole.

On the other hand, the communist component of the movement had no clearer understanding of political and organisational problems. The external articulation between party, union, and councils proposed by the Spartacist E. Ludwig to the IVth Congress of the KPD (April 14–15, 1920) on the eve of the unification with the USPD,[58] which was meant as a theoretically correct synthesis of Luxemburgian thought and of Bolshevik experiences, was only an anxious anticipation of the heterogeneity and contradictions of the future party. An easier target was found in the AAU (General Labour Unions), founded by the KAPD, which were attacked as organisms 'born in the heads of Proudhonist petty-bourgeois intellectuals; small, utopian, sectarian organisms whose perspectives would, at best, lead to a form of worker capitalism'.[59] Rather than analyse the social and political reasons which had led to the birth of these 'minority' experiences, Ludwig preferred to stick with an abstract and schematic concept of 'politics' and 'organisation', including in his critique even the USPD theorists of the councils.

> The debate around the councils has engaged at the same time both mystic-romantics and nit-picking scholastics; their fortunes have coincided

---

57   Müller 1918, p. 5.
58   Ludwig 1920, pp. 38–60.
59   Ibid.

with the period of decadence of those very councils. Däumig's and Müller's 'revolutionary factory organisations' are typical examples of council scholasticism and, furthermore, are grounded upon too restricted a base. If they are able to have some economic import, they altogether fail at the political level. Müller seeks to transform unions from craft associations into associations based on different branches of industry: this does not at all mean revolutionising the unions. The true revolutionising consists in their shifting from the ideology of labour community to that of class struggle.[60]

Subsequently, the 'ideology' of the workers' councils was criticised in terms of the ideology of a nascent Marxism-Leninism.

> The councils do not exclude the parties and the union; rather, they (and not parliament) are the ideal locus within which the discussion concerning parties must unfold. The moment in which the majority in favor of 'council dictatorship' (*Rätediktatur*) will be gained in them, the councils will change from struggling organs into organs of power of the proletarian state.[61]

Lenin's complex strategy for gaining power and for the Soviet political direction of the phase of transition, was able to generate only a very over-drawn argument in Germany.

The reality of Germany in 1920 was much more complex than Ludwig's sterile line, which could carry the majority within the party only at the price of continual breaks or of brusque shifts in political direction.[62] The documents, articles, declarations, and appeals of isolated politicians or of the groups that left the party reflect the peculiar absence of an alternative political line in the face of an awareness of the general backwardness and overall political needs of the movement.

Typical of this was the case of Paul Levi, a complex political personality who, at the beginning of the 1920s, outlined an analysis of the German political situation which was a logical and political antecedent to his pamphlet *Unser Weg*:

---

60   Ibid.
61   Ibid.
62   In February of 1921, the 51 members of the Executive Committee, with a majority of 28 to 23, eliminated from the central committee Levi, Zetkin, Däumig, Hoffman, and Brass. They were replaced by Brandler, Thalheimer, Frölich and Stoecker.

Wider den Putchismus (this marked his leaving the Communist Party and the Third International in April 1921). According to Levi, the November Revolution had not been the victim of any 'betrayal' on the part of the social democratic leaders for the simple reason that the latter had done nothing but follow the policy of servility with respect to the military apparatus, which had begun long before 4 August 1914.

> In March 1919 it was Noske who [...] filled houses of correction, prisons and military fortresses as no military dog had ever dared.[63] 'In the November Revolution the majority of the proletariat ... has been satisfied to play again the role that it has always played in bourgeois revolutions: the role of the moving force that does not pursue its own ends'. 'What came out of the November Revolution was not at all a bourgeois republic [...]. Even the bourgeois republic is impossible without the certainty of victory, without the full power and the will to hegemony of the rising class'. 'Erzberger, Scheidemann and others are old acquaintances, serfs, and shoe-shiners of the old masters; parliament has not succeeded in transforming these shoe-shiners [...] into true statesmen'.[64]

Thus, not only the bourgeoisie, but social democracy too was unable to cut its ties with the Junkers.[65] The alliance between social democracy and the bourgeoisie was unable to produce an efficient and functioning capitalist state; this was a bitter realisation, replete with indigestible implications for all the organ-

---

63 Levi 1920, pp. 118–119.
64 Levi 1920, pp. 116, 117 and 116.
65 'In the same way that the profoundly German tradition of the *Machtstaat* has turned out to be the most fragile among all political institutions of modern capital, the *bête noir* of reactionary Junkers turns out to be the road most open to the development of a certain type of democratic workers' movement. Without Bismarck there may never have been German social democracy, in its classical form', Tronti 1972, p. 31. What is relevant here is not so much the fact that the structure and the organisational model of the Prussian military state had a direct influence even upon the apparatus of the social democratic party, but that the latter shared with other political parties the general depoliticisation and authoritarian technicisation toward which they were pushed by the 'semi-absolutist' Bismarckian state, which kept them away from every specifically political question and all governmental responsibilities. This is why there was a bureaucratic technicism and economism which vitiated, to the point of bastardisation, the social democratic concept of 'politics': 'If in their practical politics the social democrats limited themselves essentially to the representation of interests, this corresponded to the general tendency of the German empire toward the "economicisation" of parties'. Matthias 1957, p. 197. What this shows is how well economism goes with a general and abstract concept of politics.

isations of the German proletariat, whose unity had been broken not by the 'betrayal' of the social democratic leaders, but rather by military defeat:

> What is the source of the internal division of the class movement? The war has not reached all the strata of the proletariat equally. It has not only spared individuals of all social extraction, but even the entire proletarian strata. It has been a happy conjuncture not only for the capitalists, but also for many proletarians. Entire categories of workers were exempted from military service and employed according to their specialisation; they were protected against unemployment by the enormous development of war production and against hunger by extremely high wages [...]. Hindenburg and Ludendorf knew their trade well.[66]

This was not an updated version of the Marxist-Leninist theory of 'labour aristocracy', which in a few years would gain wide acceptance in the Third International and which, in Stalin's politics, would function as the alibi justifying all defeats. It is instead a non-moralistic and non-ideological analysis of a singular historical relation: the concomitant growth of the working class and of German military industry, of which the war had represented the last link.

Hugo Preuss and Max Weber were as deluded as the Spartacists. The former believed themselves to have founded the bourgeois state whereas the latter believed themselves to be fighting it. The former counted upon the family of international capital whereas the Spartacists waited for the social democratic masses to finally become disabused. But 'the conditions of the armistice were clearly against pacifism ... The Treaty of Versailles should have put an end to all the chatter by Kautsky and his friends'.[67] The great bourgeois democracies (notwithstanding Keynes' plea in favor of Germany)[68] promised only unemployment and misery to the German proletariat. Yet despite the failure of the social democratic-bourgeois republic, Levi also noted the predictions of the Spartacists concerning the reunification of the working class under its leadership – and inspired by the October revolution – had been disproved by the facts. 'Some comrades, noticing that the great masses of the proletariat were very backward with respect to the movement, did all they could, even the impossible, to explain this phenomenon whose true causes they failed to grasp'.[69]

---

66   Levi 1920, pp. 119–20.
67   Levi 1920, p. 117.
68   Keynes 1919, pp. 113–225.
69   Levi 1920, p. 122.

However, Levi could not renounce the 'great idea' of a single revolutionary party of labour. In the face of the exasperated subjectivism of party comrades, the 'exemplary actions' of those who had already left the party in order to found a new one, and the practical and ideal disintegration of the movement, Levi sought to pick up Luxemburg's argument in order to enable the re-emergence of the revolutionary patterns latent in the catastrophic interdependence of crisis and workers' spontaneity: 'apparently favorable economic circumstances' – the increase of exports caused by the devaluation of the Mark – 'hid from the proletariat the collapse of capitalism and its historical task: communism'.[70] However, the days of capitalism were over: 'the crisis has erupted in Germany'[71] and the system of exploitation was forced to show to the proletariat its unveiled face.

One would seek in vain for a *positive alternative* in Levi's essay, one perhaps mediated on the politico-organisational plane by the attempt to connect the objective to the subject side of the crisis. His belaboured theoretical synthesis reflected an uneasiness widespread within the movement which had hitherto been best expressed in facts rather than words, in the complex interweaving and alternation of splits and mergers of the various labour parties: from the Heidelberg split of the KPD (which had given rise to the KAPD, while the strictly Spartacist line of Luxemburgian vintage regrouped under Paul Levi's direction), to the split of the USPD at the Halle Congress which saw the left majority, guided by Däumig, declare its adherence to the Third International and its decision to unite with the *Spartakusbund*. From this split in December 1920, there arose the United Communist Party (VKPD) which, under the direction of Levi and Däumig, seemed to have opened a new political perspective able to resolve the workers' movement's identity crisis. Once again, however, the timing of political organisation did not correspond to the class movement. The new party expressed only the need and not the *rooting* of a revolutionary mass party. The party was not born as an anticipatory science, but as the 'owl of Minerva', a tardy wisdom reflecting on recent defeats rather than on the urgent tasks of the immediate future. The organisation came 'too late' (as Rosenberg put it), when organisational voluntarism was no longer able to regain the positions the working class had lost in the frontal clashes during the years of insurrection.

Less than a year passes between the work analysed above on the German political situation (November 1920) to his pamphlet *Unser Weg. Wider den*

---

70   Levi 1920, p. 120.
71   Levi 1920, p. 123.

Putschismus (April 1921). But in that period a series of crucial events took place: the failure of the 'open letter' policy,[72] the clash with Radek,[73] his purge from the Central Committee along with Däumig and Zetkin,[74] and the 'March Action'. Let us pause for a moment over this famous and infamous episode.

In his indictment of the workers' councils, Ludwig contrasted the type of council organisation that Däumig and Müller sought to create in Berlin to the positive model of the 'revolutionary councils' of Chemnitz, in Thuringa, and of all the Halle-Mansfield district of Saxony which were controlled by the Communist Party. This was the only zone in Germany where the workers' councils had challenged the Kapp putsch, which led to the demilitarisation of the district. Only there had the workers' councils become a territorial reality outside the factories.[75] The Central Committee of the new party (Brandler, Thalheimer, Stoeker, Frölich), politically close to Radek and Bela Kun, decided to implement the 'theory of the offensive' on this battlefield.[76]

It was a case of taking advantage of a tense situation, provoked by a new attempt on the part of the state authority in Saxony to apply in the Halle-Mansfield district the law calling for the disarmament of civilians (which had already been enforced in all the other districts of central Germany), in order to remilitarise the zone. Similar attempts had been met by strikes and protests which had involving a large strata of the population that had thereby generalised the struggle's political objectives. The spark which was supposed to set all of Germany on fire, the intervention of the party as the armed wing of the class, turned out to be an unexpected boost to the state's attempt to reoccupy the zone.[77] The 'insurrectional' activity of the communist groups had been so insignificant that, after the disastrous retreat of 31 March, only the technical side of the operation was criticised and not the general political problem: the total lack of homogeneity between the workers' councils and the party. This was a sad outcome for those who had conceived of the 'March Action' and of the 'theory of the offensive' as ways to overcome the barrier between

---

72 On 7 January 1921, the centre of the KPD sent an open letter to all labour organisations (SPD, USPD, KAPD and the unions), which outlined some objectives requiring common action. On the Communist International's policy of the open letter, see Hajek 1972, pp. 10–18.
73 The dissensus arose from the Livorno split of 1921. Levi was against throwing Serrati out of the Third International – so much so that Radek defined him as the 'German Serrati'.
74 Hajek 1972, pp. 14–15.
75 Cf. Manfred Bock 1969, pp. 295–308.
76 Hajek 1972, pp. 12–18.
77 The zone was militarily re-occupied 28 March 1921. There were about 40 deaths and thousands of arrests. Cf. Rutigliano 1974, pp. 48–53.

factory and social struggles, economic and political action.[78] Ludwig's obtuse and sectarian analysis, which only a year earlier had praised the 'revolutionary consciousness' of the workers' councils in Thuringa and Saxony in contraposition to Däumig's and Müller's Berlin 'economic councils', thus met with an embarrassing historical rejection. Facts had shown the impossibility of measuring revolutionary timing by means of the ideological notions of 'class' and 'party', thus signalling a gap between insurrectional immediacy and the complex form of politics. The need for a general alternative strategy able to socialise workers' struggles by directing them towards the critical point of the relation between crisis and institutions, contrasted sharply with the theory of the offensive with which the March Action tried schematically to reverse an ideological concept of the working class into the party's immediate action.[79]

Setting aside these critical observations, Levi's pamphlet followed closely the previously analysed work of November 1920, with the obvious difference that the hopes placed in the VKPD were no longer present. In the 1920 article Levi had emphasised that at the root of the miraculous class unity of the pre-war German proletariat lay Germany's militarist politics, and so of the Prussian state which, since the beginning of the century, had become the great purchaser and driver of the whole productive apparatus. The workers' councils had believed that they could preserve unity by substituting Wilhelm II and his generals with the old social democratic party. That had been the final united gesture. Thereafter, the proletariat had fragmented into conflicting organisational experiments, each of which pretended, however, to express the needs of the whole class. If in 'Die politische Lage in Deutschland', Levi still believed in the capitalist crisis as the *deus ex machina* able to spontaneously bring about the reunification of the proletariat, in the pamphlet against putschism, the unifying element was located in the 'German national question'.[80] Levi acknowledged the Bolsheviks' success in intertwining the workers' revolutionary project with broad national questions such as the peasant problem. In the same way, the German Communist Party was supposed to make the working class the motive force of social life as whole, so as to resolve the great national questions that the war and the Treaty of Versailles had raised. Agitation and the

---

78 When they heard shooting, the workers did not know whether it was the Army or Max Hölz's gangs – with whom, in any case, relations were not very good. To avoid equivocation, they locked themselves in the factories. See Bock 1969 pp. 308–18.
79 In 'Opportunism and Putschism', Lukács 1972, p. 72, Lukács characterises putschism as the tendency to 'overrate the importance of organisation'.
80 Levi 1969, pp. 44–94.

political use of these problems could not be left to the Junkers and to the right. The nationalist Bolsheviks Laufenberg and Wolfheim were in error since they believed that they could solve the national (and international) problems of the new Germany through summit agreements (perhaps with reactionary generals eager to approach the Soviet Union out of hate for the Entente).[81] Instead, it was necessary to make the German people understand that the alliance with the USSR was supported by the VKPD, not out of deference to the Komintern (of which the party was a section), but because of its vital economic and political importance for the defense of national autonomy.[82] Finally, according Levi, the projects of political recomposition of the proletariat into a party and that of the reconstitution of a new national identity had to proceed simultaneously – otherwise they would clash, with tragic results for the working class.[83] In emphasising the 'national question' and the unquestioned need for the working class to rise to the level of political protagonist of the life of the nation, Levi had dropped the argument concerning the crisis and the way to confront the class struggle in a situation of institutional precariousness. The level of politics was thus rendered 'autonomous', but only in the negative sense of its extrapolation from the terrain of production and from the moment of direct self-organisation of the producers. The theme of general political organisation (the party) and of the 'national path' assumed a distorted and barely sketched-out form precisely because it isolated the whole issue of the councils and of socialisation: the working class' political mission was hypostatised to the level of a generality which missed the *specific task* of recomposing the different sections of the productive forces and grasping the political level *within* the objective dimension of the relations of production. In spite of its level of complexity, Levi's position displayed theoretical and political shortcomings associated with his polemical aims. Of course, the Communist Party's putschism was evident, even independently of the March Action, in its inability to establish ties and alliances with other social groups; the working class and its party operated in total isolation. Yet, beyond the fiery polemics, Levi and the putschists had something in common: the attempt to reorganise and foster the political growth of the working class and to generalise its struggles, without connecting this action to the specificity of the productive process, to the reality of the factory, to the factory councils (*Betriebsräte*), which despite their factory limitations, their

---

81 Cf. Eyck 1962, p. 250.
82 Levi 1921, pp. 51–2.
83 Tragically, Levi killed himself in 1930, when the rise of National Socialism seemed inevitable.

'productivism' and 'labour ideology', contained levels of compactness and class consciousness found neither in Levi's sketch of the 'national path to socialism' nor in Bela Kun's 'theory of the offensive'.

4 Labour Contract, Crisis and Organisation

The most serious charges brought against the council movement and their theoreticians are: labour ideology, factory-centredness, and Proudhonism. Probably Marx would have reproached them for not having been Proudhonist through to the end. This is not a paradox. Either there is the objective possibility during a revolutionary process of abolishing labour as a commodity (but this would be to eliminate the transitional phase), or it must be possible to transform labour into a general equivalent to all commodities. Marx did not accuse Proudhon of being a utopian, but of confusing the progressive socialisation of capital with socialism.[84] The progressive transformation of gold money into money-labour, which is to say, into a fundamental element of mediation between the cost of labour-power and value of social labour, cannot be found in the pages of the history of economics but it is traceable in the changing power relations between the two struggling classes. It is an obligatory path that capital undertakes in the course of its development only when it has full political control over working-class movements and ideologico-institutional hegemony over the working masses. Money, then, as the fetishised expression of the *domination of form*, tends to become – in parallel to the emergence of the state's controlling functions – the unchallenged and authoritarian arbiter in the exchange between capital and labour. Only then does the exchange between money and wage-labour tend to become total. That is, the hegemony of the value-form produces a splitting within the process of 'real abstraction' (which is expressed in the dichotomy between 'juridical abstraction' and 'real subsumption'): on the one hand, the producers are transformed into 'citizens' (whereby the specificity of class is dissolved in general equality); while on the other, capital transforms all citizens into producers, into receivers of income measured in terms of performed social labour.[85] Control and command over labour (understood not only in the factory context, but as general social labour) becomes the

---

84 In 1850, Proudhon wrote to his friend Darimon: 'The moment has come to show the bourgeoisie what advantages there are for them in socialist ideas. Socialism from the standpoint of bourgeois interests: this is what must must now be done'. Cf. Umberto Cerroni's introduction to Proudhon 1967, p. xvi.
85 Marx 1973, pp. 146–7.

determining element and the only guarantor of monetary stability. The community of producers and consumers, so desired by Müller and Däumig, might have had a concrete meaning only by anticipating and placing this very general scheme under the *political control* of the working class. It has been operating since the New Deal until today under the sign of the unchallenged domination of capital expressed on the institutional level in the form of the 'authoritarian state'.

Between 1921–3 in Germany, the revolutionary movement that goes by the name of *Rätebewegung*, despite the all the serious limitations and contradictions we have tried to analyse, was often on the point of carrying out this reversal. To focus on the parallel control of money and labour by connecting the two – keeping in mind, at the same time, the complex socio-political and economic institutional interconnections – during the period of the disintegration of the Mark, would not have entailed shifting the movement toward Proudhon, but to anticipate Keynes, i.e., to anticipate the capitalist counter-attack.[86] But in order to do so, it would have been indispensable to put the emphasis on the general direction of the process, by avoiding that separation between 'political' and 'social' which turned out to be the real obstacle to the realisation of an actual primacy of politics within the workers' movement. Let us try to reconstruct some of these developments, while not losing sight of the fact that this terrain is strewn with potential errors and risks of misunderstanding.

As mentioned, Ludwig had attacked the plan for 'revolutionising' the unions proposed by the council theoreticians, by reiterating the respective tasks of the two organisations. On the one hand, the unions were to protect the workers within a given set of productive relation, they represent the proletariat in their particular interests – subdivided according to the different trades and 'professions' – and can lead, with their action, only to the extreme limits of the sphere of capital's domination. The councils, on the other hand, were the organs of a proletarian counterpower directed towards the abolition of capitalism and the construction of the new society.[87] The question posed by Däumig and Müller, however, was much more pertinent to the specific practical and organisational problems of the German revolution. No matter how vaguely, they warned that with the intensification of the capitalist crisis, *subjectivity* emerged as the determining factor for revolutionary growth. Adequately inter-

---

86 On the relation between Keynes' and Proudhon's conception, cf. Dillard 1942.
87 Ludwig anticipated the resolutions of the II Congress of the Communist International on the union movement and the factory committees. Cf. *I congressi dell'Internazionale comunista. Testi, manifesti e risoluzioni*, Rome 1970, pp. 51–63.

preted, subjectivity could transform itself into the council's political capacity to question the unions' prerogative to regulate the power relations between capital and labour via the wage form. In other words, it was a matter of exploding the deliberations of the Nuremberg Union Congress (June 1919), which continued to be one of the cornerstones in the precarious equilibrium of power in the young republic. The labour contract was, if not the only, certainly one of the determining points of strength and mediation between workers' hegemony in the factories (expressed in the *Betriebsräte*) and the near total domination of capitalist forces over the territory – a domination made possible by the control these forces exercised over financial mechanisms that could still control the moods and purses of an altogether fragmented middle class.

On the eve of the 1923 crisis, Karl Korsch started with the fundamental concepts of labour organisation and labour contract in order to make the theoretical and organisational leap from the control of factories to the hegemony over the territory (once both the social democratic 'path to power' as well as the putschist shortcut had proven impracticable). In the 1922 writings on labour legislation for factory councils, the theory of the councils seemed to cut the last ties with the liberal-radical tradition still present in his 1919–20 writings. Yet this did not diminish but rather intensified the underlying anti-statism of Korsch's council-union project. The Rousseauian freedoms within the factory gates betrayed the class reality from which they had historically arisen. A typical example of this was work freedom: the application of this freedom ('scabbing') ran counter to the general class interests since it produced a lowering of wages. Thus, to reject this 'freedom' became imperative for class solidarity. It was in the interests of the class that the constitution did not enter the factory. The 'free' labour contract meant that the worker forfeited his own freedom in exchange for wages.

> At the end of the fourth chapter of the first volume of *Capital*, Marx has masterfully described the change in scene that takes place in front of our own eyes when from the context of 'economic commerce' (in Marxist terms: 'from the sphere of simple circulation or of the exchange of commodities') we pass to the workshop, to the factory or into the other enterprises within which ultimately 'production' or the creation of commodities take place; here, the relations among the participants are no longer in any way regulated according to the idea of freedom, equality, justice and have instead a completely different aspect.[88]

---

88 Korsch 1968, p. 32.

Thus, the extension of 'industrial democracy' only makes sense if the workers are able to place at the centre of their struggle the labour contract upon which the very system of capitalist production is based. Industrial democracy and the labour contract stood in opposition to one another within the factory: as long as the juridical-bourgeois form of the labour contract persisted, the councils were limited to co-managing a determinate form of exploitation. The labour contract is the dike between the working class ghettoed in the factory and civil society. The very representation of the proletariat's general material interests within the crisis implied, for Korsch, the breaking of that dike – the breakdown of constitutional legality sanctioned by Weimar.[89]

> [In Wilhelminian Germany] the reactionary entrepreneur was prepared to deal with 'his' labour committee, while he radically refused dealing with the union leader from 'outside the firm' [...]. Thus, until we move away from the particular meaning that the direct forms of the right to labour co-participation assume from the viewpoint of the immediate revolutionary process, up to that point one must recognise as fully justified the union's efforts to rigidly subsume the 'factory councils' as simple 'auxiliary organs' of the union struggle [...]. Only when one thinks about the particular meaning of the councils as control organs over production in a decisive phase of the struggles for power between the capitalist class and the proletarian class, and sees them as responsible centres of the future socialised economy, will this way of seeing things be overturned.

With respect to the new tasks of managing the process of transition, the predominant form of trade union organisation, the 'professional association', appeared inadequate to the needs of proletarian class organisation. The trade union needed to be 'revolutionised', radically recategorised from being a 'professional association' into an 'industrial association' that accepted the worker not on the basis of his 'professional' qualifications, but rather on the basis of his exclusively belonging to a specific factory or industrial outfit. This transformation would also profoundly change the relations between trade unions and councils:

> The factory council now no longer appears as a pure and simple 'auxiliary organ' of the unions in their struggle for the defense of the living conditions of the 'sellers of labour' within the existing capitalist class soci-

---

89 Korsch 1968, pp. 95–7.

ety but, rather, as the 'advanced position' with which the unions gain a foothold in the firms and subsequently also in the branches of industry which, although today still in the class enemy's hands, must be taken from him through revolutionary struggle and placed under the *control* and ultimately also under the exclusive *administration* of the working class organised both economically and politically.[90]

For Korsch it was a matter of generating a new 'social contract' to replace the labour contract, starting this time not from revolutionary demands from above, not from the constitutional heights of the state, but from the cells of the factory organisation. This time, too (as often during his troubled political and theoretical development) he touched upon, without fully grasping the central points for resolving the passage from political theory to organisational practice. His piercing empiricism took him to the threshold of decisive problems of which he understood the importance without having the methodological key to solve them. The insistence on the strategic nature of the factory dimension (historically understandable when one considers the concern with politics from above implicit in social democracy) led him to lose sight of the socially totalising character of the *dominance of the value-form*, the complex structure of the *juridical abstraction* that, far from being independent of the fetishism of commodities, expresses and at the same time hides and mystifies the *real* connection of the state to the general process of reproduction. Consequently Korsch's synthesis of Rousseau's 'social contract' with the Marxian concept of 'civil society' left out precisely the theory of value and that of crisis which underpins it.[91]

Thus we find ourselves at the heart of the 1923 socio-economic crisis, which we preface by noting that while Korsch's council theory relegated the problem of the state and politics to a mere epiphenomenon or 'appearance',[92] the Communist Party entered the eye of the cyclone with much the same internal divisions,[93] the same confused aims and the same tactical and strategic unpre-

---

90 Korsch 1968, p. 97.
91 Which is to say, he leaves it out from his theoretico-organisational plan, not that it is absent from his theoretico-philosophical expertise.
92 Korsch 1968, p. 39: 'The struggles between the bourgeois and the proletarian class now only *apparently* have as their object state control (and control of the remaining higher spheres of social life). In substance they have as their object the control of the *economy*, i.e., the "organisation of labour"'.
93 Brandler's leadership was strongly resisted by the left opposition in the party, composed of Thälmann, Fischer and Maslow. Cf. Hajek 1972, pp. 65–73.

paredness with which it had undertaken the 1921 *Märzaktion* (March Action). Yet, from May to November 1923, the council movement had succeeded in accomplishing even more than the most optimistic of its theoreticians had expected in the midst of the crisis: it had succeeded in displacing the trade union leadership in the organisation of large strikes. Rosenberg writes that:

> In the history of modern Germany there has never been a moment so appropriate for a socialist revolution as in the summer of 1923. In the vortex of the devaluation all traditional notions of order, property and legality disappeared, and no one could blame socialists or republicans for the terrible situation which had developed after the Ruhr occupation [...]. Not only did the working class feel ever more clearly that this state of affairs was intolerable and that the whole system would have ended up in terror, but even the middle class, robbed by inflation, was pervaded with revolutionary ferment and desired to settled accounts with capitalist profiteers. Civil servants, including the police which were also victims of inflation, would have hardly exerted much energy in case of a popular movement with truly decisive import against the existing system – and it is highly dubious that the Reichswehr soldiers would have fired on their hungry proletarian comrades in defense of speculators.[94]

This situation of generalised social crisis had immediate repercussions for the workers' movement.

> In the course of 1923, the SPD's strength continually diminished and the party went through a crisis reminiscent of the one in 1919 [...]. The masses moved so sharply toward the Communist Party that, while at the end of 1922 the new USPD still attracted the great majority of German workers, during the following semester the relation had become completely inverted and by the summer of 1923 the KPD undoubtedly had the support of the majority of the German proletariat.[95]

At the same time, the crisis had produced within the union a 'revolution' much more devastating and radical than anything proposed by the council theoreticians. Inflation, which annulled the value of union contributions, deprived

---

94   Rosenberg 1972, pp. 143–4.
95   Rosenberg 1972, p. 145.

the organisation of the capacity to provide welfare provision or payments. Not only. It also deprived the union of all contractual power: the wage contracts agreed with the employers became meaningless within a few days because of the accelerating speed of money devaluation. This led to the dismembering of the unions and the paralysis of the SPD.

A fundamentally important political fact arises here. The failure of social democracy confirmed its inability to elaborate a class-based political project, and its complete dependence upon union tactics. What had been the greatest Western workers' party began to pay dearly for its own indifference and hostility toward the proletariat's independent organisational forms. In 1923 the councils again demonstrated their vitality and efficacy after the electoral and putschist failures. The general political strike organised by the councils against the Cuno government represented the movement's acme: the government was forced to resign.[96]

The development of struggles during this period of crisis seemed to confirm Korsch's hypothesis of the success that a council attack against the juridical-bourgeois form of the labour contract could have, as well as the relative effect of imbalance within the institutional framework. This perspective seemed to receive confirmation from the other side of the class perspective, as in Dr. Schacht's hypocritical observation that:

> in the fall of 1923 the unchecked devaluation of money was at such a point that the whole German social structure threatened to collapse. Desperation had gotten the better of the workers' wives. In vain they attempted, in their shopping, to stay in step with the devaluation of the Mark. The money that the men made through labour disappeared in the hands of the housewives even after pay was adjusted day by day. It was in these conditions that I was called to put a stop to the devaluation and stabilize money. I did not decline the invitation. I gave up a profitable profession and a secure position.[97]

The hypocrisy of this position was unable to hide a profound Marxist truth: when the submission of labour to capital ceased (as in the case of the wage adjustment and the day-by-day contract negotiations), then the crisis of the monetary system tended to become a political crisis of the system, a crisis of

---

96   Cuno's right-centre government was followed by Stresemann's, supported by the social democrats. Cf. Rosenberg 1972, pp. 148 ff.
97   Cf. Schacht 1949.

the continuity of the process of realisation of surplus value. The law of value found in Schacht's diary a confirmation as resounding as it was unwanted. The old barter system could, for some brief periods, substitute for money in commodity circulation, but there is no form of barter which could substitute for the money-form in the 'exchange of equivalents' between capital and labour: the 'production of commodities by means of commodities' is fatally interrupted. As Marx wrote in the *Grundrisse*: 'It is the elementary precondition of bourgeois society that labour should directly produce exchange value, i.e. money'.[98] Hence, the specific product of the capitalist system is value in the form of money. It is precisely the nexus between the money-form and crisis that brings back into play the foundation of the entire politico-institutional framework of the capitalist system. Here lies the real reason why Dr. Schacht, at the height of the crisis of the Mark, abandoned his 'secure' and 'well-paid' profession. But let us hear once again from this livid bourgeois intellect:

> My work was crowned with success. I put the German currency back on its feet. The brink on which the people stood was pushed back. The workers began again to receive a stable income.[99]

Bourgeois order was re-established, although the real 'taking of the Winter Palace' on the part of the German working class had been *objectively* at hand. It would have sufficed to continue to deny to the state any control over the exchange-mechanism between labour and capital, over the rehabilitation of the money form, and thereby over the process of (re)production as a whole. The question of an alternative socio-political direction, which would have made a decisive impact on that convulsive phase of transition, should have been placed on the agenda. Once again, the ineffable Schacht comes to confirm this:

---

98 Marx 1973, p. 225. Here we must avoid being seduced by the apparent immediacy of the money-form, i.e., we must avoid giving a politico-revolutionary emphasis to the money-crisis relation, which would lead to the illusion of a possible subversive overturning from the overexpansion of the wage-form. Instead, the monetary morphology should be related to the general problematic of fetishism – of the *domination of the value-form* over the social relations of production – which introduces, in a necessarily mediated way, the theme of politics. On the other hand, on the very same page, Marx writes: 'In money (exchange value), however, the individual is not objectified in his natural quality, *but in a social quality* (relation) which is, at the same time, external to him' (p. 226 – emphasis added).

99 Schacht 1949, p. 2. [I have translated this passage from the Italian, as I have been unable to trace this passage to the English translation – editor's note.]

Monetary policy is not an exact science but an art.[100]

An incredible as much as involuntary paraphrase of Lenin's 'insurrection as an art'.

However, as in the 1921 March Action, the German communists sought the Winter Palace not as a mass political alternative but in the grotesque and ruinous Hamburg insurrection[101] which marked the beginning of the recomposition of the state apparatus and with it, of the general capitalist counter-attack. At different levels, class movement and party were both integral and explosive parts of events whose immanent logic they failed to grasp. The economic and political realities provided the stage upon which party and mass movement, every time they seemed to combine and generate a new revolutionary perspective, were brusquely thrown back into the isolation of their respective 'domains' and the sterility of their 'ideological oases'. Yet, it would be a serious error to take these ideologies as a pure and simple expression of backwardness that would ultimately explain the failure of the German revolution. Through what was – often incorrectly – defined as 'labour ideology', German workers expressed their real conditions of existence and their own objective political possibilities (in the absence of an alternative mass organisation able to connect the 'political' to the 'social' level); not the professional stratifications already eliminated by capital's initiative.[102] Of course, 'productivism' and 'self-management' are terms that today generate understandable ambiguities and suspicions. But it would be inaccurate (and a poor service to the revolutionary cause) to attempt to exorcise the dangers of the present through a distorted historical reading of class needs and organisational forms which, in addition to natural contradictions and ideological shortcomings, reverberated with a powerful intensity and potentiality that had no precedents in the history of the Western workers' movement.[103] In the Germany of the 1920s, 'control' and 'autonomy' expressed the will of the working class to take up the rationalisation and planning of the productive process so as to emerge from it as the hegemonic class over other social groups. This was the amibitious perspective of the council movement. To transform this need into a science of politics and into a theory of organisation was an effort as difficult as it was indispensable, not only in terms of

---

100   Cf. Schacht 1949, p. 11.
101   On the Hamburg insurrection, see the work published under the pseudonym of Neuberg 1970, pp. 81–104.
102   Only after 1924 is capital able to carry out major transformations in class composition. Cf. Arndt 2015, pp. 32–8.
103   Cf. Ihlau 1969, pp. 85 ff.

the fortunes of the German proletariat but – as Lenin himself pointed out – for the whole international workers' movement. The alternative to this project was certainly not 'communism as a minimal programme', but Stalin's five year plans, the New Deal, and Nazism.[104]

At this point, a dispassionate and rigorous analysis of the real possibilities cofronting the German workers' movement in the crucial year of 1923 to exercise real political control over labour, money, distribution and income becomes necessary. Since this would require a detailed examination of documents which cannot be carried out here, we will limit ourselves to proposing a few of the main elements (already well known) which, within the context of this work, seem to assume a somewhat different meaning from that traditionally ascribed to them.

(1) Compared to the severity of the crisis, the number of unemployed was relatively low: about 600,000 against over 6,000,000 in 1930. Thus, the determining factor in the valorisation of commodities was primarily the labour of workers – variable and not fixed capital.[105]

(2) In its strategic maneuvers to stabilise the Mark, the central bank re-established order starting from below: it no longer accepted as currency privately expended money.[106]

(3) Thus, industrialists, no longer able to trust a centralised power, were increasingly forced to regulate *in loco* the exchange between labour and

---

104 'With the abandonment of gold currency, a new currency system was gradually formed in Germany, whose essence was designated by the Führer – in an important speech – as labour currency [...]. The simple and readily accessible principle of labour-currency is: money is covered by national production. I can only make as much money as I can produce. But labour-currency needs stability as much as does gold currency. It is based on order in the national economy [...]. Evidently, the equilibrium between credit and production, money and commodities, is not the elementary principle of labour-currency'. See Winschuh 1941, pp. 55–63. But the principle of the Nazi labour-currency was even simpler than Winschuh indicated. On 2 May 1933, the 'free unions' adhering to the ADGB were dissolved. On 5 May, Ley, the head of the Labour Front, could announce to the Führer that the National Socialist movement exercised full control over all the labour-power in the Reich. On the working class under Nazism, see Roth 1974, pp. 101–56.

105 1922 records the lowest unemployment of the post-war period. In 1923, unemployment rises primarily because of the 'passive resistance' carried out in the Ruhr against the occupation troops of the French. Cf. Albrecht 1931, pp. 171–81. Only after 1924 did the progressive expulsion of the workers from the restructured factories begin. Up to 1923, German capital could only intensify the exploitation of labour through a more 'rational' use of Taylorism. But Taylorism can only reduce the workers' professionalism – not eliminate it. On the relation between labour councils and Taylorism, see Petri 1919, p. 178.

106 Schacht 1949, p. 7.

capital by releasing money coupons which were accepted by stores and public outfits. Money had slipped so low that it risked falling by the force of inertia into workers' hands.

(4) The capitalists immediately realised the danger latent in this phenomenon while the workers' movement, on the whole, was unable to understand which levers of power over the social and political framework it could have captured. The critique of political economy was rigorously banned from any party revolutionary project.[107]

(5) As for the regulation of the Mark with respect to foreign currency, the central bank followed Hilferding's old formula. It stabilised the Mark with respect to the dollar: 4.2 billion Marks to the dollar.

In this way, a defeated and rejected country, Germany, entered the community of nations with a distinctly capitalist regime, thus showing itself worthy of being saved. The country had resolved in one of the two possible ways its turbulent and troubled 'transitional phase'.

5 The 'Return to Marx' and the 'Mortal Crisis of Capitalism': From Weimar to the New Deal

When in 1920–30, 'all the factors for a great popular revolution'[108] reappeared in Germany, the gap between class movement and labour organisations was immense. The tragedy of the workers' movement ran its course precisely in these last dramatic years of the Weimar Republic and provides useful indications for social and economic theory. Consider the polemic on imperialism and the crash between Fritz Sternberg and Henryk Grossman, as well as the latter's methodological contributions reconnecting the analysis of the contradictions inherent to capitalist development to the categorical framework underpinning the critique of political economy. Consider also the works concerning the morphology of the crisis, on the Soviet Union and the 'planned economy' by economists such as Friedrich Pollock,[109] or the fundamental analyses of the *Sozialphilosophen* (social philosophers) Max Horkheimer and Theodor W. Adorno who, in the *Zeitschrift für Sozialforschung* continued the important work carried out for almost two decades by Carl Grünberg with his *Archiv für die Geschichte des Sozialismus und der Arbeiterbewegung*. To merely denounce

---

107   On the successive investments of American capital in Germany after the institution of the Dawes Plan (April 1924), see Brooks 1925.
108   Rosenberg 1972, p. 211 f.
109   Cf. the essays collected in the anthology Marramao (ed.) 1973.

the lack of mass influence of these works, to dismiss them as useless academic exercises, would be not only harsh but also simplistic and banal.[110] The effective 'separateness' of these works is not due to their alleged 'academicism', but due to a specifically political reason: the general bankruptcy of the workers' movement which, trapped in the static schematism caused by the increasingly radical and profound break between the SPD and the KPD, had generated an irremediable fracture in the relation between theory and movement, and a consequent recoiling of theoretical reflection upon itself. It was precisely this situation which led to the high levels of self-reflection in methodology and epistemology.[111]

If initially the attention of the 'council left' had focused almost entirely on self-organisation within the productive process, overlooking (as we have seen in Korsch, for instance) the theoretical analysis of the crisis, the opposite now takes place: the 'objective' analysis of economic laws leading to the crisis and to the breakdown of the system tends (primarily in the work of the most important economist of the period, Henryk Grossman) to substitute for and replace the analysis of the labour process and the self-management thematic underpinning in it. Yet, this tendency was not a *passive* attitude produced by the stasis (and, then, by the definitive defeat) of the movement. In short, it is not the sign of an 'economistic' or 'catastrophist' deformation. Rather, it was supported by a strong methodological awareness.[112] In his main work on the law of accumulation and breakdown of the capitalist system, Grossman writes: 'The great meaning of Marx's work consists precisely in the fact that he is able to explain all the phenomena of the capitalist mode of production starting from the law of value';[113] the 'Marxian theory of the breakdown is [...] a necessary presupposition for the understanding of the Marxian theory of the crisis, and it is intimately connected to it. The solution to both prob-

---

110   S. Bologna exhibits this attitude of hasty and superficial dismissal in his introduction to Moszkowska 1974, p. v.

111   [Cf. Chapter 8: 'From the Crisis of the "Self-Organised Market" to the "Authoritarian State": Notes on the Relationship between Political Economy and Critical Theory', in this volume – editor's note.]

112   For Grossman's most important methodological writings, see his 'Die Aenderung des ursprünglichen Aufbauplans des Marxschen *Kapital* und ihre Ursachen', in *Archiv für die Geschichte des Sozialismus und der Arbeiterbewegung*, XIV (1929), pp. 305–38; and 'Die Wert-Preis-Transformation bei Marx und das Krisenproblem', *Zeitschrift für Sozialforschung*, I (1932), pp. 55–84. [Translated as 'The Change in the Original Plan for Marx's *Capital* and its Causes' and 'Value-Price Transformation in Marx and the Problem of Crisis' in Grossman 2018, respectively pp. 183–209 and 304–31 – editor's note].

113   Grossman 1929, p. 608. [A complete English translation of this work in the Historical Materialism Book Series (Grossmann 2021), came out too late for the present collection – editor's note.]

lems is provided by the Marxian law of accumulation which constitutes the *key idea* of *Capital* and is in turn based on the law of value'.[114] The 'return to Marx' initiated by Luxemburg was based here on a more solid methodological foundation, which enabled the general theory of the crisis to avoid the dangers implicit in a revision. Grossman's two fundamental contributions were: 1) the direct connection of the theory of the crisis to the theory of accumulation and to the theory of value; and 2) the definition of the process of categorial abstraction as the 'method of isolation' (*Isolierungsmethode*). The economic ('objective') exposition of the *tendency* to breakdown is not presented as a pure and simple 'reflection' of the real movement, but its abstract representation (*Darstellung*) grasped via successive approximations,[115] on the level of categorical development, of the *self-contradictoriness* of the system.

The dialectical character of Grossman's method of exposition had been vigorously defended in *Rätekorrespondenz* – the theoretical organ of the 'council communists' (*Rätekommunisten*) – by Paul Mattick, in a polemic with Pannekoek on the 'theory of breakdown' and revolutionary subjectivity. In a nutshell, Pannekoek had essentially advanced two criticisms against Grossman: an alleged attempt to deduce the end of capitalism 'from a purely economic viewpoint' thus conceiving the crash 'independently of human intervention',[116] and a reduction of the class struggle to an 'economistic contest'. In his clear anti-critique, Mattick pointed out how Pannekoek failed to catch the *dialectical* character of Grossman's procedure, precisely because he was himself bound to a *restricted* ('*bourgeois*') *concept of economy*. The dialectical method of Marx's critique of political economy does not consist in a simplistic application of the criterion of the 'synthesis of opposites' but, rather, in the abstractive isolation (*Isolierungsmethode*) of fundamental moments able to define the law of movement of capitalist society. As Mattick noted: 'For Grossman too there are no "purely economic" problems; yet, in his analysis of the law of accumulation, this did not prevent him from restricting himself for *methodological reasons* to the definition of purely economic presuppositions and of thus coming to *theoretically* apprehend an objective limit-point of the system. The *theoretical recognition* that the capitalist system must, because of its internal contradictions, necessarily break down *does not at all entail* that the *real crash* is an automatic

---

114 Grossman 1929, p. 60.
115 Cf. Grossman, 'Die Wert-Preis-Transformation ...' in Grossman 2018, p. 57, and 'Die Aenderung ...', Grossman 2021, p. 337.
116 Anton Pannekoek, 'Die Zusammenbruchstheorie des Kapitalismus', in *Rätekorrespondenz*, 1 (1934), now reprinted in Korsch, Mattick, Pannekoek 1974, pp. 28 and 20.

process, independent of men'.[117] The single context defined by the interaction of production and reproduction, economy and politics, thus appeared as the inescapable objective basis of all discussions or projects of revolutionary organisation, in addition to being the key to ongoing major processes of capitalist transformation.

These last flashes of the theoretical debate in Weimar Germany became significant *after* the collapse of the German Republic and were actually already projected into a meta-European dimension. They were no longer aimed and, in some sense, functional to the movement's organisational problems, but rather confronted the Leviathan-like structures of the American New Deal and of the authoritarian Fascist state. This is the *Schwerpunkt* (cornerstone) of the analyses carried out by the groups of intellectuals associated with the now famous Institut für Sozialforschung as well as that to be found in the Marxist journal *International Marxist Correspondence* (subsequently called *Living Marxism* and then *New Essays*). This latter journal, under Paul Mattick's direction, coordinated the political work and research of many militants and theoreticians of both the American and European left (including Korsch, Rühle, and Pannekoek).[118] The 'objectivism' of the analyses which were carried out from the defeat of the revolution in Europe onwards – with greater or less conscious methodological awareness – is *for us today* all the more precious since it was the expression of the reverberation, on the categorial and analytical framework of the theory itself, of that same oscillation and ambivalence that led the workers' movement to castrate itself even before the Nazi terror sanctioned its material annihilation.

There is no red thread running from the emphasis on the tactical and organisational moment during the movement's offensive phase, and the scientific and theoretical moment (analysis of capitalist development and location of tendencies) following the defeat. The relation between them was not one of unity and continuity but, rather, of reversal. Yet, the connection was there and remained the same even if further distorted and complicated by the corporative ('massified') character of the authoritarian Fascist state: the relation between class struggle and institutions, 'councils' and 'State'. The catastrophe of the German workers' movement had dramatically posed the problem of the repurposing of theory and movement, leaving it to succeeding generations more as a spectre – the tragic poor double of October – than as a specific historical need to be met with specific political (and theoretical) answers. It is not by

---

117 Paul Mattick, 'Zur Marxschen Akkumulation- und Zusammenbruchstheorie', in *Rätekorrespondenz*, 4 (1934), now in Korsch, Mattick, Pannekoek 1974, pp. 47–8.
118 On this subject, see Bonacchi 1976, pp. 43–72.

chance that only today the workers' movement has begun to understand this connection, confronted with the gigantic structural transformations of the economy following the 1929 crisis, and has come to assume the specific form of the problem of combining the critique of political economy, the theory of crisis, and the theory of 'constitution' (of class consciousness *and* organisation). In focusing their attention on the first two elements of the connection, Grossman and Mattick had consciously isolated the objective aspect of the economic analysis as an abstract analysis (thus, not as a mere empirical description of the real movement) leaving aside, as a simple corollary, the theoretical problem of class consciousness and organisation. If this is to be seen as the historical and political limit of their efforts, it is also illusory to believe that the solution of that problem allows easy short-cuts, thus avoiding the need to pass through the 'icy desert of abstraction'.[119]

If theory, methodologically self-grounded and conscious of its own 'separateness', is sterile, if it fails to shift into the materiality of politics and the practice of class organisation – then praxis is altogether counterproductive for the revolutionary cause unless it is 'conceptualised' by theory. The unity and soldering together of the relation of theory and praxis (scientific and analytic, and not trivially empirical and/or doctrinaire), ceases to be an instance of general question begging and appears in its urgent historical and morphological specificity when confronted by the threatening progression of the crisis. Mattick's reintroduction of the Luxemburgian alternative of 'socialism or barbarism',[120] in addition to expressing the epochal catastrophe of the 'interlinking crises' and the world-historical topicality of proletarian revolution, must today be undone and articulated in a series of theoretico-political problems (and tasks). These go from a general reconsideration of the critique of political economy (updating the analysis of capitalist development for the present)[121] to a materialist theory of the forms of consciousness (of 'subjectivity'), to the identification of the organisational structures adequate to the complexity of the current real

---

119   On this, see Luporini 1974.
120   Cf. the final sentence of Mattick 1971. Cf. also 'Rosa Luxemburg's Conception of "Socialism" or "Barbarism"' in Lowy 2012.
121   An important contribution in this direction is Cassano 1973. One of the primary tasks of those who do not want to turn this reconsideration of the critique of political economy into a mere philological exercise is, according to Cassano, 'to attempt to overcome a relation between theory and class struggle that risks not only offering a limited image of the political meaning of Marx's work, but also ends up by presenting the role of theory in a mutilated and subaltern way according to a relation more reminiscent of speculative reflection than [...] *anticipation* towards the concrete unfolding of the class struggle and its needs': Cassano 1973 p. 21.

interaction of economy and politics, class struggle and institutions, and to the historico-subjective maturity of the mass movement, which can be summarised in the expression: the scientific foundation of politics.

Such a programme presupposes a real advance of the analytic possibilities contained within the nexus of present-to-past not one posed abstractly, but carried forth through specific investigations. 'Doing history' does not mean traveling in *linear fashion* the stages of a definitively closed and archived set of events from which one might draw lessons for a generic and improbable 'future', according to the extrinsically moralistic judgement of traditional historiography. Instead, it means conceptualising *through the problematic coordinates of the present* (thus not in the key of mere realisation), the past of the workers' movement as a constitutive moment of the present itself and of its non-linear possibilities of development. For this very reason this programme implies a break with the relationship of 'mirroring' between 'marxism-as-doctrine' and 'marxism-as-movement', between theory and practice, which has been so dominant in the shift from the Second to the Third Internationals – a break that imposes, at one and the same time, a 'change of the statute' of both terms of the relationship and the full recovery of the critical and anticipatory role of theoretical labour.

The tragic parabola of the German revolution is an example – still extremely relevant for us – of how the pragmatic reification of the *Organisationsfrage* generates in the class movement a paralysing break which inevitably leads it to become subjugated to capitalist initiative and to defeat.

CHAPTER 3

The Theories of Breakdown and Organised Capitalism in the Debates of 'Historical Extremism'

Introduction*

The recurring refrain of 'Breakdown or Revolution' in the various phases of the development of Marxism is rightly considered as an established fact in the recent historiography of the workers movement. What has not yet received the attention it deserves, however, is how, in the periodic re-articulation of their diverse theoretical expressions, the two terms of this alternative were taken up by various political positions, often combining under a common denominator heterogeneous and occasionally opposed currents or political positions. A correct historical understanding of the crucial moments of the western workers' movement and, consequently, of a theoretical rehabilitation of socialist strategy in the countries of developed capitalism, demands that we not be mislead by the interpretive schema which reduces this picture to the clash between social democracy and Leninism and, more generally, to a reproduction as sterile as it is mythological of the split between the reformist spirit and the revolutionary spirit, within each of the two 'domains'. A clear example of the fruitlessness of such a schema is ironically provided by the trajectory of that 'left radicalism' which, having arisen at the beginning of the century within the European socialist parties (especially the German and Dutch social democracies), later gave way in the course of its development to an array of complex and disparate positions. What interests us here, however, is not so much to emphasise the historiographical implausibility of those studies that persist in dealing with the phenomenon of *Linksradikalismus* under the generic label of 'extremism' (which is true of its defenders as often as of its opponents, as is proven by the continuing failure to distinguish, even in the most recent research in this field, between 'Left Communism' or *Linkskommunismus* and 'Council Communism' or *Rätekommunismus*, a truly serious defect). We are more interested in showing that the positions of the radical left with respect to the problem of

---

* [A version of this appeared initially as 'Teoria del crollo e capitalism organizzato' in *Problemi del socialism*, 3, 1976. It then formed chapter chapter two, part one of *Il politico e le trasformazioni*, op. cit. It was also translated by L. Fiocchi and W. Heimbach for *Telos*, 26, 1975–6, pp. 143–64. It has been revised for this volume – editor's note.]

the destiny of capitalism – which is still very relevant for us – were far from homogeneous and that it is therefore arbitrary and ideologically retrograde to presuppose the existence of a revolutionary line in its pure state, that is, beyond the day to day routine of the workers' movement and the contradictions of 'reformism'.

Of course, tracing the complex and contradictory trajectory of *Linkskommunismus* – situated at the key point of collusion and collision between the 'Marxism of the Second International' and 'Leninism' – to a large extent involves following the processes of class struggle and the theoretico-strategic debate that took place between the turn of the century and the years of the war and the October Revolution. Above all, however, it involves the later complication of the shifting positions and terms of debate evident in the period between the beginning of the 'stabilisation phase' and the great crisis of 1929 (which was also the era of the Communist International's 'Left Turn'). In the period between the wars, in the face of the resistance of the capitalist States and the stagnation of the movement, a problem arose and became increasingly obvious which was responsible for the strategic impotence of the European Left (a problem which had remained in the background as a result of the unfolding of an objective political dynamic during the years of frontal confrontations): crisis theory and the theory of development – 'breakdown' and 'organised capitalism' – were, taken separately or posed as abstract alternatives, hard to square with a precise political position. One need only consider that, if among the supporters of the *Zusammenbruchstheorie* (theory of breakdown) one finds, together with Kautsky (or at least the 'orthodox' Kautsky), an evolutionist like Heinrich Cunow and a revolutionary like Rosa Luxemburg, among its opponents we also discover, together with another one of the outstanding leaders of social democracy like Otto Bauer, one of the leading theoreticians of left communism, Anton Pannekoek, as well as the 'reformist' Rudolf Hilferding. Nor do I think it was merely by chance that it was precisely the latter who, in a report presented in 1927 at the SPD's Kiel Congress – a report rightly reckoned among the key texts in the debate on organised capitalism – insisted that in his opposition to 'breakdown-ism' he had not hesitated to embrace the activist postulate of *'Linksradikalismus'*:

> We have always been of the opinion that the breakdown of the capitalist system must not be fatalistically awaited since, far from being the product of the system's internal laws, it must be the result of the conscious action and the will of the working class. Marxism has never been fatalism, but to the contrary a maximum activism.[1]

---

1 Hilferding 1927, p. 165.

This tangle of positions, which at first glance could give the impression of a paradoxical *quid pro quo* between extremism and reformism, must not however lead us to the all-too-convenient and sterile denunciation of the 'limits' of the 'Western' left (or 'Western' Marxism). It should instead encourage us to understand the complexity and richness (although certainly not free of contradictions or shortcomings) of its problematic, which – far from constituting a dead end – interacts profoundly with the problems of Leninism and with the most advanced organisational and ideological levels reached by bourgeois hegemony.

To get an idea, even a partial one, of the complexity of this problematic, we will have to highlight three of its aspects which until now have remained obscure but, in our opinion, are nevertheless fundamental:

1. The convergences and points of intersection of certain positions of *Linkskommunismus* and certain 'varieties' of the Marxism of the Second International.
2. The non-univocity – in the determinist sense – of the 'theory of breakdown', whose fate must be viewed in connection with the distinct historical phases of the dialectic between capitalist development and the workers' movement, in which it not only plays various roles by being attached sometimes to opposed political positions, but also undergoes its own internal transformations, assuming distinct epistemological 'statutes' and distinct ways of focusing on the theme of crisis.
3. The change in function of the *theoretical moment* of the analysis of capitalism and its tendencies of development, through the work of the most sensible and advanced part of 'left communism', in the post-war era and, above all, at the end of the 1920s.

For all these reasons, the following considerations, while not limiting themselves to the positions of *Linkskommunismus*, are not on other hand intended as a specialised treatment of the debate on the destiny of capitalism within Central European Marxism. We instead propose to broadly examine the outstanding points in which this debate unfolds in the field of forces whose two poles are those of 'Leninism' and the 'Marxism of the Second International'. In the course of this study we shall try to specify the different cross-sections and moments of this complex framework of debate, with reference to polemics and thematic aspects that seem to us to be emblematic due to the particular conjuncture in which they were written or because of their periodising value.

1   Capitalism and Crisis in the Debate on Organisation: Between Lenin and Kautsky

In January 1916 Lenin's article 'Opportunism and the Collapse of the Second International' appeared in the German journal *Vorbote*.[2] The reason for starting with this article, for the purposes of the general economy of this essay, is based not so much on the fact (which is otherwise of such great historical importance) that it is a lucid balance sheet of the regression of German social democracy, but rather on the circumstance that a specific connection is adduced within it. That is, Lenin strictly relates the method and the merit of this critique of what he considers to be the extremely virulent stage of the opportunism of the Second International – social chauvinism – to the rehabilitation of the theory of the final crisis, seen as a fundamental basis for the possibility of an imminent revolution: 'The epoch of capitalist imperialism is one of ripe and rotten-ripe capitalism, which is about to collapse'.[3]

Despite appearances, Lenin was not proposing to dust off the old *Zusammenbruchstheorie*, which was integral to the doctrinal corpus of the first phase of the Second International, but was instead proposing to resolve the breakdown/revolution dichotomy in the concept of revolutionary crisis. If we situate this labour of reflection in its world-historical moment – in the midst of full-scale war and on the eve of revolution – we also discover its powerful political charge: a lot of water had passed under the bridge during the long and embittered tactical-organisational debates in Russian and German social democracies. Nor is it by accident that one of the principle targets of the Leninist critique in this article should be Kautsky's theory of 'ultra-imperialism'. The 'entirely political' character of Lenin's discourse does not arise from the contingencies of a particular historical moment, especially favourable to the revolutionary forces in Russia, but from a more than decade-long strategic inquiry, characterised by the hypothesis of a new organic connection between the theoretical and the organisational form of the class struggle on a world scale. Lenin's category of imperialism can be read, in its totality, from this perspective: it presupposes a precise interpretation of the social tendencies of development according to which the relations of force between the proletariat and the bourgeoisie were to undergo rapid dislocation, *within the new phase*, which favoured the former.[4] His theory of imperialism (which has frequently been subjected

---

2 Lenin 1964b.
3 Lenin 1964b. p. 109.
4 Cf. Lenin 1964a, pp. 345–8.

to perfectly legitimate, although abstract criticisms, as a result of their having been conducted on a purely scientific-economic terrain) follows directly from and depends upon this evaluation of the entirety of the relations of force on a world scale, and therefore fits into a tactical-organisational model which had already been prepared: the Bolshevik model.[5]

Lenin was certainly not alone in his labour of theoretical elaboration between 1905 to 1917. He neither acted nor thought within the splendid isolation of the cosmic-historical individual he has been depicted as by the complacent and sterile hagiography of a stereotyped Marxism-Leninism reduced to an empty formula, but was instead engaged in a focused and intense debate which pitted the leading exponents of the workers' movement against each other, and which had its origins in the Bernstein-Debatte. Ten years before Lenin wrote the article referred to above, Rosa Luxemburg, in her famous essay 'Mass Strike, Party and Trade Unions' (1906), had in effect made a completely analogous use of the categories of 'crisis' and 'imperialism': the imperialist and militarist phase of the bourgeoisie starkly posed the alternative 'socialism' or 'imperialism' and objectively determined a qualitative leap in spontaneous mass action. The mass strike then became a form of expression and at the same time an instrument of a relation of forces between the classes in struggle, which is the product of an objective situation. The controversy over tactics, the *Organisationsfrage*, provided an enormous impetus to the internal political struggle of social democracy, and also led to a qualitative leap with respect to the debate over revisionism, where it had originally started. It is here, the nerve centre of the polemic on the mass strike, which in effect led to a split within the party's 'orthodox front' (the break between Kautsky and Rosa Luxemburg), with the characterisation of a new 'radical' tendency (that, as we shall see, Pannekoek would join as well).

It is important to emphasise that, by combining the theory of the inevitability of the imperialist tendency of the capitalist mode of production with the debate on the tactics of social democracy, Luxemburg came to assert the organisational centrality of the *Massenstreik*, basing it on the objective evidence of a reduction in the space of maneuver for the bourgeois class, from which she deduced the consequence of the latter's increasing radicalisation in a reactionary, aggressive and anti-worker sense. As she wrote in her now-famous pamphlet, reflecting on the Russian Revolution:

---

5   On this see the noteworthy introduction to Lenin 1971, by Vittorio Strada. The volume also contains the proceedings of the second congress of the Russian Social-Democratic Workers' Party and important theoretical texts from the debate of the problem of the party.

> The mass strike is thus shown to be not a specifically Russian product, springing from absolutism, but a universal form of the proletarian struggle resulting from the present stage of capitalist development and class relations [...] the present Russian Revolution stands at a point of the historical path which is already over the summit, which is on the other side of the culminating point of capitalist society, at which the bourgeois revolution cannot again be smothered by the antagonism between the bourgeoisie and the proletariat, but, will, on the contrary, expand into a new lengthy period of violent social struggles, at which the balancing of the account with absolutism appears as a trifle in comparison with the many new accounts that the revolution itself opens up. The present revolution realizes in the particular affairs of absolutist Russia the general results of international capitalist development, and appears not so much as the last successor of the old bourgeois revolutions as the forerunner of the new series of proletarian revolutions in the West. The most backward country of all, just because it has been so unpardonably late with its bourgeois revolution, shows ways and methods of further class struggle to the proletariat of Germany and the most advanced capitalist countries.[6]

Luxemburg's text not only provides an analysis of the relations of forces on an international scale analogous to Lenin's, but also displays the belief in the irrevocably regressive and authoritarian character of the development of capitalism that made the reformist project not just mistaken but *anachronistic* and paradoxically made the revolutionary perspective of backward Russia timely for the most advanced countries. Thus the alternative 'imperialism or socialism', which Kautsky had also posed, at least verbally, in his 1909 work *The Road to Power*, made its appearance. For here too the concept of the inevitability of the end of capitalism and of the revolution was based on the prediction of an increasing polarisation in the class confrontation between a reactionary (and necessarily imperialist) bourgeoisie on the one side and the proletariat (firmly attached to the social democratic party) on the other. Beyond surface appearances and verbal similarities, however, the adoption of the 'orthodox' schema played a completely different, if not totally opposed, function for Kautsky than it did for Luxemburg. It is not always easy to grasp the difference if we restrict ourselves to textual analysis, because quite simply the center of the debate had shifted from the strictly ideological to the organisational plane. It is now on this

---

6 'The Mass Strike, the Political Party, and the Trade Unions', in Luxemburg 2008, pp. 164–5. On her polemic with Kautsky and Lenin, see L. Basso's introduction to Luxemburg 1967. On the development of Luxemburg's tactical thinking, see Warski 1922, pp. 7–15.

latter plane that the principles and the very 'statutes' of the theory were reformulated. That this was, then, the root of the movement's weaknesses, of the underestimation of the adversary's capacity for resistance and reorganisation which revealed the inability of 'orthodox Marxism' to scientifically penetrate the complexity of the historical development of the capitalist social formation is another problem, which we shall address below. It is the strategic choice, however, that reveals the clear divergence between Kautsky and Luxemburg, and the profoundly different uses to which they put the theory of breakdown. While Rosa Luxemburg subordinated the overall analysis of the catastrophic destiny of capitalism to the objective establishment of a new form of organisation and action (it was not by accident that she wrote *The Accumulation of Capital* six years after the pamphlet on the *Massenstreik*), Kautsky sought to deduce from that analysis a depiction of the relation of forces between the classes which could be harmonised with a gradualist tactic.

In an important article published in 1909 in *Die Neue Zeit*, he introduced the commonplace contrast of advanced Europe and backwards Russia precisely in order to prove, in his polemic with Rosa Luxemburg, the absurdity of an open offensive in the mature phase of the development of the class struggle: the polarisation of the conflict into a bourgeois bloc (which was increasingly prone to reaction) and a proletarian bloc inevitably produced by the imperialist tendencies of capitalism, resulted in the avoidance of the use of a form of struggle like the mass strike, as this would constitute a reckless attempt to forcibly bring about an era of rupture. Hence the necessity for Kautsky of drawing a distinct line separating the 'strategy of annihilation' from the 'strategy of attrition', as distinct responses to different situations and stages of the relation of forces.[7]

Kautsky's reasoning was undoubtedly sharp and perseptive, but not to the point of obscuring the pragmatism of the operation. I think that we would be committing a serious mistake if we see in this Kautskian distinction a foreshadowing of the subsequent theoretico-strategic reflection of the western workers' movement, or even of the Gramscian distinction between a 'war of movement' and a 'war of position'. Leaving aside the historiographical consideration of the different conjunctures, we must not to lose sight – precisely for a correct 'historicisation' – of a theoretical aspect which cannot be ignored: absent from all of Kautsky's oeuvre is the moment that provides Gramsci with the ground for the strategic decision for a war of position in the advanced capitalist countries; namely, the reactivation and rediscovery of Marx's critique of political

---

7 *Cfr.* Kautsky 1909–10, Bd. 2, p. 37. Kautsky wrote: 'Modern military thought distinguishes between two types of strategy: the strategy of annihilation and the strategy of attrition (*die Niederwerfungs- und die Ermattungsstrategie*)'.

economy and theory of revolution by way of the analysis of the *structural ruptures* and *transformations* of the mode of production, which by determining a specific relation between State and society, politics and economy in the various social formations, profoundly influence the composition and methods of struggle and the forms of consciousness of the antagonistic classes. The gradualist postulate, grafted onto the trunk of a natural-evolutionist view of the genesis and passing of society's forms, precluded Kautsky from taking into account the possibility of a productive engagement with the specific morphological threads of the distinct historical moments of capitalist development, obliging him to resort to ascribing the choice of strategy to 'superstructural' or purely 'politico-institutional' factors. If we pay close attention, we find here the root of that juxtaposition of demands (also to be found in different phases of the Kautskian conception) and of that oscillation between economism and politicism which, while typical of the Marxism of the Second International, is nonetheless not a characteristic pertaining to the Second International alone, but was passed down to theoretical tendencies and political currents that were declared enemies of that kind of Marxism, such as those later gathered together by Arthur Rosenberg, the great historian of the Weimar Republic, under the rubric *'radikaler Utopismus'*. In conclusion, although we accept the important critical observations contained in the most recent scholarship on the evolution of Kautsky's thought,[8] we must point out that not even in Kautsky at his best did the theory of breakdown ever serve as the basis for an autonomous and active strategy of the working class or for that concept of the 'imminence of the revolution' by means of which, after the 1905 Russian insurrection, the European left began to address the discontinuities of the historical process and the unevenness and chronological disjunctions of the processes of socio-economic transformation.

2   The Vicissitudes of the 'Theory of Breakdown' and the Genesis of 'Linksradikalismus'

The break within the 'orthodox' wing came about around 1910 and an autonomous 'radical' tendency took shape in German social democracy and the Second International – while Kautsky definitively opted for the path of centrism upon the occasion of the electoral success of 1912 (which was obtained

---

[8]   I refer above all to Salvadori 1974, pp. 26–80, which was then expanded into the monograph, *Karl Kautsky and the Socialist Revolution (1880–1938)*, London 1990 [Milan 1976].

by the SPD conducting a very moderate campaign, allowing it to lay claim to being the strongest party in the Reichstag with 34.8% of the vote). Above all we should not ignore a crucial circumstance, to which we already aluded in the preceding paragraph: the emergence of a new way of approaching the problematic of the destiny of capitalism, one that has little in common with the *Zusammenbruchstheorieo* of the early Second International (as eloquently expressed in Cunow's determinist breakdown-ism). Contrary to the canons of the doctrinaire corpus of Marxism (against which Eduard Bernstein had fought with a series of articles entitled 'Probleme des sozialismus', which would serve as the basis for his *Presuppositions of Socialism and the Tasks of Social Democracy* – published in English as *Evolutionary Socialism*), the theory of crisis or of 'breakdown' (as Rosa Luxemburg called it), which was elaborated and heatedly debated during these years, was not limited to the contemplation of the unfolding of an ineluctable law but was intended to activate the revolutionary consciousness of the masses. Furthermore, we have already seen that Kautsky had adapted to this new stage of the debate by dropping his previous breakdown-ism and elaborating – from his political standpoint – a pragmatic approach to the *Zusammenbruchstheorie*, in the sense of a gradualist tactic. The strong symmetry exhibited by the various possible uses of this 'objective' trend in the logic of *Capital*, which for the revisionists seemed to lead to an algebra of breakdown which was just as mythical as that 'algebra of revolution' that Lenin found contained in Hegel's Logic, thus seems to fully justify the retrospective judgment formulated by Korsch immediately after the advent of Nazism. For him, there had never been a theory of crisis that was *in-itself* revolutionary; hence the distinct positions taken on it should rather be traced back to the fundamental political attitudes underpinning them. For now we shall set aside Korsch's acute diagnosis (which was made in the context of a significant discussion of *Linkskommunismus*) for later analysis, and shall instead attempt to distinguish – precisely in order to facilitate the understanding of the various vicissitudes of the theory of the final crisis in the debates of historical extremism – the forms which the concept of the inevitable end of capitalism assumed in the different stages of the workers movement.

It is in my opinion possible to distinguish *three stages* of the *Zusammenbruchstheorie*:

1. The first stage is the theory of breakdown that we can define as the 'classic theory of the Second International', developed during the 1890s and set out in exemplary form in the pages of *Die Neue Zeit* by Heinrich Cunow. Cunow made no distinction between the objective and subjective sides of the Marxian exposition of crisis, which is why he did not hesitate to attribute to Marx the naïve catastrophism criticised by Bernstein:

'Bernstein claims [...] that we have no reason to expect an imminent breakdown of the current system because the atomization of firms, which still prevails, would set before us an unrealisable task in a scientific debate concerning the validity of the Marxian view of the capitalist process of development. This would be justified if it were a matter of provoking the breakdown by force, by way of any violent methods, an insurrection, a general strike, etc. But in this case such methods are out of the question; all we want to know is whether the preconditions for a breakdown are present or whether they are possible, and in relation to this inquiry neither our will nor our desires matter. The crux of the whole problem is whether our economic development is generating the operative tendencies leading to a general catastrophe; and in regard to this question no desire of ours carries any more weight than the desires of any other party, the national-liberals or the anti-semites, for example.'[9]

As one can immediately recognise, this is almost exactly the opposite of Hilferding's position cited above, but it is also very distant from the revolutionary breakdown-ism of Rosa Luxemburg, who set out precisely to end the divorce of science and action, theory and politics of the sort rigidly asserted in the Cunowian (and Kautskian) emphasis on the absolute *Gesetzmässigkeit* of economic development.[10]

2. The second stage began in 1905, after the Russian events, with the debate – aspects of which we have already examined above – on the role of the mass strike in the proletarian revolution in relation to the dynamic of imperialist crisis. This gave rise to the tendency which would later take the form of 'left communism'; and it was during these same years that the alternative 'breakdown or revolution' was first posed, which is to say the militant debate about whether or not the *Zusammenbruchstheorie* was compatible with an activist-revolutionary perspective. This stage lasted until about 1924 – i.e., until the *Stabilisierungsperiode* – and also contained the beginnings of so-called 'Western Marxism', which in most cases has until now been studied in an exclusively ideological, *geschichtsphilosophisch* key, but never in relation to the concrete dimension of the theoretico-political discussion of those dramatic years in Weimar Ger-

---

9   Cunow 1898–1899, Bd. 1, p. 430.
10 Kautsky's conception of historical laws can be most eloquently be found expressed in his comment to the Erfurt Programme of 1892, cfr. Kautsy 1971.

many. (Here it is legitimate to ask how it is possible to understand the 'Luxemburgism' of the Lukács of *History and Class Consciousness* and the 'radical Leninism' of the Korsch of *Marxism and Philosophy* without taking into account the impact of the *Organisationsfrage*, the contradictions of the councils movement and the 'theory of the offensive' of Radek and Bela Kun.)[11]

3. The third stage – which coincides with the decline and then the defeat of the European workers' movement – extended from the mid-1920s to the debate on crisis and state capitalism that took place during the 1920s and 1930s. This stage is emblematically expressed by the stagnation of the catastrophist theory of the Communist International on the one side, and by the development and completion of the theory of cycles 'in the bourgeois camp', on the other. Insofar as it affected the *Linksradikalen*, the crucial and theoretically most significant point is the debate over Grossman's book, which indicates the presence of an organic *Zusammenbruchstheorie* outside of the Second and Third Internationals. What distinguishes this stage from the previous one is the decline of the debate on 'tactics', which reduced the theory of breakdown to a political slogan; hence the impression of a greater separation from politics directly proportional to the requirement for a scientific-predictive focus on the developmental tendencies of the capitalist mode of production. As we shall see, this perspective would, in its mature analytic and theoretical elaborations, produce a sharp and fertile confrontation with bourgeois economic thought – Keynes in particular – and with the problematic of State intervention.

In order to understand the importance of these stages of the debate on the destiny of capitalism it will now be necessary to first of all examine the differences within 'left radicalism' in conjuncture of the second stage – already partly delineated in the polemic between Kautsky and Luxemburg.

In his 1914 book on the political strike,[12] Heinrich Laufenberg – who would later become the leader and theoretician of 'national bolshevism' with Wolffheim – while drawing up a balance sheet of the *Massenstreikdebatte* instigated by the radical left, claimed that the mass strike was the organic effect of a particular social epoch, characterised by the imperialist phase of capitalism. If it is true that in regard to this general claim, in which 'imperialism' and 'the imminence of revolution' were used synonymously, all the *Linksradikalen* were

---

11   For this set of problems we refer the reader to Chapter 2 above: 'Councils and State in Weimar Germany'.
12   Laufenberg 1914.

in agreement (they based their initial support for Lenin on precisely this issue), one cannot say the same about the consequences they deduced from this in terms of the analysis of the objective contradictions of capitalism. In reality, the corollaries of this theorem were very far from being taken for granted among the central European left, and, as we shall see, they would not even be accepted as valid within the milieu of *Linkskommunismus* when it became organisationally autonomous and separated from the Communist Party. In this connection it is significant that in the polemic that saw them unite against Kautsky, one could already discern the outlines of a divergence between Luxemburg and Pannekoek.

3 Imperialist Crisis and 'The Imminence of the Revolution': The Leninist Phase of 'Linksradikalismus'

Although he accepted Luxemburg's link between imperialism and mass action, Pannekoek tended to view the crisis-revolution problematic from a decidedly subjectivist angle. His analysis is totally concentrated on the process of the progressive emancipation of the masses from the pedagogic-enlightenment tutelage of political and trade union organisations. Pannekoek, in two articles published in *Die Neue Zeit*[13] – which moreover constituted interventions of notable importance in the debate on the tactics of social democracy – stated that while it was true that revolutionary subjectivity was the result of objective contradictions inherent in economic development, in the current phase the train had overshot the station platform: while the material preconditions for socialism were *already given* (i.e., economic objectivity had practically fulfilled and completed its proper function), what was needed now was to produce a true spiritual animation of the proletariat (i.e., the role of subjectivity had to acquire unquestionable predominance). The means for this activation were precisely those *Massenaktionen* that reformist passivism denigrated as adventurist. Urged on in this way, the autonomous action of the working class would spontaneously press towards the revolutionary break with the bourgeois state. The theme of proletarian spiritual autonomy is stressed even more in the second article, 'Marxistische Theorie und Revolutionare Taktik'. What was unique about the imperialist stage was not to be found so much in structural aspects or in a particular new morphological configuration

---

[13] Pannekoek 1911–12, Bd. 2, pp. 541–50, 585–93, and 'Maxistische Theorie und revolutionäre Tatik', Id. XXXI, 1912–13, Bd. 1, pp. 272–81 and 365–73.

of the capitalist relations of production, but rather in the fact that in – the imperialist period – the proletariat had won the chance to organise itself (its term of apprenticeship in the 'classical' competitive capitalism having come to an end) and to definitively constitute itself as an autonomous class. Furthermore, now that they had acquired the permanent disposition towards a spontaneous sense of organisation and solidarity, the workers would have to emancipate themselves from the tutelage of the party and of their historic organisations. In this diagnosis Pannekoek went far beyond Rosa Luxemburg's theoretico-political positions. While she criticised the fetishism of the organisational apparatus, without thereby denying the necessity for and the function of the party, Pannekoek saw in the latter a bad habit of the past, a superfluous residue destined to be consumed in the furnace of the 'spirit of solidarity' which would spread across the proletariat as a whole, in parallel with the tendency of the imperialist bourgeoisie to adopt more aggressive and reactionary positions out of a fear of the approaching end of their system of exploitation.

We should immediately note that, in addition to Pannekok's above-mentioned subjectivist tone, he also displays a naïve bi-polar economistic/ethicist schema that renders meaningless any need for the analysis of socio-economic structures and institutions of the capitalist system and, thus, is unable to discern the dislocations within the class structure on the basis of the modifications of the transformations that were overturning the physiognomy of nineteenth-century 'Classical' capitalism. It was no mere coincidence, then, that he proposed to integrate Marx's work – that he maintained lacked a sufficiently developed concept of emancipation – with Dietzgen's theory of the 'spirit of the proletariat'. Whereas Marx supposedly only analysed the conditioning of subjective spirit by the economy, Dietzgen focused on the way the spirit operates within the framework of its autonomous activity.[14] Were we to want to make explicit the assumption which constitutes the basis for this view, we would say that, for Pannekoek, Marx's theory is conditioned by an Enlightenment residue that was characteristic of a historical period when the proletariat still needed to be 'educated', as it had not yet achieved full independence and voluntary activity. The root of this Jacobinism was alleged to lie in the unilateral concept of science (substantially positivist and very much a product of the eighteenth century) present – as a result of particular historical conditions – in Marx's theory, which therefore remained a kind of incomplete revolution in the sphere of social thought. As Pannekok wrote,

---

14   See Pannekok 1912–13, Bd. 2, pp. 37–47.

the revolutionary significance of Marxism, consists in having made the doctrine of history and of society into a science of the same character and subject to the same strict rule of law as the natural sciences; its conclusions, which refuted all the old bourgeois conceptions, therefore assumed the certainty of universally accepted natural laws.[15]

The task now posed to the workers movement was to transfer this struggle and this inquiry from the separate plane of objective science to the plane of consciousness and ideologies. The need to 'take advantage of Dietzgen's philosophical clarity in the controversies over tactics' is negatively demonstrated by the enormous influence exercised by 'bourgeois philosophical ideas' over the revisionist current, which opened hostilities with the *Bernstein-Debatte*, that is, with the 'first theoretical discussions concerning the fundamentals of Marxism'.[16] Pannekoek justified this operation by calling for Marxism to be profoundly renovated to adapt to the new situation of the relation between objective conditioning and subjective maturation, of capitalist domination and the working class. While to this point 'the struggle of the proletariat was essentially preparation and gathering of forces' – which is why theoretical investigation during that period had to assume a predominantly historical and economic character and, symmetrically, the general theory of Marxism never went beyond the statement that 'the revolution in the mode of production is also necessarily accompanied by a revolution in the political superstructure, that the spirit is determined by the real material world and that the reality of the economic world progressively gives rise to the existence of the material preconditions for socialism'[17] – in the current imperialist stage, the primary task was instead the rediscovery of that 'active side' (*tätige Seite*) which had remained in the shadows in Marx's 'economic materialism' and which must be recovered through the analysis of the autonomy of the proletariat, of its will and its action. Only in this way could theory be fully realised, that is, find a way out of its own scientific 'separation' and materialise in the activity of the masses.

Hence, imperialism connotes the terminal stage of capitalism, the imminence of the revolution and its processual manifestation as autonomous mass action. If this general assumption contains the entire aporia of Pannekoek's discourse, it is nonetheless equally true that it is its general coordinates that

---

15   Pannekok 1912–13, Bd. 2, p. 14.
16   Pannekok 1912–13, Bd. 2, p. 46.
17   Ibid.

provide the motive for his momentary support for Lenin.[18] The reasons for the conjunctural convergence between Bolshevik praxis and the positions of *Linksradikalen* can be found in the common demand for a new tactic for the workers' movement, mediated by the critique of the 'old' theoretical form of Marxism; but, above all, it is to be found in the *political* character – discussed above – of Lenin's theory of crisis. It is this character that explains the extraordinary effect his theory had on the movement, but also the analytical weakness and precariousness of Lenin's focus on the theme of imperialism, as would become clear during the course of the 1920s and, above all, after the great crisis of 1929.[19]

In fact, between 1912 and 1917 the main reason for the convergence of Lenin's position and that of the 'radicals' was a concrete and striking fact: their attitudes towards imperialist war. Between 1911 and 1914 Kautsky defined and completed his conception of imperialist ultra-imperialism based on the alleged contradiction between finance capital, which was supposed to be the true subject and protagonist of imperialist policy, and industrial capital, which was instead said to have an innate vocation for peaceful expansion and coexistence as it is capable of expansion only when there is an harmonious extension of markets based on free trade. It was from this latter sector, then, that Kautsky saw positive impulses towards international understanding and peace. On the basis of this analysis, he arrived at the conclusion that it was possible to break the bourgeois front by promoting an alliance with the progressive sectors of the bourgeoisie, precisely those that represented industrial capital.[20] Which is why, furthermore, Kautsky predicted that, once nationalist and imperialist militarism, supported by the predatory clique of finance capital was defeated, there would be a shift from inter-imperialist competition (i.e., from that state of tension which permanently threatens to assume the form of open war) to

18 The convergence of Pannekoek and Lenin at Zimmerwald is documented in H. Lademacher (ed.) 1967.
19 It is no exaggeration to say that Gramsci is alone, amongst Marxists, in his attempt to found anew and update the strategic analysis in light of the new problems posed by capitalist reorganisation and fascism. The direction of his equiry – at the level of the 'American model' – in many ways goes beyond 'Leninism' (while being located within the historical horizon of the 'phase' the latter defines), to the extent that it confronts the new 'organic composition' of capitalist society, which is characterised by a different configuration of the relationship between politics and economics, of State and relations of production. See §6 below for more on this.
20 It should be emphasised that this position was a complete revision of his hypothesis of the polarisation of the class structure (without any attempt to verify or explicitly question his earlier assumptions), which Kautsky had affirmed only shortly earlier in his *The Road to Power* (Kautsky 1909).

a new form of international organisation of capitalist production, which we could define as a kind of cartel of states.[21]

When, at the SPD's Chemnitz Congress (1912), the party's president Haase, Ledebour, Bernstein and even Liebknecht (who would in December 1915 take a radical position, breaking party discipline with his personal vote against renewing war credits, and would be punished with expulsion from the parliamentary group) supported this position of Kautsky's (the Congress concluded with a resolution in favor of peace, understanding between nations, disarmament and free trade), Pannekoek – demonstrating impressive understanding and political farsighetedness – did not hesitate to define Kautsky's hopes illusory and restated that the only solution was a revolution carried out by the workers themselves.[22] He thus anticipated by three years the position of Karl Liebknecht, who would define Kautsky's struggle against the 'domestic truce' (*Burgfrieden*) as 'utopian'. Kautsky wanted the SPD majority who voted for war credits to support a peace without annexations and create a situation where the proletariat would have the best democratic opportunities. The war thus became the moment of truth in the political confrontation between the moderate and opportunist fraction of social democracy and the revolutionary fraction, and it was therefore the practical attitude towards the war that drew a demarcation line between the reformist right and the *Linksradikalen*.

Until 1920, the various components of 'historical extremism' were united first by their rejection of all compromise with the bourgeoisie, then by the critique of the Second International's 'exogenism', which viewed the war as a momentary perturbation of the 'normal' socio-economic course of events, with the resumption of which, as Kautsky said, the movement's internal 'disagreements' would also disappear. (It is significant that, even during the latter half of the 1920s, Hilferding still conceived of war as external violence crashing down on the natural rhythm of economic law. Once it had passed, it would have been enough to restart the mechanism, as if it were not an organic aspect of it, but a merely transitory interruption to an intrinsically perfect automatic mechanism[23]).

---

21 For the development of Kautsky's theory of 'ultra-imperialism', cf. Kautsky 1911–12, Bd. 2, pp. 107–8, and 1913–14, Bd. 2, pp. 920–1. [For extracts from these texts in English, cf. Kautsky 1983, pp. 74–96 – editor's note]
22 Cf. *Protokoll über die Verhandlungen des Parteitages der Spd 1912*, Berlin 1912, p. 423.
23 In the aforementioned lecture from 1927, Hilferding did not analyse the phenomenon of war and its impact upon economic development or upon the relations of production themselves, but saw the phase of growth and stabilisation of the 1920s like a natural or spontaneous tendency that followed the interruption of the 'economic law' (*ökonomische Gestezmässigkeit*) by the external violence of war. One should note here the extraordin-

In contrast, for the left the war was not an episodic event, just as the victorious October Revolution, which survived long enough to confirm its analysis, was the world-historical form of appearance of the system's imminent end and the reality of revolution.

In 1918, Herman Gorter, the other great Dutch leader and theoretician of *Linkskommunismus*, greeting the October Revolution as the advent of the era of workers' councils, which he said constituted 'a clear example [...] offered by the development of imperialism to the workers of western Europe, of how they must act to achieve unity and victory', declared: 'the Russian Revolution is the first revolution made entirely by Marxists according to Marxist theory. Anarchist, syndicalist, reformist and pseudo-Marxist theories (such as, for example, the Kautskyan theories) shown themselves to be useless in the revolution'.[24]

The October Revolution thus served to trigger an extraordinary acceleration in the ideological-political development of the whole European left. Starting in 1918, the activities of the *Linksradikalen*, which had till then developed within social democracy, began to play an autonomous political role. However – and here we come to a crucial point of our argument – if it can be said that, prior to the 1920s, it was a matter of complete indifference what practical positions were assumed with regard to being a defender or an adversary of the theory of breakdown, this aspect will henceforth constitute a primary rallying point, on the political plane as well, within 'left communism'.

4   The 'Two Souls' of *Linkskommunismus*

The Bremer Linke (*Internationale Kommunisten Deutschlands*) and the *Spartakusbund* merged into the KPD(S).[25] In April 1920 the more radical wing broke away from the German Communist Party and founded the KAPD (Workers' Communist Party): it was the official founding act of *Linkskommunismus* – on the organisational plane as well.[26] But within the KPD itself *two souls* continued to exist: that of the 'Bremen Left', inspired by Anton Pannekoek, and the

---

ary complementarity of the assumptions of his diagnosis: the technicist notion of the economy as mere automatism and the 'exogenous' (meta-structural) conception of crisis. Hilferding fails to grasp the function of the drive to production and accumulation exerted by war on the leading sectors of industry.

24   Gorter 1918, pp. 72 ff.
25   On the foundation of the KPD, see the volume of documents by Weber (ed.) 1993.
26   Cf. 'Erster Aufruf der Kapd (1920)', in Weber (ed.) pp. 273–4. For the history of Central European 'left communism' cf. Bock 1969 (both volumes include appendices containing documentary sources).

Luxemburgian current. So, taking up again the thread of the disagreement that we have seen run beneath the surface of the leftist front, in the form of the various inflexions of Pannekoek and Luxemburg's positions between 1906 and 1913, we see how, at the beginning of the 1920s, the internal disagreement of the radicals broke out into the open. Let us now summarise its stages of development.

In 1922, having attempted to form a left opposition in the Comintern (at the Third Congress), Karl Schröder's Berlin group – linked to what was known as the *Essener Richtung* ('Essen Tendency') – called for the immediate foundation of a communist workers' international. The *Berliner Richtung* ('Berlin Tendency') did not support the proposal, in consideration of the still-inadequate political-subjective conditions. The 'radicals'' International (*Internationale Arbeiter-Assoziation*) – which would immediately be re-baptised as the *Kommunistische Arbeiter-Internationale* – was founded only by the *Essener Richtung* and the corresponding current within the Dutch Communist Workers Party (KPAN).

The theme of the debate was precisely the prognosis for the short-term future of capitalism. While the 'Essen Tendency' embraced the 'Theory of the Mortal Crisis' (*Todeskrisentheorie*), the 'Berlin Tendency' considered the determining factor in ending the system to be the revolutionary solution brought about entirely by the autonomous subjectivity of the working class. It is interesting to observe that these two opposed wings were led by Gorter and Pannekoek respectively, whom Lenin had lumped together in his polemic against 'extremism'. In fact, the founding theses of the KAI (*Kommunistische Arbeiter-Internationale*) substantially reiterate positions set forth in the 'Open Letter to Comrade Lenin', written by Gorter in 1920 in response to Lenin's 'Extremism' essay.[27]

In this work of the Dutch 'Tribunist' we find – besides the thesis, common to all *Linkskommunismus*, of the 'bourgeois' character of the Russian Revolution as a peasant revolution – a nexus between the strategic need to guarantee and safeguard the 'pure' working class character of the European revolution and the prediction of the 'mortal crisis', which is why it is of such vital and immediate importance to form a 'workers' international'. As Gorter wrote:

> Theory teaches us that capital is formidably concentrated in banks, trusts and monopolies. In the West and especially in England and Germany,

---

27 [Marramao is referring to the essay – or rather short tract – which in English has been translated as 'Left-Wing Communism: an Infantile Disorder'. The Italian translation, which is more faithful to the German, appeared as 'L'estremismo, malattia infantile del comunismo' or 'Extremism, the infantile disorder of communism' – editor's note.]

these banks, trusts and cartels have integrated almost all the capital of the different branches of industry, commerce, transportation and even large swathes of agriculture. For this reason, industry as a whole, whether large or small, all the relations, large and small, the whole of commerce, large or small, and most of agriculture, both large-and small-scale, has beome totally dependent on big capital and been incorporated within it.[28]

The conclusion which he drew from this analysis of capitalist concentration was undoubtedly that of the imminence of the final crisis and of the advent of the revolution. Nevertheless, a doubt remained which signalled a serious theoretical impasse:

> Capital is certainly terribly weakened. The crisis is coming and, along with it, the revolution. I believe that the revolution will be victorious. But there are still two factors upholding the stability of capitalism: the spiritual slavery of the masses and finance capital.[29]

Gorter's diagnosis thus exemplifies the oscillation between capitalism's breakdown and its authoritarian reorganisation which would characterise *Linkskommunismus* throughout the period between the two wars, and whose roots are to be found precisely in that Marxism of the Second International, that the radicals believed to have been definitively superseded. It was not by chance that in his response to Lenin the Dutch Tribunist once again took up the theory (previously championed by Kautsky) of the predominance of finance capital as the ultimate factor in the concentration and coordination of all industries and as the common fabric, which is all the stronger for its elasticity, of all the social strata with an anti-worker function:

> [...] modern western European (and American) society and state, form a vast whole articulated with its most distant sectors and branches, and that is ruled, put into motion and regulated by finance capital; [...] here, society is an organised body, organised according to the capitalist model but organised nonetheless; [...] finance capital is the blood of this body which flows through all its limbs and nourishes them; [...] this body is an organic whole and [...] all its parts owe their extreme vitality to this

---

28   'Offener Brief an den Genossen Lenin. Eine Antwort auf Lenins Broschüre: Der Radikalismus, eine Kinderkrankenkheit des Kommunismus', in Gorter 1969, p. 77.
29   Gorter 1969, p. 79.

unity, so that they will remain bound to it until death. All except the proletariat, which is the creator of the blood, surplus value. Due to this dependence of all classes upon capital and the formidable power at its disposal, all the classes are hostile to revolution, leaving the proletariat standing alone. And since finance capital is the most elastic and malleable power in the world and knows how to multiply its influence a hundredfold by means of credit, it succeeds in keeping the capitalist class, society and state united, even after this horrible war, after the loss of millions, and in a situation which appears to reveal its bankruptcy. Even so, it succeeds in unifying all the classes – with the exception of the proletariat – more solidly around it, organising their common fight against the proletariat. This power, this elasticity, and this mutual support of all classes, are capable of lasting a very long time even after the outbreak of the revolution.[30]

The lack of any relation between the two moments of the analysis – the revolutionary crisis, as a phase inherent to autonomous workers' action, and the tendencies toward concentration, under the aegis of finance capital – explains the absence in Gorter's discussion (which is otherwise so stimulating and rich in insights) of any interest in the *structural-institutional effects of the passage from the anarchy of competition to the 'despotic' reorganisation of society and economy* under the control of a single authority. But if the growing emphasis – which is in many respects ideological, insofar as it is not supported by specific economic research – on the importance of finance capital must be seen in relation to the theoretical limitations of the workers' movement of those years (which also characterises Lenin's *Imperialism, the Highest Stage of Capitalism*),[31] the simplistic diagnosis that reduces the complex problem of the class

---

30 Ibid.
31 The precarious theoretical basis of Lenin's analysis lies in the excessive emphasis given to the parasitic aspects of the capitalist system, the effect of which can be registered in the discrepancy between the diagnosis of the processes of concentration and reorganisation of the relations of production and the characterisation of imperialism as 'capitalism in transition, or, more precisely, as moribund capitalism' ('Imperialism, the Highest Stage of Capitalism', in Lenin 1964c, p. 302). To this extent, we share F. Claudin's observations that, on the one hand, Lenin grasps the monopoly aspect, on the other, he accentuates the concept of the *cumulative worsening of contradictions* (cf. Claudin 1974, p. 51). This does not mean that Lenin draws upon the idea of the maturity and agony of western capitalism from the orthodox or 'centrist' theorists of the Second International without revision. A doctrinaire hypostasisation of catastrophy, reproducing some *leitmotives* of Second International Marxism, can indeed be met with in later ideological systematisations of the Communist International (particularly between 1928–34) – but not in Lenin. He falls into

structure of western societies to a fragile bi-polar schema juxtaposing proletariat and bourgeoisie (in which the support of all the other social layers for the policies of finance capital is taken for granted), was in reality a motif derived from the Kautskian tradition of the Second International, which we shall rediscover – after the 'left turn' of 1929 – in the 'class against class' tactic of the Communist International. Hence, at the root of the aporias of *Linkskommunismus* was undoubtedly a profound inadequacy of the tools of the analysis of capitalist development, which prevented it from understanding the endogenous, which is to say, organic character of the crisis and the intimate relation between crisis and politico-institutional reorganisation. Consequently, this also inhibited it from grasping the changing tendency of the class dynamic and its roots in the reorganisation of the factory system and social labour as a whole. The fact, however, that this theoretical difficulty was so flagrantly manifested among the classic representatives of 'left communism' does not mean that it was an exclusive attribute of the latter. Rather, it was a limitation it shared with the 'majority tendencies' – socialist and communist – of the workers' movement, something which, to say the least, paradoxically, 'historical extremism' had in common with the Third International. As we shall see, few and far between were the reflections in the Marxist camp able to measure themselves against the highest levels of the social and economic reorganisation of capitalist relations in order to reformulate – at this level – their theoretical discourse on crisis and its relation to strategy.

5 The Theoretical Phase of Left Communism and the New Terms of the Problem of Crisis

The internal division within *Linkskommunismus* – officially sanctioned by the 1924 split[32] – between those who engaged in further elaboration of the subjective aspect (and, therefore, emphasising the possibility for economic crises

---

what we have defined as the 'second phase' of the theory of crisis, which is rooted not in scholastic or metaphysical prejudices but rather in a political analysis of the relations of forces on a world scale, which Gramsci – reflecting in his years of incarceration on the reasons for the defeat of the revolution in the west – would relate to the strategic phase of the 'war of movement'.

32 On the split of 1924 (between the Essen-tendency, which professed the theory of the mortal crisis of capitalism and the need for an international working class organisation able to catalyse the imminent explosion of insurrection, and the Berlin-tendency, which was contrary to the formation of the KAI and tied to the Dutch 'council commun-

to be absorbed and for the progressive concentration of the world system of exploitation) and the 'neo-breakdown-ists', concealed an unresolved issue that both sides had in common: in neither of the two tendencies could one find a combined analysis of structural transformations and socio-political mutations. Instead, both turned to the classic dualism of economic law and the subjective factor which, by dissolving the problem of the state into that of 'ideological' or 'spiritual' 'domination' of the proletariat by the bourgeoisie, rendered both sides politically sterile. It is not by chance that even in Gorter's reflections discussed above, the hypostasis of the process of concentration of finance capital corresponds – on the field that was supposed to be political – to that aspect of 'spiritual power', of *geistige Macht*, which played a decisive role in Pannekoek's 'anti-breakdown' conception (and which, in the final analysis, was not so different from the social democratic position, which sought the reason for the crisis or the success of capitalism in the 'moral factor').

The fact that, in the tragic Weimar years, this inability to achieve a strategic refoundation drew upon the most fundamental postulates of the movement's *Weltanschauung*, was already clear to the most lucid and well-known intellects of the 'west European left'. It is enough to recall that, precisely at the beginning of the 1930s, an intellectual such as Karl Korsch unhesitatingly began to speak of a 'crisis of Marxism':

> Marxism today is in the midst of an historical and theoretical crisis. It is not simply a crisis within the Marxist movement, but a crisis of Marxism itself. This crisis reveals itself externally in the complete collapse of the dominant position – partially illusory, but also partially real – that Marxism held during the pre-World War I era in the European working class movement. It reveals itself internally in the transformation of Marxist theory and practice, a transformation which is most immediately apparent in Marxists' altered position vis-à-vis their own national state as well as with respect to the bourgeois system of national states as a whole. It is deceptive and even false to see the theoretical origins of the present crisis as resulting either from a perversion or an oversimplification of Marx and Engels' revolutionary theory at the hands of their successors. It is equally misleading to juxtapose this degenerated, falsified Marxism to the 'pure

---

ists' that embraced Pannekoek's critique of *Zusammenbruchstheorie*), and the varied currents and tendencies of 'left communism', and, more specifically, on the differences between *Linkskommunisms* and *Rätekommunismus*, cf. C. Pozzoli 1976. On *Rätekommunismus*, one should note the important pages by the eminent exponent of council communism, C. Brendel, prefacing the works of Pannekoek 1974.

theory' of Marx and Engels themselves. In the final analysis, today's crisis is the crisis of Marx and Engels' theory as well. The ideological and doctrinaire separation of 'pure theory' from the real historical movement, as well as the further development of theory, is itself an expression of the present crisis.[33]

What nonetheless remained concealed in the Korschian denunciation of the split which had opened up between theory and movement, was the problem of the verification of the methodological assumptions and conceptual framework of the analysis of capitalist development accepted at that time in the workers' movement. Such a verification was all the more necessary when one considers that it was precisely during the 1920s and '30s that bourgeois social and economic thought showed itself to be extraordinarily fecund. It was precisely this circumstance that made the poverty and inadequacy of the internal debate within *Linkskommunismus* so striking.

The work of Henryk Grossman, occupying the point of intersection between 'bourgeois theory' and the workers' movement, heralded a decisive turning point, facilitating a partial escape from this impasse and opening a new phase of debate, characterised by a different approach to the problematic of the destiny of capitalism, and bequeathing a heritage which – during the years of workers' defeat and fascism – would permit a host of Weimar intellectuals and 'council communists' to confront the new tendencies and organisational forms of the capitalist economy, from the nazi-fascist regimes to the New Deal, by deepening the category of 'state capitalism'. Grossman's book *The Law of Accumulation and Breakdown of the Capitalist System* was published in 1929,[34] the year when the depression began, and circulated during the phase of the movement's reflux and liquidation. His elliptical revision of *Zusammenbruchstheorie*, however, could not (and furthermore did not attempt to) serve as a direct instrument of political combat: that is, it was not a book for activists in the strict sense of the term. This fact, however, does not detract from its historical importance, which can only be understood by those who make the effort to grasp its innovative aspects in connection with the general problems of the workers' movement of those years. The Grossmanian programme of a scientific exposition of the developmental tendencies of capitalism is not formulated on the basis of (or at the same level as) the earlier crisis theories. What is more, the latter are at first subjected to a dual critique: 1) because they remain anchored in

---

33 Korsch 1971, p. 167.
34 Grossman 1929.

a rigid preconceived assumption of underconsumption; 2) because they did not differentiate (and therefore made unjustified inferences) between the 'logical plane' and the 'historical plane' (the scientific exposition of the tendential laws and the real movement), both in defense of as well as in the criticism of the Marxian analysis of capitalism. We cannot take the time here to consider the extremely well-articulated way Grossman develops this two-pronged critique in his major works and in his 'epistemological' essays,[35] but shall simply aim to provide an outline of their most general aspects, which will nonetheless give the gist of their originality and qualitative rupture with respect to the previous debates on crisis.

The characteristic feature of Grossman's theory – which stands out when compared with Rosa Luxemburg's *The Accumulation of Capital*, or with the analyses of imperialism made during the 1920s by the Luxemburgian Sternberg[36] – is the deepening of the elements of epistemological discrimination between the logical structure (and internal functionality) of Marx's categories and that of classical political economists. This allowed Grossman to recover the *hermeneutical capacity of the theory of value in relation to the nexus of production and reproduction*. From this standpoint, he turns his critique against the various forms of underconsumption and registers the common 'exogenist' cast of the breakdown-ist and plan-ist explanations of the mechanisms of capitalist development. Despite the continuing survival of vestiges of Second International sociologism (visible in the definition of the abstract-concrete relation in terms of 'procedures of approximation' or 'methods of isolation'),[37] Grossman's critique of the displacement of the axis upon which the crisis turns towards that of the *realisation* of surplus value (the market), expressed a powerful demand that Marxist analysis should measure up to the complex character of the system's development, and that this should be grasped in its productive-reproductive unity, rather than by means of the dual schema of production-underconsumption.

Grossman's work was already being read and debated at the start of the 1930s, not only within the European left but also among the *Linksradikalen* groups who emigrated to the United States. It was precisely during this period that the United Workers of America published a manifesto that adopted Gross-

---

35 These have been collected in Italian translation in Grossman 1975. [In English see Grossman 2017 and 2019 – editor's note.]
36 Cf. Sternberg 1926 (in relation to which see Grossman's extremely perceptive critique in 'A New Theory of Imperialism and the Social Revolution' in Grossman 2019., pp. 120 ff.).
37 On Grossman's *Annäherungsverfahren* and the *Isolierungsmethode*, see G.M. Bonacchi's introduction to Farnetti 1970.

man's theory as the theoretical basis for a new orientation of the workers' movement. This manifesto provided Pannekoek with the opportunity to reopen the polemic concerning the theory of breakdown in the theoretical organ of European 'council communism', *Rätekorrespondenz*.

In this article, Pannekoek substantially reiterated the anti-collapse arguments he had employed twenty years earlier in the crisis debates and accuses Grossman of having a bourgeois view of economic necessity, which Pannekoek claimed was for Grossman a mythical, extra-human power. The theoretical basis for the critique was, once again, the abstract postulate (that is, it was not analytically mediated) of the unity and reciprocal interpenetration of the objective side and the subjective side, the economy and politics:

> Economics, as the totality of men working and striving to satisfy their subsistence needs, and politics (in its widest sense), as the action and struggle of these men as classes to satisfy these needs, form a single unified domain of law-governed development.[38]

It is thus evident that Pannekoek's activist subjectivism was not only incapable of confronting the methodological framework of Grossman's book, but when faced with the need to set forth theoretical alternatives, was obliged to fall back on the safe haven of the Second International's old concept of *Gesetzmässigkeit* [law-like], of which economism and ethical voluntarism were ultimately variants.[39] But the aspect we would most like to emphasise here is the appearance, in the last part of his article, of the prediction of an 'organised capitalism' of an authoritarian type, which, however, would still not necessarily result in the integration (or irreversible defeat) of the working class, but in the acceleration and spread of the process of its total unification.

> It is not due to the economic collapse of capitalism but to the enormous development of its strength, to its expansion all over the Earth, to its exacerbation of political oppositions, to the violent reinforcement of its inner strength, that the proletariat must take mass action, summoning up the strength of the whole class. It is this shift in the relations of power that is the basis for the new direction for the workers' movement.[40]

---

38   Pannekoek 1977, pp. 62–81.
39   For the theoretical terms of the debate, see Chapter 4 below: 'Theory of the Crisis and the Problem of Constitution'.
40   Pannekoek 1977, pp. 80–1.

Even though it is possible to discern in this prognosis the faint outline of that excessive ideologisation of the category of 'state capitalism' that would take place during the 1940s by some theorists of the ultra-left (among which we must include Korsch), in which the process of the total socialisation of the working class was the mirror image of the process of capitalist concentration,[41] Pannekoek's intervention once again proved extremely weak in indications concerning the strategic question of the analysis of the new aspects of capitalist development. Nor was it by chance that this critique of Grossman should denounce an approach to theory and crisis in a way that was methodologically much less differentiated and articulated than the attempt made years before by Korsch in the journal *Proletarier*, in his essay 'Some Fundamental Presuppositions for a Materialist Discussion of Crisis Theory'.

> A great shortcoming of the form in which the discussion of crisis took place hitherto, especially in the circles of the left and far-left wings of the workers' movement, was to be found in their search for a 'revolutionary' crisis theory per se, just as in the middle ages one searched for the philosopher's stone. Historical examples, however, can demonstrate quite easily that possession of such a supposedly highly revolutionary crisis theory says little about the actual level of class consciousness and revolutionary preparedness for action of a group or an individual believing in the theory.[42]

If we momentarily disregard the implicit assumption of Korsch's approach (which is immediately obvious when compared to the earlier piece on the crisis of Marxism), one cannot help but appreciate the implicit novelty of the distinction between political positions and the scientific 'paradigms' of *Krisentheorie*. The distinguishing feature of the various crisis theories that competed for attention within the workers movement is not to be found in their inner conceptual construction or their methodological bases, but in the *attitude* animating them. It is from here that Korsch drew the criterion to orientate his balance sheet of the debates on crisis, distinguishing two basic types of *Krisentheorie*:

1. The first kind was the 'official social democratic crisis theory', which – descended directly from Bernstein – found its greatest representatives in Hilferding, Lederer, Tarnow and Naphtali;

---

41 The debates in Paul Mattick's journal, *New Essays*, are emblematic in this respect. For the later developments of Korsch's position, see Rusconi's 'Introduzione' to Korsch 1975.
42 'Some Fundamental Proposition for a Materialist Discussion of Crisis Theory' (1938), in Korsch 1977.

2. The second kind was the 'objectivist theory of crisis', classically formulated by Rosa Luxemburg in *The Accumulation of Capital*, and later upheld by Sternberg and Grossman.

The characteristic trait of subjectivist crisis theories – which culminated during the 1920s in the concept of 'organised capitalism' – is that they '*ideologically reflect* the phase of the real movement of capitalist economies that was just past and place it vis-à-vis the changed present reality as fixed rigid "theory"'.[43] Unlike Pannekoek, Korsch had a good grasp of the political risks of such a conception, which in reality amounted to a destruction of 'all the bases of the proletarian class movement', reducing socialism's strategy to a mere 'moral demand'.[44]

On the other hand, the objectivist theory of crisis which conceives of '*an objectively given economic tendency of development whose ultimate goal can be grasped* in advance employs pictorial notions rather than unequivocally determined scientific concepts. Furthermore, it is founded inevitably on insufficient induction' and appears to Korsch 'as not suitable for bringing forward that full earnestness of self-disciplined activity of the proletarian class struggling for its own goals, which is as much necessary for the class war of the workers as it is for every other ordinary war'.[45]

To these two attitudes Korsch opposes a 'materialist-activist attitude'[46] that:

> alone deserves the designation of a truly Marxian materialist stance. This position explains the whole question of the objective necessity or avoidability of capitalist crises *as a senseless question in this general form* (within the framework of a practical theory of the revolution of the proletariat). It agrees with the revolutionary critic of Marx, Georges Sorel, who will not consider Marx's general tendency of capitalism to catastrophe generated by the insurrection of the working class – colored in a strong idealist-philosophical 'dialectical' manner of speech – as valid scientific prognosis, but merely as a 'myth' whose whole significance is limited to determine the current action of the working class.[47]

Despite his strong subjectivist inflection, Korsch was not attempting here to dissolve the categorical framework of Marxist analysis in a generic activism;

---

43 Korsch 1977, p. 184.
44 Korsch 1977, p. 185.
45 Ibid.
46 [No such expression is to be found in the English translation in *Telos*, which merely speaks of a 'truly *materialist* stance' – editor's note.]
47 Ibid.

much less was he seeking to reformulate a new form of revolutionary syndicalism. He was instead provocatively expressing the requirement for a disaggregation of Marx's morphological prediction (consider, furthermore, the function of 'myth' within Gramsci's rehabilitation of Marxism, after the real 'split' reflected in the *Revisionismus-Debatte*) as a *conditio sine qua non* for rendering it hermeneutically and practically effective.

> The materialist stance, is, however, not in accord with Sorel when he quite generally wants to *limit* the function of any future social theory of revolution to form such a myth. The materialist stance rather believes that certain, if only always limited, prognostic statements sufficient for practical action can be made on the basis of always more exact and thorough empirical investigation [*empirische Erforschung*] of the present capitalist mode of production and its recognizable immanent tendencies of development.[48]

However, by defining the 'activist-materialist attitude' in such an undoubtedly evocative way (which hearkens back to Lenin's 1894 critique of 'the subjectivism of the popular revolutionary Mikhailovsky and the objectivism of the then-leading Marxist theoretician Struve'),[49] Korsch overlooked a basic theoretical problem: the non-linear nature of the relation between what is 'logical' and what is 'historical' in the Marxian analysis of capitalism. As I will show in the subsequent chapter,[50] this aporia in Korsch's thinking – manifested in a declared indifference towards the specific modality by which the 'laws' which explain capitalist reality operate[51] – must be viewed in the context of a lack of understanding of the strategic role that the distinction between the mode of research and the mode of exposition (*Forschungs und Darstellungsweise*)[52]

---

48   Ibid.
49   Ibid.
50   See Chapter 4, 'Theory of the Crisis and the Problem of Constitution', § 3 in particular.
51   In defining the objectivist theory of the crisis (that allows him to join Sternberg and Grossman, despite the fact that the two had argued over the analytico-methodological explanations of crises), Korsch wrote: 'It is of no consequence from which assumed objective system of laws of the capitalist method of production the objectively guaranteed economic necessity of its imminent collapse is derived in detail' (Ibid).
52   On this problem (and in general for a critique of Korsch's Marxism), see Ceppa 1974, pp. 1231–59. One should also bear in mind the recent critical comments by Giuseppe Vacca – cf. 'Una figura della scissione tra tematica delle forme e analisi dei processi nel marxismo europeo fra le due guerre (Karl Korsch 1923–1938)', in Vacca 1976, pp. 129–204. Bearing in mind Vacca's penetrating insights, it is worth noting that this 'lack' in Korsch

plays in *Capital*. In this connection, the important theoretical points made by Paul Mattick in *Rätekorrespondenz* in defence of Grossman sound like a response not only to Pannekoek's critique, but also to the more complex Korschian attempt to carry out a 'pragmatization of the dialectic'.[53] What was criticised in Grossman as an 'economistic' perspective, as a limitation of analysis to 'purely economic' aspects, was in reality the result of a scientific application of the Marxian idea of dialectics, which coincides with neither a generic 'holism' nor with the philosophical postulate of the 'unity of opposites'. As Mattick wrote,

> For Grossman, too, purely economic problems do not exist. This does not prevent him, however, in his analysis of the law of accumulation, from limiting himself for *methodological reasons* to the definition of purely economic assumptions, and thus from theoretically grasping an objective limit-point of the system. The theoretical understanding that the capitalist system through its internal contradictions must necessarily move towards collapse, by no means leads him to consider that the real collapse is an automatic process, independent of men.[54]

The Marxian analysis of the capitalist system is scientific not because it *reflects* the real history of the mode of production, but because it defines its structural prerogatives through the study of the *forms* in which the basic contradiction between productive forces and relations of production are reproduced in the passage from simple reproduction to extended reproduction.

If, on the one hand, imbalance and crisis do not arise from the disproportion between production and market (that is, as a result of the difficulties of realisation) but are already present in simple reproduction, on the other hand, what is

---

      does not affect his *stricu sensu* methodological grasp of the problem. What he misses is the *strategic function* of this distinction, which is critical for establishing the correct relationship between (morphological) theory and (scientific) theory of politics.

53   I borrow this expression from Rusconi's 'Tensione tra scienza e azione politica in Karl Korsch', which forms the introduction to Korsch 1974. 'Pragmatisation', to our mind, indicates the lack in Korsch of that *theory of reproduction* that represents the connective support for the *critique* of political economy and the *science* of politics. From here springs too – as Vacca argues in the above cited article, p. 158 – the gap (and immediate translation) between 'epochal' phases of the mode of production and empirical analysis of the concrete class struggles, which stands in the way of an 'integrated' and differentiated (economico-political) analysis of the processes of development within the capitalist *social formation*.

54   Cfr. Mattick 1934, 4, and now in Korsch, Mattick, Pannekoek 1974, pp. 47–8.

constant in this process of transformation is the *affirmation of the value-form as a totality on the scale of society as a whole*. Hence Mattick concludes that the 'movement of capital on the basis of value is nothing but [...] the dialectical movement of society itself'.[55] The mis-recognition of the irreducible specificity of the Marxian dialectical method has prevented the orthodox as well as the revisionists from grasping the profound meaning of this 'self-movement of capital' on which the Marxian theory of crisis is based.[56] It is interesting to note that via this route Mattick would later come to denounce the 'epistemological vice' that lay at the root of the celebrated controversy between Böhm-Bawerk and Hilferding concerning the problem of the transformation of values into prices. Mattick examined Marx's efforts in this regard:

> his efforts relate to the theoretical need to test the validity of the law in confrontation with a reality which seemed to contradict it. Finding out whether or not value relations do, in fact, underlay market and price relations required a theory of prices consistent with the theory of value. The 'transformation' of values into prices of production satisfies this theoretical need. The problem of individual price determination was of no real interest to Marx; only value relations mattered, plus the assurance that the difference between value and price as encountered in reality would neither logically, nor actually, invalidate the value concept as the *key* to the 'essential fundamental laws' of capital production.[57]

The divergence of value and price therefore does not invalidate the labour theory of value, precisely because the essential nature of the concept from which the 'fundamental laws' of the system and its dominant developmental *tendency* are deduced are not determined in linear fashion with respect to the historical phenomena of development. This central epistemological assumption of Marxian science remained outside Hilferding's purview, which is why, precisely when he takes up the defence of the theory of value, he actually empties it of its critical substance in order to accept it as an interpretive schema for real market relations:

> For Hilferding, social necessity turns into a law of value in capitalism because social relations between persons are attached to things and a-

---

55   Mattick 1934, p. 49.
56   Mattick 1934, p. 50.
57   Mattick 1969 [available in English at: https://www.marxists.org/archive/mattick-paul/1969/marx-keynes/index.htm, from 'Chapter 4: Value and Price' – editor's note].

ppear as things, as commodity relations, and not as what they really are, namely, social production relations between persons. By doing away with the fetishism of commodity productions he believes the law of value would be revealed for what it really is – the necessity to regulate the social labor process in accordance with social needs directly recognized in the needs of persons. And it is only in this sense, according to Hilferding, that the law of value is historical.[58]

The analytical effect of this epistemological deformation of the law of value is the inability – shared, as we have seen, by almost all parties to the debate – to explain the crisis as an *organic phenomenon* of the capitalist system. This inability to penetrate the contradictory dynamic of development fed not only naïve catastrophism but also the success of the idea of an 'exogenous' *Regulierung* enjoyed during the 1920s, which gave rise to the famous 'theory of organised capitalism'. As Grossman wrote to Mattick in 1937,

> That the clique of neoharmonists, Hilferdings and Otto Bauers, tried for decades to systematically distort Marx, that passages such as the ones cited above were systematically concealed and that there is no trace of them to be found in the Marxist literature, is not a reason for us to go along with the neoharmonists. Once you think through Marx's concepts consistently to the end, how can a crisis arise at the level of simple reproduction in which such a harmonious equilibrium appears to prevail? Then you will find in Marx many more theoretical concepts of which the 'philosophers' have not dreamed, even those such as Karl Korsch, who imagine that they understand something of Marxist economics.[59]

Significantly, these harsh words came three years after the important anti-critique in which Mattick, polemicising with Pannekoek, indirectly called attention to the fact that despite the insightfulness of his summary of the debates concerning crisis theory, Korsch had not grasped the novelty and originality of Grossman's work in a workers' movement which was divided and oscillating between underconsumptionism and plan-ism.

---

58   Ibid. [From 'Chapter 3: Marx's Labor Theory of Value' – editor's note.]
59   Letter to Mattick, 18 July 1937, Grossman 2019, pp. 272–3.

6 Grossman's Dynamic Model and the Common Source of Plan-ism and Collapse-ism. From 'Generalised Imperialist Crisis' to 'State Capitalism'

While, in the period between 1928 and 1934, the Communist International established an extremely close connection between imperialism and crisis which clearly pointed towards a theory of collapse – assuming, above all in Varga's works, an underconsumptionist reading of crisis – the debate concerning organised capitalism took shape within European social democracy. In the report to the Kiel Congress mentioned above, Hilferding defined this controversial concept in the following terms: 'Organised capitalism means [...] *the replacement of the capitalist principle of free competition by the socialist principle of planned production*'.[60] Such a task immediately posed the problem of the relations between the programme of economic planning and the state as the centralised technical hub of organisation and fulfillment of that programme by means of which the working class takes the productive apparatus under its control: 'This means nothing less than the fact that our generation is faced by the task of transforming, with the help of the state, that is, with the help of conscious social regulation, this economy organised and directed by the capitalists into an economy directed by the *democratic state*'.[61] Hilferding integrates this scheme of (techno-)political democracy by combining the elements of 'corporate democracy', or *Betriebsdemokratie*, with those of 'economic democracy', or *Wirtschaftsdemokratie* (the latter theme having been most fully developed by Naphtali), which were to be realised by way of trade union action, and which were to be related to the state in accordance with a ready-made rigorous framework of representation, which – symptomatically – says not one word about the councils or any other instrument of rank and file democracy.[62]

The fact that the plan-ist perspective failed to discuss the sources of surplus value and the 'simple dynamics' of the system (which was considered to be exempt from any disequilibrium or disharmony), and thus remained imprisoned within the 'juridical illusion' whereby the cyclical downturns of the economy would be resolved by way of a conscious regulation of the anarchy

---

60 'Die Aufgaben der Sozialdemokratie in der Republik', in Hilferding 1927, p. 168.
61 Hilferding 1927, p. 169.
62 Interesting incites on this issue can be found in G.E. Rusconi, '"Capitalismo organizzato" e Stato democratico nella socialdemocrazia di Weimar', a talk given at the II Settimana internazionale di studi marxisti organised [Second international week of Marxist studies] by the *Fondazione Basso-Issoco* on the topic of *Lo stato capitalistico contemporaneo alla luce del pensiero di Marx*, Florence, 3–7 March 1975. Rusconi went on to further elaborate this issue in Rusconi 1977 [see especially pp. 177–229 – editor's note].

of circulation, was made clear not only in Hilferding's version, but also by other planning projects such as those of Henri de Man or the 'French socialists' (Deat).[63] In any case, despite its serious theoretical limitations and the ideology with which it was saturated, the theory of organised capitalism reflected, in a certain sense, all the difficulties and contradictions of the workers' movement confronted by the vast processes of economico-institutional reorganisation of western societies. It was this aspect that completely overshadowed the prickly class-ism of the European communist (and socialist) left as well as the sectarian perspective of the Communist International.

In 1934, barely one year before the Seventh Congress, Varga liquidated the problem of the planned economy displaying total indifference to the organisational forms of capitalist society, which he viewed as equivalent in that they were utterly incapable of eliminating the exploitation of the workers and crisis. But what is of more interest within the context of our discussion is the fact that, in order to supply a bit of 'scientific' support to his polemic, the official economist of the Comintern was obliged to resort to the 'classic' underconsumptionist explanation which had dominated the *Zusammenbruchstheorie* field of the Second International debates:

> [...] capitalism, whether it is based in whole or in part on free competition, or is totally or partially spiced with ingredients of State capitalism, necessarily leads to periodic crises [...] the 'nationalisation' of credit or a state monopoly in raw materials changes nothing in the framework of the bourgeois state; and 'underconsumption' cannot end because the working class will continue to receive only a part of the value it produces in

---

63 These planning proposals were linked to the 'anti-capitalist' alliance between proletarians and a 'new middle classes', which was supposed to be limited to 'action against the monopoly power of financial capital, without touching upon other forms of private property' (H. de Man 1934, p. 12). In 'plan-ist' ideology as well, that autonomisation of the role of finance capital – of Second Internationalist origin – as monopolistic excrescence of a harmonious market capitalism – that, as we will see, can be linked back to the 'exogenist' postulate of the entire debate on 'crisis'. On the *Plan du Travail* and its revisionist character, see Agosti 1969, pp. 241–60. For further confirmation of the debate on the 'de Man plan' within the 'socialist milieu' of the Thirties, cfr. L. Luzzato and B. Maffi, 'La politica delle classi medie e il planismo', a partial draft of which was published in *Politica socialista*, August 1935, 4, pp. 357 ff. under the signature 'x.x.x.' It then appeared in full as a pamphlet in October 1938, as n. 5 of the imprint *Echi* of the *Centro socialista interno*. It can now be read in Merli 1975, pp. 76 ff. On the theoretical interest in the 'de Man plan' within the milieu of corporativism, see Ciliberto 1977. (It is significant that it was an intellectual of the stature of Cantimori who translated and commented upon the 'Plan du Travail' in the *Archivio di Studi corporative*, VI, 1935, pp. 31–50.)

the form of wages, while the other part remains with the capitalists in the form of surplus value and will be used to augment their capital. There is no capitalism without underconsumption, without the limitation of the earnings of the workers to the minimum, as determined by the profits of the capitalists.[64]

Aside from the starightforward denunciation of the political incompatibilities and the democraticist ideology of the theory of organised capitalism, the new historical fact that the Communist International failed to grasp was precisely that tendency on the part of the capitalists to introduce elements of regulation and control of the economy which, far from being mere tactical instruments for the purpose of obtaining a temporary adjustment of the anarchic market mechanism, implied a direct intervention of the state in the social reorganisation of production and, consequently, an increasingly closer connection between the 'political' and the 'economic'. But the fact that this 'detail' escaped its notice was only a consequence of an inability to provide a rigorously 'endogenous' explanation of the *dynamic of the capitalist crisis*; that is, of grasping the contradictory nexus of crisis and development, 'anarchy' and 'planning', as an inherent structural connotation of the mode of production. Viewed in this light, if we look closely, there was not much difference between the thinly disguised breakdown-ism of the Comintern and the plan-ism of the social democrats. To have provided all the elements for a demonstration of the common source (and of the paradoxical interchangeability) of the opposed theories of 'generalised imperialist crisis' and 'democratic planning' constitutes the most original aspect of Grossman's contribution.

It is no accident that his critique applies equally to breakdown-ist supporters of the underconsumptionist hypothesis and to the 'neo-harmonists'; both proved incapable of grasping the consubstantiality of crisis to capitalist development, explaining the vicissitudes of the period extending from 1914 to 1919 as 'catastrophes' or as 'disturbances', produced in any event by external causes. Both Hilferding and Varga understood the war as an external accident, a hiatus or momentary interruption of the accumulation process. For Hilferding, Marx's nexus between crisis and the process of reconstituting the conditions for accumulation disappears; for Vargas, the crisis does not represent a process of reconstitution of the processes of accumulation but rather a distribution of the already-attained level of capital accumulation, a mere regression or relapse

---

64 Varga 1934, p. 48. It is symptomatic how from here Varga ends up rendering 'plan' and 'fascism'. See Galli Della Loggia 1974, cit., particularly pp. 1004–9. For Varga's critique of 'organised capitalism' cfr. also the collected articles in Varga 1969, pp. 11 ff.

to a previous stage.⁶⁵ The ostensible contrasting objectives of the two positions do not contradict this symmetry (Varga's absolute indifference to any kind of plan corresponds to Hilferding's exclusive attention to the mere organisational form), which Grossman even connects to the Hilferdingian tendency – already outlined in *Finance Capital* (1910) – to extrapolate the analysis of monetary phenomena and financial concentration from the context of the Marxian theory of value, elaborating his own theory of money. As a result, neither the debates concerning imperialism nor the investigations into monopoly forms of organisation really came to terms with the authentic theoretical structure of the Marxian undertaking, which 'explains all of the phenomena of the capitalist mode of production on the basis of the law of value'.⁶⁶

Although his final statements – with their drastic denial of the possibility of any capitalist control over the economy⁶⁷ – betrayed his participation in the debates' historical limitations, Grossman's theory possessed the rudiments of the instruments that would prove decisive for the purposes of analyses of the 'morphological' changes of the system. It fell to Friedrich Pollock – who had also, like Grossman, been formed by that extraordinary meeting-point of the bourgeois social sciences and Marxism represented by the *Grünberg-Archiv* – to verify, over the course of the 1930s and 1940s, the possibilities and limits of a capitalist planned economy, on the basis of a complex and highly-articulated analysis of the morphology of the international crisis; and to detect a new mode of the functioning of the economy, based on a *displacement* of the Marxian contradiction between the productive forces and the relations of production.⁶⁸ If the novelty of Pollock's research resides in confronting the real historical form of 'organised capitalism' which represents state capitalism within the framework of an 'endogenous' explanation of the crisis (which is therefore viewed strictly in relation to developmental trends) this was nonetheless unthinkable without Grossman's fundamental *prolegomena*, which constituted the enduring methodological background to the work carried out by that Weimar intellectual left that would later become famous under the name of 'The Frankfurt School'.

Another aspect of Grossman's work that would prove seminal not only for the analyses of the Frankfurt School but also for those of Paul Mattick and his group in the United States, is the attention devoted to the problem of dynamics which, in certain respects, aligns the Polish economist with the research on

---

65 Grossman 1929, pp. 498 ff. and 604 ff.
66 Grossman 1929, p. 608.
67 Grossman 1929, p. 606.
68 Cfr. Pollock 1973, pp. 135 ff.

cycles carried out during those same years by Schumpeter and Mitchell, rather than with the Marxism of that time. This research presupposed the rejection of static systems and the central position of dynamics as the scientific criterion for the analysis of capitalist development.[69] In this context, what Grossman wrote to Mattick in a 1933 letter seems highly significant:

> all Marxists to date have had a 'little' accident, in that they have not noticed simple reproduction in Marx, have not noticed its real meaning. All engage only with expanded reproduction as a problem. In the schema of simple reproduction everything works. And it is precisely the opposite that Marx wanted to demonstrate. Even under simple reproduction, crises are unavoidable. This, precisely, is why Marx is a really dynamic thinker, in contrast to bourgeois economics, which is essentially static ([affirming a] 'tendency to equilibrium' which is automatically produced – the crisis must therefore come from outside the system as a deus ex machina). In Marx, disequilibrium is bound up with the nature of the system.[70]

As confirmation of the links, despite notable differences, between Grossman's research and the theory of cycles, it is enough to again cite his continuing engagement with Tugan-Baranowski, whose text on commercial crises in England had become established as a not merely analytical but also methodological acquisition of bourgeois economic thought.[71]

In light of our considerations on Grossman's work, let us now turn our attention to a diagnosis of the debate on the destiny of the capitalism in the years straddling the Twenties and Thirties. In so doing, we cannot but be surprised by the position of those who believe it is possible to conveniently draw a sharp dividing line between a stance which affirmed the necessity of breakdown through 'purely economic' causes, and another which instead links the downfall of the system to the 'proletariat's subversive intervention'.[72] Setting out with

---

69 For Grossman's interest in the work of W. Mitchell, *Business Cycles: The Problem and its Setting* (Mitchell 1927), see the letter to Mattick of 21 June 1931, in Grossman 1929, pp. 227 ff.
70 Cf. Letter to Mattick of 17 June 1933, Grossman 2019, p. 249.
71 A notable European contribution to the theory of economic cycles came from Ernst Wagemann and the *Institut für Konjunkturforschung* in Berlin, the work of which is referred to in Moszkowska 1935. The book has been translated into Italian with the title *Per la critica delle modern teorie della crisi*, with an introduction by Sergio Bologna, Turin 1974 (see pp. 37 ff. for a discussion of Grossman's theses). For more on these aspects see my 'Razionalizzazione capitalistica e soluzione totalitaria. Il fascismo tedesco nell'analisi di Alfred Sohn-Rethel', the final chapter of Marramao 1979.
72 Cfr. S. Bologna's introduction to Moszkowska 1974, p. vii.

such a yardstick amounts to erasing in one stroke the characteristic note of the 'third phase' of the debate concerning capitalism's destiny: the not only politico-strategic but also 'epistemological' line of demarcation within theories of crisis. In short, after 1929, what was imposed upon the movement was not so much an empirical updating or 'adjustment' of the analysis (as proposed by the Communist International) but, rather, a new foundation and a change of form for Marxism: a distinct expression of theory with respect to the entire capitalist social formation as precondition for a new relation to revolutionary politics and praxis. These were the problems of the movement that certainly could not be considered to be merely academic: the redefinition of the 'systemic' function of the theory of value, the establishment of the moment of *reproduction* at the centre of strategic elaboration and, thus, the displacement of the centre of gravity of a debate which had till then revolved in a vacuum, prisoner of the production/consumption opposition. Untying the thorny problem of reproduction therefore implied elaborating a theoretical model capable of explaining the dynamic of the whole capitalist mechanism on the basis of that accumulation-crisis nexus, which were rejected by both social democratic 'revisionism' as well as by 'left radicalism' (from the Comintern to Hilferding and Varga), and – *therefore* – capable of providing a *foundation, by means of a series of scientifically determined steps, for the terrain of politics.*

All of this, for obvious historical reasons, could only have been present in Grossman in an embryonic state. It would be Marxist economists of the stamp of Mattick and Kalecki who would continue, during the following years, the discourse which began at the end of the 1920s, tackling the problems of state intervention and the dynamics of the capitalist cycle, in a frontal confrontation with Keynesianism and bourgeois economic thought.[73] The analyses carried out between the wars by Paul Mattick and the working group he organised and led, which published the 'councilist' journals *International Council Correspondence*, *Living Marxism* and *New Essays*, are important because – as we shall attempt to highlight in the next chapter – they reformulated crisis theory in a manner that was no longer ideological and/or empiricist, but by way of a more profound understanding of the *circulation-production nexus* and of the *relation between the state and the process of reproduction*. In this sense, they also provided the key to an interpretation which is not purely sociological, but 'structural-morphological', of fascism and the various forms of state capitalism.

---

73 Cfr. Mattick 1969; 1973 [and in English, https://www.marxists.org/archive/mattick-paul/1974/crisis/index.htm]; Kalecki 1971. Cf. also Mattick, Korsch and Langerhans 1976.

If, then, during the 1930s and 1940s the most vital component of *Linkskommunismus* could productively engage with phenomena and aspects unknown to the debate of the 1920s, this was due in no small part to the fact that – in the study of the various forms of capitalist concentration and organisation – it had taken from Grossman the theoretical instruments required to avoid the repeated suggestions offered by the underconsumptionist hypotheses (which, in a new guise, made notable headway during the 1960s with Baran and Sweezy's *Monopoly Capital*). It also enabled it to go beyond the Hilferdingian conception, which had weighed just as heavily on the development of the breakdown-ist theory of imperialist concentration as on the plan-ist theory of organised capitalism. In subjecting this last point to closer examination, we shall attempt to arrive at some kind of conclusion.

Grossmann's critique of Hilferding allowed him to specify the relation between finance capital and industrial capital and also to recover an aspect of Lenin's analysis that he considered to be valid and useful. As he wrote in a letter to Mattick dated 21 June 1931:

> Regarding the questions put to me, I want to establish first that I do oppose Hilferding's concept of 'finance capital' but not Lenin's concept. The two are *fundamentally different*. Hilferding understands finance capital to be *bank capital*; he does not ask who stands *behind* this bank capital. I oppose this conception of the decisive role of bank capital. Lenin, on the other hand, understands finance capital not as bank capital, but as the merging of monopoly capital, primarily *industrial* capital, with state power and policy, which is a tool of this capital. That is something quite different. That the banks are *facilitators* of the expansion of capital is clear. But one has to ask whether, for example, the American bankers play the chief role in America's economic life, *deciding the direction of expansionist American policy*. Or are they mere organs of the industrial magnates, who have their representatives in the bank administrations? In my book I have tried (admittedly only briefly) to show how, in the early stages of industrial development, bank capital has autonomous influence. In the advanced stage, the industrial magnates have the decisive influence. I affirm the mighty role of finance capital in Lenin's sense, because he does not speak of 'bank capital' dominating industry any more than I do, but rather of industry dominating the state and its policies.[74]

---

[74] In Grossman 2019, pp. 231.

However we judge the strictly economic merit of this statement on Lenin's concept of imperialism, Grossman intended to assert – using Lenin against the 'neo-harmonists' – a theoretical demand that was also implicitly (for the whole European workers' movement) a strategic demand: the analysis of the mode of functioning of capitalist society on the basis of the mutual interpenetration of circulation and production, reproduction and production, politics and economics. Setting out from the process of restructuring which, at the highest levels of development, was then taking place in the big factories and seemed to be the *conditio sine qua non* for grasping and verifying the efficacy of this interweaving of the process of the social reorganisation of labour *and* capital as a whole, which reproduced on an extended scale (and, as Pollock would later define it, *displaced*) the contradiction between forces of production and relations of production. In the final pages of his book Grossman sees the relation between banks and big industry in a way completely opposite to Hilferding. The resulting accumulation allowed very high rates of self-financing; the administration and distribution of surplus value is carried out directly from the brain of the large enterprise, as a result of which – as has been observed – 'the bank lost its unifying, centralising and controlling power, which according to Hilferding's hypothesis created the conditions of a pre-socialist economic organisation'.[75] But if one acknowledges that the implicit subject of Grossman's analysis is the large enterprise which revolutionises the techniques and organisation of labour, one must also conclude that the natural theoretico-political complement of his 'model' is not the attitude of waiting characteristic of the Second International, but the analysis of the structural effects of Taylorism and Fordism carried out by Gramsci in his *Quaderni dal carcere*.[76] The fact that Gramsci understood the importance of Grossman's book (with which he was

---

75 Bologna, introduction to Moszkowska 1974, p. ix.
76 Cfr. Gramsci 1975, pp. 2139 ss (on Grossman see pp. 890 and 1279). [Passages in English from 'Americanism and Fordism' can be found in *The Gramsci Reader*, edited by D. Forgacs, New York 2000, pp. 275–99 – editor's note]. 'Americanism and Fordism' is a text that has remained long-neglected in the reception of Gramsci's work and only today is the richness of its problematic and the breadth of its implications beginning to be appreciated. Indirectly expressive of the need to relaunch these themes as an object of historico-critical inquiry is the work of L. Villari ('Per una ricerca del taylorismo delle origini') and A. Accornero ('Dove cercare le origini del taylorismo e del fordismo'), which appeared in the journal *Il Mulino*, in number 239, May–June 1975 and 241, September–October 1975 respectively. For a rereading of Gramsci's work as a whole from this thematic standpoint, permit me to refer you to Marramao 1975, pp. 23–5. But see above all the section dedicated to Gramsci (or rather, to the relationship between *Form of crisis and theory of hegemony*) in De Giovanni 1976, pp. 265 ff. See also the introduction by F. De Felice to Gramsci 1978.

only indirectly acquainted) and that he treated 'Americanisation' as a *countertendency*, although of vast ('epochal') proportions, to the fall of the rate of profit, is by itself indicative of how the solution to the great strategic problems of the movement necessarily had to return to the categories of the critique of political economy and to the new theoretical foundation of Marxism at the level of the new morphology of the mode of production.

With Gramsci, we are certainly far beyond the limitations of *Linkskommunismus*, as we are far beyond those of the 'Marxism of the Third International' (including its most 'heretical' variants) – but we also find ourselves in a perspective which addresses and explains the problems, the contradictions, and the fearsome backwardness of the western workers' movement as a whole. From Gramsci, we have not only obtained a great contribution to the generic demand for a creative development of Marxism; we have also learned the strategic importance of the relation between the critique of political economy and the science of politics: that is, of the problem of how the crisis dynamic functions in the current phase of 'state capitalism' and, within that phase, the dynamic of that reproductive process which is not just the reproduction of 'dead labour' and wealth (the commodity), but of relations of production – therefore: the *reproduction of classes*. To grasp the complexity of this tangled knot, it is indispensable to retrace the secular history of Marxism and the workers' movement; to undo the knot today it is necessary to theoretically penetrate the internal dynamic of that 'integral politicity' (the 'political cycle', as Kalecki calls it) which is the unique mechanism of contemporary capitalism. Without taking these steps it is impossible (or it will remain a mere ethical postulate) – as the contradictory trajectory of 'historical extremism' shows us *ex negativo* – to translate the problem of the destiny of capitalism into the political problem of the revolutionary transformation of the existing relations by organised subjectivity.

CHAPTER 4

Theory of the Crisis and the Problem of Constitution: Notes in the Margin to the *Konstitutionsproblematik*

Cautionary Note*

The term *Konstitutionsproblematik* (problematic of the constitution) – which may well appear obscure to many readers – relates to the theoretico-political debate taking place in the Federal Republic of Germany. Developed in particular by two young scholars of the Frankfurt School (while subjecting it to Marxist re-elaboration) – Hans-Jürgen Krahl (who died tragically in February 1970) and Oskar Negt – it indicates the problem of class consciousness as the objective fabric of experience in relation to the dialectical relationship of production and class struggle. In the discussion below, however, I adopt a very different standpoint from that of the federal-German debate. In the latter, the concept of 'constitution' tends to become autonomous from the strictly Marxian context, making way for a division between a scientific analysis (marked by the logical 'model' of *Capital*) and a theory of subjectivity (conditioned by the phenomenal variable of the experiential universe). In betraying its 'Kantian' provenance, this standpoint to my mind risks being caught in 'transcendental' aporeticism, bearing within it an unbridgeable gap between theory (*subjective* scientific abstraction) and politics, where the latter ends up being relegated to the purgatory of empiricism. The perspective that I outline in these notes – while it retains the demand to not treat the theory/practice relationship as unemediated – calls for a deepening of the theme of constitution (that tends to approximate to Marx's notion of *Bildung*, or at least to establish with it a complex reciprocal relation), in the sense of a redefinition of the relationship of the critique of political economy and the theory of class consciousness. I aim at a *scientific foundation* for the discussion of politics and the state, in the sense of one that refuses a linear flattening (in evolutionary-historicist form) of

---

* [This appeared originally in *Critica marxista*, XIII, 2–3, March–June 1975, pp. 115–45. It then formed chapter two, part one of *Il politico e le transformazioni*, op. cit. It was then translated by L. Fiocchi and W. Heimbach for *Telos*, 26, Winter, 1975–6: pp. 143–64, and revised here. – editor's note.]

the processes of socialisation and at a materialist critique of real abstractions, and of the forms of objectified consciousness. The morphology of crisis can be theoretically investigated via the adoption (and reactivation) of Marx's structural-genetic method. Such a method is the only one I believe capable of overcoming the present impass in social analysis, one whose origin lies in the Second International crisis of the relationship between 'Marxist theory' and 'practical socialism', which produced the division of the 'science of history' into a sociologising empiricism and speculative (and/or ethicising) abstractivism. The scope of these notes is limited in a number of respects: the aim is only to indirectly demonstrate – that is, via a historico-critical examination – the emergence of these links from the expository morphology of *Capital* and the theoretico-political weight of a delimitation (or 'critical circumscription') of the dialectic.

I tried to develop this theme – only set-out or hinted at here – in an earlier work: 'Dialettica della forma e scienza politica', in *Critica marxista*, 1975, 6. For historico-political exploration of the *konstitutionsproblematik*, see 'Councils and State in Weimar Germany' (Chapter 3 above).

1 *Immanence of Crisis* and Gesamtkapital

It is still widely held that the theory of crisis and breakdown of the capitalist system is inherited from the positivist deformation of the 'Marxism of the Second International', and that it thus implies ideological support for reformist politics. Ten years ago, Raniero Panzieri wrote:

> As a matter of fact, Marxist thought since Marx has recognised the appearance of a 'turn' in the system with the development of monopoly capitalism and of imperialism around the 1870s (which today appears to us as a transitional period in relation to the 'turn' that began in the 1930s and is still being completed). But the analysis and representation of the new phase emerging with that turn was immediately framed in terms of laws that such a phase tended to overcome. Thus, it was interpreted as a 'last phase'.[1]

And, in a note, he added:

---

[1] Panzieri 1964, p. 287. [An English translation of this piece appears in Panzieri 1972, pp. 329ff. – editor's note.]

The mythology of the 'last stage' of capitalism exists with differing, even opposite, ideological functions both in Lenin and in Kautsky: in Lenin, to 'legitimise' the breakdown of the system at the less advanced points of its development; in Kautsky, to sanction the reformist postponement of revolutionary action until the 'correct time'. Since the 1917 revolution failed to consolidate itself with revolutions in more advanced countries, it fell back on objectives realisable at levels of development Russia could achieve. And the lack of clear explanation of the possible presence of capitalist social relations in planning (a shortcoming remaining in the whole development of Leninist thought) will later facilitate the repetition, whether in the factories or in total social production, of capitalist forms behind the ideological screen identifying socialism with planning and the possibility of 'socialism in one country'.[2]

Here, in addition to the *Zusammenbruchstheorie*, Panzieri attacked the method that was being consolidated in the shift from the Second to the Third International of an optimistic conception of the historical process that appealed to the automatic realisation of the 'highest phase' of capitalism. He sought to reintroduce the active, political, revolutionary perspective of Marx's thought as against the vulgar positivism that regarded the mortal crisis of the system as an unavoidable phenomenon resulting from the simple quantitative development of the productive forces. Panzieri's polemic was aimed against the instrumental use, within the workers' movement, of the argument for the 'objective' and 'necessary' character of the laws governing capitalist development. This instrumental use tended to overshadow or render secondary the contradiction between capital and labour, and the urgency of developing 'workers' control' over the entire productive process. The desire to provide a theoretical foundation for this project had Panzieri excavating the Marxist critique of political economy in order to trace the lines of analytical development that lead unambiguously to an identity of the 'law of the plan' with the 'law of value'. From the first to the third volume of *Capital*, the development of Marx's argument thus coincided with the historical development of contemporary capitalism from its competitive to its monopolistic phase. The 'plan' was not considered as a single or concrete programmatic project but, rather, as social capital's mode of functioning in the historically determined form of its development. Thus, in order to eliminate every 'naturalist' residue from the theory of development, it was necessary to demonstrate the previous overcoming of the dichotomy (still

---

2 Panzieri 1972, pp. 286–287n.

present in Marx, especially in the first volume of *Capital*) between despotism in the factory and anarchy in civil society. It was also necessary to show that the 'dynamic of the capitalist process is essentially dominated by the law of concentration'[3] and, going beyond Marx, that the highest stage of development whereby capital becomes 'autonomous' (*Verselbständigung*) is not finance capital but 'planned capitalism'.[4] According to Panzieri's conclusions, every trace of the origins of the capitalist process disappears with the advent of generalised planning because of the obsolescence of a 'mode of production which is "unconscious", anarchic, and tied to the uncontrolled activities of competition'.[5] On this level, the increasing cohesion of the system can be seen in its entirety as completely autonomous with respect to the agents of production. On the overall social level, this process is characterised by the same despotic rationality at work in the modern factory – a rationality which avails itself of the immense possibilities of the capitalist use of science and technology.[6] Here Panzieri, sidestepping a fundamental problem whose complexity Marx himself had emphasised in the *Grundrisse*, concluded that the 'immanent contradictions' had completely lost their naturalist character, typical of the competitive period: the '"immanent contradictions" are not in the movements of capitals, they are not "internal" to capital: the only limit to the development of capital is not capital, but the resistance of the working class'.[7]

---

3   Id., p. 235.
4   Id., p. 286.
5   Id., p. 284.
6   This can be seen in Panzieri's other important work, 'Sull'uso Capitalistico della Macchine nel Neo-capitalismo', in *La Ripresa del Marxismo-Leninismo in Italia*, op. cit., pp. 148 ff. [An English translation of this article can be found here: https://libcom.org/library/capalist-use-machinery-raniero-panzieri – editor's note.]
7   Panzieri 1972, p. 270. The substantial revision of Marx's statement that the '*true barrier* of capitalist production is *capital itself*' (Marx 1991, p. 358) was not merely an historical correction (i.e., an adjustment of Marx's theory in terms of post-war capitalist developments). It upset the methodological foundations of the dialectical presentation (*Darstellung*) of the critique of political economy. This *Darstellung* is 'dialectical' in that it expresses the movement of a negativity *immanent* to the general concept of capital (*allgemeiner Kapitalbegriff*) and to the (dynamic) structure of commodities as the 'elementary form' of capitalist society. Thus, the dialectical quality of Marx's chosen 'method of presentation' consists in the comprehension of the movement of categories as a self-contradictory movement of capital, as the self-criticism of the system in terms of the very categorical objectivity, of the 'bourgeois standpoint' (cf. Marx 1981, p. 368). This self-criticism refers to the historical, and thus transitory character of the mode of production based on commodity exchange. For Marx, '*First of all, there is a limit, not inherent to production generally, but to production founded on capital*' (cf. Marx 1973, p. 415). The horizon of this limit, which is represented by capital itself, and the self-contradictory movement of capital is shown by Marx in the dialectic of limit (*Grenze*)

We will see whether and to what extent this reading of Marx can actually found a comprehensive social theory of revolution once it eradicates the 'naturalness' of the capitalist process. For the present, we want to show, at the beginning of the 1960s in Italy, an argument common to a large part of the European left opposition in the 1920s and 1930s was proposed by a militant of the inner opposition of the workers' movement: that revolutionary action should not attempt to leverage the presumed weaknesses and 'internal contradictions' of the system, but only the active autonomy, the *Selbsttätigkeit* (today's 'insubordination') of the working class – its exclusive organisability.

2 Korsch's Critique of the 'Theory of Breakdown'

Proceeding in orderly fashion, I want to return to the problem that I began with: that of the theoretical (and political nature) of the theory of crisis and of 'breakdown'. If we scan the documents of the 1920s and 1930s dealing with this problem, we notice that the equation of the *Zusammenbruchstheorie* with a reformist and opportunistic conception of politics is based on a rather schem-

---

and barrier (*Schranke*). 'To begin with: capital forces the workers beyond necessary labour to surplus labour. Only in this way does it realize itself, and create surplus value. But on the other hand, it presupposes necessary labour only *to the extent* and *insofar as* it is surplus labour and the latter is *realizable* as *surplus labour*. It posits surplus labour, then, as a condition of the necessary, and surplus labour as a *limit* [*Grenze*] of objectified labour [*vergegenständlichte Arbeit*], of value as such. When it can no longer posit value it cannot posit necessary labour; and, given its foundation, it cannot be otherwise. It therefore restricts labour and the creation of value – by an artificial check, as the English express it – and it does so on the same grounds as and to the same extent that it posits surplus labour and surplus value. By its nature, therefore, it posits a barrier [*Schranke*] to labour and value-creation, in contradiction to its tendency to expand them boundlessly. And in as much as it both posits a barrier *specific* to itself, and on the other side equally drives over and beyond *every* barrier, it is the living contradiction' (ibid., p. 421). Marx continues in the note: 'Since value forms the foundation of capital, and since it therefore necessarily exists only through an exchange for *counter-value*, it thus necessarily repels itself from itself. A *universal capital* [*Universalkapital*], one without alien capitals confronting it, which it exchanges – and from the present standpoint, nothing confronts it but wage labourers or itself – is therefore a non-thing. The reciprocal exclusion of capitals *is already contained in capital* [emphasis added – G.M.] as realized exchange value' (ibid.). It is evident that the profound dialectical significance (not reducible to an 'allegory' or to a 'metaphor') of this 'exposition' would collapse if the limit to the development of capital were not provided by 'capital itself'. The collapse of the limit-barrier dialectic would present difficulties for an analysis of the movement of capital and thus also for the theoretical possibility of a critique of political economy. This is something to which we shall return over the following pages.

atic and reductionist conception of the history of Marxism and of the workers' movement.[8] The example of Luxemburg can help break down this historiographic scheme. Even if it was claimed that Luxemburg's conception of the breakdown itself reflects Second International themes, the question of the relationship – which at this level can only appear paradoxical – between economic theory (deterministic-catastrophic) and political theory (activist-spontaneist) in her work would remain unresolved. The problem is thus considerably more complex and intricate than is indicated by traditional and convenient simplifications provided by European and 'Western' Marxism.

In a 1933 essay addressing precisely this problem, Korsch already pointed out the impossibility of reconciling opponents and supporters of crisis theory within a *political* common denominator. The *Zusammenbruchstheorie* had in fact been challenged with surprisingly similar arguments both by the founder of revisionism, Eduard Bernstein, as well as by the council communist, Pannekoek; while it was supported by Luxemburg as well as the 'arch-reformist' Heinrich Cunow.[9] But then Korsch himself ended up by proposing a solution which traced all positions back to the common ideological denominator of *Krisentheorie* and, having established their determinist and passive character, rejected them *en bloc* as simple *reflections* of the class struggle.[10] Within the context of the theory of crisis, Korsch distinguished two *attitudes* corresponding to two different ways of understanding the catastrophic mechanism of development: the *subjectivist* attitude, corresponding to the official

---

8   This argument was developed by Dario Lanzardo in his introduction to Panzieri 1972, pp. 72–3.
9   See Korsch 1977, pp. 181–2. For a discussion of crisis theory in the Bernstein Debate, see Colletti 1972, pp. 45–108. For the historical and political background of the debate see K. Mandelbaum's dissertation, Mandelbaum 1926, pp. 32–42.
10 For Korsch it could be said that the 'whole historical development of socialist crisis theories from *Fourier* to *Sismondi* to the various subsequent temporal phases of Marx-Engels and the later Marxists (and the crisis theories of Marx epigones up to Sternberg and Grossman, Lederer and Naphtali), in their ultimate theoretical details, can be seen as merely a passive reflection of the respective previous objective economic development. From the same viewpoint one could also, beyond the framework of crisis theories, represent all the important struggles over direction which have arisen within the socialist movement during the last fifty years as *mere consequences and reflexes* of the immediately preceding *conjuncture* within the capitalist crisis cycle' (Korsch 1977, pp. 182–3). Clearly, Korsch's critique is more complex and articulate (especially since he is not hindered by the illusion of being able to find a crisis theory that would be *in-itself* revolutionary) but essentially no different from that appearing anonymously in the same journal under the title: 'Die Grundlagen einer revolutionären Krisentheorie', *Proletarier Zeitschrift*, 1 (1993); now in Korsch, Mattick and Pannekoek 1974, pp. 71ff.

social-democratic version typical of theoreticians such as Hilferding, Bernstein, Lederer, Tarnow and Naphtali; and the *objectivist* attitude, represented by the 'classic' *Zusammenbruchstheorie*, of Rosa Luxemburg, Fritz Sternberg and Henryk Grossman. The subjectivist attitude maintains that the crisis can be overcome within the capitalist system, with the help of a general cartel (Hilferding's *Generalkartell*) and by means of the regulation of capital-labour relations. According to Korsch, not only the social democrats but Bolshevik and Soviet economic planners as well, who are also subjective theorists of the crisis, revert to Hilferding's theory.[11] 'It is just the characteriastic of this kind of crisis theory', he writes, 'that they always *ideologically reflect the* just *past* phase of the real movement of capitalist economies and place it vis-à-vis the changed present reality as a fixed and rigid "theory"'.[12] The practical consequences of these theories is the '*complete destruction of all the objective bases of the proletarian class movement*'.[13] The objectivist attitude – which Korsch considers only *apparently* counterposed to the subjectivist – was articulated in its 'classic form' by Rosa Luxemburg in the *Accumulation of Capital*. This theory 'cannot be recognized as truly materialist, and, as regards it practical efficiency, [cannot be recognised as a truly] revolutionary position on the crisis question'.[14] The 'objectivist' deformation of this position cannot be suppressed by claiming, with its supporters, that the existing system can be overturned only by means of active intervention by the proletariat. '*Such a theory*', writes Korsch, 'appears to me as not suitable for bringing forward that full earnestness of self-disciplined activity of the proletarian class struggling for it own goals, which is as much necessary for the class war of the workers as it is for every other ordinary war'.[15]

Korsch counterposes the 'materialist attitude' to the other two:

> This position explains the whole question of the objective necessity or avoidability of capitalist crises as a *senseless question in this general form* (within the framework of a practical theory of the revolution of the proletariat). It agrees with the revolutionary critic of Marx *George Sorel* who will not consider Marx's general tendency of capitalism to catastrophe generated by the insurrection of the working class – colored in a strong idealist-philosophical 'dialectical' manner of speech – as a valid prognosis, but merely as a 'myth' whose whole significance is limited to determine the

---

11   Cfr. Korsch 1977, p. 184.
12   Korsch 1977, p. 184.
13   Korsch 1977, p. 185.
14   Ibid.
15   Ibid.

current action of the working class. The materialist stance is, however, not in accord with Sorel when he quite generally wants to *limit* the function of any future social theory of revolution to form such a myth. The materialist stance rather believes that certain, if only always limited, prognostic statements sufficient for practical action can be made on the basis of always more exact and thorough empirical investigation of the present capitalist mode of production and its recognizable immanent tendencies of development.[16]

Thus, in order to determine his action, the materialist must empirically explore the present situation, the level of consciousness, the level of organisation and the working class's readiness for struggle. The basic principles of this *'theoretical and practical materialist fundamental stance'*[17] were given their classic formulation in 1894 by the young Lenin in his polemic on Michailowski's populist subjectivism and Struve's objectivism. Lenin counterposed his own 'activist-materialist standpoint' to these two positions.[18]

2 Dialectical Exposition and Theory of Crisis

Let us pause a moment to examine the salient points and implications of this interesting work by Korsch. First of all, we must question the meaning of reducing all the theoretical positions of German Social Democracy and of the Second International (whether right or left) to passive conceptions and attitudes of waiting [for the arrival of the 'right' moment] that limit themselves to *reflecting* on the elapsed stages of the 'real movement' (which for Korsch is represented by class conflicts, by practico-political clashes among the various tendencies and currents within the workers' movement). Certainly, it helps here to consider the particular time in which Korsch wrote these lines. We are in 1933, the period immediately following the rise of Nazism in Germany. The success of the national-socialist dictatorship had not yet destroyed the residual hopes for a workers' insurrection. This is why it is necessary to carry out the *whole* theoretical discussion in terms of an analysis of the present in its most empirical, specific aspects, which can in no way be deduced from a general and abstract theoretical construction: on the basis of 'the situation, the level of consciousness, the organization, and the readiness for struggle of the

---

16 Korsch 1977, p. 186.
17 Ibid.
18 Ibid.

working class'.[19] Even the appeal to the Sorelian 'myth' and to Lenin's 'activist-materialist' position must be seen as a way to stress the need to mobilise workers for the struggle against fascism.[20]

However necessary, this rigorous historical consideration is not enough. In fact, this work contains a contradictory motive that cannot be resolved purely by reference to the political exigencies of the moment, since it is a constant of Korsch's discourse which, despite its greater complexity and breadth, he shares with a large part of the communist *and* socialist left between the two wars.[21]

Korsch seems to grasp the need for a politico-revolutionary interpretation of the 'scientific representation' of *Capital*, and thus to read the critique of political economy in connection with the theory of classes and of revolution. But in the rush to bring the discussion *immediately* back to the requirements of a 'practical theory of proletarian revolution', he ends up side-stepping the crucial dimensions of the mature Marx's problematic. It is precisely by this evasion that he can uncompromisingly reject all theories of the crisis, *regardless* of their methodological and epistemological foundations, as abstract constructions which, *as such*, can only be passive reflections of the real movement. Korsch thus avoids the complex problem of the 'method of presentation'[22]

---

19 Ibid.
20 This *positive* reference to Lenin is rather surprising in that by the end of the 1920s Korsch had already broken with Leninism and, in the *Antikritik* of 1930, he had even stated that his adherence to the Leninist concept expressed in *Marxism and Philosophy* was the result of a misunderstanding. Cf. 'The Present State of the Problem of *Marxism and Philosophy*', in Korsch 1970, pp. 98–144. If the use of Leninist theory (or at least the reference to Lenin) has survived the theoretical and political *Selbstverständigung* of the late 1920s, then it cannot really be explained through the subjectivist category of 'misunderstanding'. As usual, the solution to this problem in Korsch requires a deeper and more disenchanted theoretical and historiographic analysis of this thinker. Above all, it would be important to analyse his position in the light of the theoretical discussions and perspectives of *Linkskommunismus* and *Linkssozialismus* in the inter-war period. Cfr. Bock 1969; Drechsler 1965; Tjaden 1964; and Ihlau 1969.
21 It would be useful to trace the analogies between Korsch and Max Adler – an author to whom insufficient attention has been paid. Cf. Zanardo 1960, pp. 153–65 [and now in Zanardo 1974, pp. 73–164 – editor's note] as well as the interesting comparative treatment of the council conceptions of Korsch and Adler developed by Cerroni 1973, pp. 75–83. (In the years following the composition of this essay, a number of important works by Max Adler have come out in Italy: Adler 1974 and Adler 1976. On the parallel between Korsch and Adler I refer you again to Chapter 2, 'Councils and State in Weimar Germany', in the present volume.)
22 The difference between the *method of inquiry* and the *method of presentation* is spelled out by Marx in the Postface (January 1873) to the second German edition of *Capital*: 'the method of presentation must differ in form from that of inquiry. The latter has to appro-

when, in his urgency to work out an economic analysis able to provide a 'practical theory of revolution' supported by an 'activist-materialist standpoint', he reads the dialectical method of presentation of the mature Marx as a mere *allegory*[23] meant to rouse the proletariat's will and revolutionary spirit.[24] Thus, Korsch ruled out the possibility of differentiation between the various methodological and epistemological foundations of the different theories of the crisis which throw light on their function within the general vision of the historical movement and the relationship between theory and practice. As a result, Korsch did not see that Luxemburg's theory of the crash was different from the one formulated by Kautsky in the 1906 preface to the fifth German edition of Engels' *Socialism: Utopian and Scientific*, not only because of a difference of 'attitude' (which is, in the final analysis, a subjective difference), but rather because of a different value assigned to the function of economic 'description' within Marxist theory. Luxemburg never conceived of the model she described in the *Accumulation of Capital* as a pure and simple "reflection" of historical and empirical evolution of the capitalist mode of production. Rather, against Kautsky, she always refused to attribute to economic laws the character of fetishistic objectivity. One could discuss (apart from the economic 'errors' con-

---

priate the material in detail, to analyse its different forms of development and to track down their inner connections. Only after this work has been done can the real movement be appropriately presented. If this is done successfully, if the life of the subject-matter is now reflected back in the ideas, then it may appear as if we have before us an *a priori* construction' (Marx 1976a, p. 102). For problems connected to the above distinction and the general relation between Logic and History in Marx, cf. 'Marx secondo Marx', in Luporini 1974, pp. 213 ff.

23 This pragmatic reduction of the dialectical and morphological aspect of the critique of political economy is a *topos* which connects the European 'theoretical left' (often through Sorel, but in forms and ways which still need to be historically specified) to Bernstein and to the revisionist current of social democracy. Korsch's reference to Sorel should be historically (and theoretically) understood in relation to the Bernsteinian revision of the theme of 'industrial democracy', which constitutes, next to the anarcho-syndicalist thread, the other source of Korsch's 'conception of the councils' derived from the Fabian Society. Cf. Korsch 1912, pp. 422–7; Korsch 1975; and Korsch 1969. For Korsch's theoretical and political formation, see Michael Buckmiller's 'Marxismus als Realität. Zur Rekonstruktion der theoretischen und politischen Entwicklung Karl Korschs', in Pozzoli (ed.) 1973, esp. pp. 19–35. For a comprehensive if peremptory treatment of the European council movement in relation to *Linkskommunismus*, cf. Cacciari's 'Sul problema dell'organizzazione. Germania 1917–1921', which appeared as an introduction to Lukács 1972. The same points are developed by Bologna 1972, pp. 3–27; and De Masi 1972, pp. 86–118.

24 Cf. Korsch 1977, pp. 185–6. Here Korsch probably has in mind the famous passage in *Capital* (ending with *the expropriation of the expropriators*) in which Marx connected the concentration-impoverishment process and 'working class rebellion'. Cf. Marx 1976a, pp. 763–4.

tained in her book) the completeness of her methodological self-reflection and the oscillations and incongruencies present in her various formulations of the relationship between economic and political moments, between spontaneity and the political and revolutionary direction of the masses. But such a discussion would lead us too far from our present subject matter.[25]

3 'Tendency to Decline' and Relations of Production in Grossman's Analysis

Returning to Korsch, there is another surprising point in his exposition which indirectly confirms the shortcomings of his approach to the theory of the crisis: the association of Fritz Sternberg and Henryk Grossman as 'epigones of the Luxemburgian theory'.[26] In truth, these two economists were so far from being epigones that – at the acme of the problem of crisis, the epicentre of which was 1929 – they engaged in one of the harshest and most intriguing polemics on imperialism.[27] In his vast work on imperialism, Sternberg had taken up and incorporated Luxemburg's partial revision of Marxist theory which related expanded reproduction and expansion in 'non-capitalist areas'.[28] Grossman,

---

25 In the above-cited essay, Bologna observes that 'Rosa finds herself caught between the sociology of organisation and the theory of the party' (Bologna 1972, p. 17). This type of 'ambivalence' can be reduced to the fact that 'What for Luxemburg was a problem of the social composition within the party, was for Lenin a problem of programme, or even of party statute. For Lenin, workers' revolutionary direction was to be attained by tying militants to this programme and thus disciplining them to centralisation. Rosa and Lenin speak to two different types of working class, against two different types of reformism' (Bologna 1972, p. 21). More scholastic and formalistic is Cacciari's approach, which dismisses Luxemburg's argument as 'democratic-libertarian' (cf. Cacciari, in Lukács 1972, p. 62). Moreover, Cacciari provides a rather inadequate treatment of the *Zusammenbruchstheorie*, which he equates entirely with the Luxemburg model characterised by 'a constant tendency to under-consumption' and by 'an unbearable production-market contradiction' (ibid., p. 63). But it is precisely this incongruence and this dualism (producing a splitting of the politico-strategic dimension) in Luxemburg which was criticised by the 'theoretician of collapse', Henryk Grossman. [The discussion of Cacciari in this note only appears in the 1975–6 *Telos* translation. The Italian version published later – 1979 – as chapter two, part one of *Il politico e le transformazioni*, op. cit., ends with the discussion of S. Bologna – editor's note.]

26 Korsch 1912, p. 92.

27 Cf. Sternberg 1926.

28 Sternberg's appropriation of Luxemburg's theory involves identifying the phenomenon of surplus-population as a constitutive condition of capitalism (without a reserve army of labour there cannot be an excess of wage labour and therefore a surplus of value).

conversely, maintained that the capitalist system's tendency to crisis and 'breakdown' could only be explained *on the basis of the Marxist theory of value*:

> The law of value dominates the entire economic process of the capitalist mechanism and, since its dynamic and developmental tendencies cannot be understood except on the basis of this law, its end – breakdown – must also be explained on the basis of the *law of value*.[29]

The error of Luxemburg and Sternberg – which led them to a revision and 'appropriation' of Marx's work on expanded reproduction – was the result of an erroneous assumption: in Luxemburg's *Accumulation of Capital* as well as in Sternberg's *Imperialism*, the crisis was not explained in terms of *production*, but in terms of the *market*. This is why it is impossible to grasp the continuity and structural connection between the reproductive process and the capital-labour relation on the one hand, and the need to introduce the safety-valve of 'non-capitalist areas' (resulting in a significant thematic twist to the Marxian problem of production and reproduction into a problem of 'realisation' of surplus value.) Through a meticulous reflection on methodology, however, Grossman succeeded in posing the question in terms of an analysis of the *relations of production*, within whose dynamic he sought the general developmental tendency of the capitalist mode of production.[30] Basing his analysis on the two-fold

---

In addition, Sternberg affirms that Luxemburg committed important errors, especially in the conclusions of her analyses. He does not accept, for example, her claim of the impossibility of expanded reproduction in 'pure' capitalism and – agreeing with Bukharin's criticism in *Imperialism and the Accumulation of Capital* (cf. Bukharin and Luxemburg 1972) – asserts it is possible in state capitalism, since the latter can destroy part of the surplus value (see Sternberg 1926, p. 102).

29 Grossman 1929, p. 13. In this work, Grossman returns again, in a broader context, to the brilliant critique of Sternberg's work he published the previous year: 'A New Theory of Imperialism and Social Revolution' (1928), Grossman 2019, pp. 120–76. Sternberg responded with a pamphlet entitled *Eine Umwälzung der Wissenschaft? Kritik des Buches von Henryk Grossman. Zugleich eine positive Analyse des Imperialismus* (Sternberg 1930). For an analysis of underconsumption from the perspective of Marx's theory of value and, in general, for all of the specifically economic aspects of the problem, see Cogoy 1987, pp. 11–37; and 'Ueber einige Aspekte der Akkumulations- und Krisentheorie bei Grossman und Mattick', in Hermanin, Lauer, and Schurmann 1973, pp. 85–111.

30 Among Grossman's theoretical and methodological works are 'Marx, Classical Political Economy and the Problem of Dynamics', in Grossman 2019, pp. 469–533; 'The Change in the Original Plan for *Capital* and its Causes' (1929), in Grossman 2019, pp. 183–209; 'The Value-Price Transformation in Marx and the Problem of Crisis' (1932) (pp. 304–31); 'Gold Production in the Reproduction Schema of Marx and Rosa Luxemburg' (1932) (pp. 276–

dimension of determining reality and of abstract generality (with respect to the historico-empirical movement) of the law of value, he ended up connecting it to the theory of crisis *by means of the law of accumulation*. 'The great significance of Marx's work lies precisely in the fact that it is able to explain all the phenomena of the capitalist mode of production on the basis of the law of value'.[31] 'Marx's theory of breakdown is [...] a necessary supposition for the comprehension of Marx's theory of crisis and it is intimately connected to it. The solution to both problems is in the Marxist law of accumulation, *which constitutes the central idea of Capital* and is in turn founded on the law of value'.[32]

Thus, far from being the work of an 'epigone', Grossman's book carried out the 'return to Marx' advanced by Luxemburg against the reformist revisionism of Bernstein and the Austro-Marxist 'neoharmonists'[33] as well as Kautsky's pseudo-orthodox and positivist scholasticism. Thus, Grossman salvaged Luxemburg's political demand, recasting it on a more solid analytical and methodological basis. Not by chance, it is this work of Grossman which, in the early thirties (a year after the appearance of the previously discussed article by Korsch), revived an important discussion within *Linkskommunismus* on the connection between the theory of breakdown and revolutionary subjectivity.

4 Breakdown or Revolution: A Debate between Anton Pannekoek and Paul Mattick

The protagonists of the polemic carried out in the columns of the *Rätecorrespondenz*, the theoretical organ of the 'council communists', are Anton Pan-

---

303); 'The Evolutionist Revolt against Classical Economics' (pp. 556–99). For an analysis of the epistemological basis of Grossman's theory, see my 'From the Crisis of the "Self-Organised Market" to the "Authoritarian State": Notes on the Relationship between Political Economy and Critical Theory' [Chapter 8 below – editor's note].

31 Grossman 1929, p. 608.
32 Grossman 1929, p. 60.
33 H. Grossman to P. Mattick, 18 July 1937: 'That the clique of neoharmonists, Hilferdings and Otto Bauers, tried for decades to systematically distort Marx, that passages such as the ones cited above were systematically concealed and that there is no trace of them to be found in the Marxist literature, is not a reason for us to go along with the neoharmonists. Once you think through Marx's concepts consistently to the end, how can a crisis arise at the level of simple reproduction in which such a harmonious equilibrium appears to prevail? Then you will find in Marx many more theoretical concepts of which the 'philosophers' have not dreamed, even those such as Karl Korsch, who imagine that they understand something of Marxist economics' (Grossman 2019, pp. 272–3).

nekoek and Paul Mattick. In his contribution to the discussion, Pannekoek[34] addressed a criticism to Grossman – with greater scientific-economic pretensions but with much less clarity – that was analogous to the one that Korsch had made regarding theories of crisis as a whole. Starting with the assumption that the 'question of the necessity and the inevitability of the collapse of capitalism, and the way in which this is to be understood, is the most important of all questions for the working class and its understanding and tactics,'[35] he then ended up criticising Grossman from a basically external perspective.[36] Pannekoek's criticisms of Grossman are basically that he wants to 1) deduce the end of capitalism 'for purely economic reasons'[37] (*rein wirtschaftlich*) and thus of conceiving the crash 'independently of human intervention',[38] and 2) of reducing the class struggle to an 'economic' contest, i.e., of defining it as a struggle for wages and reduction of working hours.[39] Thus, he ended up liquidating, more thoroughly and radically than Korsch had done, the whole theory of breakdown from Luxemburg to Grossman, by anchoring the theory to a deterministic and 'bourgeois' concept of natural necessity. On a closer analysis, however, it turns out that this criticism of Grossman's 'economism' could be addressed to Pannekoek since *it was he who was tied to a restricted ('bourgeois') concept of economics*. This is precisely the point of Mattick's important criticism.

Pannekoek, Mattick points out, did not succeed in understanding the *dialectical* character of Grossman's development, founded on a strictly Marxian methodological basis. The method by which the critique of political economy proceeds is not aimed at the historical and empirical description of real processes, but at the abstract isolation of certain fundamental moments, in order to define the unity of the laws of movement of capitalist society. As Mattick notes:

---

34 Cf. Pannekoek 1934. [now: https://www.marxists.org/archive/pannekoe/1934/collapse.htm]
35 Pannekoek 1934.
36 Pannekoek uncritically restated the objection to Grossman made by many 'professional economists', i.e., of having shown the inevitability of breakdown on the basis of O. Bauer's schema; cf. Pannekoek 1912–13, pp. 831–8, 862–74. The objection would make sense only if Grossman had really meant to provide a schematic representation of breakdown. But Grossman denied the possibility of such a description. His actual aim was to show the impossibility of harmonious development starting from Bauer's premises. Cf. Grossman 1929, pp. 95 ff. The same objection to Grossman was put forth by P.M. Sweezy in *The Theory of Capitalist Development* (Sweezy 1968), pp. 209–13. On this subject see also Rosdolsky 1980.
37 Pannekoek 1934.
38 Ibid.
39 Ibid.

For Grossman, too there are no purely economic problems. Yet that does not prevent him, in his analysis of the law of accumulation, from limiting himself for *methodological reasons* to the definition of purely economic presuppositions so as to grasp *theoretically* a limit-point of the system. The *theoretical cognition* that the capitalist system must necessarily breakdown because of its internal contradictions *does not at all imply* that the *real breakdown* is an automatic process, independent of men.[40]

Mattick's clarifications are of enormous importance, not only because they stand in contrast to a general tendency of left communism (and socialism), but also and above all because, thanks to their breadth of range, they go beyond its restricted theoretico-politcal confines and are able to grasp, perhaps unknowingly, a general political incapacity of European Marxism that is met with in the wavering between a speculative and a pragmatic relationship between theory and praxis. The limits of Pannekoek's Marxism are evident when, after having ruled out any 'practical utility' for the theory of the crisis, he goes on to propose a positive solution to the problem of the connection between economics and politics, between the objective and subjective moments. Starting from the assumption that 'Marx's economics cannot be grasped without an understanding of the historical-materialist way of thinking,'[41] he *immediately* seeks to resolve – in an undifferentiated unity – the relationship economy-politics, objectivity-subjectivity, being-consciousness:

> The economy, as a totality of men who work and labour for their vital needs, and politics (in a broad sense) as a totality of men who work and struggle as a class for their vital needs, constitute a single sphere developing according to precise laws.[42]

Here we have, on the one hand, an undifferentiated unity and, on the other, an abstract dualism of two camps which, in terms so defined, cannot in any way be *mediated*. If the economy can be reduced to a simple labouring and instrumental activity, and politics to a mere autonomous and voluntary activity, their unity cannot be nothing other than an empty form or a moral postulate. In answer to the declared unity of theory and practice we find, in

---

40   Mattick 1934, now in Korsch, Mattick and Pannekoek 1974, pp. 47–8.
41   Pannekoek 1934, p. 38.
42   Ibid.

Pannekoek, the opposite couple, or better, the hypostatised polar co-presence of economism and voluntarism. But what is most important, this incongruence is neither the result of personal deficiency and even less is it an excusive historical limitation of the debate of the 1930s.[43] Actually, the *same type of critique* of the theory of breakdown and *the same type of appeal to subjectivity* can be found in reformist theoreticians of social democracy such as Hilferding and Braunthal.

Even before the *Marx-Renaissance* characterised by the works of the young Lukács and Korsch, and destined to assume major proportions with the publication of Marx's early philosophical writings, the Austro-Marxist theoreticians were the ones who inaugurated in European Marxism that 'season of subjectivity' consisting of an active re-reading of Marx's work, filtered through neo-Kantian themes.[44] Although it represented a change in emphasis in the

---

43 To demonstrate the timeliness of this aporia one need only examine the polemics generated by the Habermasian critique of the concept of 'labour' in Marx. Cf. Habermas 1971, Part 1, chapter 2. In this respect, see also Krahl's polemic, 'Produktion und Klassenkampf', in Krahl 1971, p. 392 ff. 'Habermas', notes Krahl, 'can throw a restricted concept of praxis in Marx's face only because he has a restricted concept of production. According to Marx, production includes all the elements of social praxis, i.e., the relation of subject-object and intersubjectivity, labour and the division of labour. Habermas, instead, reduces the concept of production to a non-intersubjective subject-object relationship of instrumental activity, i.e., to an instrumental concept of labour. The price paid by Habermas for such a reduction of the concept of production is the dematerialisation of intersubjectivity, the forms of which he designates with the abstract title of interaction or, in other words, of the dematerialisation of revolutionary praxis' (Krahl 1971, p. 394).

44 Within the workers' movement, neo-Kantianism (and, in general, the influence of all those philosophical currents characterised by the centrality of the subject) did not emerge, as the history of ideas would require, from the new results of scientific and epistemological research, abstractly demonstrating the 'erroneousness' of the evolutionist and determinist viewpoint. Nor did it emerge as the subjectivist viewpoint itself maintains, from a revisionist 'deviation' or 'degeneration'. Rather, it can be seen as a recoil, on the level of theoretical consciousness, of the processes of capitalist organisation and 'dissemination' of power which, by contradicting in reality the positivist conception of an ineluctable evolutionary passage to socialism, had precipitated a crisis in the flatly objectivistic interpretation of Marx's theory. If one reads Max Adler's work, one notes – much more than in Bernstein or, to mention a neo-Kantian Marxist, in Vorländer – the peculiar connection between the crisis of the Second International (which is both a crisis of a canonic framework based on the absolute legitimacy – *absolute Gestezmässigkeit* – of the historical process, and of the *objectivist-economistic* conception of politics which this framework supported) and the birth of so-called 'Western Marxism'. The latter emerged at the same time as a critique of every determinist concept of history and of every reformist practice, while seeking an activist-revolutionary reconstitution of the forms of subjectivity. Max Adler's attempt to find an autonomous theoretical and political

theoretical and political debate within the workers' movement, this appeal to subjectivity by both the neo-Kantian Austro-Marxists and the majority wing of the *Linkscommunismus* resulted in an *epistemological restriction* of the field Marx defined as the social relations of production. The sociological and empirical analysis of the 'multiple or the real' comes up against the vindication of the (ethical-universal) subjective factor. Thus, instead of identifying the tendential laws of the mode of production, economic analysis ends up as an exercise in microsociology. To the empiricist reduction of categorical abstractions, which draws from reality its structuring moments, corresponds the de-objectified resolution of the political moment into an ethico-transcendental moment. The same doubling also appears in the definition of *class*: the latter splits into a 'material' moment within production (labour-power), and a 'spiritual' moment which, thanks to its universality transcends the empirical levels of the material and productive condition of class (the universal human 'will' of the proletariat, 'class consciousness' as a reassembling of the *disiecta membra* of the human essence). Thus, the genesis of class consciousness is not *explained* in terms of the process of production and reproduction, and from within the objectivity of social relations, but is *presupposed* as a result of an irreducible autonomy that at a certain point of development, makes the qualitative jump which cracks the quantitative uniformity of the empirical world.[45]

In the polemic around Grossman's book we are confronted by a sharp contrast between two theoretical perspectives. On one side is Pannekoek's, which

---

way (a sort of 'third way' between social democracy and Bolshevism) based on a broad and comprehensive philosophical refounding of Marxism, took place at this delicate point in time characterised by the war, the October revolution, and the theoretical crisis of 1923. Of great significance in this respect is, above all, Adler's collaboration with *Der Kampf*, the theoretical organ of the *Sozialdemokratische Partei Österreich*: see for instance the debate with K. Renner on the tactics-strategy link (Jg. IX, 1916, pp. 87–97; 129139; Jg. XI, 1918, pp. 18–30; 39–56; Jg. XXI, 1928, pp. 53–59; 142–63; 197–206; 245–56; 256–62) and the discussions with E. Zilsel and W. Frank on materialism (Jg. XXIV, 1931, pp. 68–75; 125–31; 163–6; 213–20; Jg. XXVI, 1933, pp. 112–21) and with O. Leichter, O. Trebitsch, R. Kassel and H. Deutsch on the role of intellectual workers (Jg. XII, 1919 and XIII, 1920). In addition, for this entire range of issues, cf. in addition to the aforementioned review by A. Zanardo on neo-Kantian socialism, the (openly social-democratic exposition) contained in the voluminous Leser 1968. For Max Adler, cf. pp. 513–561. Finally, also worthwhile is the extensive – and important – introduction by L. Paggi to Adler 1975.

45 While this aporia also appears in Lukács' *History and Class Consciousness*, it nevertheless has the merit of *positing* the problem of a materialist treatment of *Bewusstseinsformen*, as well as grasping the idea of the structuring-real character of abstraction (as in the categories of *Daseinsformen* and *Existenzbestimmungen*).

sees the process of autonomisation of the will from economic and empirical conditions according to the aforementioned dualist scheme (subsequently resolved in the claim of an *undifferentiated* unity of the two moments). The other side is represented by Mattick, who sees the genesis of class consciousness (and thus the passage from the 'class in itself' into the 'class for itself') as the *result of an objective process*, whose laws of movement are *neither resolved nor reflected in a movement of abstract consciousness or in an abstract unity of consciousness and objective conditions*, but in the articulated and differentiated context of *relations of production*. Only within this dynamic can the class struggle be explained, since it is none other than the 'active side' of the contradictions inherent in these productive relations.

5   The Unity Development-Crisis against the Dualism Production/Market

In a letter to Mattick dated 21 June 1931, Grossman clarified this controversial point in his theory in opposition to the Austro-Marxists.

> Of course, I am far from thinking that capitalism must break down 'of itself' or 'automatically', as Hilferding and other socialists (Braunthal) assert, in criticising my book. It can only be brought down by the class struggle of the working class. But I wanted to show that the class struggle alone is not enough. The will to bring it down is not sufficient. In the initial phases of capitalist development such a will cannot even arise. [...] Of course, as a dialectical Marxist, I know that both sides of the process, the objective and subjective elements influence each other. In the class struggle these factors merge. One cannot wait until, eventually, the 'objective' conditions are present so that, only then, the 'subjective' ones can operate. That would be an inadequate, mechanical perspective, which is alien to me. But, for the purposes of the analysis, I have to use the process of abstracting and isolating individual elements to show the essential functions of each element. Lenin often speaks of the objectively revolutionary situation that must be present as the precondition for the active, victorious intervention of the proletariat. My breakdown theory is not intended to exclude this active intervention but rather aims to show when and under what conditions such an objectively revolutionary situation can and does arise.[46]

---

46   In Grossman 2019, p. 230.

Here Grossman lays the foundations for a possible connection between the critique of political economy and the theory of revolution. A fundamental and irreducible moment of this connection should have been the dialectical *Darstellung*. As Roman Rosdolsky has shown in his work on the genesis of *Capital*, the distinction between 'method of research' (*Forschungsweise*) and 'method of exposition' (*Darstellung*) in the critique of political economy – a distinction which underlies the other, also decisive distinction between the genetic and morphological levels, the historical and the logical moment[47] – does not have purely epistemological significance, but also political and revolutionary relevance.[48] If the selection of an abstract criterion of exposition is not arbitrary (nor the result of purely methodological considerations), but is connected to the need to conceptually represent the process of *real abstraction*; and if the dialectical exposition of *Capital* describes the development of categorical norms which, in their logical structure, express the *real domination* of abstraction in capitalist society, then the critique of political economy is, *through the dialectical Darstellung*, a penetration and at the same time a criticism of an *a-subjective totality* regulated by the domination of the abstract (abstract-commodity labour). Thus, the critique of political economy is, on the one hand, a penetration of categorical objectivity as a 'mode of being-there' (*Daseinsweise*) of a totality specified in a historically determined present and of its reified 'forms of thought' (*Denkenformen*);[49] while on the other hand, it is an immanent critique of this 'objectivity' (*Gegenständlichkeit*) in as much as it is the theoretical expression of a real negativity and refers to an alternate logical and historical process having its genesis in the ambit of abstract labour.[50] It is at the same time a critique of 'consciousness' and a critical theory of revolution.

To the extent that they reconstruct the fundamental components of Marx's mature research (the theory of value and of money, the essence/phenomenon

---

47   Cf. Schmidt 1971, pp. 41 ff., as well as Luporini 1974, pp. 84–112.
48   In addition to the already mentioned work on the genesis of *Capital*, cf. Rosdolsky's recently published collection of essays on the theory and practice of the Second International, Rosdolsky 1973. Concerning the problem of a political reading of the *Darstellung*, cf. Reinicke 1974. This book takes up and develops several of Krahl's ideas.
49   On the relationship between the commodity form (*Warenform*) and the thought form (*Denkform*), cf. A. Sohn-Rethel's controversial but stimulating considerations in Sohn-Rethel 1971a, pp. 101 ff., and 1971b, pp. 24. The publication of Sohn-Rethel's writings, written during the 1930s in the context of the internal discussion of Critical Theory, but 'discovered' only recently, may constitute the most relevant theoretical event of the last decade in West Germany. Cf. Reinicke 1974, pp. 103–18, and Reinicke 1971, pp. 22–33.
50   Cf. De Giovanni 1970, pp. 173–202.

relation, logical time/historical time, use value/exchange value), recent studies on the genesis of the structure of *Capital* and on the epistemological *status* of Marxist theory offer the possibility of deriving from the critique of political economy itself, the fundamental categories of political theory, of the theory of classes and of the state. The critique of political economy, in its dual character of theory of real abstraction and a critique of the forms of reified consciousness (understood, not subjectively, but as effective 'modes of being-there' [(*Daseinsweise*)] of individuals and classes in the historically specified totality of capitalist society), constitutes the obligatory point of departure for a *scientific foundation of class consciousness*, or for what today is called 'the problem of constitution'.[51]

Returning this complex of problems (and tasks) to the theoretical and political discussion connected to *our* historical present, urgently demands the theoretically elaborated and historically specific recognition of the *Methodenstreit* within Marxism and the workers' movement. This is necessary so as to locate the epistemological moments and efforts where the problem of constitution (and the connection between political economy and the revolutionary theory at its foundation) is postulated. Or at least where the presuppositions for the problem's materialist treatment can be found.

Initial signs in this direction can be traced works, until recently neglected, by Henryk Grossman and Paul Mattick. Despite their theoretical limits and historical conditions, ironically it is precisely the fact that their economic 'models' appear 'closed' and unified (because, unlike 'neo-Marxist' theories of capitalist development, they do not present any dualism between *production* and *market*), which allows them to provide a potential foundation for a specific, non-generic (ethico-subjectivist) level of politics.[52] The categorial re-examination

---

[51] Marxist theory is rigorously analysed in the works of Rosdolsky already cited; Morf 1970; and, more recently, in the work of Reichelt 1970; Backhaus 1980, pp. 99–120; and Backhaus 1974, pp. 52–77. Concerning the relation between the critique of political economy and the theory of history, the dialectical *Darstellung* and the theme of class consciousness (*Konstitutionsproblematik*), the contributions of A. Schmidt are relevant. In addition to the already cited *Geschichte und Struktur* (Schmidt 1971), see Schmidt 1968, pp. 30–43; and Negt 1971. But, above all, see the volume written in collaboration with A. Kluge: Kluge and Negt 1972. All these authors develop (often with sharp polemical points) central themes of Critical Theory.

[52] Cf. N. Badaloni's perceptive article, Badaloni 1973, pp. 23–5. Here Badaloni takes up and clarifies several central points of his contribution to the conference on Marxism of the 1960s, Cf. *Il marxismo italiano degli anni sessanta e la formazione teorico-politica delle nuove generazioni*, 1972, pp. 19 ff., subsequently developed in Badaloni 1972, which along with the

of the capitalist system as a contradictory unity defined by the process of social reproduction as a whole, and expressed on the historico-structural level as a tendency to crisis (*Krisenzusammenhang*), brings us back to the very current theme of the state and of its function within the mechanism of valorisation and socialisation of labour. To the extent that it is a specification – and thus an *anticipation* – rather than a 'reflection' of the essential structural factors of the real historical process of capitalist society, the abstract categorial representation is not self-sufficient but refers back to the dimension of class struggle.

6 Crisis and Commodity-Form

Pannekoek had been able to accuse Grossman of being tied to a positivist and bourgeois conception of '*geschichtliche Notwendigkeit*'[53] [social necessity] because he had omitted the *critical* aspect of Grossman's exposition, taking it instead as an abstract, empirical and descriptive model, and thus he ended up by treating it as a manual of political economy.[54] Thus, in the same manner one could accuse Marx of economism for having described, in the four volumes of *Capital*, the development of *bürgerliche Gessellschaft* as the development of categorial forms transformed from economic science. This type of objection does not take into account the preliminary methodological warning implicit in

---

aforementioned works by Luporini and De Giovanni, constitutes the major recent contribution to Italian Marxist debates. For Mattick's critico-methodological conceptions, see the recent collection of his essays, Mattick 1974.

53 Cf. Pannekoek 1977.
54 The anonymous author of the article on crisis theory which came out in *Proletarier* together with Korsch's, had accused Grossman of not understanding Marx's method. 'Marx', he wrote, 'does not mean to *explain* capitalist reality through a "procedure of approximation" (*Annäherungsverfahren*). His theory is not meant as a means to reconstruct economic reality in its totality. It is meant, rather, to unveil the absurdity of the economic foundations of the system [...] and, furthermore, to give to the proletariat the chance to examine concretely its reality from the perspective of revolutionary transformation' (Cf. 'Die Grundlagen einer revolutionären Krisentheorie', reprinted in Korsch-Mattick-Pannekoek, 1973, p. 75). After having read this article, Grossman wrote to Mattick in a letter dated 7 May 1933: 'For Marx – the critic assures us – it is not a matter of *explaining* capitalist reality (as I maintain). Yet the same critic wants to offer a "theory" of crises. But what does theory mean other than that the facts of the capitalist mechanism are not simply *described* but also understood in their functional context, that is, *explained*!' (Cf. Grossman 2009, p. 246).

the subtitle to *Capital*, '*critique* of political economy'. At the same time, it precludes the possibility of understanding its profound *political* significance (not to be understood as plain instrumentality). Thus, Pannekoek's critique stems from his failure to grasp the *ars maieutica* that underpins the *Darstellung* of the critique of political economy:

> What is visible here in a *purely economic* manner, i.e., *from the bourgeois standpoint*, within the limits of capitalist understanding, from the standpoint of capitalist production itself, are its barriers, its relativity, the fact that it is not an absolute but only a historical mode of production, corresponding to a specific and limited epoch in the development of the material conditions of production.[55]

Having understood the 'theory of breakdown' as the self-criticism of the capitalist system at the level of 'abstract representation' and, hence, refering it to the transient, historical character of the mode of production based on com-

---

55   Marx 1981, p. 368 [emphasis added by GM – Ed.]. Pannekoek's methodological misunderstanding is further clarified if we examine the more theoretical and political side of his critique. Challenging Grossman's claim that breakdown is neither an alternative to nor in contradiction to the class struggle (cf. Grossman 2009, p. 602), Pannekoek accuses him of having a reductivist conception of the latter, i.e., of seeing it as a simple struggle for wage increases and for the reduction of labour time (cf. Pannekoek 1977). Actually, as follows from Gossman's line of argument, which Pannekoek ignores, the reference is not solely to factory struggle but to the overall dynamic of the capitalist system. Grossman connects the class struggle, in all of its complexity, to the process of *reproduction* and not to the simple productive process: 'precisely because, in Marx, the entire analysis of the process of reproduction leads to the class *struggle*' (Grossman 2009). Here, Grossman quotes a final passage from a letter by Marx to Engels dated 30 April 1868, concerning the structure of the second and third volumes of *Capital*. In this letter, after having shown the phenomenal appearance of the 'independent movement' of the economy, which makes economic categories appear as if they followed an objective, autonomous, and self-determining process; then concludes that, when one relates wages and profits to the three classes (landowners, capitalists and workers), which constitute the sources of income, the result of the entire dialectic of the forms is 'the *class struggle*, as the conclusion in which the movement and disintegration of the whole shit resolves itself' (Marx and Engels 1988, p. 25). To the extent that this conclusion implies the totality of the *reproductive* process, it rules out all restricted conceptions (economistic or factory-centred) of the class struggle. And Grossman uses it in order to demonstrate that, at a high level of capital accumulation, *the struggle for the distribution of income* 'is not only a struggle for the betterment of the standards of living of the classes in struggle; but *a struggle for the very existence of the capitalist mechanism*' (Grossman 2009).

modity exchange, Grossman can avoid the error usually committed by many Marxist economists: to separate the theory of value – the cornerstone of the critique of political economy – from the materialist conception of history. The 'becoming science' of historical materialism coincides with the understanding of the transitory nature of bourgeois society, which Sismondi 'foresaw' on the plane of the philosophy of history: in the 'cell form' (*Zellenform*) of the mode of production, in the form of commodity production, in the value form of commodities, and in value taking the form of capital.[56] Grossman's 'method of isolation' (*Isolierungsmethode*) represents the contradictory unity of use value and exchange value *only* in its economic aspect, thus as a problem of the organic composition of capital and, finally, as an *economic tendency* to crisis (tendential fall of the rate of profit) – a result of the contradiction inherent in the very mechanism of accumulation. The historical past of the capitalist social formation thus appears, in its 'naturalness' (*Naturwüchsigkeit*), as a tendency within the economic heart of the material base, as a 'natural' connection to crisis (*Krisenzusammenhang*) which leads to breakdown.[57] But from within this critical 'self-representation' (*Selbstdarstellung*) of the system – underpinned by the historico-materialist *self-foundation* of the critique of political economy, marked by the passage from the level of the philosophy of history to categorial-dialectical *Selbstverständis* of the determined and fleeting historical character of *bürgerliche Gesellschaft* – Grossman *deduces* the *social* tendency through which this economic tendency is realised: the contradiction between productive forces and relations of production. To the extent that it defines the *essential* contradictoriness of the capitalist mode of production at the general social level, this contradiction between productive forces and relations of production can neither be relegated to the competitive capitalist phase (as affirmed, for instance, by Panzieri and more schematically still by other 'New Left' theorists) nor reduced to a metaphorical objectification of the capital/labour conflict (as many exponents of *Linkskommunismus* maintained). In the same way that it is impossible to escape 'pre-history' by remaining within the milieu of com-

---

56   Grossman wrote a sizeable study on Sismondi: 'Simonde de Sismondi and his Economic Theories (A New Interpretation of his Thought)', in Grossman 2009, pp. 55–119. Some important considerations concerning the Swiss economist can also be found in the essay 'W. Playfair, The Earliest Theorist of Capitalist Development', Grossman 2009, pp. 600–23.
57   The dialectical representation reveals the contradiction within the very appearance of 'naturalness' of the system. That *Naturwüchsigkeit* that conferred the appearance of 'natural' immutability on the realised totality (*fertige Totalität*) of the capitalist mode of production now contradicts itself *in the level of its own fetishistic objectivity*, turning itself into *naturwüchsiger Krisenzusammenhang*, in its 'natural' tendency to breakdown.

modity production, so there is no way to suppress – from within the capitalist system – the 'naturalness' of the process or to control it through planning. And, if the autonomous moment of *Darstellung* is not to result merely in an empirical abstraction but is to express the effective 'becoming autonomous' of the dominion of the abstract within bourgeois society, then the constitution of the proletariat as a 'class for itself' cannot be something given *ab originibus* in the 'relations of production' as the cause-effect of a manichean split between capital and 'workers' autonomy; it is rather the result of a long historical process of emancipation from within the *real* domination of *abstract* labour. To put this in philosophical terms: the process whereby the proletariat becomes-subject is the result of a process without a subject. Thus, this process has produced a historical present characterised and specified by a growing protagonism of the masses; but without the 'naturalness' of capitalism this protagonism would be a mere idealist category – i.e., something practically inconceivable both in the past (in its genesis) and in the present (as realised today). Despotic socialisation does not supress but fulfills in its *contradictory unity* the fundamental historical contradiction between productive forces and relations of production (which is not limited to the competitive phase but is inherent in the dichotomous structure of the system's 'cell-form': the *commodity*). State intervention in the economy functions as a 'plan' only in the technocratic ideology of late capitalism. In reality, it acts as mediator of counter-tendencies (itself too being a counter-tendency) to the tendency of the rate of profit to fall. The *formally* unifying character of despotic socialisation results in the real function of the state as regulator of the overall process of production being understood through the ideological category of the 'plan'. It thus impedes the comprehension of the unity/contradiction of the productive forces and of the relations of production within the new *Gestalt* that this process assumes in modern organised capitalism.

7 Scientific Representation and Historical Process: The Problem of Constitution

Paradoxically, the weak point of Panzieri's argument (which, apart from the obvious historical differences, turns out have a striking resemblance to Korsch's) lies in its most vital political contribution: the call for an anti-dogmatic reprise of Marx's discourse based on the simultaneous translation of the categories of the critique of political economy into those of revolutionary theory. Despite starting from the Marxian connection between the theory of capitalist development and the theory of social revolution which Korsch had violently criticised,[58] Panzieri finds himself in the company of Korsch's theoretical Leftism in misinterpreting the significance and the function of *Darstellung*. If in Korsch the categorial representation is reduced to a mere reflection and the theory of the crisis to an objectifying allegory of real class conflicts, in Panzieri the development of Marx's presentation from the first to the third volume of *Capital* is directly associated with the real historical development of capital from the competitive to the monopolistic phase. In support of his reading of the three volumes of *Capital* as a description of the 'historical process of the growing cohesion of the system',[59] which would have led, beyond Marx's own prognosis, to the complete realisation of the law of value as the 'law of the plan', Panzieri quotes an important passage from the chapter on the trinity formula in the third volume:

> In presenting the reification [*Versachlichung*] of the relations of production and the autonomy [*Verselbständigung*] they acquire vis-à-vis the agents of production, we shall not go into the form and manner in which these connections appear to them as overwhelming natural laws, governing them irrespective of their will, in the form that the world market and its conjunctures, the movements of market prices, the cycles of industry and trade and the alternation of prosperity and crisis prevails on them as blind necessity. This is because the actual movement of competition [*die wirkliche Bewegung der Konkurrenz*] *lies outside our plan*, and we are *only* out to present the internal organization of the capitalist mode of production, its ideal average, as it were [*in ihrem idealen Durchschnitt*].[60]

But the meaning of this passage takes precisely the opposite direction from that taken by Panzieri: here we are not dealing – even 'abstractly' – with reproducing the phases of a real historical movement, but with abstracting from it understood as a complex of empirical phenomena, in order to describe the capitalist mode of production in its essential moments, in its purity, in its *idealen Durchschnitt*. The fact that the *Versachlichung* [reification] of capital in the trinitary formula 'appears [...] only at the highest level of capitalist development: characterised by interest-producing capital',[61] does not mean that the trinitary

---

58   Cf. in this regard P. Mattick, 'Marxismus und die Unzulänglichkeiten der Arbeiterbewegung', in Pozzoli 1973, p. 195, where Korsch's refusal to connect the theory of social revolution with that of capitalist development is sharply criticised.
59   Panzieri 1964, p. 283.
60   Marx 1981, pp. 969–70. Italics added.
61   Panzieri 1964, p. 282.

formula reflects or captures the real historical complexity of this level of development. Rather, in the general framework of the Marxist dialectical representation, the trinitary formula represents the synthesis of the forms of 'necessary appearance' deduced from the abstract totality of the concept of capital.[62] The relation between the essence and phenomenon obtaining between the general concept of capital (*allgemeiner Kapitalbegriff*) and 'independently existing capitals' (*für sich seiendes Kapital*) – competition – does not concern the historico-genetic plane, but rather the logico-cognitive one.[63] If, on the one hand, the categorial structure cannot be considered a blunt reflection of the real movement, on the other hand, the logico-structural domination of a form of the process defines, but does not resolve within itself, or suppress, the variety and complexity of an historical phase. The political function of the *Darstellungsweise* [method of presentation] does not lie in mechanically superimposing itself on the *Forschungsweis* [method of inquiry], but in forming its foundation and background. The dimension of political tactics has a real meaning and place only within this distinction, in the same way that – on the 'cognitive plane' – science has a meaning and a place in the hiatus existing between essence and phenomenal form: 'all science would be superfluous if the form of appearance of things coincided with their essence'.[64]

8 The Process of Reproduction and the Role of the State

In drawing some provisional conclusions (as a first framing of the problematic), we shall briefly consider the *status* of the theory of crisis in relation to the theme of 'constitution'. Grossman's and Mattick's theories, whose importance we have emphasised, are not without defects and ideological distortions produced by the historical circumstances within which they developed. Thus, in Grossman, despite repeated theoretical warnings, the genesis of proletarian class consciousness is directly and exclusively connected with crisis periods. Similarly, Mattick sharply separates revolutionary periods defined by economic crises from non-revolutionary periods defined by productive expansion and the resulting prevalence of reformist tendencies within the workers' movement.[65]

---

62 Cf. Reichelt 1970, pp. 243 ff.
63 Cf. Schmidt 1971, pp. 41 ff.
64 Marx 1981, p. 956. For all of these problems, cf. Luporini 1974, pp. 99–101. [The page range given to Luporini is to an entirely different chapter, which does not concern itself with the issues discussed here. Reference should be to Luporini's essay 'Marx secondo Marx' that is indeed concerned with these issues – editor's note.]
65 Cf. Mattick 1969 and 'Marxismus und die Unzulanglichkeiten der Arbeiterbewegung',

These claims undoubtedly run the risk of an objectivist and mechanical reduction of the problem of constitution.[66] Yet, this direct linking of periods of crisis with the genesis of class consciousness cannot be regarded as peculiar and limited to Grossman and Mattick as 'theoreticians of breakdown'. The same 'catastrophist' interdependence can be found in Lukács, who was the first to pose the problem of constitution in the light of *Capital*:

> The proletariat is then at one and the same time the product of the permanent crisis in capitalism and the instrument of those tendencies driving capitalism toward crisis [...]. By recognizing its situation it acts. By combating capitalism it discovers its own mission in society.
>
> But the class consciousness of the proletariat, the truth of the process 'as subject' is itself far from stable and constant; it does not advance according to mechanical laws. It is the consciousness of the dialectical process itself: it is likewise a dialectical concept. For the active and practical side of class consciousness, its true essence, can only become visible in its authentic form when the historical process imperiously requires it to come into force, i.e., when an acute crisis of the economy drives it to action.[67]

Thus, even in their shortcomings, the works of Grossman and Mattick belong with the most advanced level of discussion of the 1920s and 30s. Although Mattick only poses the problem of the state within the form of capitalist organisation of the time, the so-called 'mixed economy',[68] the richness of his approach can be measured *ex negativo* by comparing it with some of Korsch's essays on the state written during his American exile and published in *Living Marxism* (edited by Mattick himself).[69] Here Korsch develops some ideas on the

---

Mattick 1973b, pp. 192 ff. For a look at Mattick's theoretical-political positions considered as a whole, see the French anthology af his work edited by R. Paris, Mattick 1972.

66   The presence of such a risk is confirmed by the absence in Grossman and Mattick of an analysis of the labour process and of the capitalist organisation of labour.

67   Lukács 1971, p. 40. For a discussion of the political implications of this work of Lukács, see the important discussion in Cerruti, Claussen, Krahl, Negt and Schmidt 1971 (especially pp. 18–25).

68   For a discussiin of the economic model that follows from Mattick's *Marx and Keynes*, see Hermanin 1973.

69   *Living Marxism*, which was first known as *International Council Correspondence* and then as *New Essays* [all the issues of these journals have been reprinted by Greenwood Publishing Company (Westport, Conn., 1971)], published political, economic and social theories of some of the better-known exponents of *Linkskommunismus* during the 1930s and 1940s. Besides Mattick and Korsch (both in emigration in the United States), both Pannekoek (articles were periodically translated from *Rätekorrespondenz* of Amsterdam in it), and

state by developing ideas from some of his other works. The importance of these articles lies in the fact that they demonstrate the overriding importance of the level of *Darstellung* for the theme of the state. In his 'Marxism and the Present Task of the Proletarian Class Struggle',[70] Korsch counterposes Marx as a 'proletarian theorist' to Marx as a 'spokesman' for 'radical democratic' policies (referring to Marx's contributions in the *Neue Rheinische Zeitung* and in the *New York Daily Tribune*), and traces this dualism to the Jacobin model of revolution adopted by the founders of scientific socialism.[71] Korsch can advance this schema because he hypostatises as a final and permanent theoretical result the ideas on the state expressed by Marx and Engels in the *Vormärz*, without seeing the possibility of reconsidering the problem on the basis of their later critique of political economy.

Having established a relation of simple reversal of civil society and the state, with an explicit anti-state bias,[72] Korsch runs into what he considers the original contradiction of Marxism: since, *as theory*, it is the *reflection* of a *real* process it cannot also be a theory of proletarian and communist revolution (since the latter has not yet occurred). Thus, up to now Marxism has existed as the reflection of another revolution, the capitalist and bourgeois revolution. Unable to grasp the practical and political function of the dialectical mode of exposition as distinct from the 'method of research', Korsch posits a relation of mere 'reflection' or simple 'correspondence' between the level of categorical abstractions and that of empirical facts.[73] Hence, the essential simplicity with which he sees that specific historical form of *real abstraction* represented by the state. The latter is not considered in the light of the overall structure

---

Otto Rühle (the Proletarian Party of America, from which another group – the United Workers' Party – broke off to publish the journal, had grown close to the *Einheitsorganisation*, which was born of a split in the KPD) wrote for the paper. There has been an anthology in French of articles from this journal, although it is dedicated almost entirely to studies critical of the USSR: *La contre-révolution bureaucratique*, Paris 1973. There is also a comprehensive collection of articles from the journal on all the themes covered in the journal in Italian: *Capitalismo e fascismo verso la guerra* (Bonacchi and Pozzoli (ed.) 1976). See also the excellent account in Bonacchi 1976, pp. 43–72.

70 In Korsch 1977, pp. 190–1.

71 According to Korsch, the adoption of this model explains the polemics with Proudhon and Bakunin, which are based upon the privileging of the political, party, and state-centred moments of the class struggle.

72 Cf. 'Economics and Politics in Revolutionary Spain', *Living Marxism* IV (May 3, 1938), and 'Collectivisation in Spain', ibid., IV (April 6, 1939).

73 Cf. my essay, 'Kritische Bemerkungen zur Korsch-Reception in Italien', in Pozzoli 1973, pp. 238–9 [and as the next chapter of this book – editor's note].

of the abstract in Marx's mature conception, but in terms of the immediate counterposition of state and civil society paralleling that between speculation and reality.[74] Thus Korsch, in attempting to diachronically dilute the dialectical categories of Marxism in order to re-adapt them pragmatically to the needs of a 'practical theory of proletarian revolution', flattens the dialectical problems of historical constitution (which demarcates the indirect phases of the passage from factory struggles to overall social struggle, from economic to political struggles) onto the positivist problematic of empirical 'specification'. The class struggle is thus simplified in a series of empirically observable actions scattered across different spatio-temporal locations, the multiplicity of which is never connected with the morphological context of the crisis, to the unifying moment of the historical present.

The tragically impotent result of Korsch's thought shows how the unhooking of the theory of social revolution – the theory of classes and of the state – from the critique of political economy and its resulting theory of the crisis, paradoxically produces a loss of *specificity* in precisely that political dimension which initially was to be privileged.[75] Above all, what remains unexplored is the function of the state in the mature Marxian conception: this is a problem that theory must finally deal with.

The state emerges from the *Darstellung* of the entire process of social reproduction as the supreme expression of the reality of abstraction, of its effective

---

74   From this perspective, the parallel drawn in *Marxism and Philosophy* between the abolition of philosophy and the abolition of the state is to be seen as a theoretical and political failure linked to a somewhat limiting reading of Marx's early philosophical works. On this point cf. De Giovanni 1973, p. 49.

75   The flipside of Korsch's 'critical' programme is his dogmatic understanding of the critique of political economy. The latter is considered finished once and for all with the analysis of the essence of the mode of capitalist production elaborated by Marx in *Capital*; one need only restate its fundamental concepts each time. Marxist theory, however, must be constantly rediscovered and updated (*die lebendige Weiterentwicklung*) as the theory of the class struggle. Once separated from the structural analysis of capitalist development and from the consequent critical reflexion on the logical apparatus of Marxist categories in relation to the changed 'morphology' of the mode of production, the theory of revolution ends up wavering – impotently – between the extreme poles of dogmatism and empiricism. In this respect, see Negt 1975 [which appears in the same issue in which this chapter was first published in English by *Telos* – editor's note]. The importance and originality of *Marx and Keynes* (especially if compared to the model of Baran and Sweezy, which has conditioned international discussion for many years) lies, on the contrary, in the fact that it makes possible a unitary theoretical and political discourse grounded in a comprehensive economic analysis connecting production with markets, distribution, reproduction and the state – all on the basis of the Marxist theory of value.

domination over society, and of the complex structure of that domination. The state as the final shore of the logico-historical process of the socialisation of capital, and thus of the real universalisation of the domination of the abstract; it returns as backdrop to the critique of political economy: a regulating instance and, at the same time, a generalised expression of crisis.

CHAPTER 5

Korsch in Italy

Before 1966, Italian Marxism was influenced by Lukacs's 'socialist realism' rather than by *History and Class Consciousness*.* This predominant interest in aesthetic questions can be ascribed to the lingering influence of Croce's neo-idealism over Italian Marxist intellectuals. Only with the translation of *The Destruction of Reason* and *The Young Hegel* immediately after de-Stalinisation in the 1960s did discussion of Lukács's philosophical work begin, along with that of Western Marxism in general.

The Italian translation of *Marxism and Philosophy* appeared in 1966, even before that of *History and Class Consciousness*. Mario Spinella's introduction to Korsch's work was very general and revealed the extent to which Italian Marxism still lagged behind the many problems central to 'critical Marxism'. As he wrote there:

> Korsch, together with the Lukács of *History and Class Consciousness* and the Lenin of the famous letter [to the journal] *Under the Banner of Marxism*, is one of the initiators of that Hegel-renaissance within Marxist thought which, despite all contradictoriness ... has increasingly influenced an essential current of Marxist research of the last forty years.[1]

Spinella did not fail to locate the concrete historical causes for this new departure within 'theoretical Marxism'. When Korsch was writing *Marxism and Philosophy*, the spread of the October revolution to Germany could not yet be ruled out. The re-emergence of the 'philosophy of revolution' was borne out by major historical events: Germany's military defeat, the monarchy's fall, the serious economic and financial crisis, and the shock that ran through the world market, world politics and the international workers' movement as a result of the Bolshevik revolution in Russia. Nonetheless, Spinella's points of departure remained general and were not followed by a thorough analysis. Thus, he iden-

---

* [This essay appeared initially as 'Kritische Bemerkungen zur Korsch-Reception in Italien', in *Jahrbuch Arbeiterbewegung – Theorie und Geschichte*, Bd. 1, *Über Karl Korsch*, edited by Claudio Pozzoli, Frankfurt a. M. 1973, and was then translated by David J. Parenti for *Telos*, 26, Winter 1975–6. Like all essays, this version has been revised for this volume.]

1 Spinella 1966, p. i. [The letter is published under the title of 'On the Significance of Militant Materialism', Lenin, *Collected Works*, vol. 33, pp. 227–36 – editor's note.]

tified Korsch with Lukács, and both of them with Lenin, under the common denominator of the 'Hegel-renaissance'.[2] This diluted Korsch's work to a translation of Lenin's 'On the Significance of Militant Materialism' and *State and Revolution* into the jargon of Western Marxism. Thus, it was only logical for Spinella to misconstrue the meaning of the 1930 '*Antikritik*' and to reduce its theoretical and political significance to a simple work of enlightenment:

> The '*Antikritik*' once again passes through this critical route [the decline of Leninist theory into a legitimating science – G.M.] and discovers its immediate political and theoretical causes, *not the least of which* is the choice of that formulation which Lenin gave, in *Materialism and Empiriocriticism*, to the relation between Marxism and philosophy.[3]

The radical political difference between Korsch and Lenin had thus been reduced to a purely philosophical disagreement. By not paying sufficient attention to the concrete, historical and political aspect of the question, Spinella side-stepped the problem of elucidating the important way Korsch understood himself in relation to Lenin and Leninism in 1929. He dissolved the entire process of clarification which Korsch had gone through between 1923 and 1930 into the abstract process of a mere psychological reflection. As for the later development of Korsch's thinking, Spinella was satisfied with the statement that 'Korsch's decision led him into practical isolation despite the not insignificant role that he played in some circles as a scholar'.[4]

The Italian translation of *Marxism and Philosophy* was followed by numerous reviews stemming from the most varied tendencies of Italian theoretical Marxism.[5] What is most important for the following discussion is undoubtedly Lucio Colletti's trenchant critique.[6] Colletti reproached Korsch for failing to

---

2 Spinella 1966, p. iv.
3 Spinella 1966, p. x. Emphasis added.
4 Ibid. More precise is the 'Nota storica' of Giorgio Backhaus printed in the appendix to the book, and acting as the first – though unsuccessful – attempt to draw Korsch into the debate of the 'New Left'; cf. Spinella 1966, pp. 161–76.
5 Among these, cf. especially that of Luciano Amodio, who attacked *Marxism and Philosophy* from a Lukácsian standpoint and claimed that the dialectic was not sufficiently developed in Korsch.
6 Colletti is presently the main representative of Galvano Della Volpe's school of thought. This trend gained prominence in Italy in the second half of the 1950s. Della Volpe's most important theoretical work – *Logica come scienza positive* – had a major influence on Italy's young Marxist intellectuals as a rejection of Stalinism as well as of the subjective idealism of Croce and Gentile. However, in arguing that Marx, by 1843, had laid the logical foundation for his historico-materialist science in the *Critique of Hegel's Philosophy of Right*, which he then used

untie the Gordion knot binding Marx to Hegel; for not seeing the unbridgeable difference between the two. For Colletti, Korsch did not distinguish between Marx's and Hegel's theory of alienation *and* the theory of fetishism:

> Korsch does not have a correct concept of Marx's notions of fetishism and alienation, he therefore cannot understand how Marx differs from Hegel. Thus, he confuses Marx's analysis of fetishism, i.e., the critique of capital and of the state, with Hegel's critique of 'scientific reason' and 'positivity'. He thus confuses the critique of *bourgeois society* with idealistic and romantic critiques of science.[7]

Thus, Colletti saw *Marxism and Philosophy* as a reduction of Marxism to a 'restored philosophy' and predicted for it 'the same fate as *History and Class Consciousness*'. In fact, up to the Italian publication of *Karl Marx* three years later, *Marxism and Philosophy* was not discussed as an independent work, but as a mere appendage to the young Lukács.

After the Italian translation of *Karl Marx*, the Dellavolpeans renewed their discussion of Korsch. Impressed by his designation of Marxism as the 'science of society', they began to revise decisively their previous estimation of Korsch, without, however, questioning the reasons for Korsch's theoretical shift. Their aprioristic interpretation prevented them from grasping the connection between theory and politics in Korsch. Instead of retracting their former judgment of *Marxism and Philosophy*, they merely modified it. While they had formerly regarded his work as a relapse into idealism, they now were satisfied to claim that in 1923 Korsch had looked upon 'the scientific analyses of *Capital* with a certain suspicion'.[8] The revised judgment, however, remained external. The Dellavolpeans used Korsch to confirm the coherence and validity of their own approach. In effect, they said: 'It is not us who have changed, but Korsch'. Again, the relation between Hegel and Marx was the crucial point: 'In *Karl Marx*', Bedeschi wrote, 'the way the Hegel-Marx relation is under-

---

positively in *Capital*, Della Volpe reduced Marxism to scientific theory on the model of the natural sciences. In establishing an unbroken continuity in the Marxist corpus, grounded in a methodological unity, Della Volpe ruled out the possibility of a historico-political interpretation of theory. It is Colletti's Dellavolpean heritage that has prevented him from treating Korsch in a historical context.

7 Cf. Colletti's review of *Marxismo e filosofia* in the journal, *Problemi del socialismo* 10, 1966, p. 777.
8 Bedeschi, 'Introduzione' to Korsch 1969.

stood shows new essential developments'.[9] The dialectic was no longer seen as a closed metaphysical model, but in terms of its function for understanding experience. Bedeschi's remarks were not without a certain sagacity: the significance of Hegel's works for Korsch was no longer seen as merely methodological, in the sense of having to turn Hegel's dialectics upsidedown – i.e. to interpret them materialistically in order to grasp the entire world-historical series of stages in overall perfection, but as a material one. It is based on the organic entanglement of Hegel's philosophy with the bourgeois system:

> In other words, Hegel's work is of fundamental significance for Marx to the extent that he finds in it the contents and ideological reflexes of bourgeois society, or, to the extent that Hegel is the spokesman and theorist of this society.

These remarks are confirmed by Korsch:

> While still formally basing his criticism of Hegel's glorification of the state on the realistic statements concerning the nature of civil society embodied in the same Hegelian work, Marx now definitely abandoned Hegel and all his idealistic philosophy. Instead, he associated himself with those great enquirers into the social nature of man who, in the preceding centuries, had first set up the new idea of civil society as a revolutionary slogan, and had even unearthed, in the new science of political economy, the material foundations of that new and 'civilized' form of society.[10]

But if Bedeschi went on to characterise Korsch's critique of Hegel as exclusively philosophical rather than political and revolutionary, and if he dealt with the relation between Hegel and Marx simply in terms of the thesis of the 'break', he was expressing precisely the Dellavolpean weakness: he neglected Korsch's important initiatives which deserved to be further developed and did not see Korsch's theoretical shortcomings, especially concerning the understanding of *ideology* in its relation to the base (of the social conditions of production) as well as his designation of Marxism as a 'class science'. But these very historical and theoretical shortcomings made it possible for the Dellavolpeans to appropriate Korsch. According to Korsch, too, Marx essentially broke with Hegel's idealist philosophy – despite his flirtation with Hegel's mode of expression.

---

9 Bedeschi, 'Introduzione' to Korsch 1969, p. xviii.
10 Korsch 2016, p. 9.

Korsch also refused to speak of a 'break' between the young and the mature Marx, and argued for the substantial unity between the theory of alienation and the theory of fetishism. Thus, Bedeschi was led to claim a correspondence between Korsch and Della Volpe.[11] But this is tenable only if one disregards the abstract and scholastic nature of this approach. It presupposes that Della Volpe really saw the development of Marx's thought as a progressive self-clarification in relation to the shifting movements of the class struggle, as Korsch had done, and took into consideration Marx's second reading of Hegel in the light of a more mature conception, which understood the critique of the economy as the 'critique of the weapons' of the proletariat. Furthermore, it assumes that Korsch had really rid himself of all 'neo-Hegelian' (or neo-Kantian?) subjective-idealist elements of his thinking.

Actually, Della Volpe depicted the 'theoretical field' of the critique of political economy in a simplified and undialectical way. Thus, he read *Capital* from the perspective of a strictly logical Aristotelianism, abstractly focusing on the principle of non-contradiction. Furthermore, Korsch did not actually give up all ethical-subjective traits, which remain on the political level as voluntarist tendencies.[12] Despite the clarity of some of his arguments, Bedeschi's attempt ultimately was bound to fail. Della Volpe's rigorous and obstinate 'anti-Hegelianism' could hardly be reconciled with Korsch's dynamic theory, which is so closely linked with the events of the class struggle and the problems of political militancy, that it resists all systematisations.

It is no accident that the most important attempt to reclaim Korsch in Italy was made by another exponent of the second generation of Dellavolpeans, who was led by his study of *Karl Marx* to break with the fundamental tenets of the Della Volpe school, and thus to initiate a new phase: the 'post-Dellavolpean' period. Despite the flexibility of this theoretical approach, it ultimately ended up pouring more water on the mill-wheel of the so-called 'Italian way to socialism'.

Three central concerns emerge from Giuseppe Vacca's pamphlet *Lukács o Korsch?*: (a) the elucidation of the relation between Korsch and Lukács in 1923 when their works appeared; (b) the elucidation of the relation between

---

11   Bedeschi, 'Introduzione', to Korsch 1969, p. xxv, note 14.
12   Of course, this cannot be abstractly determined but can only be explained through a confrontation with the *specific historical situation*, the state of the class struggle, and the long 'economic slump' of the international workers' movement under the hegemony of Leninism and Stalinism. The decisive factor for Korsch's change of position is the failure of the German revolution: it is at the basis of the *ethical emphasis* of revolutionary subjectivity typical of Korsch.

Hegel and Marx, as well as of the specific dialectical function of the concept of totality in their works; (c) the determination of the relation between *Marxism and Philosophy* and *Karl Marx* and the problem of the correct reading of the two works in the context of Korsch's intellectual and political biography.

On the first point, Vacca's view is that although *History and Class Consciousness* and *Marxism and Philosophy* have had a common destiny in the history of Marxism ('both were criticised by the ideologists of the Russian Communist Party as "deviations" and "revisions" of the sort that was labeled "the new Marxist school" or "Western Marxism" – which included Revai and Fogarosi as well'),[13] they actually took basically different positions toward the politically decisive problem of the European revolution, the validity of the Leninist model of the party for the working class of highly developed capitalist countries, and especially the relation between the development of theoretical and practical Leninism in the USSR and in the Western Communist movements. According to Vacca,

> Korsch's starting point is the need to materialistically historicise the whole experience of the workers' movement and its theory, including the Russian revolution and Leninism. Therefore, his objective lies in providing an original interpretation and re-evaluation of Marx's thought. Lukács, on the contrary, believes that the experience of the Russian revolution and of Lenin's work contains a 'theoretical legacy' of extraordinary relevance which provides the key to the correct understanding of the Marxist method. [This] 'correct method of knowing society and history' must be restored as an inalienable precondition for the development of the proletarian revolution in the West.[14]

---

13   Vacca 1969, p. 15. It may be surprising to find such violent attacks against the institutionalised Marxism of the Russian Communist Party coming from a militant intellectual of the Italian Communist Party. But, unlike the French Communist Party, the PCI's cultural policy was always extraordinarily flexible and therefore able to absorb some aspects of even the most 'heterodox' theoretical views. This can be explained by the familiarity of the Italian Communist tradition with bourgeois thought such as subjective idealism (Croce and Gentile). In fact, subjective idealism exercised great influence on party leaders such as Gramsci and Togliatti.

14   Vacca 1969, p. 35. Vacca can claim this gap between *History and Class Consciousness* and *Marxism and Philosophy* because he backdates the ideas of the *Anti-kritik* of 1930. Here his analysis betrays a certain apriorism and an inadequate historical articulation of the problem.

The relation between Hegel and Marx, as well as the theme of the totality (the second point), are also treated differently in the two works. Korsch sought to determine the specific 'theoretical' level of the revolutionary proletarian struggle. For him, to pose the question of the relation between philosophy and Marxism meant to not 'to pose the problem of a specific philosophy of Marx' but, rather,

> to go back to those theoretical models (Classical German philosophy) which, to the extent that they were the ideal organic means of a revolutionary process (of the bourgeois revolution), provide a historical example for the organic and critical function of theory, i.e., they present a model for the global theoretical reconstruction of the formation of a society from the standpoint of a particular class (the modern bourgeoisie). Recourse to that theoretical model makes it possible to determine the analogous historical function which the Marxist critique of bourgeois society as a whole must have for the proletariat and its revolution.[15]

According to Vacca, already in *Marxism and Philosophy* the critique of political economy of the mature Marx is given primacy over the philosophical critique of bourgeois representative government in the young Marx. For Marxism, there is a connection between the abolition of philosophy and the abolition of the state. For Korsch, this connection entails investigating the practico-revolutionary significance of philosophy and of all social forms of consciousness for historical reality. This is why Korsch concentrated on investigating the reality-character of ideology. According to Vacca, such a view of the reality of forms of consciousness constitutes the dialectical nature of Marxism:

> Dialectics is, for Korsch, the theoretical position which introduces a continuity and articulation between the social conditions and the forms of consciousness as an expression of them, by fixing precisely the reality of these forms of consciousness.[16]

Only from this viewpoint is there, for Korsch, a continuity between Hegel and Marx: if the 'continuity of the dialectical method from Hegel to Marx in Korsch's

---

15   Vacca 1969, pp. 42–3. The political content of Vacca's interpretation is hidden precisely at this point. It thus intervened in the discussion in progress within the Italian Communist Party concerning the relations between the party and mass movements.
16   Vacca 1969, p. 46.

analyses merely designates their analogous views of the *reality* of the forms of consciousness', then what necessarily follows is 'the regaining of the category of *totality*, which Korsch prescribes when he re-problematises the relation between Marx and philosophy'.[17] In *Marxism and Philosophy*, regaining the category of totality does not imply the 're-establishment of a philosophical category, of a general "purely" epistemological principle', but the reconstruction of the complex unity of Marx's critiques

> as an organic whole, outside of which it is impossible to understand the historical movement of the formation of bourgeois society and the revolutionary nature of the proletariat's social practice. Regaining the totality thus means to reconstruct Marx's *critical* thinking, understood in its irreducibility to a form of particular science or philosophy and in its authentic nature as the theoretical critique of bourgeois society.[18]

Starting from a similar appraisal of the historical situation, Lukács posed instead 'a problem of theoretical orthodoxy'. He also started with a basic canon of historical materialism, which positivist Marxism as well as the neo-idealism of the Second International had lost sight of: the reality of the forms of consciousness and of ideology in general. For Lukács, the epoch-making character of historical materialism consisted in seeing that the apparently independent systems of English political economy and of classical German philosophy 'were recognised as mere factors of a comprehensive whole; that their apparent independence could be abolished'. According to Vacca, the possible abolition of their 'apparent independence' in Lukács' analysis departs

> increasingly from the practical critique of bourgeois society as a whole, as it is advanced by the struggle of the revolutionary proeltarian class and becomes a viable task within a correct theory.[19]

For Lukács, the 'apparent independence' of those systems implies their ideological nature. Although he admitted the reality of ideologies, he also tended to conceive of them as 'false' by virtue of being *partial* forms of consciousness

> and so to relegate the problem of the truth of knowledge – which for Marx was a problem of 'social practice' – implicitly to the independent level of

---

17 Vacca 1969, pp. 48–9.
18 Vacca 1969, p. 51.
19 Vacca 1969, p. 53.

pure theory whereby the problem of theory is posed as the problem of a dialectic between partial and total forms of knowledge.[20]

The proletariat no longer stands in the centre of contemporary history by constituting in its real movement the constant 'truth-criterion' of theory (as in Korsch) but, rather, insofar as it alone is capable of correctly posing the problem of the relationship to society as a whole. According to Vacca, once truth as a totality is associated with the proletariat as the absolute subject-object of the course of history, and falsehood is associated with the forms of consciousness of the social reality of the bourgeoisie, we are on 'a dangerous path' which ultimately reduces the Marxist theory of ideology to the historicist relativism of the 'sociology of knowledge'. Thus, Lukács' totality does not refer to the totality of historico-empirical analyses whereby Marxist theory grasps the knowledge of an entire epoch of social economic formation, but to 'the general knowledge of the processuality of the real and of the general context of the "phenomena"'.[21]

Having shown the wide gap between *Marxism and Philosophy* and *History and Class Consciousness*, Vacca analysed *Karl Marx* as the last confirmation of his thesis concerning the 'radical difference between Korsch and Lukács' (the third point). Here, Vacca denies any substantial changes in Korsch's intellectual and political biography. Instead, he argues for a definite continuity between the approach to the problem in *Marxism and Philosophy* and in *Karl Marx*: the 'scientificity' of Marxist theory discussed in *Karl Marx* is based on its *critical* character, which for Korsch is closely related to its *dialectical* character. The scattered elements of Marxism cannot be reunited by a purely mental process. The analytico-theoretical *corpus* of Marx has an organicity (always in the *negative* sense, to the extent that it is *critique* of social conditions and of bourgeois forms of social consciousness) only because 'the social struggle of the modern proletariat increasingly explains the inner movement of this organism'.[22] Unlike Lukács, Korsch saw the critical nature of Marxism rooted in the specific form of knowledge of the proletariat and related to the problems that appear in its struggle.

Despite the acuity of this interpretation, which met with considerable resistance in the political and intellectual atmosphere of the Italian Communist Party,[23] Vacca's interpretation concludes with an attempt to instrumentalise

---

20 Vacca 1969, p. 54.
21 Vacca 1969, p. 58.
22 Vacca 1969, p. 99.
23 Symptomatic, in this respect, was C. Pasquinelli's attack on Vacca. Cf. Pasquinelli 1970,

Korsch's positions as political weapons in controversies within the party such as the relation between party and mass movements provoked by the outbreak of the 1968 mass struggles. This instrumentalisation was possible to the extent that the debate remained abstract and detached from the historical relation between Korsch and the official workers' movement. Despite the provocative and apparently radical posture,[24] Vacca's insistence on the priority of the class struggle and the lack of any concern for the *anticipatory* nature of theory betrays a historicist adaptation of theory. Any such account of the anticipatory nature of theory would have entailed a concrete political revision of the relationship between the Italian Communist Party, which was still oscillating between badly hidden manipulation and open rejection, and the mass student movement, as well as the new forms of proletarian struggle which achieved a new peak of 'autonomy' in Italy in 1969. It is no accident that in this historical context, Vacca's theoretical critique was aimed mainly at 'economism': the so-called Workerist current which had considerable influence within and outside the workers' movement since the publication of the theoretical journal *Quaderni rossi* in the early 1960s.[25] Moreover, Vacca fell into an uncritical glorification of Korsch's work for having overcome the relapses into the fetishism of the productive forces by the Second and Third Internationals. Yet, Vacca's interpretation left unclarified the question of a real political historisation of Korsch's work and the question of the possible limits of Korsch's thinking about the *anticipatory* nature of theory.

A serious historical and political thematisation of Korsch's intellectual development was provided shortly thereafter by Gian Enrico Rusconi's introduction to the Italian translation of *The Materialistic View of History* (*Anti-*

---

      pp. 178–96. Made from an 'Althusserian standpoint', this attack was based on the very polemical interpretation of 'critical Marxism' evident also in Vacatello 1968.

24   The foreword to Vacca's *Lukács o Korsch?* closed as follows: 'The confidence with which Vacca decides on a delicate point linking theory and practice perhaps proclaims for the first time a possible opening of the Communist camp to an unprejudiced debate on one of the last taboos which survived de-Stalinisation: Leninism' (Vacca 1969, p. 4).

25   The 'New Left', in turn, committed the serious mistake of paying only scant attention to Korsch or (like the followers of Mario Tronti), it even hastened to reject him as a subjectivist utopian and reactionary. The main target of this polemic was Korsch's conception of the workers' councils. The 'reactionary' character of the workers' council idea in general (and that of Korsch in particular) was seen to consist in the fact that it found its *material basis* in the figure of the 'professional worker', i.e., in a particular type of 'worker aristocracy'. 'Korsch's writings reveal the connection between administration and its productivist function. Control over the economic cycle by the worker-producer is wholly directed to growth of production of goods by increasing the productivity of labour: the worker administers the entire process of production in the name of development' (Perulli 1970, pp. 366–7n).

Kautsky).[26] By closely analysing Korsch's historical development as that of a militant revolutionary, Rusconi reiterated and elaborated a thesis which he had already outlined three years earlier:

> The science of society of Korsch's Marxism, though it does not exclude elements which could bring about a positive construction of such a science, itself contains none. Korsch's Marxist theory is so 'critical and negative' that its final goal, the liberation of man, becomes contentless, although this is one of the bases of the theory.[27]

This impotence of Korsch's critical and analytical tools cannot be understood merely through a philosophical reflection on his 'thinking' – which would wrongly deal with his thoughts as if they constituted an organic and homogeneous whole – but rather, it expresses the effect on his theory of the 'revolution which did not happen'. The tragic political impotence of Korsch's analysis characterises the impotence of a man who waited in vain for the crisis to erupt, for the collapse, or – in the years of his American exile – for the awakening of revolutionary consciousness in the proletariat as a result of the capitalist accumulation process. But 'ironically, this very political impotence generates the historical fertility of Korsch's Marxism',[28] for it negatively derives the need for a critical theory of bourgeois society and of a class science of the proletariat from the historically realised alternative to revolution. Today, more than ever, *all* the questions Korsch asked are still unanswered:

> What deformations does the theory of revolution, i.e. Marxism, undergo in a historical context and with organisations that are not objectively revolutionary? What conceptual arsenal does the revolutionary 'movement' need to achieve the necessary level of revolutionary 'theory'? How can the problem of the 'science of society' be reformulated in Marx's sense? How are Kautsky's and Lenin's theories related to it?[29]

From this perspective, Rusconi analysed Korsch's intellectual development, from his council experiences to his critique of Leninism, in the light of his *political radicalisation* during the decisive events of 1919, 1923, 1926, and 1929 –

---

26   Rusconi 1971.
27   Rusconi 1968, p. 204.
28   Rusconi 1968, p. 121.
29   This was the 'missing link' in Vacca's interpretation: as already mentioned, Vacca backdated the ideas of the *Anti-kritik* from 1930 to 1923.

which Rusconi calls the 'turning point' of Korsch's theoretical evolution. The relevance of the polemic against Kautsky consists in the fact that it is 'one of the constant elements in Korsch's theoretical and practical works'.[30] This is because of the historical incorporation of Kautskyism into the German workers' movement and because of the discovery of a few pervasive factors in the relation of theory and practice in the Second International, which will also reappear in Third – though in a changed global context. In dealing with Kautsky, Korsch 'created the analytical and theoretical tools for that critique which was politically closest to his heart: his critique of Leninism-Stalinism'.

This does not mean that, for Rusconi, Korsch develops a complete foundation or an organic, systematic formation for a revolutionary theory of advanced capitalist societies. On the contrary, Rusconi shows how the idea of workers' councils and the permanent attachment to the mass movement (i.e., to theoretical and political anti-vanguard positions) have a central place in Korsch;[31] how Korsch's interest shifts to the 'science of society', of which *Capital* is the model, and thus differs considerably from the naive thinking of his contemporary Pannekoek; and, finally, how Korsch equates Kautskyism and Leninism. Rusconi thus indicates the vitality as well as the limits of Korsch's positions, his inability to the end of his life to give a *positive* answer to the burning problems of contemporary Marxism. The simple recourse to the proletarian mass movement as the central axis of theory remains an empty assurance when it gives no analytically exhaustive answers. Rusconi concludes:

> But by what criterion can one decide on the validity or invalidity of Lenin's thinking if, for both Lenin and Korsch, theory has a simply *functional* character for the proletariat? It can be neither a merely theoretical nor only a pragmatic criterion. Here we are at the heart of the problem of the dialectical relation of theory and practice. Korsch's indications are important but inadequate.[32]

To the end of his life, in the despair of his repeatedly frustrated expectations for the outbreak of revolution, Korsch considered the workers' council movement

---

30   Rusconi 1971, p. x.
31   Rusconi 1971, pp. xii–xxiii. Rusconi had already written an article on the problematic of workers' councils in Korsch on the occasion of the publication of the Italian translation of Karl Korsch's *Schriften zur Sozialisierung* and *Arbeitsrecht für Betriebsräte* in a single volume under the title *Consigli di fabbrica e socializazzione* (Bari, 1970). See Rusconi 1969, pp. 762–77. The same subject is treated in an article by Manganaro 1969, pp. 74–7.
32   Rusconi 1971, p. lx.

as the authentic proletarian model of revolution as contraposed to institutionalised Marxism and Leninist 'Jacobinism'.

> But doesn't Korsch thereby run the danger of clinging to an ideal model of proletarian revolution, of exposing himself to the charge of abstraction, and of contradicting the principle of 'historical specification' in the analysis of social phenomena, which constitutes one of his central positive points? If the specific contribution of Lenin's revolutionary theory is seen only negatively, then not only do we lose an essential factor of real contemporary history, but also the possibility to 'apply' the Marxist method of investigation emphatically affirmed in the abstract.[33]

Through his brief but intensive discussion of Korsch, Rusconi has finally created in Italy the preconditions for a balanced evaluation of this great revolutionary. Although it leaves open the fundamental theoretical questions, it has at least posed them correctly, thereby exposing the uncritical glorification of Korsch's work typical of the Dellavolpeans and post-Dellavolpeans. Can it be claimed, as Vacca and Bedeschi do, that Korsch in 1938 (*Karl Marx*) had given up all the idealist elements of his thought?[34] As already suggested, the basic flaw in the Dellavolpean interpretation of Korsch is that for political reasons it neglects the most important features of Korsch's theory and shares in its theoretical shortcomings, as expressed in his understanding of ideology's relation to the base in the social relations of production. For the Dellavolpean and post-Dellavolpean interpretation, the relation between Hegel and Marx in Korsch is reducible to the critical use of the realistic (i.e., economic, social, and political) content of the Hegelian system insofar as Hegel was the ideologist of bourgeois society, and Marx's radical critique and the fundamental change he effected in Hegel's methodology (the concept of 'historical specification'). But in Korsch, this relation is further determined and it leaves a few questions unsolved. It is *further determined* insofar as he is inclined to deal with *Hegel in relation to Ricardo* by making both the object of the critique of ideology. Thus Korsch writes in *Karl Marx*:

> Even Hegel, in dealing with the material conditions of existing society, nowhere passed beyond the range of bourgeois thought. Still this new world of the bourgeoisie, with its internal oppositions ranging themselves

---

33   Manganaro 1969, p. lxii.
34   Cf. Bedeschi, 'Introduzione', it Korsch 1969, p. xxif., and Vacca 1969, pp. 110–11.

like so many unbridgeable chasms philosophically exposed by Hegel under the direct influence of Ricardo, stood in a striking contrast to that 'best of all possible worlds' into which even the most daring among the bourgeois thinkers of the preceding generation had ideologically transfigured the hard facts of existing social life. In Ricardo's economic system and in Hegel's philosophy, bourgeois society reached the highest grade of critical self-consciousness of which it was capable without violating its own principles.[35]

Korsch leaves unanswered questions insofar as he merely tends to subsume and ascribe theories and ideologies to social classes. Moreover, he blurs the distinction between theory and ideology by letting the first correspond to its underlying phase of the social development of the class, while dissolving the second into the way the class can stand in an inadequate and illusory relation to its own activity (as in the case of the 'vulgar Marxism' of the Second International and the 'Diamat' of the Third International). Consequently, despite the 'Copernican revolution', which moved the proletariat and the class struggle to the centre of historical development as a permanent reference point whereby theory must be tested, Korsch's conception runs the danger of losing sight of the anticipatory content of theory and its critical-emancipatory potential.[36]

Furio Cerutti recently joined in the dispute over these problems and even reversed the thrust of Vacca's interpretation (though he stays within the perspective of 'critical Marxism'): in Lukács and not in Korsch one can find the *positive* elements for a reconstruction of revolutionary theory for advanced capitalist societies. In Korsch, it is possible to abstract the problem of class consciousness, i.e., the formation of the proletariat into a 'class by itself'. The fact that Korsch did not do justice to his own programme of a materialist dialectic of forms of consciousness is explained in the fact that he was unable to trace the dialectical genesis of these forms from the economic structure.[37] According to Cerutti, Korsch ends up by abstractly separating the economic

---

35 Korsch 2016, p. 38.
36 These reservations are quite different from those of Negt 1975–6. The 'theoretical deficiency' in Korsch lies not in the separation of production and class struggle, and therefore in the failure to develop a 'materialist social science'. Rather, it lies in the *lack of a structural context between the critique of philosophy and ideology, and the critique of the economy*. This lack is expressed in a division of the class into a material side within production and a spiritual side. The genesis of the independence of the latter is not analysed from the specific historical dialectic of the material process of production, but is the result of a mysterious 'qualitative outburst' of a neo-Kantian ethico-transcendental subjectivity.
37 Cf. Cerutti 1975, pp. 165–74.

social structure from the intellectual dimension, to subsequently establish an extrinsic relation of 'correspondence' between them (the forms of consciousness as 'forms of expression' or 'reflections' of the economic base). But what Korsch calls 'forms of consciousness' are in Marx's *Introduction* (1857) to the *Grundrisse*, 'forms of existence' (*Daseinsformen*), and determinations of existence (*Existenzbestimmungen*) of a certain phase of socio-economic formation. The scientific foundation of revolutionary subjectivity is impossible unless, as in Lukács, the unity of the genesis of thought-determinations with the history of the concrete contents is conceptually understood and developed. Contrary to Vacca's premature liquidation of *History and Class Consciousness*, Cerutti stresses that 'in spite of any "messianic" Leninism', the 'dialectical penetration of organisational problems, i.e. the theoretical expression of the early Lukács' anti-bureacratic and anti-institutional thought saves his theory of revolution from degenerating to the level of a legitimating science of power'.[38]

Although Cerutti's remarks are useful and important, the problem remains unsolved. A great deal of Korsch's work, perhaps even the most important, is still practically unknown. But today there is a greater need than ever before to investigate the development of this theoretician and revolutionary from a concrete and historical viewpoint. It is difficult to foresee whether in the future the ideas of Korsch will succeed in advancing beyond the closed atmosphere of political and purely intellectual discussions to which the 'leadership' of the Italian Communist Party has condemned him, or whether his ideas can become an object of authentic theoretical and political reflection. One thing is certain: a critical analysis of Korsch cannot develop without precise answers to the most pressing questions posed by the concrete history of the workers' movement in the West – questions and problems that comprise an important part of *our* current political consciousness (and 'false consciousness').

---

38 Cerutti 1975, pp. 173–4 and p. 172. Italian extraparliamentary groups have made far greater use of the thematic of the young Lukács than that of Korsch. Cf. e.g., the essay by Daghini (Daghini 1971, pp. 47–154).

CHAPTER 6

Gramsci's Marxism and the Theory of Transition

1. It is not easy to condense into a few observations the richness of the problematic outlined in Badaloni's *Il marxismo di Gramsci*.* I shall limit myself to a necessarily rough sketch of what I take to be the core themes of the volume. I shall then linger over some of the many complex theoretico-political implications of the reading of Gramsci in the book.

There is one motif that it seems to me appears with particular emphasis: that of *genesis*. Rooted in this theme are the complementary problematics of 'transition' and 'socialisation', which constitute the peculiar – yet vast – terrain of Gramsci's thought. Here Badaloni locates the red thread that, in spite of disorder and internal divisions, runs through Italian Marxism. Since Labriola, there has been a tendency to separate the subjective moment from the objective necessity of the 'laws of motion', and to deal with Marxism as the 'theory of the historical space for the proletarian revolution'.[1] Setting out from 'genesis', Labriola brought about a speculative overturning of the traditional (Jacobin) relation between theory and the working class, locating in the latter the bearer of socialism as that which *forms history anew*: a 'new formation' that progressively tends to displace the old one. Thus, with Labriola, we have the first great attempt to translate the Marxian critique of political economy (the science of the laws of movement of the natural-social whole) into a theory of transition. Such a translation is left at the stage of a first draft because of the 'persistence of a kind of mechanism' that limits the growth of the new formation to the rhythm of development of the old.[2] In other words, Labriola does not complete the programme of *appropriation* of the old civilisation because he is unable to turn its problematic into the meaning of the new one. Despite this limitation, Labriola attained some fundamental results for the theoretical construction of Marxism.

First, he demonstrated the *morphological* rather than chronological character of prediction in Marx. That is to say, he does not prophesy an automatic collapse but locates in crisis the structural aspect, which connotes the *qual-*

---

* [This review of Nicola Badaloni, *Il marxismo di Gramsci*, Turin: Einaudi 1975, was originally published in *Aut-Aut* 148, July–August 1975, pp. 68–76. The English translation in *Telos* 31, Spring 1977, was originally by Franca Bernabei. Translation has been revised for this volume.]
1 Badaloni 1975, p. 16.
2 Badaloni 1975, p. 51.

ity of the capitalist epoch, and in the impossibility of indefinitely deferring its resolution the *substance* of that quality. Although Labriola did not develop a concept of imperialism, i.e., an understanding of a new form of regulated and controlled competition, he had a clear notion of the *historical validity* of the tendential laws of the mode of production. His polemic against Croce[3] and the revisionists of the Second International,[4] was prefaced by this preliminary methodological warning: to refute Marxism, it is not sufficient to set against it an army of 'facts'. As Badaloni points out, it is necessary rather:

> to deny that the history of our century has been a progressive and increasing introduction into society of instruments of social direction of the economy, of production, etc., necessitated by the class struggle, i.e., not only by the working class, but also by its antagonist, in order to perpetuate the domination of its own formation.[5]

The expansion and multiplication of 'countertendential' interventions is an indirect confirmation of the fundamental 'tendency' and, with it, of the historical character of Marx's prediction (which does not mechanically exclude the 'subjective intervention' of the masses but, rather, considers it as a fundamental, *structuring* component of the objective process itself).[6]

Equally important is the concept of *formation*, which underpins the connection between theory and tactics. Croce and the revisionists magnified 'facts' – and, although starting from objectively observed historical phenomena, they did not insert them into the context of 'sociological data' (which reveals the point of historical development where the succession of social forms can be distinguished), and thus were unable to move from empirical analysis to morphological prediction. Labriola's thought, on the other hand, rotates around the notion of the 'form of production', thus opening the way to a theory of the transition.

2. In the course of his polemics with revisionists and with Marx's critics, Gramsci attaches himself to these concepts of Labriola – which are constitutive of the autonomy and self-sufficiency of Marxism – not in order to re-establish a sterile orthodoxy, but to solve the theoretical and political aporias of revisionism, beginning with its objective roots and its rational nucleus. Gramsci did not

---

3   See Labriola 1975, pp. 265–6.
4   Cf. Procacci 1960, pp. 264 ff.
5   Badaloni 1975, p. 46.
6   For this problematic see Grossman, *Saggi sulla teoria delle crisi*, edited and introduced by G.M. Bonacchi (Bari, 1975) [all of which can now be found in Grossman 2019 – editor's note].

reject but examines from within the 'rupture' of the dialectical unity brought about by the critics of Marxism (Bernstein, Croce, Sorel). The break of the link which Labriola, following Engels, presupposed between the 'rhythm of things' (the objective historical process) and the development of 'socialist consciousness', was justified by the tendencies of the capitalist economy and the emergence of the controlling functions connected with the domination of finance capital. Gramsci acknowledged the new situation which, instead of encouraging the automatic expansion of socialist consciousness (correlated, in the predictions of classical Second Internationalism, to the 'dialectical' effects of mechanism of competition), accentuated the separation of the working class from the social totality. Only by starting from such a separation – the 'rupture' indicated by Sorel – is it possible to regain the unity of the doctrine. Gramsci's re-elaboration of Marxism, Badaloni remarks, is neither a philosophical nor a philological fact. It does not overlook 'the rupture within Labriola's philosophy brought about by Sorel and Croce', but sets out from this rupture because it 'represents an objective process of social reality'.[7] The result, however, is the reversal of the relation between 'logical' and 'historical' that exists in Marx: the starting point is no longer the logical order (as the hermeneutic key and overturning of the structure of chronological succession) but the historical. If the political programme is to suture anew the fabric of unity from the position of rupture, in the medium term the theoretical programme is to recompose 'Marxism, its logical order upset by the phenomenology of reality, [...] at the level of the latter, i.e., of the historical order'.[8] While *from the viewpoint of logical order* the rise of capitalism implies – through the separation of the producers from the means of production – a break and a contradiction with communal organisations (and, therefore, the expansion of the separation and the slow erosion of pre-capitalist forms of existence), the question is different *from the viewpoint of historical order*. From this viewpoint, the perspective of the community is taken as predominant and 'the growing break brought about by capitalism becomes an internal fact of its dissolution'.[9] By stressing Sorel's influence, Badaloni introduces the theme of the 'bloc' in terms of the reconstitution of the logical order through history as the reintegration of the voluntarist element. Yet, while this reintegration in Sorel resulted in the perspective of myth, in Gramsci it is articulated in a complex programme of re-connection with Marx's model and of the critical regaining of the unity of Marxism.

---

7 Badaloni 1975 p. 130.
8 Badaloni 1975, p. 59.
9 Badaloni 1975, p. 72.

3. In order to carry out this programme, it was necessary to reintroduce the key concept of *genesis* (of which Labriola had provided a first outline), formulating it rigorously and in terms adequate to the logical structure of Marx's theory. Thus, Gramsci singles out the *subjective side of the productive forces* (the bearer of which is the revolutionary class) as the objective and, at the same time, the genetico-propulsive element that enables him to push through to the very end the reading of the historical order, faithfully retreading (even if in reverse direction) Marx's path. According to Badaloni, the notion of 'absolute historicism' synthesises Gramsci's view of reality as already charged with tensions, of a set of actions and reactions generated by the subjective side of the productive forces (i.e. of *objectivity*). This does not mean that Gramsci tacitly becomes a vehicle for revisionist categories: he does not oppose historical facts to a theoretical model hypostasised on a meta-historical level, but restructures theory starting from the *new* and *specific* element produced by the irruption of the subjective side (the 'political consciousness of the new producers') of the productive forces in the relations of production.

If the confrontation with Croce's conception of the 'ethico-political' allowed Gramci to retranslate in an original way Lenin's 'primacy of politics', his confrontation with Sorel allowed him to elaborate, in addition to the concept of the 'historical bloc', that of a 'new common sense', which he related to 'Marx's theme of the enrichment of faculties'.[10] Moreover, if Gramsci inherited Sorel's concepts of communal morality and self-control, from Croce he drew the demand for recomposition as the regaining of the totality. The fusion of these two aspects leads the totality to coincide, in an epoch of transition, with the *socialisation of the political*, whose nucleus is constituted by the 'collective intellectual'. Such a formulation of the theme of the intellectuals marks Gramci's break from Sorel, who had seen their function only in the negative sense of a cover-up and dissembling of the rupture (and had hence deluded himself into thinking that he could solve it by radicalising the separateness and subaltern status of the working class). At the same time, however, it marks his break from Croce who, although facing the problem of recomposition, conceived the latter as the activity and task of the Spirit, i.e., of intellectuals as functionaries of the ruling classes.[11]

---

10   Badaloni 1975, p. 67.
11   Moreover, one should also note that for Badaloni, this framing of the problem of the intellectuals in Gramsci underpins an analagous reversal of the relation theory/working class (and, on the theoretical plane, of the relationship logical order/historical order) when compared to Lenin. Whereas Lenin had fought the populists by reasserting the primacy of the logical order that was capable of imposing itself historically within the Russian com-

Far from being merely 'superstructural', the concept of the intellectual is connected with the previously outlined concept of the subjective side of the productive forces. Thus Gramsci is not, as it is generally claimed, the 'theoretician of the superstructure' but, rather (and this is the main thesis of Badaloni's book), the *theoretician of the productive forces*, who in his analysis privileges the 'social figures closest to the base'. (At the origin of this statement lies the opposition between *wage-earner* – characterised by the separateness and subaltern status of his position – and *producer*, who has consciousness of the totality, i.e., of himself as the active side of the productive forces – as well as for the ability to direct the historical process).[12] Given these premises, it follows for Badaloni that socialisation does not take place through the state or political and juridical institutions, but through the productive forces themselves: 'Gramsci has not arrested socialisation at the state stage'.[13] Thus, the extinction of the state (and of the transition), far from resulting in a falling back into the private, is the full regaining of communal life (not by chance, he relates the concept of 'public' not to the party and the trade unions – which are private organisations – but to the councils, conceived as organs of the social direction of the productive forces). According to Badaloni, by pointing to the *social* dialectic of dissolution and recomposition (mediated by the growing shift of intellectuals towards the hegemonic area of the working class), Gramsci indicates the historical necessity of the 'masses to learn the science of politics', but does not go so far as to 'consider democracy as the whole political locus of the historical transition'.[14] With Togliatti we have the complete recovery of democracy no longer as an instrument or a transitory vehicle, but as an indispensable element of socialism: the specific locus of growth of workers' hegemony and, with it, of the masses' political and intellectual faculties. The preservation and strengthening of democracy is no longer the class adversary's exclusive ground, but the battleground onto which he is forced and within whose boundaries there occurs 'a complex process in which the social figures change their roles and in the historical order there come into being, in forms not immediately recognisable, the changes foreseen in the dialectical articulation of Marx's logical order' (p. 129).[15]

---

munity, Gramsci – operating within Western Europe – found in the intellectuals the 'key to *communitarian* structure through which a divided society could imagine itself': the function of the intellectuals in the face of the people and the peasant masses consists in their 'ability to give the appearance of community to a world divided' (Badaloni 1975, p. 72).

12   Badaloni 1975, p. 103.
13   Badaloni 1975, p. 182.
14   Badaloni 1975, p. 128.
15   Badaloni 1975, p. 129.

5. Leaving aside – for reasons of space – a whole series of complex themes that Badaloni develops (such as, just to cite a few of the most interesting ones, those relative to the notion of 'determinate market' and the suggestive parallels of Croce and Sraffa and Popper and Keynes), I would like to attempt to advance some observations on the theoretico-political implications of the book.

The main point lies in vindicating the *Marxist* (even more than Leninist) character of the notion of Gramsci as theoretist of the productive forces and, *therefore* (i.e. secondarily), as scientist of politics. Such an approach allows, first, to explode the legend of Gramsci as the 'theoretician of the superstructure' (not to speak of Gramsci as the theoretist of the cultural revolution in the West, recently proposed with scanty political and intellectual seriousness, as a new fashion item). Second, it throws light on the current debate concerning the question of the state and the transition in terms of the more general problem of the theory-strategy nexus. The consequences of Badaloni's claims are that Gramsci's reading of the historical order, although grand and ingenious, still leaves room for a theoretical reconstitution of Marxism as a morphological rereading of society (one that is self-sufficient and *founded upon itself*). In this respect, the reproposal of genesis as a hermeneutic criterion and, consequently, of *historicism* (understood as the appearance of the new fundamental class), risks ending up being inadequate and to generate misunderstandings. Ironically, the 'genetic' criterion itself, instead of favouring, risks hampering the construction of that theory of history which is the irrepressible condition of a theory of (revolutionary) transition. This is because the only possible starting point for a structural theory of history is the 'non-history' of capital ('first there was history, now there is no more', writes Marx in the *Grundrisse*),[16] the fulfilled and 'classical character' of the process of production, which gives birth to a *new level of historicity*, in which the 'laws' of events are correlated with the rhythm of development of the social formation. We find here the nexus of the theory of history and the theory of transition, in the historical present characterised by the relation of economy to politics, and of capital (the process of production/reproduction) to the state. That is why, in order to meet this need postulated with great rigour by Badaloni, to provide a firm theoretical foundation for *trans-forming* praxis, it would be necessary to start, instead of from the historical appearance of an irreducible quality (the 'new fundamental class'), from the *morphological* conditions of such an emergence and from its 'structural' effects on social formations (the relationship of class struggle-institutions, masses-politics, and workers-state).

---

16 [The quotation actually comes from Marx 1976b, p. 174 – editor's note.]

To move, as Labriola does,[17] from the *manner* (rather than from the *fact*) of genesis means, moreover, setting aside all subjectivist and empiricist reductionism, to face the problematic of 'consciousness' as a dialectical thematic of the *constitution* of the proletariat into a 'class for-itself', and to scientifically ground the materialist demand to place 'politics in command'.[18] If the substance of Gramsci's polemic with Croce lies, as Badaloni points out, in the claim that Marxism is able to overcome 'its free-trade and economist phase',[19] this means that the problem of the state must be confronted by theory as the central theme of the transition phase. In this regard, one might disagree with Badaloni that the state does not resolve itself either *entirely* or *immediately* into its 'economic and social matrices';[20] i.e., it cannot be set in the straits of the function of 'ownership' by one of the 'two fundamental classes' (in the same way as the class struggle cannot be resolved or simplified into the sociological conflictual of capitalists and workers), because it survives even after the bourgeoisie has died out as a traditional class. For the existence and function of the state the (sociological) relation to a 'class' is not as indispensable as the (structural) link with capital and its reproduction process.[21] At this point,

---

17   Incidentally, one should note here that the 'genetic' lens through which Badaloni reads Labriola leads him to underline the continuity with [Johann Friedrich] Hebart's themes which are, from the historical standpoint, highly questionable and, above all, confines the originality of Labriola's conception to the milieu of the 'Marxism of the Second International'; whereas, for us, his originality is due to the deep assimilation of the Hegelian dialectic. For further confirmation of this, see the recent complete edition of the letters to Croce (note 3 above).

18   In this regard, cf. Luporini 1974, from which the following considerations have benefited.

19   Badaloni 1975, p. 159.

20   Cf. Badaloni 1975, pp. 20–2.

21   If one looks into the question carefully, it is exactly such a reductive view of the topic of the state that leads Badaloni to overemphasise Sorel's influence and to dismiss Gentile's uncomfortable presence. 'Stressing the importance of philosophy within Marxism', Badaloni writes, 'Gentile was not praising Labriola, but was trying to leave no path open to socialism' (p. 84). The point is, however, whether Gentile's ideology was not more effective than Croce's *from the viewpoint of an organic* relation to a stage of development of capitalist domination; that is, whether it is better able to weld together the intellectual and the state, relegating to a subaltern position Croce's influence on the intellectual class. Equally, Badaloni tends to over-emphasise the 'influence' of Sorel's mental *outillage* on Gramsci, by stating that the logical armour of common sense requires that the implications of Marx's turning of compulsory cooperation into free cooperation, in the sense of an 'enriching of the faculties' (p. 67), must be underlined. But Badaloni then cautions that, since in Marx's view the human faculties can be *historically* enriched, the 'new common sense' is not, in Gramsci, a primordial voluntarist element or a natural-behaviorist datum. And yet, if the positive evaluation of the voluntarist element is not as a *causa sui* (i.e., an irreducible *quid*, as in Sorel's anarcho-syndicalism), but is instead 'rendered indispensable by the function

it has to be pointed out that the (structural) theme of the productive forces and the (historical) one of genesis become detached in Badaloni. This can be seen in the failure to probe into the *form of the contradiction* (i.e., the *way* in which the productive forces intertwine with the relations of production in a contradictory unity which has different configurations according to different historical phases). To use Gramci's terminology: 'disintegration' and 'historical bloc' are not the extreme limits of the parabola of transition, but constitute the opposing poles of a dialectical constellation within which the *field of objectivity of politics* is captured. Now, this recovery of the substantial materiality and objectivity of politics presupposes that the context in which it carves out a space for itself is *effectively dialectical*. To be dialectical, however, the contradictory 'totality' needs a *real mediation*. Such mediation is provided by the moment of 'organic crisis' – i.e., what in Marxist terms is the characterisation of the capitalist system as an 'interlinked crisis' (*Krisenzusammenhang*). If the moment of mediation is not called into play, one must necessarily – as it seems to me occurs in Badaloni – displace the sphere in which revolutionary subjectivity is founded from the analysis of the organic contradictions produced in the 'interlinked crisis', resulting in the mere acknowledgment of the (primarily horizontal) movement of self-development and self-growth of the 'new formation', with the risk of a 'neo-historicist' flattening and the destructuration not only of the concept 'formation', but of the very notion of subjectivity.[22]

The link between theory and tactics can be realised only by passing through the *real objectivity* of the contradiction, *never outside of it*, since there is no model available that can avoid the objective necessity of the *immanent resolution* of the 'interlinked crisis'.

Although the theoretical work to be done is still immense, the first foundations of this programme of the 'morphological reconstruction' of Marxism have been laid. In fact, the suggestion of a correct – and analytically fruitful – formulation of the problem is provided by Badaloni himself when, commenting on Labriola's effort to define the relation between praxis and knowledge, tactics and theory, he writes: 'The proletariat is not situated [...] in an indetermin-

---

of social direction which the "producers" are called upon to assume' (p. 68) – so as to prevent the dissolution (*Auflösung*) of capitalist society from turning into a catastrophe – is one then not urgently confronted with the problem of advancing further, at the present level of the development and *crisis* of capitalist social formation, into the relation of state and capital, of institution and class struggle; which, in practice, is to say, into the theme of *politics today* and its relation to theory?

22 On the 'structuring' character of subjectivity, see Luporini 1974.

ate historical time, but in that particular historical time which is dominated by the crisis of the bourgeois social formation'.[23] Is it not exactly this theoretical warning – in which Labriola saw the distant historical source of Marxism in the 'world-historical' development of humanity – that roots *for us today* the need to analyse the relation between state and crisis, in order to scientifically ground politics?

Consequently, the Gramscian theme of the 'collective intellectual' and his historical role during the phase of transition, should be re-examined in relation to the 'conception of the state according to the productivity [function] of social classes'.[24] Following Gramsci along this path, it is perhaps possible to seek the roots of our conception (i.e., in Marx himself), the nucleus of a scientific theory of the political (in the sense refered to as the 'problematic of constitution'), linked to the need for a unitary recomposition of Marxism which Badaloni has had the courage to advocate. He has proposed a fertile critique of 'revisionism', not aimed at banishing it as a mere ideological falsehood, but rather so as to recover its specific levels of reality: in Marx's terms, its 'rational core'. This is quite remarkable and full of implications today, if one still believes that the space and function of theory must be neither that of a legitimising ideology nor that of a justificatory screen for existing political practice.

23   Badaloni 1975, p. 13.
24   Gramsci 1992, p. 229.

CHAPTER 7

Corporatist Pluralism, Mass Democracy and Authoritarian State

What can it mean, today, for the workers' movement to reflect on the theme of the transformations that followed the Great Crash?* It is a commonplace on the Left – or at least among a large part of it – that studying the turning point of the 1930s means having the possibility of drawing out the general characteristics that marked a whole era of economico-social-institutional reordering. That is to say, a whole phase of the history of the 'welfare state' whose crisis we see today. But however apt it may be to emphasise the 'epochal' character of the 1929 rupture, we should add that too often – among our circles no less than among the Socialist milieu – we have failed to go beyond mere repetition of general formulas on the 'new' physiognomy of contemporary capitalism and the 'new' relation established therein between politics and the economy, the state and social classes. Far from wanting to deny the validity of such claims, I do however think it necessary to make clear that the Left will struggle to emerge from its current *impasse* – an *impasse* of its strategy and project, as well as of analysis – if it does not succeed in determining the characteristics of this turn in a critical and contextualised manner. It is telling, in this regard, that some historians have already in recent years warned of the insufficiency of a purely historiographical – or even only historico-economic – approach to the problematic of the 1930s (this being one of the rare cases, we might add, in which historians' contribution has been adequately balanced by that of economists and sociologists). Hence the need for an, at least tendentially, 'interdisciplinary' approach to this 'object', one that aims to identify those specific aspects that 'gave shape' to the socio-economic and politico-institutional restructuring of the 1930s. Even so, it is precisely when we proceed with determining the peculiar characteristics of this new phase that we understand the insufficiency of that interpretative schema which identifies the 1929 rupture as the emblematic date of the transition from a generic 'market system' to a likewise generic 'planner-state'.

---

* [This lecture was first presented at the workshop at the *Istituto Gramsci* called 'Stato e trasformazioni capitalistiche negli anni trenta', 18–19 November 1978. It was then published with the conference proceedings in *Stato e capitalism negli anni trenta*, Rome: Editori Riuniti 1979 – editor's note.]

This hermeneutic model – of which there now exist the most varied versions – has easily its most creditable representation in Karl Polanyi's suggestive portrait,[1] where in seeking to bring into relief the caesura leading to the 'great transformation', he hypostatised what had gone before as the 'self-regulated market system'. Much as this homologation of 1920s capitalism within a nineteenth-century 'classic' type of competitive mechanisms does aptly throw light on the subjective backwardness of the political leadership of Western countries – including that of the workers' movement, which shared in the bourgeois political elite's traditional, static vision of crisis – it also presents two fundamental limits. First, there are holes in its periodisation (World War I and the October Revolution and their effects are considered as the final offshoots of the convulsions of the 'old world', linked as it was to the deflationist philosophy of the gold standard). Second, it runs the risk of burying under an ideal-typical schema the comparative analysis of different social systems (the New Deal, fascism, the USSR), even though Polanyi did also have the merit of such analysis.

So, if we do not want to reduce the discussion of the 1930s to an *a prioristic* banal generalisation about 'the new functions of the state' (as we often – unfortunately – see even many Marxists doing), and we really intend to develop an interpretative key capable of bringing to fruition a *differentiated analysis* – and, at the same time, to get some useful perspectives on the dynamics of transformation in the postwar period – then we must begin by first stripping the formula of the 'crisis of capitalism' of any transcendent aura so as to *grasp, within the 1929 rupture, the crisis of a historically (and morphologically) determinate phase of capitalism*. That is to say, a capitalism that – far from being summarised in terms of an undifferentiated 'self-regulated market system' – already exhibits, after the Great Depression of 1873–96 and still more emphatically after the world war, traits no longer reducible to the classical free-trade-competitive model. In proposing this more articulated periodisation, it is not my intention to downplay the significance of the 1930s rupture, but instead to introduce new elements of reflection appropriate to delineating its transformative dynamic in more developed (and analytically fruitful) forms. As such, in my exposition I intend to touch upon three aspects, which I will summarise as follows: 1) the rationalisation/crisis relationship in the passage from the 1920s to the 1930s (with particular attention to the problems of periodising the 'German case'); 2) the crisis of democracy and the attempted revisions of the Marxist 'paradigm'; and 3) corporatist pluralism and the totalitarian state.

---

1   Polanyi 1944.

1   The Relationship between Rationalisation and Crisis in the Passage from the 1920s to the 1930s. The 'German Case', from Weimar to National Socialism

Recent contributions to social history and political science in West Germany and the USA have shown just how difficult it is to unravel the knot of the passage from the 'stabilising structures' of the 1920s, to the new order of the 1930s, via a mechanical application of traditional Marxist cataegories. Rather symptomatic, in this respect, are the difficulties that an economist of the standing of Friedrich Pollock[2] faced in adapting Marx's predictive schemas to the complex texture of the great crisis. Indeed, he was one of the first to attempt to examine the relationship between the crisis and the tendencies towards the 'planned reordering' of the economy, amending the 'breakdown' implications of Grossman's schema.

No less significant is the fact that, already in the first half of the 1920s, Weimar social democracy and Austro-Marxism had made significant revisions of the old vulgate, precisely on account of the difficulties they had encountered in applying the classical theorem of proletarianisation to the changes brought about by state intervention in the forms and rhythms of development, and to the social structure that the increasing growth of 'intermediate strata' and the emergence of new oligopolistic 'powers' made ever less reducible to the Second International's classic 'dichotomous' schema.[3]

At the core of these debates was the set of processes that go under the name of 'rationalisation'. From these processes there issued a set of changes that, having taken shape already before the turn of the century (not by chance, being concomitant with the debate on revisionism), culminted precisely in the 'stabilisation' period of the 1920s. For this reason, it is necessary to bear its effects in mind, if we are to avoid the risk of considering as a peculiarity of the 1930s, economic and politico-institutional organisations that had actually already emerged between 1873–1929. These include the rationalisation of the labour process and the new role of technico-scientific management (revolutions introduced by Taylorism and Fordism); the progressive separation of ownership and control of the firm; expansion of the bureaucratic

---

2 See, above all, Pollock 1933, II, pp. 321–53.
3 These themes were the object of an important early debate in the *Verein für Sozialpolitik*, documented in a series of *Schriften* and in the *Archiv für Sozialwissenschaft und Sozialpolitik*. See, in this regard, Böse 1939 and Plessen 1975. In his research, Georges Haupt has lucidly captured the non-linear relation between the history of the workers' parties and organisations and of the history of 'social complexity': see Haupt 1986.

and administrative sphere (and a consequent complication of social stratification); the dislocation (even if in a limited and contradictory manner) of the relationship between the state and certain important sectors of the economy; a new link between intellectual labour and institutions; the intervention of state power in labour conflicts (think of its 'arbitration' functions in the Weimar Republic), and so on. While these restructuring processes had already begun to take place from time of the Great Depression of 1873–96 (as amply documented in the research carried out by Hans Rosenberg and his school),[4] we can also say that *they reached their culmination around the middle of the 1920s*, when the contours of modern mass society had clearly taken shape.

In what way did the authors who adopted Marxism's crisis theory (and those who still do), denounce the stalemate into which this 'rationalised' capitalism had fallen by the end of that decade? Almost all of them interpreted the crisis as the effect of the disarticulation of its two sides, production and the market. In this view, the crisis is a consequence of the fracture between production and consumption, between a 'productive economy' characterised by the 'socialisation' of the Taylorised labour process, and a 'market economy' that was still governed by the traditional mechanisms of valorisation. For example, in his book *The Economy and Class Structure of German Fascism*[5] (important, in my view, above all on account of the first-hand documents he brought to public awareness), Alfred Sohn-Rethel saw in the crisis-years impasse of the Steel Union (the largest company in Europe at the time, with over 200,000 employees), an emblematic expression of the growing gap between the productive economy based on fixed costs and the market economy of demand and prices. This uncoupling of the two sides – which we find again, in our own time, in Baran and Sweezy's model[6] (here, it matters little that they start out from the market and Sohn-Rethel from the transformations of the production process) – is

---

4 Cfr. Rosenberg 1967; Wehler 1973a, 1970, 1973b 1971, 1974; Winkler 1964. For an outline of the fundamentally Weberian 'paradigm' to which these studies hark back (their methodology in many respects converging with the results arrived at by the 'critical' Marxist research of Habermas and Offe), see Kocka 1972, pp. 316 ff.

5 Sohn-Rethel 1987. Sohn-Rethel had the great merit of basing his analysis on the transformations that Taylorism and Fordism had produced on the entire physiognomy and internal structure of capitalism. Very useful on the question of 1920s rationalisation, also for the purposes of a non-'ideal-typical' comparative study, is the essay by Fano 1978.

6 On this point, and more generally for a critical discussion and reconstruction of Sohn-Rethel's account, I take the liberty of referring the reader to the final chapter, 'Razionalizzazione capitalistica e soluzione totalitarian. Il fascismo tedesco di Alfred Sohn-Rethel' in *Il Politico e le trasformazioni*: Marramao 1979.

symptomatic of two fundamental limitations of an approach to the economy of the crisis that continues to hold firm to the classical Marxist paradigm:

a) reducing capitalism to the abstraction of exchange and its identification with 'blind', 'anarchic' market mechanisms (this reduction is not the exclusive monopoly of orthodox Marxism, but also operates in the 'critical' revision of Marxism carried out by the majority current of the Frankfurt school, which sees the new state intervention as an exogenous function compressing 'crisis tendencies'. Indeed, in his famous essay on the 'Authoritarian State', Horkheimer attempts to square the circle between the hypostatisation of the paradigm of the critique of political economy and the change in the form of the state, pointing to its inverse confirmation of *Capital*'s prognoses).[7]

b) a restricted technico-economic vision of rationalisation, tending to reduce it to a simple restructuring of the process of labour and exchange, without grasping its effects in reorganising productive relations as a whole, i.e. of the entire capitalist 'social brain'.[8]

It is worth considering whether a liberal vision of capitalism might still be at work behind the interpretations that see the 1930s as a drastic inversion of the relationship between the economy and politics – and, more generally, behind the rigid opposition of 'the primacy of economics' (or industry) and the 'primacy of politics' (as seen, for example, in the important debate among Western and East German historians on fascism, taking place in the journal *Das Argument* between 1966 and 1968).[9] From such a perspective, the state's new functions are understood as something absolutely 'other' than the economy's 'laws of motion'.

In reality, it is impossible to understand either the experience of Weimar's 'organised capitalism', or the determinate forms of its crisis, without analysing the interferences and asymmetrical relations that come to be established between the different sectors of the economy, pressure groups in society, and

---

7 'The Authoritarian State' in Horkheimer 1978.
8 On the non-'economistic' meaning of the concept of *Rationalisierung* in Weber and Schumpeter, see *Il Politico e le trasformazioni* [a number of essays from which are translated in this volume – editor's note] as well as Cacciari 1977.
9 See Mason 1968, pp. 193–209; 1972; Czichon 1968, pp. 168–82; Eichholtz and Gossweiler 1968, pp. 210–27. For a useful review of the West German discussion on fascism, see Rabinbach 1974, pp. 127–53.

public authority, belonging to an order that the American historian Charles S. Maier has defined – in his comparative study of stabilisation in France, Germany and Italy – as 'corporatist pluralism'.[10] To affirm, not merely the economic, but also the political significance of the battle between different sectors that characterised the development of the Weimar Republic, it is necessary to – taking the lead of a recent tendency in social history[11] – first distinguish two determinate phases of the process of monopolistic concentration. In the first phase (1918–23), there developed a vertical concentration, which was also encouraged by the union leaderships' wages policy – that supported the formation of monopolies because they saw in this the guarantee of higher salaries (and hence the policy of agreements with entrepreneurs like Stinnes, representing the heavy industry that solidly played a leadership role ever since the onset of 'monopolisation' in Bismarck's Reich). In the second phase (1924–8), the guiding role passed into the hands of the chemical and electrico-technical industries. In this period, basic and light industry did indeed bring the rationalisation process to completion,[12] while in heavy industry (thanks to the credits conceded by the Dawes Plan) there was a rapid expansion of productive capacities, which soon proved out of all proportion to the actual realisation possibilities afforded by the domestic and international market. The German Social Democrats did not wholly grasp the significance of the conflictual tension that follows from this, seeing the advent of stabilisation as the triumphal advance of a process of socialisation-democratisation that could already be defined as the 'transition to socialism'.[13] In reality, in the crisis years began heavy industry's

---

10   See Maier 1975 (on Germany, pp. 355–420 in particular). See also Maier's important paper at the 29th Congress of German Historians (Regensburg, 5–6 October 1972), which anticipates in summary form the main theses of Maier 1974.

11   See H.A. Winkler, op. cit. and Mommsen, Petzina and Weisbrod (eds.) 1974. Moreover, for a general picture of this question, see Hoffman 1965; G. Hallgarten and Radkau 1974; and Maschke 1964. As for contributions from the time, let us just note Krüger 1927; Berkenkopf 1928; Beckerath 1930; and Brady 1933.

12   Some companies – the most significant case being Siemens – could draw on a particularly early assimilation and application of the new scientific methods for organising and directing the production process. See above Kocka 1969. A. Sohn-Rethel draws attention to the Siemens case in Sohn-Rethel 1987.

13   In this regard, we should remember – as many others do not – that the theory of 'organised capitalism' systematised by Hilferding in these same years, grew on the soil of the fallacious conviction that the guiding role of the great chemicals industry, with its reforming line open to collaboration with the unions, was now definitively secured. See R. Hilferding, 'Politische Probleme', *Die Geselleschaft*, III/10, October 1926, p. 292. On the 'Weimarian' Hilferding, see Rusconi 1977.

massive counterattack, gathered as these sectors were in the 'Harzburg Front', under the able and discrete leadership of Hjalmar Schacht, a real *eminence grise* of the bloc of alliances that would later raise Hitler to power. But the 'intersectorial contest' continued even under the National Socialist regime, up until 1936, with a further turning-point in the inauguration of the Four-Year Plan, the unseating of Schacht and the consolidation of the Goering-IG Farben bloc, which marked a drastic shift in the centre of gravity towards the chemicals industry. It is no coincidence that it was precisely on the basis of this turn that the English historian Tim Mason advanced his own interpretation of German fascism in terms of 'the primacy of politics' (later partially revised in light of his far-reaching, well-documented research on National Socialism's 'working-class' policies).[14] But a far more effective key for explaining this dynamic appears, as we shall see, in the cues given by Michael Kalecki, who sees in the 'fascist conjuncture' the emergence of the first historical form of the capitalist 'political cycle'.

2   Organised Capitalism and the Crisis of Democracy: The Attempts to Revise the Marxist 'Paradigm'

Before examining in any greater depth this aspect – and its complex politico-institutional consequences – I would like to briefly dwell on certain social-democratic theorists' attempts at a revision of the Marxist problematic of the relation between democratic form and 'organised capitalism'. My thesis is that these attempts were heavily conditioned – despite their considerable theoretico-political differences – by a limitation that we can define as 'neo-classical'.

In order to get to the heart of the problem wrapped up in the 'neo-classical paradigm', it is not enough to criticise the ideology of the *homo oeconomicus*, or the 'hedonistic' assumption. Rather, it is necessary to elaborate a historical understanding that sets this paradigm in relation to the specific phase of capitalist development of which it is the expression. This phase is defined

---

14   See Mason 1993. This is a very valuable work both on account of its far-reaching introductory essay and its vast documentary appendix, which allows him to reconstruct – beyond metaphysical claims of total domination – the concrete organisational forms of Nazi authority on the basis of the 'disciplining' of working-class labour. On the 'systemic' consequences of the regime's 'working-class' policy, see the sixth part of his introductory essay.

by the process that Schumpeter called 'the changed function of the entrepreneur', the separation between ownership and management of the means of production.[15] It is precisely from the outlining of this process that the theories of 'organised capitalism' and 'economic democracy' took their cue, as elaborated by two of the most distinguished theorists of German and Austrian social democracy: Rudolf Hilferding and Karl Renner. At the outset of the stabilisation period, Hilferding and Renner looked back to the lessons of Weber and Kelsen in order to fill the void in Marxist political theory that had previously proven literally unfillable within the terms of a mechanistic Kautskyian perspective. Both understood the macro-historical process as the effect of a movement of disequilibrium/re-equilibration in the relations between the fundamental tendency (which Kautsky had hypostatised in a deterministic, linear theory of progress), and the countertendencies to it. They saw these countertendencies no longer as simple obstacles to or brakes on the fulfilment of the fundamental tendency, but rather as dynamic and autonomous factors, agglomerations of new social needs and imperatives that *gave shape* to development.

Already in their writings of the early 1920s,[16] they had established a closely interdependent relation between the inversion of the tendency towards breakdown and the intervention of the organised masses ('the great historic fact of the workers' movement') in the evolutionary dynamic of the social system. This new element had the capacity gradually to alter the physiognomy and qualities of development, in that it compelled the state to become ever more 'social' and 'reforming'. The struggle for socialism thus came to coincide with the struggle for the liberation of the state from the limits placed on it by private and monopolistic power.[17] It was perhaps Renner who went furthest in his revision, seeing

---

15   Even before World War I, Schumpeter had underlined the insufficiency of a critique of marginalism as mere 'hedonism' or 'psychologism', and tended to set the marginalist paradigm in close relation with the hypothesis – in fact, a post-classical one – that saw the market as a field of equilibrium-neutralisation of forces, as a terrain on which the various subjects and factors combined under the mark of 'equivalence'. See Schumpeter 1908, 1911, 1942, 1952, 1954. On its connection to the theory of 'organised capitalism', see his important essay 'The Instability of Capitalism', Schumpeter 1928, pp. 361–86. The thesis as to the 'changed function of the entrepreneur' as a characteristic note of the transition to socialism is most completely and explicitly expressed in *Capitalism, Socialism and Democracy* (Schumpeter 1942).

16   I have developed and documented a more extensive discussion of this parallel between Hilferding and Renner in Marramao 1977, pp. 83 ff.

17   K. Renner had made this argument already during the war years: Renner 1917, p. 29.

the 1920s as the epoch of the 'rationalisation of circulation' (whereas Weber's had been the era of 'the rationalisation of production', as Renner wrote in a 1924 book),[18] and viewing the function of the 'political' as entirely resolved by the juridical formalisation of socialisation. Hence, the true subject of the transition from rationalised capitalism to socialism was the democratic state (understood as a formal mechanism of 'guarantees', and, at the same time, as a 'community' – *Gemeinwesen*); the working class was only its material bearer (*Träger*).[19]

Social democracy's 'revised' Marxism of the 1920s betrayed its own limitations in two fundamental respects: a) in its failure to overcome (in spite of numerous empirical adjustments) the Second Internationalist dichotomous vision of the social structure. This limit, manifestly apparent in both Austrian and German social democracy, can be attributed to the rigidity of the assumed 'worker/industrialist' relationship,[20] and explains the foreignness of the workers' movement to wide layers of the 'intermediate' strata[21] (Jürgen Kocka has dedicated a recent comparative study on white-collar employees and technicians in the USA and Germany to the changes that took place between the two wars in terms of their social composition and political positioning, which have still hardly been studied). And b), it also betrays a limitation in its 'negative' conception of the crisis, which reduces it to exogenous factors or to conjunctural imbalances and disproportions.

---

18   Renner 1924, p. 369.
19   See Renner 1924, pp. 378–9. For an introduction to the 1920s state debate, see R. Racinaro, 'Introduzione' in Kelsen 1978.
20   I take the expression from Rusconi 1977.
21   The theoretico-strategic significance of the problem of *Mittelstand* was lucidly and acutely captured by Theodor Geiger. Cf. Geiger 1931, pp. 617–35. But also notable in many regards is his 1932 research on social stratification in Germany (Geiger 1932), in which, though continuing to hold firm to the Marxian dichotomous schema, he forcefully underlined the need to make recourse to various indicators of social class and to pay attention (an attention almost entirely lacking on the Left at the time) to the 'mentality' of the different layers and to the multiple variables that combined in determining the complex character of social stratification (see ibid. pp. 77–138, in particular). The general lines of development of Geiger's important work are known in Italy thanks to the studies performed by Paolo Farneti (Farneti 1966), who has also edited and wrote an introduction to a collection of writings on industrial society: Farneti 1978, pp. 774–82 also offers a recent look at Geiger.) On the changes occurring in the social composition and political positioning of the 'middle strata' in the interwar period, see the recent comparative study Farneti 1977, and the extensive bibliography it presents and discusses. On the role played by the 'middle layer' in the dynamic that led to the advent of National Socialism, see Winkler 1972.

It is rather symptomatic, in this regard, that in Hilferding's conception of 'organised capitalism' the divarication of crisis and development results in a sharp division between politics and the economy, taking the form of a "bad" autonomy of the political – that is, the now-autonomous functions of the state apparatuses having an extrinsic relation to the economic. The democratic state can only organise from outside the imperatives of economic 'legality', accompanying and safeguarding via a formal-institutional apparatus that guides the evolutionary metamorphosis of political democracy into social democracy. The state must on no account 'intervene' in the economic process, because this would violate the 'bonds' that are also the technical, 'quasi-natural' conditions of the harmonious development that will gradually arrive at socialism.[22] Hence the rigid deflationary postulate which led Hilferding to reject the anti-crisis plan being put forward within the union by Woytinsky, Tarnow and Baade.[23] The radical tone in which Hilferding struck down Wagemann's positions (fruit of his important and in many ways innovative research at the Berlin *Institut für Konjunkturforschung*),[24] and denounced bourgeois anti-cyclical measures

---

22   Hilferding argued in this sense even before the Kiel Congress (where he systematised his theory of 'organised capitalism'), at the 1925 Heidelberg Congress. See *Protokoll über die Verhandlungen des SPD-Parteitages Heidelberg 1925*, Berlin, p. 5. Hilferding is a classic example of the cordial discord that characterised the relations between the leadership of the workers' movement and that of the bourgeois parties in the 1920s with regard to the diagnosis of the crisis and the appropriate medicine for it. He did not, indeed, go beyond the traditional recipe of monetary measures, though these were accompanied by the slogan 'social policy': see 'Unheimliche Tage', Die Gesellschaft, VIII, 131, p. 107; 'In der Gefahrzone', Die Gesellschaft, VII, 1930, p. 290.

23   The 'WTB plan' underpinned the conflict between the Party and the union, which develops from 1931–32. The bitter polemic between the 'Hilferding line' (promoted within the ADGB principally by Fritz Naphtali) and that of the 'reformers' took place in both *Vorwärts* and the union's monthly *Die Arbeit* (see Woytinsky's article 'Aktive Weltwirtschaftspolik' in no. 6 of 1931, and Naphtali's 'Neuer Angelpunkt der Aktive Konjunkturpolitik oder Fehlleitung von Energien?' in the same issue). Woytinksky referred to this conflict in his memoirs as follows: 'The Plan gained more and more popularity in the nation, but the S-D party remained adamant and refused to use the slogan of public works in the Reichstag election campaign in July 1932. It preferred to stick to Bruning's guns – defense of the currency' (Woytinksy 1961, p. 470). On the '*avant la lettre* Keynesianism' of the *reformers*' positions, cfr. Grottkopp 1954, p. 259.

24   See, in this regard, the talk given by Ernst Wagemann on the 52nd anniversary of the *Deutsche Vereinigung für Staatswissenschaftliche Fortbildung* (Harms 1931). Friedrich Pollock also made repeated references to the *Institut für Konjunkturforschung*'s analyses (see Pollock 1933, pp. 321–52). In light of this brief reconstruction, it is incomprehensible that Winkler sees in Hilferding's theory of 'organised capitalism' a sort of anticipation of

as illusory, should not mislead us, or make us forget the fundamental fact that the strategic frame of reference of concepts like 'organised capitalism' and 'economic democracy' was *not yet at the level* of Keynes's critique of 'Say's law'.

Only this subordination to the old deflationary postulates can explain why the European workers' movement's relationship with the state always ran aground on the terrain of economic policy. This was the case not only for Weimar Social Democracy and Austro-Marxism, but for also the Popular Front in France and the Labour government in Britain (while the experience of Swedish Social Democracy's experience in government starting in 1932 would require a whole other discussion).

In Hilferding's technocratic model (or the organicist one of Naphtali, official theorist of Weimar trade unionism),[25] there was no space for a dynamic-immanent analysis of the crisis of democracy, which was reduced to the irrational rebellion of social forces that had not been integrated into the institutional formalism of the democratic state. In the Marxist camp, Bauer and Gramsci clearly produced more advanced attempts to diagnose the 'dark ills' of the parliamentary form, taking their lead from Marx's analysis of Bonapartism as a temporary solution, balancing class forces by making the executive autonomous (other important pointers in the same direction can also be found in Paul Levi and in Thalheimer and Stawar's analyses of fascism).[26] But however much this perspective represented a titanic effort to revise the old 'reductionist' the-

---

Keynesianism: see his introduction in Winkler (ed.) 1974, particularly p. 13, where he identifies the novelty and timeliness of Hilferding's analysis in his concept of the adaptive self-regulation of the system.

25 See *Protokoll der Verhandlungen des 13. Kongress der Gewerkschaften Deutschlands (3. Bundestag des Allgemeinen Deutschen Gewerkschaftsbundes), abgehalten in Hamburg von 3. bis 7. September 1928*, pp. 20–2, 170–224, and *Wirtschaftsdemokratie, ihr wesen, weg und ziel*.

26 See Thalheimer 1930; and Stawar 1973. Some analogies with these interpretations are also present in the important analysis carried out – within the ambit of the central European socialist Left – by Richard Löwenthal (under the pseudonym Paul Sering) in *Zeitschrift für Sozialismus*, II, 1935, pp. 765 ff. and 839 ff. As for the analogies between Bauer and Gramsci, these should not be understood as a direct influence of one on the other (which was not the case), but rather in terms of their both seeing a need for theoretico-strategic redefinition, on account of the reflux of the revolutionary wave in Europe and the advent of the stabilisation period. The analogy, moreover, does not concern only their points of merit, but also the historical limits of such positions, which both looked – starting from different positions – to construct a 'third way' alternative to both the official social-democratic line and the rigidities of Stalinist 'Leninism'. I elaborated on the comparisons between the two in my paper to the Vienna conference organised by the Austrian Socialist Youth in November 1978, on occasion of the fiftieth anniversary of Bauer's death: 'Zum problem der Demokratie in der politischen Theorie Otto Bauers' in Detlev Albers, Josef Hindels,

ories of the state apparatus, it too appears, ultimately, to have been vitiated by the 'neo-classical' limit inherent to a descriptive functionalism that upholds a conception of democracy as a direct expression of the 'balance of class forces'.[27]

The problem that none of these 'revisions' manage to answer concerns, in the last instance, *the specific dynamic* that leads to the 'entropy' of the democratic form. The heart of this question was the relation between the dissemination-socialisation of power and the concentration of the moment of decision. This was something which completely eluded the workers' movement, which instead held firm to an ingenuously 'participatory' vision of democratisation. The identification of the system's 'dark ills' in a *lack of decision* can be found, not by chance, only in a student of Carl Schmitt active in social-democratic ranks: Otto Kirchheimer. For Kirchheimer, the root of the crisis lay in the fact that the Weimar Constitution 'lacked decision' ['*Verfassung ohne Entscheidung*']:[28] the state's old external 'neutralising' apparatus was no longer up to the task of governing the 'reduction to zero' of the power of decision induced by the paralysing effects resulting from pluralistic-corporatist conflict. Nor was there any hope to be had for 'the political' in the juridico-reactionary illusion of restoring the *Obrigkeitsstaat*: the old state authoritarianism of the pre-WWI period (this illusion being cultivated by Brüning and the presidential governments in the final phase of the Weimar Republic). No 'solution' worthy of the name was going to be found short of recognition of the anachronism of the liberal reduction of 'enemy' to 'competitor', and recognition of the need to set out from 'relations of force' as 'the political's' only 'laws of motion' and spirit. Kirchheimer had learnt – from the 'reactionary' Schmitt – the need for a ruthless critique of any ideology of the ethical state, even that being reproduced in a new guise within the workers' movement.[29] From this point of view,

---

and Lucio Lombardo Radice (eds.), *Otto Bauer und der "dritte" Weg. Die Wiederentdeckung des Austromarxismus durch Linkssozialisten und Eurokommunisten* (Frankfurt/ Main: Campus, 1979).

27 In *Il Politico e le trasformazioni* I addressed Mach's critique of mechanicism, the foundation of the 'theory of equilibrium' on the terrain of political reflection as well [cf. Chapter One of this volume – editor's note].

28 See Kirchheimer 1964, p. 32. In this text, Kirchheimer took inspiration principally from the writings of Max Adler and his splitting of the concept of democracy into 'political democracy' and 'social democracy'.

29 The 'political scientists' of the social-democratic Left who collaborated on *Die Gesellschaft* (the journal directed by Hilferding, which from 1924 took the place of *Die Zeit*) in many respects borrowed their critique of the Weimar constitution from Carl Schmitt, in particular *Die geistesgeschichtliche Lage des heutigen Parlamentarismus*, Munich-Leipzig 1923 as well as *Legalität und Legitimität* (with which Kirchheimer polemicised) and his *Weiterentwicklung des totalen Staates in Deutschland*, collected together in *Verfassungsrechtliche*

the great lessons of Weber and of normativism, lifting the spell of the ethical state's universality, were truly irreversible – a point of no return.

3   'Corporatist Pluralism' and the 'Totalitarian State'

We thus arrive at the final aspect: the relation between corporatist pluralism and the totalitarian state. From the 1930s to 1950s people of various and sometimes even opposed political viewpoints upheld the so-called *Totalitarismustheorie*, the theory of the authoritarian planner-state. The kernel of this thesis lies in interpreting the 1930s as being characterised by the primacy of the political, understood in radical antithesis to the laws of 'economic necessity' that governed the classical (free-trade) phase of capitalism. This viewpoint reached its most extreme expression in the analyses conducted by the circle around *Die Tat*, the monthly directed by Ferdinand Fried. The *Tatkreis*'s positions were the exact inverse of the neo-classical paradigm: the epoch of the industrial revolution had now been left behind for good, and the 'totalitarian political revolution' was to supplant it. This latter 'revolution' was characterised by a constant technological transformation of the social organism, and through its completion the 'political' would take the place of the 'economic' as the nerve centre and beating heart of society.[30] A sociologist of social-democratic training such as Emil Lederer would express himself in this same way *post festum* (in 1940), identifying in fascism an entirely bureaucratised and homogenised society: a totality 'without classes', fed by the charismatic relationship between the amorphous masses and the *Führer*.[31] We can find similar reasoning behind the theory of the managerial elite as advanced by Rizzi and Burnham; and with rather different accents and articulations, in Pollock, Gurland and Horkheimer. For them, the state of the 1930s was the state of planned administration, characterised by the despotic subordination of private profit, a 'derisory' socialisation of power ('fascism', wrote Horkheimer, 'fixes in place the social results of capitalist breakdown'), and an unprecedented expansion of the bureaucratic sphere, which functioned as a repressive support for the process of technological rationalisation.[32] Though some of these authors repeatedly referred back

---

Aufsatze aus den Jahren 1924–1954, Berlin 1958. [In English cfr. Schmitt 1988, 2003 and 1999 – editor's note.]

30   See Sontheimer 1968.
31   See Lederer 1940.
32   Note, in this regard, the important discussion taking place in the early 1940s within the ambit of the group around the Institute for Social Research, now having emigrated to the

to Weber, their theses in reality betrayed a deformation – if not even an abandonment – of his teachings, which instead held firm to the connection between the becoming-autonomous of the sphere of 'power' (*Macht*) and the overall dynamic of the 'rationalised' social system. Rather, we see in these positions – which I have only very briefly summarised – the ultimate effect of the idea of the 'malign' autonomy of politics, which had established itself in the social-democratic analysis of the late 1920s; that is, an ideological emphasis on the role of bureaucracy and an undifferentiated view of the political system, which often stopped at the external façade of processes and, on this basis, made forced analogies between different systems, to the point of losing sight of the specific differences between the New Deal, fascism, and Soviet 'state socialism', all subsumed under the generic label 'totalitarianism' (hence the singular confusion present in such expressions as 'black Bolshevism' or 'bureaucratic collectivism').

Not by chance, this 'ideal type' advanced in *Totalitarismustheorie* would play a certain politico-ideological role in the Cold War years. It is worth adding, however, that the fortune that these interpretations subsequently enjoyed – and which we again see today – is in large measure to be explained by the inadequacy of the orthodox and Third International Marxist analysis that presented fascism as a 'puppet' of big finance and monopoly capital (which is still today reproduced in *Stamokap* theory [state monopoly capitalism]). The revised perspective advanced by Habermas and Offe seems an undoubtable innovation with respect to such a mechanico-instrumentalist vision of the relationship between the state, economic transformations, and social classes.[33] However, the limit of their models for interpreting the crisis tendencies of 'mature capitalism' resides in their reproposing a paradigm of the political that is at the same time both weak (lacking in specificity) and formalistically all-embracing: the thesis of an institutional system characterised, from the 1930s onward, by 'selective filters' orienting the governance of social conflict *as a function* of the interests of capitalism as a whole, is, at root, marked by the 'orthodox' equation of capitalism with the 'need for valorisation', an equation which had already negatively conditioned the 'classic' Frankfurt school theories of the 'authoritarian state'. In spite of their methodological openness and the flexibility in their use of categories, Habermas and Offe shared with Horkheimer and Pollock the idea of the 1930s as the onset of an 'epochal' trend towards state capitalism; as

---

USA: Gurland 1941, Kirchheimer 1941a, 1941b, Pollock 1941, Marcuse 1941, Pollock 1941. For a precise and very well-documented reconstruction of these debates and the different positions taken, see Jay 1973.

33   See in particular Habermas 1976; Offe 1972, and Offe 1973.

the beginning, that is, of a *linear process of the authoritarian homogenisation of the political system*, which would progressively absorb civil society, dissolving its original boundaries (and, with them, the traditional 'liberties' of the Western individual).

I will note that in discussing this thesis we enter the heart of the current debate in Italy amongst a significant section of radical-socialist culture, taking its cue from critiques of 'mass democracy' by conservative theorists rooted in the Legitimist thinking of the Restoration (Tocqueville). It is useful, here, to consider one of the central points of these theses: the way in which they relate, however explicitly, to the analyses developed by the Frankfurt school in the late 1930s. And here we should clearly state that *among the 'Frankfurters' who emigrated to the USA, there was no unity around the thesis of 'authoritarian planning'; instead, it divided them*. Indeed, the strongest critique of the idea of the authoritarian homologation of the political system came from the political scientists at the Institute for Social Research who had most engaged with empirical studies: Otto Kirchheimer and Franz Neumann. Indeed, it was Neumann who – in polemic with Lederer, but also with Pollock and Horkheimer – sharply demystified the concept of the 'total state', signally with respect to the case that was considered its paradigmatic expression: the National Socialist regime.[34] Neumann's vivisection of the Behemoth looked behind its monolithic, one-dimensional façade, and brought to light the struggle between different pressure groups who shared out power by duplicating the functions of command in the *non-parallel but symmetrical* spheres of politics and the economy. The permanent state of conflict between entrepreneurs, the state bureaucracy, the army and the Nazi Party, signalled the institutional system's non-homogeneity, the impossibility of planning its imperatives long-term, and thus the utopian character of any pretence of reducing the state to the sphere of 'political exchange', i.e. to the mere mechanism of 'neutralising' mediation. Neumann thus introduced an interpretative key that was no longer univocal, but differentiated, no longer static, but dynamic and applicable to all the developed politico-institutional systems of the 1930s.

The hypothesis that I wish to advance concerns the possibility of extending into the 1930s the concept of 'corporatist pluralism' that Maier coined to denote the stabilisation of the 1920s. In my view, this hypothesis is supported by the post-Cold War developments in so-called *Pluralismustheorie*, which, taking their lead precisely from Neumann's *Behemoth*, run from Schweitzer's book to Bollmus and Broszat's studies on the internal structure of the National Social-

---

34   See Neumann 2009. See also the important essay Neumann 1937, pp. 542–96.

ist state.[35] The 'authoritarian state' *did not suppress but rather internalised the conflictual order inherited from 1920s mass society.* The 1930s – as certain 'reactionary' theorists had precociously noted (think, in the Italian case, of Santi Romano),[36] unlike the Marxists – did not mark the arrival of the 'planner-state', but rather the *full entry of contradiction into the political system.* The new form that contradiction assumed was, rather, the consequence of the dissemination of power within 'specialisms' and of the extension of the state into 'civil society'. But once again, not in the sense of an indistinct unity of economy and politics (as neo-Marxist 'holism' would have it) but rather in the sense of a complex interaction between the dynamic of the economic cycle and the imperatives of the political system. The institutional selectivity of which Offe speaks is neither an anonymous operation characterised by the planned administration of conflict, nor simply a 'market of plural interests', but rather expresses the vector resulting from the alternating conflicts and alliances between the different corporate 'autonomies' into which the ruling bloc is pathologically divided. To the complex – non-linear – relation between political imperatives and economic development, there corresponds the end of any possible flatly 'functional' and one-to-one relation between the state and the economically dominant class, and the reaffirmation of 'political compromise' as the institutional prerequisite of the state adopting interventionist anti-crisis policies.[37]

This problem was already intuited by Kalecki in his 1943 essay 'Political Aspects of Full Employment',[38] where he made a distinction between the economic aspect (for which a full-employment policy could only be a good thing, in terms of the overall system's functioning) and the political aspect; it was at *the latter* level that the entrepreneurial classes' resistance to the *maintenance* of full employment could be understood (for within it they saw the possibility of their own social power being diminished relative to the working class),

---

35 See Schweitzer 1964; Broszat 1981; Bollmus 2006; Mommsen 1966; Höhne 1969; Diehl-Thiele 1969; and Petzina 1968 are also important works. However hampered they are by their 'descriptive' limitation, these works – shaped by the *pluralismustheoretische Deutung* of the Nazi regime – display a richness and incisiveness much greater than is to be found in the 'Stamokap' interpretation predominant in East German historiography of fascism, its model being the research in Gossweiler 1971.

36 On the significance of the changes in Italy's politico-institutional form and structure under the fascist regime's 'corporatist state' and the need to distinguish this contradictory and segmented reality from the various corporatist ideologies, cf. Cassese 1974.

37 Cfr. De Brunhoff 1978.

38 See Kalecki 1971 and 1996.

explaining their pressure for a return to more 'orthodox policies', in an interchange that Kalecki defined as the 'political cycle'.[39]

Faced with this complex *dynamic*, the old Marxian critique of the 'abstraction' of the representative state now seems rather ineffective, as do the attempts at a *'neo-classical' refoundation* of the 'essentialist' paradigm of the critique of political economy, which see 'the political' as the mirror image or functional description ('parallelogram') of relations of force already established within the economico-productive sphere. Moreover, given the social complexity that has sprung forth from the immense transformations of the last fifty years, the workers' movement and Left must urgently update not only their empirico-analytical outlook, but also the entire *theoretical form* inherited from their tradition. In this regard, Giorgio Ruffolo has rather aptly underlined the need to test the interpretative limits of the Marxist model in relation to the metamorphoses of the capitalist social system.[40] Though not sharing Ruffolo's confidence in the applicability of 'systems theory', one cannot doubt that critical engagement with its most recent developments is more important than ever,[41] precisely so as to adopt as a central problem *the governance of complexity and the crisis in function of a strategy of transformation.* The Left debate must today concentrate on this node, abandoning any propagandistic and sterile opposition between 'family trees', and should instead move to a critical re-examination of the movement's entire historical baggage – including that of the great experiences of the social democrats in government, which pose us a whole range of problems of burning contemporary relevance. But to take on these questions (which the Italian communist movement seems ready for, more than elsewhere) cannot, and must in no case, mean an uncritical acceptance of 'solutions' (which, wherever they have been given, also themselves seem to be in crisis).

A further consequence, for anyone who wants to start out on the basis that these transformation processes are irreversible, is to recognise the impossibility of translating into the old dichotomous schema the plurality of social subjects and phenomena 'constituted' across the whole arc of the capitalist state's his-

---

39   I refer the reader to D'Antonio 1978, pp. 17–45 for a point-by-point analysis of these aspects of Kalecki's conception.

40   See Ruffolo 1978, pp. 56–66. Ruffolo does not, however, seem to grasp that the 'systems-theory' outlook, though undoubtedly an innovation in the European cultural context, does not go beyond the mere 'governmentality' of social complexity, and thus fails to take into consideration the theoretico-practical node of the *transformation* (in the strong sense) of the system itself, which by definition seeks to optimise its 'self-adapting' mechanisms.

41   Especially when we look without dogmatic lenses at the wealth of implications arising from the polemic between Habermas and Luhmann (cfr. Habermas and Luhmann 1974).

tory, even if this schema were to be carefully integrated and updated. But does such a consideration not perhaps demand a serious redefinition of the party-form itself? And is it not perhaps decisive, in order to determine the modes and extent of this *redefinition of organisation and of politics*, to think again about the specific traits that the contemporary world has inherited from the great turn of the 1930s?

CHAPTER 8

From the Crisis of the 'Self-Organised Market' to the 'Authoritarian State': Notes on the Relationship between Political Economy and *Critical Theory*

That today men are unable to rationally regulate economic relations, i.e. their mutual relations to the production and reproduction of social life, to the degree of understanding available in other fields, cannot simply be explained as theoretical weakness. The existence of economics as a self-enclosed special discipline, which is increasingly less affected by the whole set of social issues, is the expression of a profound state of affairs whereby present-day power relations are opposed to regulation for the benefit of the majority of humanity. It is a problem of praxis the solution of which will shape the content of the history lying immediately before us. The fortunes of the coming generations depend on its outcome.

Written by Max Horkheimer in 1934, these words appear in the introductory remarks to Kurt Mandelbaum's and Gerhard Mayer's study, 'Zur Theorie der Planwirtschaft'.*,1 The intervention of the most important exponent of 'Critical Theory' in what appears to be an exclusively economic debate, was itself symptomatic of the complexity of the theoretical and political questions at the roots of the problematic of economic planning in the 1930s. Stimulated by, on the one hand, the Soviet experience and, on the other, by the monopolistic-totalitarian tendencies in the German economy, the discussion had already begun with the first volume of the *Zeitschrift für Sozialforzchung*, in Friedrich Pollock's essay on 'Die gegenwärtige Lage des Kapitalismus und die Aussichten einer planwirtschaftlichen Neuordnung'.[2]

---

* [This chapter first appeared as the introduction to F. Pollock, *Teoria e prassi dell'economia do piano: Antologia di scritti 1928–1941*, Bari: De Donato 1973. It was also revised for *Il politico e le transformazioni*, op. cit. A translation by R. Morrow appeared with the title 'Political Economy and Critical Theory' in *Telos*, 24, 1975, pp. 56–80 – editor's note.]
1 In *Zeitschrift für Sozialforschung*, vol. III, 1934, pp. 228–62.
2 In *Zeitschrift für Sozialforschung*, vol. I, 1938, pp. 8–27. Among the most important contributions to the discussion af the 'planned Economy', cf. Gerhard Meyer's many reviews, especially 'Neue englische Literatur zur Planwirtschaft', in *Zeitschrift für Sozialforschung*, vol. II, 1933, pp. 257 ff.

All the participants in the discussion presented different 'ideal types'[3] of the planned economy that could be abstractly hypothesised or were realistically realisable, deliberately abstracting from the empirical forms of historically determined economic processes. Despite the reference to the necessity of praxis (emphasised in the above quote from Horkheimer), this tendency to describe different 'models' of economic planning in historical terms meant a clear retreat of theoretical analysis as a consequence of the failure of the German revolution. We are far removed from the controversy over accumulation and breakdown provoked by Rosa Luxemburg's book, and by the heated exchanges on the future of capitalism which presupposed a still open dialectic and different ways of conceiving and practising revolutionary tactics. The 'freezing' of the historical movement produced by Nazi totalitarianism manifested itself in the heightened interest in economic planning efforts undertaken in the Soviet Union.[4]

The studies by Meyer, Mandelbaum, and above all Pollock, contain important new elements which – considering the influence they have had on the most important theorists of the *Zeitschrift* (Horkheimer, Adorno, Marcuse) – must be clearly brought out. The basic novelty stems from the choice of the central elements of economic analysis; they are the following: (1) a *dynamic* aspect: the tendency of capitalism to overcome the crisis by means of an economically planned new order; (2) a *static* aspect: the 'model' of the planned economy; (3) *state capitalism*, understood as an abstract form of economic organisation, i.e., as an 'ideal type'.

Underlying this analysis lies the presupposition that capitalism can definitively abandon the competitive phase and develop toward a planned eco-

---

3 Weber's expression is not employed by chance. Pollock explicitly refers to it in the essay 'State Capitalism' in *Zeitschrift für Sozialforschung*, vol. IX, 1941, p. 200n. [In English, Horkheimer 2005. The note reads: 'The term "model" is used here in the sense of Weber's "ideal type"', p. 173 – editor's note.]

4 In the above quoted passage, Horkheimer himself referred to the necessity to correctly pose the *theoretical* problem of the planned economy by linking up 'with the great experience which mankind is presently undergoing with planned economic efforts'. Evidently Horkheimer was thinking of Pollock's book *Die planwirtschaftlichen Versuche in der Sowjetunion* (Leipzig 1929; reprinted as Pollock 1971). Of course, within the limits of this essay we cannot go into the important contributions to the theory of transition in the *Zetschrift für Socialforschung* and the Asiatic mode of production. Particularly relevant are the following: Borkenau 1987, pp. 109–27 (cf. Grossman's critique of it in the article Grossman 1987, pp. 129–80), whose theme is taken up again in Borkenau 1934: reprinted as *Wissenschaftliche Buchgesellschaft*, Dramstadt 1971; and Wittfogel 1935, pp. 26–58, 1938, pp. 90–120, 1939, pp. 138–83, and, above all, Wittfogel 1931.

nomy. This presupposition marks the fundamental difference between Pollock's theory and that of the most important economist of the *Zeitschrift für Sozialforschung*, Henryk Grossman.[5] In order to understand this difference, a short excursus is necessary to show how Grossman had participated in the discussion of the collapse of the capitalist system.[6]

1 The Critique of Political Economy and the Scientific-Theoretical Foundations of the Analysis of Capitalism. The Effort of Henryk Grossman

Paul Mattick has justifiably marked the year of appearance of Henryk Grossman's fundamental work, *Das Akkumulations- und Zusammenbruchsgesetz des kapitalistischen Systems* (1929), as an important historical event.[7] It is the date of the world economic crisis which forced the leadership of the most important capitalist states to undertake a radical shift, then realised in Roosevelt's New Deal which, next to the Soviet experience, constituted the most important reference point for Pollock's analysis. But this date has yet another meaning, which is immanent in Grossman's work: it coincided with the outbreak of the final crisis of the competitive phase of capitalism. At the same time, it marks the end of an entire series of debates in the context of one of the most eventful periods in the history of the European workers' movement. At the level of economic analysis, it also coincided with the highest point of the critical reappropriation of Marxian 'orthodoxy' known as Western Marxism.

Through his sharp critique of the revisionist separation of the theory of value and the theory of breakdown, Grossman put the Marxian theory of accumulation at the centre of his analysis and, thus, cleared the field of numerous ambiguities which had been produced by resorting to '*ad hoc* hypotheses'.[8] In this way he was able to simultaneously:

(1) recover the essentially *political* kernel underlying Rosa Luxemburg's *Accumulation of Capital*, where the assumption of economically unlim-

---

5 Biographical and bibliographical information on Grossman can be found in Trottmann 1956. Cf. also Jacoby 1975, pp. 3–52. [For a more recent study, cf. also, Kuhn 2007 – editor's note.]
6 This debate got mixed up with the one on imperialism which had begun at the 1907 Congress of the Second International in Stuttgart. Cf. Mandelbaum 1926, esp. pp. 32–42.
7 Mattick's remark appears in the afterword to another study by Grossman which first appeared in 1941: Grossman 1969, p. 115.
8 The 'necessity of the breakdown', writes Grossman, is 'to be established [...] from Marxian theory itself, therefore on the basis of the law of value' (Grossman 1929, p. 283).

ited capital accumulation, and thus the endless perfectibility of the system (held by Bernstein, Otto Bauer, and Tugan-Baranowski), would have meant for socialism the removal of 'the granite foundation of objective historical necessity';[9] and

(2) criticise Luxemburg's false starting point which had forced her to a kind of integration of Marxian theory with respect to the problem of expanded reproduction.[10]

In a nutshell, Luxemburg explained the crisis in terms of the *market* rather than in terms of *production*. From her viewpoint, the relationship between capital and labour was inadequate to explain the full realisation of surplus value; hence, the need to introduce 'non-capitalist areas' as safety valves to relieve the stress. As a consequence, the focus is shifted from the production of surplus value to the *realisation* of surplus value. Grossman, who based his reading of Marx on solid methodological foundations,[11] redirected the problem to the *relations of production*. For it was in the relations of production (and proceeding from them) that the answer to the *vexata quaestio* as to the objective tendency of the 'future' of capitalism was to be sought.[12]

In order to understand Grossman's position, it is necessary at this point to turn back to his studies on the genesis of the critique of political economy and its scientifico-theoretical foundations. In this regard, two writings dating back respectively from 1929 and 1932 are important: 'Die Aenderung des ursprünglichen Aufbauplans des Marxschen *Kapital* und ihre Ursachen'[13] and

---

9   Luxemburg 1973, p. 76.
10 According to Luxemburg, Marx had 'only posed the question of the accumulation of gross capital, but his answer went no further' (Luxemburg 1973, p. 62). On the history of the question, see along with the dissertation by Mandelbaum mentioned, pp. 34–57, Wittfogel 1924, pp. 264–72.
11 Cf. Mattick, in Grossman 1969, pp. 120–21.
12 On the general aspects of the problem cf. Grossman 1929, ch. 2; section 11, 'Die Ursachen der Verkennung der Marxschen Akkumulations- und Zusammenbruchslehre', pp. 190–8; and for the critique of Rosa Luxemburg, see section 16, pp. 278–86 [Unfortunately, the Brill/Historical Materialism edition, Grossman 2021, did not come out in time to be taken into account in this translation, so the sections mentioned here are to the earlier, abridged addition: *The Law of Accumulation and the Breakdown of the Capitalist System*, London 1992: 'The the Marxist Theory of Accumulation and Breakdown was Misunderstood', pp. 101–3, and 'The Marxist Theory of Imperfect Valorisation', pp. 12–17 – editor's note.] The critique of Luxemburg is again taken up in the essay 'Gold Production in the Reproduction Schema of Marx and Luxemburg' in Grossmann 2019. Cf. also Neusüss 1972, p. 9 ff.
13 Cf. Grossman, 'The Change in the Original Plan of *Capital* and its Causes', Grossman 2019.

'Die Wert-Preis-Transformation bei Marx und das Krisenproblem'.[14] Although the first essay has been surpassed by more recent works on the historical genesis of *Capital*,[15] it is indicative of Grossman's interest in the form of Marxian theory – its 'mode of presentation' (*Darstellungsweise*) of the material analysed. Inasmuch as he relied upon Marx's letters discussing the different outlines and, above all, the abandoning of the original project of writing six volumes on six specific problems in favour of a more 'abstract' procedure eventually used in *Capital* and in the *Theories of Surplus Value*, Grossman came to the conclusion that

> Marx's reproduction schema is intimately connected with the methodological procedure that underlies all three volumes of Capital. For this reason, the change in the plan for Marx's life's work and the construction of the reproduction schema arose from the same fundamental idea.[16]

From this Grossman derived a kind of parallel between the cyclical representation of the reproduction process and the structuring of the material treated in *Capital*.

The publication of the *Grundrisse* has shown, however, that this hypothesis was false.[17] As Mattick has correctly remarked in this context,[18] the controversy of the 'Marxologists' over the supposed changes in Marx's work plan would then have a meaning only if, with Grossman, *Capital* is seen as a 'fragment' or a 'torso' yet to be completed (Luxemburg).[19] Grossman had very clearly perceived the kernel of 'scientific essentialism' which constitutes the foundation of the Marx's *Darstellungsweise*: the dialectical procedure of *Capital* does not portray the movement of capitalist production in terms of its *historical immediacy*, but rather, 'what was essential about capitalist production [...] to use Hegel's language' (*das Wesentliche der kapitalistischen Produktion*), the 'essential, fundamental form of the process of reproduction and accumulation' (*die wesentliche Grundform des Reproduktions- und Akkumlations- prozesses*).[20]

---

14 Cf. Grossman, 'The Value-Price Transformation and the Problem of Dynamics', Grossman 2019.
15 Cf., for example, Morf 1951; revised and expanded edition entitled *Geschichte und Dialektik in der politischen Oekonomie*, Frankfurt am Main and Vienna, 1970; and Rosdolsky 1977.
16 'The Change in the Original Plan ...', Grossman 2019, pp. 208–9.
17 The nature of this mistake has been explained with exemplary clarity in Rosdolsky, *The Making of ...* op. cit., pp. pp. 53–55. A sharp criticism of Grossman's essay can also be found in Morf 1951, pp. 75–78 (new ed., pp. 104–108).
18 Mattick, 'Nachwort', in Grossman 1969, p. 120.
19 'The Change in the Original Plan ...', Grossman 2019, p. 208.
20 Ibid. Eugen Varga, in his official party critique of Grossman, believed he had refuted him on the methodological level by claiming that Marx's 'method of research' did not have cat-

This constitutes the Marxian *method of isolation* (*Isolierungsmethode*) through which the necessary abstractions can be derived leading then to the identification of the concrete, i.e., to the tendential laws of the capitalist system. Marx writes:

> In a general analysis of the present kind, it is assumed throughout that actual conditions correspond to their concept, or, and this amounts to the same thing, that actual conditions are depicted only in so far as they express their own general type.[21]

In the second essay, devoted to the transformation problem, Grossman applies in practice his interpretation of Marx's method in the controversy over the 'contradiction' between the first and third volumes of *Capital* (i.e., between the analysis of value and the reality of the domination of prices), which Böhm-Bawerk had discovered in his well-known essay.[22] Grossman was aware of the significance of Böhm-Bawerk's critique: the confusion which it occasioned was one of the chief factors in the misunderstandings which appeared in the controversy over the reproduction schemes. The danger of a regression to Ricardo was evident in Luxemburg's solution. It was therefore necessary to regain, through an analysis carried out in accordance with the 'logic of science', the originality of Marx's formulation of the value concept as distinct from that of the classical economists.

We have already seen how the Marxian model of accumulation abstracted from many empirical elements in order to penetrate to the laws of movement of the capitalist economy. Moreover, for Grossman, it hypothesises an equivalency of exchange whose measure is labour time. Thus, the system results in the confrontation of workers and capitalists. Resting exclusively on value, this conception is not merely a 'simplifying hypothesis', since it presupposes concrete reality, nor is it a 'provisional hypothesis', since it remains valid even when the previously bracketed concrete aspects are included. The law of value is therefore *part of reality* and not simply an instrument of research.[23] Despite termin-

---

egorical abstractions as its object but, rather, 'concrete reality' (cf. Varga 1930, p. 62). Thus, he showed that he had not understood the underlying complex dialectic moving 'from the abstract to the concrete'.

21   Mark 1981, p. 242.
22   Böhm-Bawerk 1896 [*Karl Marx and the Close of His System*, New York 1949 – editor's note.]
23   In the 'Supplement to Volume 3 of Capital', Engels argues against Conrad Schmidt's reduction of the law of value to a pure hypothesis: 'The law of value has a far greater and more definite importance for capitalist production than that of a mere hypothesis, let alone a

ological differences, Grossman's method coincides with that of one of the most important defenders – and penetrating interpreters – of the dialectic, Roman Rosdolsky. 'Not only for Rosdolsky, but also for Grossman, Marx's abstract view of value is not just a presupposition for knowledge of the empirical world, but contains in kernel form the entire secret of capitalist development and its inevitable end'.[24] If Grossman described Marx's method as a 'method of successive approximations' (*Annäherungsverfahren*),[25] he does not understand by it some kind of one-way and rectilinear movement from thought (concepts) to reality, but the gradual process of the 'rising from the abstract to the concrete' as outlined in the 'Introduction' (1857) to the *Grundrisse*.[26]

Marx's *Isolierungsmethode* is the presupposition for understanding the nature of Grossman's argument concerning the reproduction schemes. The reproduction schemes are to be understood as a necessary moment in the 'method of isolation' adopted by Marx. In his critique of Otto Bauer, Grossman had shown that even setting out from the Automarxist's own assumptions, one can likewise arrive at the breakdown of the capitalist system (even if after a longer period of time).[27] With this, Grossman did *not* want to claim the possibility of

---

necessary fiction. [...] what is involved is not just a logical process but a historical one, and its explanatory reflection in thought, the logical follow-up of its internal connections' (Marx 1981, pp. 1032–3).

24 Mattick, in Grossman 1969, p. 124.
25 'The Value-Price Transformation ...', in Grossman 2019, p. 305. Alfred Schmidt has rightly referred to the scientific and epistemological relevance of this essay (in the introduction, 'Geschichte und gegenwärtige Bedeutung', to the reprint of the *Zeitschrift für Sozialforschung*, Munich 1970, p. 54). These theoretical inquiries are developed in the book on dynamics where Grossman clearly makes the conception of the economic structure of capitalism, depend upon the *Dopplecharakter* of labour, as the basis of the *qualitative* difference between Marxian theory and that of the classical economists. In the two-fold character of labour, Marx sees 'a decisive break between his conception and that of all his predecessors. And in fact, from the new standpoint of a two-dimensional conception of economic processes, he repeatedly criticises the classical political economists in principle, reproaching them for their one-dimensional theory, exclusively concerned with value' ('Marx, Classical Political Economy ...', Grossman 2019, p. 479). Hence Grossman forcefully rejects the thesis whereby Marxian value theory represents the further development and completion of the presuppositions of classical theorists (a thesis defended, for example, by Maurice Dobb in Dobb 1937).
26 [Marx 1973, p. 101 – editor's note].
27 Bauer 1912–13, pp. 831–8; 826–74. According to the Polish economists O. Lange and T. Kowalik, Bauer's history has been vindicated and Marx refuted: 'a considerable part of social production', writes Kowalik, 'can alternatively be used as a means of production and for the purpose of private consumption'; this fact is confirmed by the practice of socialist countries where accumulation takes place above all in Department II, while the major part of Department I is invested (cf. Kowalik 1963, p. 208 – in Polish). This predilection of Polish

a schematic presentation of breakdown (thus Sweezy's criticism in *The Theory of Capitalist Development* turns out to be *methodologically* unfounded),[28] but only to do away with the revisionist illusion that one could provide a 'scientific' proof for the unlimited developmental capacity of accumulation. In a letter to Mattick dated July 18, 1937, Grossman wrote:

> That the clique of neoharmonists, Hilferdings and Otto Bauers, tried for decades to systematically distort Marx [...] is not a reason for us to go along with the neoharmonists. Once you think through Marx's concepts consistently to the end, how can a crisis arise at the level of simple reproduction in which such a harmonious equilibrium appears to prevail? Then you will find in Marx many more theoretical concepts of which the 'philosophers' have not dreamed, even those such as Karl Korsch, who imagine that they understand something of Marxist economics.[29]

However, as Mattick – student and disciple of Grossman – later remarked,[30] Grossman's intervention in the controversy over the reproduction schemes helped obscure the core of his interpretation, which was not based on the harmony/disharmony of exchange proportions in the reproduction schemes, but on the law of the tendential fall in the rate of profit as related to the growing organic composition of capital.[31] Grossman's lack of success in subsequent

---

economists for a representative of the 'clique of new-harmonists' is by no means surprising given that in the Soviet editions of Luxemburg's *Accumulation of Capital*, Bauer's scheme is printed as an appendix – obviously as an antidote (e.g. in the edition of 1934, pp. 339–58).

28 Sweezy 1968, p. 209 ff. See also Grossman's unmistakable formulation: 'The neo-harmonists glorify the equilibrium scheme, not because it is a useful methodological tool, but because – in confusing the method of research with the phenomena to be investigated – they believed they could read out of the equilibrium scheme the tendency of capitalism towards equilibrium' (Grossman 1929, p. 95fn.). Rosdolsky has correctly shown that this mistake can only be explained by a false understanding of Marxian methodology on the part of the Austro-Marxists (cf. Rosdolsky 1981, p. 521). That this methodological deficiency is found again in Sweezy is by no means accidental.

29 Grossman to Mattick, 18 July 1937, Grossman 2019, pp. 272–3.

30 Mattick, in Grossman 1969, p. 119. See also Mattick's article, 'The Permanent Crisis. Henryk Grossman's Interpretation of Marx's Theory of Capitalist Accumulation' *International Council Correspondence*, no. 2 (Nov., 1934), esp. pp. 4–9. [Available online: https://www.marxists.org/subject/left-wing/icc/1934/11/permanent-crisis.htm, accessed 28 December, 2018 – editor's note].

31 That Grossman's theory was based upon the tendential fall in the rate of profit has already heen pointed out by Natalie Moszkowska, who rejected it (cf. ch. 4 of her book Moszkowska 1935). In regard to the revision of the law cf. Ibid., p. 46. See also her earlier

developments of Marxist economic criticism must be traced back to this not unambiguous intervention. Even if we accept that Sweezy's careless disposal of his theses represents neither a solution of the substantive problems, nor touches upon the critical and methodological basis of Grossman's analysis, we are forced to conclude at the same time that even today (aside from Mattick) a genuinely *critical* reception of his works is still lacking.[32]

Another widespread prejudice concerning Grossman is that he, together with Luxemburg, was one of the most radical defenders of capitalism's 'automatic' breakdown – a view which would contradict the 'radical' and 'spontaneist' inclinations of both because it would result in the denial of revolutionary subjectivity.[33] Despite the ambiguities and misunderstandings which had arisen from his critique of Bauer, Grossman had neither said nor thought that the breakdown would follow 'automatically', or that it would be possible to predict the exact point in time. Rather, it is the class struggle which must be

study, Moszkowska 1929, p. 118, where it is suggested that the law of the tendential fall in the rate of profit is not an historical, but a dynamic law which does not confirm any facts. Instead, it simply formulates the mutual dependence of two quantities: that of surplus-value and the rate of profit, such that if the first remains constant, the second falls and whenever the second remains constant, the first rises. According to Moszkowska, this law would consequently have to be characterised as the 'law of the tendential rise of the rate of surplus value'. An analysis which shows, on the contrary, remarkable similarities with Grossman's position is Preiser 1924.

32   Although holding an ambivalent position, Colletti himself manifests a certain propensity for Sweezy's critique of Grossman. Cf. Colletti and Napoleoni 1970, p. 443. A further confirmation of the strictly Marxian basis of Grossman's theory is found in his two-fold polemic: on the one hand, with Kautsky and Luxemburg (and then Sternberg), who consigned to the past the tendency toward immiseration and derived the betterment of the living conditions of the working class from competition, i.e., from the market; and, on the other hand, with Bukharin, who 'spatially' displaced the tendency toward immiseration by asserting that the position of the working class in the highly developed countries is improved at the expense of colonial countries (a thesis defended even today by 'fashionable' economists). In his book (Grossman 1929, pp. 587–603), Grossman shows that both these theses rest on a misunderstanding of Marx's wage theory. Interesting in this contest is the polemic against Fritz Sternberg, a defender of Rosa Luxemburg's theory and author of an important book on imperialism (Sternberg 1926). This book was sharply criticised by Grossman ('A new Theory of Imperialism and the Social Revolution', in Grossman 1929). Sternberg answered two years later with the pamphlet *Eine Umwälzung der Wissenschaft? Kritik des Buches von Henryk Grossmann. Zugleich eine positive Analyse des Imperialismus*, Berlin: R.L. Prager, 1930.

33   A good example of it is the criticism by A. Braunthal in Braunthal 1929, as well as in his recently republished book Braunthal 1972, esp. pp. 28–39. It should be added that the position of the Left Communists in general and the Council Communists in particular was not uniform, especially with reference to the question of breakdown, as is confirmed by Karl Korsch's criticism of Grossman (Korsch 1933, pp. 20–5) and the exchange between Mattick and Pannekoek in *Rätekorrespondenz* (cf. Pannekoek 1977, pp. 62–81; and Mattick 1954).

activated within the cyclical crisis process, thus interrupting the reconstruction of the capitalist contradiction by transforming it into an active, *autonomous* moment: the revolution for a new society. This is the true meaning of the alternative 'socialism or barbarism'. '[N]o economic system, no matter how weakened, collapses by itself in automatic fashion. It must be "overthrown"'.[34]

It is here that the political aspect of Grossman's effort emerges. The abstract analysis of capitalism and the determination of the tendential laws are nothing other than the *prolegomena* to the problem of class consciousness, the necessary presupposition of which would be described today as the 'problematic of constitution'.[35]

> Of course, as a dialectical Marxist, I know that both sides of the process, the objective and subjective elements influence each other. In the class struggle these factors merge. One cannot wait until, eventually, the 'objective' conditions are present so that, only then, the 'subjective' ones can operate. That would be an inadequate, mechanical perspective, which is alien to me. But, for the purposes of the analysis, I have to use the process of abstracting and isolating individual elements to show the essential functions of each element. Lenin often speaks of the objectively revolutionary situation that must be present as the precondition for the active, victorious intervention of the proletariat. My breakdown theory is not intended to exclude this active intervention but rather aims to show when and under what conditions such an objectively revolutionary situation can and does arise.[36]

It is no accident that it is precisely in Lukács' *History and Class Consciousness* that one finds the philosophical equivalent of Grossman's great attempt at a critical-revolutionary re-appropriation of Marxian categories.[37] For the 'Lux-

---

34 Grossman, 'The Evolutionist Revolt against Classical Economics', Grossman 2019, p. 596.
35 Cf. Krahl 1971, pp. 82–97 and 323–9.
36 H. Grossman, letter to P. Mattick on June 21, 1931, in Grossman 2019, p. 230. Here once again Grossman's strictly Marxian approach is evident: 'What is visible here in a purely economic manner, i.e. *from the bourgeois standpoint*, within the limits of capitalist understanding, from the standpoint of capitalist production itself, are its barriers, its relativity, that fact that it is not an absolute but only a historical mode of production, corresponding to a specific and limited epoch on the development of the material conditions of production' (Marx 1981, p. 368). My emphasis.
37 On the question of the theoretical and political meaning of Lukács' book see the discussion in Cerutti, Claussen, Krahl, Negt and Schmidt 1971, esp. pp. 18–25.

emburgian' Lukács of 1923, the 'catastrophe theory of history'[38] is the continuing impetus for 'the process of proletarian knowledge' (*proletarischen Erkenntnisprozess*) and for the effect of class in the dialectical context of the historical process:

> The proletariat is [...] at one and the same time the product of the permanent crisis in capitalism and instrument of those tendencies which drive capitalism towards crisis [...]. By recognizing its situation it acts. By combating capitalism it discovers its own place in society. But the class consciousness of the proletariat, the truth of the process 'as subject,' is itself far from stable or constant; it does not advance according to mechanical laws. It is the consciousness of the dialectical process itself; it is likewise a dialectical concept. For the practical and active side of class consciousness, its true essence can then only become visible in its authentic form when the historical process imperiously requires its coming into force, i.e., when an acute crisis in the economy drives it to action.[39]

Even with their traditional elements, Grossman's and Lukács's efforts represent for us today the sole reference points to be taken seriously for the reconstruction of a critique of political economy which is appropriate both for the present context of *social* capitalist organisation and for a scientific reconstitution of class consciousness.

2 From the Crisis of Competitive Capitalism to Its Transformation. The 'New Object' of Pollock's Analysis

As I pointed out in the beginning, Grossman's work represents not only the best attempt at a critical re-appropriation of Marxian 'orthodoxy' on the level of economic ('abstract') analysis, but it also marks the closing of an epoch, of an historical cycle which encompasses both the development of capitalism and of its theory. Grossman's effort stands *before* the profound structural

---

38 The expression comes from Schmidt 1971, p. 132.
39 Lukács 1971, p. 40. In another place Lukács writes: 'The objective economic evolution could no more than create the position of the proletariat in the production process. It was this position that determined its point of view. But the objective evolution could only give the proletariat the opportunity and the necessity to change society. Any transformation can only come about as the product of the – free – action of the proletariat itself', Lukács 1971, p. 209.

transformations capital undergoes after the 1929 crisis, i.e., *before* the features of *monopolistic* and *state capitalist* forms gradually emerged in the course of the 1940s. And this divides us from his work and from the last crisis of overproduction generated by the anarchy of the competitive mechanism and the uncontrollable convulsions of the old 'automatic character of the market'.

Grossman's book closed with the radical claim of the 'impossibility of "regulating" production on the basis of the existing economic order'.[40] Pollock's analysis, carried out in the broad and contradictory context of the crisis, proceeds instead from the inverse presupposition: the crisis which had broken out in Wall Street on 'Black Thursday', spreading to all capitalist countries, is not the beginning of the final catastrophe but the end of a phase, the competitive phase of capitalism. 'What is coming to an end is not capitalism, but its liberal phase'.[41] A closer examination of the dynamic of the crisis prefigured the prospects for a 'planning of a new economic order'. These prospects indicate, however, only a tendential direction which in itself is not necessary: the style of the 'planned re-ordering' cannot be concretely determined beforehand, but only abstractly outlined. Economic theorists can only outline different models of planning as a contribution to the construction of a 'closed theory [...] which could serve a future economic policy as a means of orientation'.[42] Drawing on Lorwin,[43] Pollock arranged these models in a scheme whose criteria are characterised by two main types of planned economy: the capitalist type (resting on the 'general cartel' of Hilferding and the preservation of private ownership of the means of production), and the socialist (resting on the collective ownership of the means of production). These models have in common the replacement of the old automatism, based on 'self-regulation', with a plan. Pollock's 'abstract' description was by no means the result of a technocratic deformation; it was grounded in the historical circumstance of the simultaneity of the crisis – and also in a theoretical phenomenon which was closely

---

40 Grossman 2009, p. 623. In the introduction to the new edition of Grossman's book (Frankfurt am Main 1967), Wolf Rosenbaum pointed out the limits of the work stemmed from the failure to treat the remaining causes which bring forth the crisis and the tendencies counteracting the tendential fall in the rate of profit. On this point see the discussion of the Gillman's book (*The Falling Rate of Profit* [London, 1957]) in the anthology edited by C. Rolshausen *Kapitalismus und Krise. Eine Kontroverse um das Gesetz des tendentziellen Falls der Profitrate* (Rolshausen (ed.) 1970, esp. the contribution by Mattick, 'Werttheorie und Kapitalakkumulation', pp. 7–34).
41 Pollock 1933, p. 350.
42 Pollock 1933, p. 27.
43 Cf. Lorwin 1931.

bound up with this circumstance: in the profound proces of revision to which the most important representatives of liberalism subjected their theories.[44]

> Without a doubt it can be established that the crisis can be overcome with *capitalist means* and that 'monopolistic' capitalism will be able to continue at least for the forseeable future.[45]

With that, Pollock did not want to maintain that the system was able to realise a perfect steering of the cyclic movement and a total transcendence of all contradictions:

> There is considerable evidence, to be sure, that in this administered capitalism the depressions will be longer, the boom phases shorter and stronger, and the crises more destructive than in the times of 'free competition,' but its 'automatic' collapse is not to be expected. There is no *purely economic* irrepressible compulsion to replace it with another economic system.[46]

The statement of the problem is more complicated than it appears at first sight. Pollock does not deny the 'catastrophic' character of the crisis – on the contrary, he sharply polemicises against the harmonising representations of 'pre-war capitalism' in which the massive destruction produced by the automatism of the market were defined as 'friction';[47] but, at the same time, he did not view it (like Grossman) as the *memento mori* of the system and felt that it could be overcome by *capitalistic means*. The market mechanism is no longer able to realise the 'optimal adjustment' to demand of the productive forces; hence the need arises for an economically planned new order:

> The manifest difficulties of the capitalist system, as well as the Russian planning efforts whose collapse was wrongly prophesised by nearly all experts, are the main reasons why today economic planning is being discussed everywhere.[48]

---

44 Cf. here the detailed review of Keynes' *General Theory* which Pollock, together with Mandelbaum, had written under the pseudonym Erich Baumann: 'Keynes Revision der liberalistischen Nationalökonomie', *Zeitschrift für Sozialforschung*, vol. V (1936), pp. 384–405.
45 Pollock 1933, p. 18. My emphasis.
46 Ibid. My emphasis.
47 Pollock 1933, p. 15.
48 Pollock 1933, p. 17.

The 'abstract' statement of the problem thus flows into the laborious process of economic and social transition in which, on the one hand, the western capitalist states (above all the United States) and, on the other, the Soviet Union, began to discover new forms which could again set in motion the process of accumulation. But it is the Soviet experience which persists as the reference point for the 'new course' of the capitalist economy.[49]

> It is part of the fundamental notion of Marx's economic theory that a new economic system can come into being only when its economic and social presuppositions, or at least their seeds, are planted beneath the surface in the old system and when the relations of production have become fetters on the productive forces.
>
> Just as in France, toward the end of the 18th century, where the elimination of the old bonds resulted in rapid economic development because, under the rubble of the residual feudal economy, the socio-economic presuppositions of the system of laissez-faire were already in place. In the same way, the unleashing of existing forces of production by an economically planned new order is only to be anticipated when its presuppositions are already given. Keeping to this level of generality, the economic preconditions for this re-ordering (leaving aside the political ones for now) can be formulated as follows: the major weight of industrial production must be shifted to large-scale firms and the process of centralisation must reach a certain level; the technical and organisational means for mastering the tasks of a centralised economic administration must be already known; and a considerable reserve of productivity must be available to be utilised through the application of the methods of economic planning. It can be easily demonstrated that all these economic presuppositions are to a great extent at hand in the great industrial nations, as well as in the world economy.[50]

This same development, which had proven fatal for the 'normal' operation of automatic market mechanisms, created the presupposition for the planned steering of the economic process. The timing and character of this steering could take many different forms, which are devolved to complex political con-

---

49 Cf. on this point the pages on 'war communism' and the NEP in the previously cited book, *Die planwirtschaftlichen Versuche in der Sowjetunion* (Pollock 1971, esp. pp. 96–111 and 126–70).

50 Pollock 1933, pp. 19 ff.

ditions, or to the initiative of 'economic subjects'. Possibilities for a 'socialist' orientation of economic planning are 'slight so long as the influence of those strata, which are interested because of their class position, is not sufficient for an overthrow of the current social order'.[51]

Although Pollock's analysis was carried out with exemplary clarity and precision, it left the underlying problems open, rather than resolving them. The principles from which it departed were, to be sure, those of Marx: they were based upon the conflict between the forces and relations of production. Yet, the new qualities of contemporary processes rendered necessary if not a revision, at least a contemporary supplement to the old theoretical premises. The historical rupture of 1917 had led to a decisive change within the world economy by introducing a new element in the overall dynamic of the process: a *political* element which necessitated a similarly *political* reaction from the side of capital. Had this not been the case, the end of the *laissez-faire* system would have meant the end of capitalism. A mere retreat to orthodoxy, where the decisive role of the political factor would have been left in the background, would have been absolutely inadequate because it would have given no answer to the *new* problems and would not have grasped the *morphological novelty* of the international situation. Horkheimer correctly noted in the first issue of the *Zeitschrift für Sozialforschung* that the objective weight of the general crisis was represented subjectively in an 'inner crisis of science'.[52] One has to realise the following: it was a matter of critical circumstances in conjunction with the special historical situation (Russian Revolution, defeat of the Revolution in the West, tendency toward monopoly capitalism) without which the genesis of Critical Theory and its *political conditioning* cannot be understood. As Horkheimer wrote:

> To the extent that we can speak of a crisis of science, it is not to be separated from the general crisis. Historical development has brought with it a fettering of science as a force of production, which affects accordingly its parts, the content and the form, the material, as well as the method. Furthermore, science as a means of production is not correspondingly utilised. The understanding of the crisis of science depends on the correct theory of the contemporary social situation, for presently science, as a social function, mirrors the contradictions of society.[53]

---

51 Pollock 1933, p. 27.
52 Horkheimer, 'Bemerkungen über Wissenschaft und Krise', *Zeitschrift für Sozialforschung*, I (1932), p. 4.
53 Horkheimer, 'Bemerkungen über Wissenschaft und Krise', *Zeitschrift für Sozialforschung*, I (1932), p. 7.

Symptomatic of this difficulty in adapting 'science' to the new reality is Pollock's essay, 'Bemerkungen zur Wirtschaftskrise'.[54] Here, Pollock found himself confronted with an especially resistant object of investigation which also was not adequately treated by Marx. Although the defender of an 'endogenous' crisis theory, he still did not overlook – in agreement with Marx – the 'exogenous' factors which could explain the particularities of the crisis. He rightly viewed the crisis as a complex phenomenon produced by a variety of causes,[55] which partly explains the lack of an adequate level of abstraction. Unlike Grossman, however, he lacked a consideration of the law of accumulation and any reference to the law of the tendential fall in the rate of profit (although, as we will see, the consequences of his approach seem to suggest an *implicit* revision of this law). Consequently, this complicates the locating of Pollock within the old and new discussions of crisis theory.

Marx had demonstrated the 'general, abstract possibility of crisis'[56] in the separation of supply and demand. But the most general form of the crisis is not its cause. In order to explain the phenomenon of the crisis, one must go back to the distinction between simple commodity production and capitalist production – a distinction which represents not only a qualitative difference but also an actual break between Marxian theory and the theories of the classical economics.[57] The *effective* cause of the crisis lies in the fall of the profit rate, this

---

54 Pollock 1933.
55 Pollock 1933, pp. 325 ff.
56 Marx 1968, p. 509.
57 The possibility of crisis is already contained in simple commodity circulation (C-M-C), i.e., where the transition is made from a simple commodity exchange (C-C) to the most developed forms of exchange, and where then money emerges, having the function of separating in time buying and selling. Thanks to money, the producers no longer need to search for 'buyers', and *vice versa*. Also, though simple commodity circulation already contains the possibility of a disruption (through the separation of buying and selling) of the exchange process, there is still no cause for this actually to occur. In the investigation of the forms which commodity circulation assumes, Marx notices that these forms include the possibility – but only the possibility – of crisis, because for their concretisation an entire context of relations is necessary which do not yet exist in simple commodity exchange. Proof for this is the fact that – even if there are no crises without commodity and money circulation – there was commodity and money circulation long before capitalist production, without this resulting in crisis. Therefore, it is important to hold to this point because the failure to differentiate clearly between simple commodity production and capitalist production (with all the historical implications which go along with it), constitutes the reason why classical economists came to reject the phenomenon of crisis. Without explicating this argument any further here, I would like to note that for us the places where Marx polemicises against Say and Ricardo have as a *critique of economic science* an enormous *epistemological* significance (Cf. Marx 1968,

determines the tendency of capitalists to retain capital in monetary form (a tendency characterised by Keynes as 'liquidity preference'). Nevertheless, the 'determinant' of the falling rate of profit is still hotly debated. In the famous third section of *Capital* vol. III, Marx connects it to the inadequacy of the rate of surplus value compared to the organic composition of capital. In this case, the value system would remain unchanged. The other cause for the fall of the profit rate could lie in the impossibility of selling the product according to its value, i.e., it could be a matter of the lack of 'real demand' (or, with Marx, of the lack of 'effective consumption'). Both these possibilities correspond to two different interpretations of crisis which we can schematise as follows:[58] (a) that interpretation which depends on the tendential fall in the rate of profit; and (b) the theory of the 'realisation crisis' which can be differentiated into two types (b1) 'disproportionality theory'; and (b2) 'underconsumption theory'.

We will now attempt to summarise the theses contained in these interpretations and describe them in a very simplified manner.

(a) The cause of the crisis is not in the disproportionality between production and consumption, but is to be sought within production itself, i.e., in the basic contradiction between the forces and relations of production. The crisis then represents a reaction enforced by the system to the decline in the profit rate; it is the means which capital reverts to in order to repair the damages of 'prosperity'. The transformation of crisis into a depression, the consequent reforming of the reserve army, and the devaluation of capital are the connecting links of the cyclical chain through which the profitability of production and the bases for the resumption of accumulation are reconstituted. (Among the most important representatives of this theory are Preiser, Grossman, Mattick and, with considerable differences, Dobb.)[59]

(b) The fall in the profit rate is not to be explained by accumulation and the increase in the organic composition of capital, but by the impossibility of *realising* surplus value because the capitalists do not succeed in selling commodities at their value. (One must at the same time be aware of the internal divisions within this interpretation, because it is precisely in the realm of the

---

pp. 507–13.) [Only a version of the final sentence of this note appears in the original Italian chapter one of part two of *Il politico e le trasformazioni*, op. cit. The substantial discussion of 'crisis' in the first part of this note was added to the *Telos* translation – editor's note.]

58 This formulation is based largely on comments by Sweezy 1968, pp. 147–86.

59 Cf. *Capital*, vol. I. ch. 7 and vol. III, ch. 15, in which crisis theory tends to assume the form of a *theory of cycles*.

'realisation crisis' that the different currents of right and left revisionism as well as more 'up to date'[60] economic analyses operate.)

(b1) The crisis is caused by 'unbalanced' production, i.e., by an uneven division of social labour among particular spheres of production. The increase or decrease of market value on the basis of this disproportionality results in the migration of capital from one branch of production to another. (Marx himself had not excluded the possibility that this disproportionality was traceable to *the lack of a 'plan'*, inasmuch as the entrepreneur in competitive capitalism can determine the level of real market demand only *a posteriori*. And if it affects an especially important sector of production, this leads to disequilibrium in the spheres essential to life and would in the end bring forth the crisis.) Tugan-Baranowski accepted the hypothesis of disproportionality as the sole explanation for crisis and thus contested the theory which depended upon the tendential fall in the profit rate, as well as the theory of underconsumption. Thus he came to deny the pathological character of the diseases of the system; he even tried, on the basis of the reproduction schemes in the second volume of *Capital*, to prove the possibility of unlimited stabilisation, owing to the maintenance of proportionalities – a maintenance which would be guaranteed ever more strongly by the development of monopolistic concentration, by the trusts and growing state controls, whereby the anarchy at the societal level would be continuously reduced. (The theory of 'disproportionality crisis' has played an important role in the Second International – see Hilferding – as well as in Russian Marxism – see Lenin's polemic against 'economic romanticism'.)[61]

(b2) The crisis arises from the inability of capitalism to create an adequate market for the requirements of its own production. Let us read the statement of this now classic thesis in the words of its most famous current representative:

> The real task of an underconsumption theory is to demonstrate that capitalism has an inherent *tendency* to expand the capacity to produce con-

---

60   One is reminded here of Emannuel 1972, which has aroused a considerable stir.
61   Cf. Tugan-Baranowski 1901, and 1966; Hilferding 1981; Lenin 1960a, pp. 129–332. As Rosdolsky notes (Rosdolsky 1981, p. 481, n. 97), Lenin not only leaves the theories of Bulgakov and Tugan untouched, but even defends them against their critics. Thus, for example, against Struve who had raised the objection that they had derived 'the harmony between production and consumption' from the Marxian schemes (cf. Lenin 1960b, p. 83). Despite the objective difficulty of finding a unified solution to the crisis problem, it must be pointed out that Lenin's postulate of the necessary subsumption of the relations between production and consumption under the concept of 'proportionality', comes dangerously close to the theory of the 'lack of proportionality' (or the 'lack of a plan', as one would say today) that is typical of Tugan-Baranowski's interpretation of crisis.

sumption goods more rapidly than the demand for consumption goods. To put it another way, it must be shown that there is a *tendency* to utilize resources in such a way as to distort the relation between potential supply of and the potential demand for consumption goods.[62]

The general theoretical ground of this interpretation is that the logic of capitalism is one of *production for consumption* – and not, as Marx in various places explained, that of *production for production*. ('Underconsumption theory', strongly influenced by the teachings of Sismondi and Malthus, spread in the second half of the last century in Germany through the work of Rodbertus and, with Lassalle and Dühring, was transformed from the classical ideology of landowners into the 'staple' of the interpretations of German social democracy and the Second International. Among its most important defenders are Fritz Sternberg and, today, Sweezy.)[63]

Only with difficulty can Pollock's interpretation be situated within this schematisation of crisis theories. This could be easily explained from an historical viewpoint by the 'crisis of science', of which Horkheimer spoke and which expressed itself in the difficulties of economic theory after the First World War and the October Revolution. From a *theoretical* viewpoint, however, numerous problems arise. As we have seen, Pollock specifically starts out from the classical scheme which rests upon the basic contradiction between the forces and relations of production. He is inclined, nevertheless, to unite this scheme with the hypothesis which is typical of the 'disproportionality crisis'. According to this hypothesis, only a *plan* or regulations (those *Regulierung* which for Grossman were absolutely impossible in a capitalist system) could bring to a halt the ruinous process caused by the continuous migration of capital from one sector of production to another, and thereby eliminating the *Disproportionalitäten* that constitute the greatest obstacle to overcoming the crisis. Attempting once again a schematisation, we could conclude that with Pollock's analysis we find ourselves in a new and original combination of the classical Marxian interpretation re-elaborated by Grossman (a) and the 'disproportionality crisis'

---

62   Sweezy 1968, p. 180.
63   In his presentation, Sweezy also relegates Rosa Luxemburg (who he even characterises as 'the queen of the underconsumptionists', Sweezy 1968, p. 171) to this subcategory. Even if there is no doubt that Rosa Luxemburg is a representative of the theory of the realisation crisis, in my opinion one cannot include her with the 'underconsumptionists'. Although in parts of *The Accumulation of Capital*, she approaches such an interpretation, the characterisation of her theory as 'underconsumptionism' is tantamount to flattening the theory and robbing it of its political meaning.

(b1).⁶⁴ This allows Pollock to establish a connection between controllability and the reciprocal correction of the two theories, whereby onesidedness can be avoided while introducing the concept of 'plan'. This connection forces Pollock to revise the dialectic between the forces and relations of production. In this 'adjustment' of the conflict Pollock recognised the menacing authoritarian consequences of the planned control of all economic processes as they appeared to be assumed by the state to an increasing degree. But let us consider the decisive points of Pollock's analysis somewhat more closely.

In the fifth section of the essay on crisis, Pollock refers to the tendency of capitalist planning to intervene actively in the dynamic of the conflict between the forces and relations of production (a conflict which 'has become more intense than it has ever been before'), introducing a kind of 'adjustment process'. This process operated in a twofold manner: through the forcible destruction of excess productive forces (which Pollock described as the 'Procrustean method'), and through the 'relaxation of the fetters' with which capital binds productive relations. Both these methods 'leave the *foundations* of the capitalist system untouched'; they allow themselves to be 'differentiated sharply only in thought', since they are in fact united in the practise of capitalist steering.⁶⁵ For Pollock, the method of 'relaxing the fetters' appears to be the one that wins out in the long run: in practice it works itself out in an increasing limitation of the individual owner's control over his own capital, for this control is increasingly transferred over to 'large-scale units', or even to the state. Pollock's train of thought gets complicated at this point because he does not succeed in clearly determining the *limits* of the process of concentration. When the steering of the economic process is carried out by a central state authority, we reach an extreme point where the relations of production cannot be further modified

---

64 Cf. Pollock 1933, p. 338. To be sure, Pollock is not the only theorist where one finds a combination of different crisis theories. Lenin, for example, as an adherent of the disproportionality theory which he derived from the anarchy of capitalist production, supplemented his conception with the theory of underconsumption: 'the irregular production of a surplus-product (crises) is inevitable in capitalist society as a result of the disturbance in proportion between the various branches of industry. But a certain state of consumption is one of the elements of proportion' (Lenin 1960c, p. 16n). The theory of the disproportionality crisis is modified here in such a way that the proportionality between the different branches of production also depends on the relations of consumption. A similar combination is found in Bukharin, for whom the crisis derives from 'disproportionality of social production', of which the factor of consumption is one 'element' of these disproportions (N. Bucharin, 'Imperialism and the Accumulation of Capital' in Luxemburg and Bukharin 1972, p. 236 [see the entire chapter 3, 'The General Theory of the Market, and Crises!', pp. 203–38 – editor's note]).

65 Cf. Pollock 1933, p. 338.

without eliminating the foundations of the capitalist system.[66] Pollock's uncertainty mirrored a real process. Through his investigations of the developments in the German and American economy, he had come to realise that capitalist steering was on the verge of giving its 'sardonic' answer to the crisis. That is, it was realising in 'inverted', 'upside down' form the model of a planned economy which the theorists of the *Zeitschrift* had seen as the only possible way out of the catastrophic crisis. Rather than placing such processes under the control of 'associated individuals' and using them for the welfare and happiness of the 'majority', the 'rational' steering of economic processes resulted in further control by the strongest 'monopolistic groups' in German National Socialism and, with different methods, in the U.S. New Deal. It was up to these monopolistic groups to arbitrarily decide on 'the fate of all remaining economic subjects, owners of capital, and workers'.[67]

Thus, that tendency which Pollock and Mandelbaum had emphasised in their essay 'Autarkie und Planwirtschaft'[68] began to take shape. It proved to be the determining element of the present form of the capitalist social order: state interference in the economy. Insofar as National Socialism corresponded to this process (although it only expressed the first and most primitive phase), it was by no means the sign of a 'backward step' or mere barbarism, but rather the logical result of the *concentration process*:

> Parlamentarianism was poorly suited to this end [...], inasmuch as it corresponded to a less advanced concentration of economic power. As a consequence of the release from the constraints of parlamentarianism and of having the entire apparatus of the psychic domination of the masses at their disposal, during this period governments appear to be independent from classes and to stand impartially above society.[69]

Despite these important observations, the descriptive aspects of Pollock's analysis predominated over the critical. This is particularly apparent in the essay 'State Capitalism'.[70] Here, the pure description empties the object of all its

---

66   Pollock 1933, p. 348.
67   Pollock 1933, p. 349.
68   Under the pseudonym 'Kurt Baumann' in the *Zeitschrift für Sozialforschung*, vol. II, 1933, pp. 79–103.
69   Pollock 1933, p. 363.
70   Pollock 1933, *passim*. An investigation of the leading tendencies of state capitalism which is symptomatic of the resonance of this theme since the beginning of the 1930s appears in Carl Steuermann (the pseudonym of Otto Rühle), Rühle 1931; cf. esp. pp. 213–55 (also very interesting is the chapter on the Soviet Union, pp. 183 ff.).

contradictory components, lending it the character of 'bad' abstraction as in Weber's 'ideal type'. One has the clear impression that Pollock has driven to an extreme point his own tendency (which was already evident in his first work)[71] to rehabilitate the 'mask', i.e., the different fetishised forms of capitalist economic processes: money, state, technology.[72]

The historical violence with which the tendency toward 'state capitalism' had manifested itself, giving rise to the monstrous possibilities of despotic controls linked to the institutionalised forms of violence, had prevented him from critically appraising the new developments and locating the latent dialectical elements within the breast of this new 'totality'. Thus, he mistook as the essence the apparent character as 'alien power' of the fetishised forms of the economic process, while accepting as reality the a-contradictory and 'one-dimensional' façade of socialised despotism:

> Government control of production and distribution furnishes the means for eliminating the economic causes of depressions, cumulative destructive processes, and unemployment of capital and labor. We may even say that under state capitalism economics as a social science has lost its object.[73]

The connections between Pollock's conclusions and those of the major philosophical representatives of the *Zeitschrift für Sozialforschung* are evident. These connections exist not only with respect to conclusions, but also in regard to the complex development of the *Zeitschrift*. We do not make this observation

---

71   Cf. Pollock's essay on Marx's money theory in *Grünberg's Archiv*. XIII, 1928, pp. 193–209, which takes up again the theses from his unpublished dissertation (Pollock 1923). His approach was in any case correct and strictly 'orthodox' Marxist insofar as it rested on the dialectic of essence and appearance, and on the close connection between money and commodity analysis in Marx. That is all the more significant since the most astute contemporary scholars have recently demonstrated, on the basis of the *Grundrisse* (which Pollock could not have known at that time), the constitutive meaning of the relation between the analysis of money and that of the commodity for the structure of Marxian theory. Cfr. Rosdolsky 1981, pp. 123–9, and Wygodski 1967, p. 54. Despite the tendency of theory to withdraw from the essential level (i.e., the investigation of the categorial forms as a function of the social relations of production) to the phenomenal (i.e., the privileging of the 'mask' of the economic process as a whole), Pollock's analysis is anything but methodologically naive.

72   Investigations of the social consequences of the automation of work processes have almost exclusively preoccupied Pollock's interest in the post-war period, culminating in the well-known book Pollock 1957.

73   Pollock 1933, p. 87.

only in order to formulate a historico-cultural judgement (which could never truly 'do justice' to the imprecisely named – but extremely important – Frankfurt School). We do so to provide a valid contribution to the analysis of this important current of thought from the standpoint of *ideology critique*.[74] This means, first, distinguishing the historical phases of the development of Critical Theory in terms of it theoretico-economic contributions, which have, up to now, been unfairly overlooked. Second, to turn to an investigation into the causes of the inadequate elaboration of the theory/practice relation of the later phase (that of the 1930s).

3 The Socialisation of Work and Critical Theory. The Critique of Political Economy as a Condition of the 'Making of History'

In the essay 'The Struggle Against Liberalism in the Totalitarian View of the State' (1934), Marcuse described – with explicit reference to Pollock's analysis – the nature of the substantial continuity between the liberal and the totalitarian conceptions with the following words:

> This rough sketch of liberalist social theory has shown how many elements of the totalitarian view of the state are already present in it. Taking the economic structure as a point of reference, we see an almost unbroken continuity in the development of the social theory. We shall here assume some prior knowledge of the economic foundations of this development from liberalist to totalitarian theory (reference to Pollack's analysis): they are all essentially part of the transformation of capitalist society from mercantile and industrial capitalism, based on the free competition of independent individual entrepreneurs, to monopoly capitalism, in which the changed relations of production (and especially the large 'units' such as cartels and trusts) require a strong state mobilizing all means of power [...]. The turn from the liberalist to the total-authoritarian state occurs within the framework of a single social order. With regard to the unity of this economic base, we can say it is liberalism that 'produces' the total-authoritarian state out of itself, as its own consummation at a more advanced stage of development. The total-authoritarian state brings with

---

74 With this I by no means intend to subscribe to the subsumption of 'Critical Theory' under the concept of the 'idealistic reaction against science' with which some authors believe they have disposed of it (cf. Therborn 1970, pp. 65–96; and Colletti 1973, pp. 173–7).

it the organisation and theory of society that correspond to the monopolistic stage of capitalism.[75]

The reciprocal relation of influence of the investigations by Marcuse and Pollock appears also to extend beyond the 1930s, when Pollock writes in his book on *automation*:

> We tried to explain why, in our view, one ultimate result of the continued advance of automation might be the spread of authoritarian forms of government. It may be useful to indicate some specific ways in which our lives and ways of thought may in future be affected by the spread of automation. This of course is only one aspect of the social consequences of the new industrial revolution. Another social change that may be expected to follow in the wake of automation may be the abolition of poverty and soul-destroying drudgery. And this change will affect not only the advanced industrial states but also – in the not too distant future-every country in the world. Such a policy may indeed appear to be Utopian in the light of the strains and bitter conflicts which result from the very low standard of living of the vast majority of the human race, yet the abolition of poverty need not be just a dream if only the world would use its reasoning powers to make sensible use of the economic assets at its disposal.[76]

The gap between the aspect of theoretical 'representation' and that of critical-praxis has reached the highest point. The denunciation of the system, as in Marcuse's *One Dimensional Man*, is a fact of ethical reason, which is itself outside 'the existent' and, hence, is unable to exert an *immanent* critique.

More interesting still – but also correspondingly more difficult – is the relationship of Pollock to Adorno. On the one hand, while Adorno always kept Grossman in mind as the more profound and versatile of the economic theorists who worked on the basis of Marxian categories from the standpoint of *methodology*; on the other hand, he took over Pollock's *Darstellung* of authoritarian socialisation as produced by the oligo-/mono-polistic developments of contemporary capitalism. Viewed abstractly and theoretically, the dialectic between the forces and relations of production remains the fundamental principle for explaining capitalist society. As Pollock had shown in his essay on the

---

75 Marcuse 1969, pp. 18–19. In the essay written with Mandelbaum, Pollock refers to this important essay by Marcuse (Mandelbaum and Pollock 1933, p. 402).
76 Pollock 1957, pp. 205.

economic crisis of 1933, however, this dialectic appears to have been suspended, ushering in a kind of 'adjustment process' which, if it does not disprove the Marxian law of the tendential fall in the rate of profit, at least removes the concrete temporality upon whose foundation the law's validity must rest. In the introduction to *The Positivist Dispute in German Sociology*, Adorno explains unmistakably that the theory of breakdown (or 'collapse') continued to represent one of the most important questions of the social sciences.[77] He makes similar remarks with respect to value theory.[78] The Marxian laws appear, however, to have strangely lost their object and with it the means for their practical verification. With the 'freezing' of the dialectic of the real, critical thinking appears to be damned to the exile of contemplation for an unforeseeable future. Even as Adorno's theory holds to Marxian orthodoxy, at the same time it is unable to become effective in the new form of the capitalist organisation of domination. It thus becomes a negative totality, the reflex of the *absence of historical movement (Stillstands der historischen Bewegung)*, of that objective process which Grossman had outlined in his rigorous interpretation, and which appears to be blocked by a series of counter tendencies:

> Through the absolute rule of negation and in accordance with the pattern of immanent antithesis, the movement of thought, as of history, becomes unambiguously, exclusively, implacably positive. Everything is subsumed under the main economic phases and their development.[79]

The 'sardonic' realisation of mankind as 'generic thing' in the planned economy, has subtracted the object of the practico-critical moment of revolutionary humanism:

> The culture industry has sardonically realized man's species being [*Gattungwesen*]. Everyone amounts only to those qualities by which he or she can replace everyone else: all are fungible, mere specimens.[80]

One finds a similar description of this phenomenon in those pages of Pollock's automation book where he speaks of the military-type organisation of the modern factory and describes this as the cellular form of the 'despotism' of society as

---

77 Adorno (ed.) 1976, p. 42.
78 In Horkheimer and Adorno 1962, p. 117. Cf. in this regard the important essay by H.G. Backhaus: Backhaus 1980, pp. 99–120.
79 Adorno 1974, pp. 150–1.
80 Horkheimer and Adorno 2002, pp. 116–17.

a whole. Adorno's analysis represents the mirror of these structural processes. The process of the socialisation of labour assumes a completely 'caricatured' form; it is expressed in the absolutisation-separation of both moments of the process: an abstract rationalisation in which variable capital is treated as constant capital and the worker as a machine, and an increase in the hierarchical power of despotism in the factory.[81]

This parallel between an economist such as Pollock and an 'abstract' philosopher like Adorno can only astonish those who are not familiar with the real problematic (or even just with the texts) of critical Marxism. From the very beginning it has tried to interpret the dynamic of the modern production process by recourse to the Marxian analysis of commodities:

> We are concerned above all with the *principle* at work here: the principle of rationalisation based on what is and *can be calculated*. [...] Rationalisation in the sense of being able to predict with ever greater precision all the results to be achieved is only to be acquired by the exact breakdown of every complex into its elements and by the study of the special laws governing production. [...] This destroys the organic necessity with which inter-related special operations are unified in the end-product. The unity of a product as a *commodity* no longer coincides with its unity as a use-value; as society becomes more radically capitalistic the increasing technical autonomy of the special operations involved in production is expressed also, as an economic autonomy, as the growing relativisation of the commodity character of a product at the various stages of production.[82]

The mechanical fragmentation of the production process also shatters those ties which, within 'organic' production, united individual subjects of labour into a community. Mechanised production transforms these subjects into abstract, isolated atoms whose association is increasingly mediated by the abstract laws of the mechanism. In the system of socialised labour, time loses its qualitative character, its mutability, congealing into a quantitatively measureable continuum, which is filled with equally measureable 'things' (the alienated operations of workers). The quantifying abstraction of work – the subsumption of the production process under the concept of calculability – is in the society

---

81 Cf. Pollock 1957, pp. 205–46. The sole comparison between the analyses of Pollock and that of Adorno which I have found until now is in Panzieri 1972; cfr. pp. 184 and 195.
82 Lukács 1971, pp. 88–9.

of planned capitalism the *concretion* of the abstract presupposition which is implicit in exchange relations:

> Bourgeois society is universally situated under the law of exchange, of the like-for-like of accounts that match and that leave no remainder. In its very essence exchange is something timeless; like ratio itself, like the operations of mathematics according to their pure form, they remove the aspect of time. [...] Similarly, concrete time disappears from industrial production [...] and hardly requires accumulated experience any more.[83]

Such an abstraction of the production process and of the internal organisation of the industrial enterprise would be impossible 'were it not for the fact that it contained in concentrated form the whole structure of capitalist society'.[84] The sphere within which 'rational calculation' is effective is not only subjected to strict laws, but also presupposes the absolute lawfulness of all events; i.e., this means the satisfaction of social needs is completely realised in the form of commodity exchange. The atomisation of individuals is therefore, only the mirroring in consciousness of the fact that the 'natural laws' of capitalist production have seized all the manifestations of the life of society. For the first time in history, all of society has been subjected to a unitary and uniform economic process that controls and decides upon the activities and the fate of all of its members. The commodity structure of 'things' and the lawfulness of their relations, lends to social relations the character of an innate naturalness which appears to the individual consciousness as an insurmountable fact:

> The thesis that society is subject to natural laws is ideology if it is hypostatized as immutably given by nature. But this natural legality is real as the laws of motion of the unconscious society.[85]

This *Naturgesetlichkeit* of society has a specific repercussion in the dimension of theory: what the philosophers once termed 'Life' – the leitmotif of *Minima Moralia* – has been reduced to the sphere of the private, of mere *consumption*, which at the same time is the appendage and estranged form of the material production process.

---

83   Adorno 2005, p. 344, n. 11.
84   Lukács 1971, p. 90; cf. Pollock 1933, *passim*, and 1957, p. 249.
85   Adorno 1973, pp. 355–6. [Translation slightly altered – editor's note.]

The change in the relations of production themselves depends largely on what takes place in the 'sphere of consumption', the mere reflection of production and the caricature of true life: in the consciousness and unconsciousness of individuals. Only by virtue of opposition to production, as still not wholly encompassed by this order, can men bring about another more worthy of human beings.[86]

Nevertheless, Adorno appears here to have forgotten the point of departure. His attention is directed toward the *socialised* form of reification and of exchange, to the disadvantage of what is in reality the hub of this process of socialisation of labour: the modern factory. In clearly distancing himself from Lukács, from whom he had set out, he tends to reduce the analysis of the modern capitalist firm, based on the processes of automation and of the segmentation of production activity, to a purely micro-sociological problem, instead of seeing the firm as the cellular form of the entire capitalist relation. Consequently he can ask himself the 'grimly comic' question: where is the proletariat? This cannot be explained simply by recourse to, doubtless important, historical causes.[87] The failure of revolution, the crisis of 1929, fascism and the development of the Soviet Union can perhaps explain some of the characteristic features of Adorno's thought: the jelous conserving of the fundamental categories of Marxian analysis (which were suspended by the thwarting of the 'objective movement', i.e., the tendency toward crisis and to the breakdown of the system); the de-materialisation – and nominalist reduction – of the concept, and the frustrating of history in *Negative Dialectics*, to the point that it approaches the empty categories of Heidegger. But historical factors *do not* explain how the 'fall' of the historical movement is reflected in Adorno's theory by an inexorable absence of the intermediate link that should unite it with praxis; they do not explain how this absence becomes a factor *internal* to the theory, which points to the inadequacy of the critical appropriation of the real antagonistic totality. In order to take a step beyond Critical Theory, it is necessary to proceed via the *critique of ideology* and so to grasp the weakness of the link with praxis as the immanent limit of the theory itself. If one tries, however, to escape from the limbo of completely general expressions in order to see how this limit is actually constituted, then one finds that it is not simply a matter of peculiarity of the thought of Adorno and Horkheimer, but that it goes back even further, to the beginnings of 'critical Marxism', to Lukács's *History and Class*

---

86   Adorno 1974, p. 15. [This citation does not appear in the original Italian – editor's note.]
87   The most thorough analysis in this sense appears in Krahl 1974, pp. 164–7.

Consciousness. It derives from the dialectical relationship between the abstract (quantitative) rationality of 'the existent' (of capitalist domination) and the bursting forth of the qualitative dimension. As is well known, Lukács solves the problem through a re-translation of the relationship into a dialectic of the consciousness of an absolute subject-object – the proletariat – that then becomes the guarantor of historical development and of the ineluctability of revolution. Critical Theory decisively rejects this idealistic and Hegelianising interpretation of Marxism and confronts it with the *contingent character of the materialist dialectic*,[88] without being able to point to a positive solution.

The question is still far from being solved – even with the most 'modern' Marxist interpretations which have often turned out to be satisfied with a 'scientistic' or 'theoreticist' reduction of the concept of praxis, thereby amputating the problematic of class consciousness completely. As a consequence, the basic problem of Critical Theory – the relationship between the 'block', the 'structuring' of the historical process (which Alfred Schmidt describes as the 'congealing of historical movement'), and the bursting forth of the qualitative dimension – is still *our* problem today. The mere harking to the *form* of the dialectic not only offers no solution, it even dissimulates the difficulties inherent in this relationship upon which the entire problematic of revolutionary subjectivity rests. Nor can the conflict be solved by a confrontation between the 'immediate needs' of human 'essence' and the capitalist plundering of it. Marx's analysis of commodity fetishism does not have as its outcome the 'rediscovery, beneath the mask of fetishized objectivity, of the alienated human subject',[89] but rather the unveiling of the fact that behind commodity exchange are hidden determinate *relations of production*. One must, therefore, set out from the *determinate* process of the capitalist socialisation of labour in order to correctly pose the question of class *consciousness*, which is itself inseparable from the given *material* level of class *composition*.

As noted, the problem is still far from being solved, but – and this is important – its solution cannot remain within 'philosophy' (any less than it can be exhausted in a critico-philological textual reappraisal). Nor can the solution be given by the – often appealed to – supersession of the disciplinary boundaries which isolate economics and philosophy. It cannot be a matter of translating both fields reciprocally into one another (with that one would not succeed in

---

88 Interpreting this 'contingency' empirically, Habermas has begun an explicit revision of Marxian value theory, thus breaking with Adorno's static orthodoxy (cf. Habermas 1988, pp. 227 ff.).

89 Thus, Colletti renews repeatedly – without really knowing it – the *real weak point* of Lukács analysis of alienation. Cf. Colletti 1972, p. 89.

getting much beyond traditional 'syncretism'), but of transcendening of both from the perspective of the critique of ideology.

The condition for the return of theory to historical praxis consists in making theory put its categories into motion, i.e., subsuming within it the new material created by the 'real totality' and, thereby, recovering its own analytical capacity. This presupposes, however, *the reappropriation of the critique of political economy*, as the sole means to ascend – in Marx's words – from the abstract to the concrete.

The engagement with Critical Theory, today, will have a significance (that is more than merely historical or generically cultural), if it proceeds through an exploration of its relationship to economic analysis.

CHAPTER 9

Political System, Rationalisation, and 'Social Brain'

One of the central points of Althusser's article is his assertion that the state (meaning, the modern state) is 'always been being "expanded"'.*,1 The expansion of the state and its penetration into the body of 'civil society' were already visible in the age of absolute monarchy. It is odd that none of his interlocutors have raised the need to explicate the double consequence of such a statement within the economy of Althusser's reasoning. First (and in general terms), it means unhooking the 'crisis of Marxism' from the transformations of capitalism across this century (its exclusive anchoring to the 'lacunas' at the origin of this doctrine and the Stalinist tragedy of 'actually-existing socialism'). Second, that the concept of 'ideological apparatuses' cannot help us specify the state's (historical, determinate) *modes* of being and the role it assumes in the various phases of capitalist society's development. Certainly, to some extent these consequences can be put down to the effect on Althusser of the historical experience of the French state (or better: the way in which this experience was 'internalised' by the French Communist movement). However, this alone does not suffice to grasp their specific theoretical impact – their function in both limiting and distorting the set of problematic fields (and practical tasks) that the European Left must today address.

But let us proceed in orderly fashion. I, too, believe that in establishing the difference between the state and political spheres, between the institutional and the social, Althusser still remains enmeshed in the traditional (Third Internationalist) strategic orbit of the party *qua* anti-state. And I also agree with the critical judgement that in the recent Althusser there is a sort of 'practical purism', pathologically afflicted by an oscillation between 'neo-Leninism' and 'movementism'. But what meaning do such objections have, if we hold on to the schema of Marxism's crisis-expansiveness? If it is true that Althusser's limit lies – as I also hold – in his promotion of a theoretical problematic that is inadequate to the state's transformations (and changes of form), then we must address the terms of this 'new constellation' and start to *name them*, rather than limit ourselves to repeating what is now becoming a well-worn rhetorical adage

---

* [This lecture appeared in *Discutere lo stato: posizioni a confronto su una tesi di Althusser*, Bari: De Donato 1978 – editor's note.]
1 [Althusser 1977, available in English: https://www.viewpointmag.com/2017/12/14/marxism-finite-theory-1978/ – editor's note.]

among Marxists: namely, that Marxism has always been in crisis and has overcome this crisis by rediscovering itself and developing. This schema risks turning into the umpteenth surrogate philosophy of history – with the consolatory functions that we can expect from all philosophies of history – and dangerously over-simplifying what is in fact a rather more complex and multi-faceted question. The now more-than-a-centennial itinerary of Marxism has not been only a matter of crises and development/overcoming mediated by 'returning to Marx' every now and then; it has also been marked by irrevocable collapses and the *persistence* of those acquisitions inherited by the whole contemporary world (and common sense), to the point of being 'internalised' even by the most advanced and perceptive of the so-called 'bourgeois sciences'. Bobbio is quite right, therefore, to criticise Marxists' inclination to look at things as if in every crisis we were starting again from zero, as if a hundred years of the history of capitalism (and of development of theoretical and scientific thinking) had not produced a more complex framework than the one posed in the choice: with Marx or against him. Hence the absence in this debate of non-conventional references to the most significant social scientists of this century: from Weber to Kelsen.[2] I do not believe, however, that this deficiency is reducible to a lack of cultural or epistemological openness (though this does undoubtedly afflict a great part of Marxist philosophy today). It is something rather more profound, which concerns *the very manner in which theory is developed in relation to politics* – and not incidentally, it forms a single whole with the absence in this debate of any *conceptualisation* of the history of the workers' movement (which, in Europe, has above all been a history of tragic defeats).

In the first two decades of the twentieth century, the European workers' movement was not only linked to a new *intelligentsia* that – unlike the first generation, the Kautskys, Lafargues and Plekhanovs – was formed in close contact with the most advanced currents of bourgeois culture and science. It also found itself (especially after World War I) *practising* on the new terrain of a revolutionary capitalism based on the rationalisation processes whose greatest theoretical systematisation (and anticipation) had appeared in the works of Max Weber. If we do not want to reduce Weber's reflection to a chapter of the history of thought – that it is possible to eliminate, in fine Marxist tradition, with a ritual 'ideology critique' – then we must set it in relation with the reality (with the phase of capitalist transformation) of which it was the expression. Weber's theme of 'rationality' (the oppositional couple of formal/material

---

2 It is not by chance that only Altvater and Kallscheuer have felt the need to make reference to Carl Schmitt and Ernst Forsthoff – political thinkers usually labelled as reactionaries – and an analyst of democratic theories such as Ernst Fraenkel.

rationality) broke with all positivist metaphysics of 'reflection' and forcefully introduced the dimension of *planning* [*progettualità*] into the social sciences. But what was the historico-real referent of this demand for science-planning, which constituted its own object, as against the science-reflection that limited itself to recording how social processes unfolded? To *what* crisis was it meant to be the response? The political meaning of Weber's theory is *literally impossible to grasp* outside the context of his historical period, characterised as it was by the *crisis of automatic market mechanisms* (which had regulated capitalist development up until the Great Depression) and, with this, the decline of the (more or less tacit) teleological paradigm that had represented its *twin* at the level of the historico-social sciences: the idea of an objective process endowed with an immanent direction and directed towards an End. The specific effect of the emergence of the moment of projective [*progettuale*] rationality was that science opened up to the sphere of *reproduction*. Reproduction became simultaneously the site of operation and the specific aim of science. Weber's 'rationalisation' was far from reducible to merely 'using' science so as to subdivide the production process into calculable parts; it entailed a restructuring of the entire 'social brain' by way of its institutional segmentation into special fields of knowledge ('specialisms'). And it was precisely thanks to the eminently political character of rationalisation that Weber could perfectly coherently state that 'the party of the bourgeoisie is science'. However, behind this statement, hid the seed of an incipient change in the form of the capitalist state, which had the double effect of a dissolution of the boundaries of 'civil society' and the becoming-autonomous of the 'political' in the strict sense (the politico-state sphere). The more the state inserted itself into 'civil society', thus weaving its 'private woof' into it, the more autonomous became its claims to decision and control of the social dynamic.

It would of course be farcical here to attempt to separate these implications of the formalism of reason from the problem of 'Caesarism', thus separating out Weber the scientist from the political Weber. But while it was clear to Weber that this 'autonomisation-effect' – with all its dramatic import – formed a single whole with the rationalisation of the 'social', the workers' movement was dazzled by it and, thus, lost sight of the context of morphological changes that had produced this effect. It is rather symptomatic, in this regard, that Weimar Social Democracy *theorised* and *practised* what I have elsewhere called the '"bad" autonomy of the political'[3] – understanding this to mean the reduc-

---

3 [Cf. Chapter 7 above, 'Corporatist pluralism, mass democracy, authoritarian state' – editor's note.]

tion of the latter to a technico-instrumental instance of organising economic 'legality' (note, in this regard, the role the category 'power' plays in Hilferding: an exogenous, extra-economic factor that regulates the social dynamic from without). This explains why the strategies that divided the workers' movement between the two World Wars reduced the complexity of the processes of the state's extension to the sharp alternative between 'the primacy of politics' and 'the primacy of the economy'. If Weimar Social Democracy fetishised the form of the democratic state – which it set in relation to the multiplicity of specialisms into which the 'social brain' was structured as if it were the neutral mechanism through which tasks were 'democratised' – the Communists emphasised (especially after 1928) the primacy of the economy, posing as the representatives of social insubordination against the state.

No less of a failure than the Weimar experience was that of Austrian Social Democracy, which had also tried to hold firm to the Party's class autonomy by developing, around the mid-1920s, an idea of the state as expression of the relation of class forces, thus setting it in polemic with both the German Social Democracy's hyper-institutional strategy and the 'Sovietist illusion' that had so miserably collapsed along with the council republics of Bavaria and Hungary. The symmetrical failure of the two opposing strategies followed by Central Europe's two great social-democratic parties after the shipwreck of the councilist alternative, was neither a matter of chance nor reducible to external causes (however important a role they played). The fact that Austro-Marxism[4] only drew from its theorem of the state as a parallelogram of the relation of class forces the weak corollary of entrenching the autonomy of the working class *in the social* (to the point of organising armed self-defence with the creation of the 'Schutzbund' paramilitary organisation), demands that we seriously reflect on the limits of the many of the doctrinaire positions advanced by the so-called 'third way'. That is to say, the intermediate tendency (equally critical of social democracy and of Stalinism), that brought together at the level of ideas sectors as significant as the social-democratic and communist opposition (from Paul Levi to Thalheimer and from the Left Austro-Marxism to Gramsci).

But how is it possible to measure the limits of these strategies, and their tragic outcomes, outside of the context of capitalist transformation referred to above? It is in relation to these transformations – and the complications they induced in the entire body of capitalist social organisation – that *everything that the workers' movement did not manage to see* becomes evident; and thus

---

4 Cf. Otto Bauer and Max Adler, who carried out a point-by-point critique of the institutionalist ideologies of the 'democratic state'.

also the tragic inadequacy of not only their instrumental vision of 'the political', but also the view that identifies the political as a 'reflection', 'condensation', or 'function' of the relation of class forces *in 'the social'*. No 'reflection' or 'correspondence' can overcome the dichotomy of political moment and socio-economic moment that condemned the 1920s workers' movement to subalternity and defeat. In failing to understand the intensely political content of the rationalisation process, the workers' movement allowed its adversary the possibility of *managing on its own* the contradictions that this same process – interwoven with class struggles – had induced in the mechanisms of reproduction, and the various segmentations of the 'social brain', from industrial workers to technicians and the new layer of 'specialist intellectuals' and 'intellectual functionaries'.

The emergence of a situation of 'corporatist pluralism' was the logical consequence of *this* lack of initiative from the workers' parties on the terrain defined by the new institutional tools of diffusion of power and restructuring of the social by way of its subdivision (as well as through a corporatist management of the contradictions that were thus generated in particular circles). The tragic rise and fall of the Weimar Republic directly relates to questions that are still today very important for the workers' movement. Precisely in the sense that this history amply demonstrates that when the corporatist conflicts among various sectors lead to the nullification of their decision-making powers, and so to the sclerosis of the mechanism of social reproduction – then it is always the 'decision' of those forces that prove able to maintain control of the levers of state that will prevail.

It is significant, indeed, that precisely in these years Franz Neumann and Otto Kirchheimer – two among the most important Marxist political scientists of the Weimar Republic – established a direct relation between 'pluralism' and 'the crisis of parliamentarism', conducting a critique of the Weimar Constitution as a 'Constitution *without* decision'. There is, then, a very close connection between the pluralisation of reason, the diffusion of power in specific circles, and the crisis of the traditional institutions of liberal democracy. Namely, the crisis of the illusion of governing the different 'knowledge-powers' by promoting an *only external* democratisation of the latter, as if it were a matter of neutral and non-contradictory instances that could be entirely translated into the universal-abstract forms of 'parliamentarisation'.

It is wholly legitimate to see, in these processes, the definitive crisis of the 'synthesising' function of the state-form (what Rathenau called 'political Politics') in relation to the multiplicity of specialisms – but *it is not enough*. And I say this, not so much on account of the consideration (which is, in the last analysis, voluntaristic) that the mere recognition of the existence of a 'plurality of languages' can have paralysing effects; but as much as because it fails to grasp that, from the 1929 rupture onwards, the 'political' plays again a determining role in the dynamic of conflict among the various sectors of the 'general intellect'. To push the limits of schematisation a little, we could say that while the 1920s was the period of rationalisation (issuing in 'pluralistic-corporatist' sclerosis and the jamming of the reproductive mechanisms), the 1930s were the years in which 'the political' assumed a decisive position in the governance of the crisis and the contradictions of society. *It was not, however, any sort of return to an operation of recomposition in the absolute sense.* Hence, the 'disenchantment' of the ethical universality of the state carried out by normativism and institutionalism truly did reflect an irreversible process, a point of no return. Far from coinciding with the birth of a 'total state' or 'new Leviathan', the 1930s marked the transition to a 'pluralist' order of a different type (and this also goes – as demonstrated by Neumann's 1942 research, later confirmed by other studies – for what we are accustomed to calling the 'totalitarian state' *par excellence*, the National Socialist regime).

But to say all this also means to take a sharply critical position with regard to the interpretative line that sees in the 1930s the emergence of a 'planner-state', an *authoritarian homogenisation of the political system* functioning as a 'filter' of the social dynamic. There can be no doubt that, following the 1929 crisis, there took place not only an extension of institutional apparatuses (which completed the process of the 'politicisation of the social' that had already begun with rationalisation), but a veritable change in the form of the state, which now – with the introduction of anti-cyclical policies – became an 'interventionist' state in the full sense of the word: the ultimate vector of decisions and site of a 'conscious governance' of the crisis. But this site – and here we touch on the crucial point – was not a homogeneous unit (a self-referential subjectivity) or a 'filter' devoid of contradictions, but rather the site where the conflict between the corporatist 'autonomies' (pressure groups) within the ruling bloc were unleashed, the site where they were tactically composed and recomposed. While 'the political' can take charge of the contradictions that traverse the segments of the 'social brain', it *is not able to* suppress these contradictions and it pays a high price for its 'intervention': namely, internalising – *volens nolens* – the conflict and, thus, itself fully becoming a field of contradiction. The state cannot 'plan' the contradictions (except in the ideology of its technocrats); it can only *govern* them. The result is a structural complication that involves – at the same time and *in different ways* – both the 'social' and the 'political'. What is political, here, is the very *morphology* of crisis, not the chimera of its 'suppression'. The historical significance of this change in form (which is also the origin – as Luporini has aptly noted – of the welfare state whose crisis we are today witnessing), was that it broke all residual instrumental, functionally linear relationships that still connected – like a sort of umbilical cord – the capitalism of the 1920s to the automatisms of the phase of competitive capitalism. The breaking-up of the functional relation that made the party the 'class nomenklatura' was thus dislocated 'upwards', and now also concerned the relationship between the state and the ruling class. The state became no longer the *exclusive* dispensation of the economically dominant class.[5] The problem of hegemony came to coincide – *for the capitalist class no less than for the working class* – with the question of *constructing* a ruling *bloc*.

It was here that the new terms in which the problem of political compromise was posed from the 1930s onwards laid their roots. As Suzanne de Brunhoff has rightly noted in her intervention, this compromise is the very precondition of 'Keynesian' economic policies. Is it, perhaps, a matter of chance that the crisis of these policies coincided with the decline of the social bases of the compromise that has sustained the ruling bloc until then – that is, at a moment when it was necessary to relaunch it on new bases (as in the cases of the USA and France)? And what chance can the workers' movement hope to have if it recoils from the institutional terrain that is the very theatre of *this* contradiction, leaving it up to others to play the card of compromise?

In relation to this, it is curious to note the extent to which Althusser's theory of 'interstitial social forms' conserves the inheritance of the old vision of the state as an all-embracing and uncontradictory form. Despite all their differences, this groups him with those positions – buoyant in the Italian debate today – which upholds the revolutionary character of the struggle to defend civil liberties and interprets the capitalist transformations of the last half-century as the authoritarian absorption of 'civil society' into the state. The emergence of such positions is hardly surprising when we consider that they arise from the contradictory context marked by the crisis of the welfare state (and a concomitant crisis of Marxist theory, which has proven incapable of grasping the political morphology of the contradiction and its effects 'disseminated' at the social level). It is thanks to this contradictory context (and the unpredictable alliances that result from it) that the president of Confindustria[6] had no trouble taking on the 'new economist's' clothes and offering us his own theory of 'interstices', under a banner opposite to Althusser's:

---

5 This class often was in dispute with state-interventionist policies. Exemplary in this regard was the conflictual tension that characterised entrepreneurs' relations with Roosevelt's 'New Deal'.
6 [The Italian industrialists' confederation – Editor's note.]

It seems to me that the progressive introduction of elements of socialism into our society has not produced the effect of making it a socialist society, but rather has succeeded in making it a society in which there are increasingly limited interstices into which the propulsive forces of economic activity can fit.[7]

This notwithstanding, we cannot simply wish away the fact that the relation between the politico-institutional and regional demands produced by the politicisation of the social represent an open problem of decisive significance. No longer can we put off getting to grips with this. Nor should we underestimate the significance of Althusser's critique of the concept of the 'socialisation of the political', where he highlights a real risk entailed in this latter. Namely, that it ends up advancing the socialising the political *as is*. In my view, equally important is his invitation to 'listen to politics where it happens' and where it is being made. It is possible that this passage betrays – perhaps more than Althusser would be ready to admit – a debt to the late Foucault. I do not believe, however, that Althusser goes – as has been written in this debate – *beyond* Foucault, for the simple reason that in reality he does not manage to translate Foucault's problematic of power into that of politics but remains behind on the question of 'specialised knowledges'.

Foucault's merit is not only that of having driven forward a radical critique of negative, narrow, skeletal conceptions of power, but also in shedding light on the fact that the ideology operating behind this *reductio* endows power (more or less explicitly) with a *juridical status* (according to which power is always and everywhere a power of 'veto', a 'repressive' power). For Foucault, power has a productive character – it is the production of *nexuses* and of *knowledges* – and the state is a codification of multiple power relations: 'The theory of the state and the traditional analyses of their apparatuses certainly don't exhaust the field where power is exercised and where it functions'.[8] On this point, the stimuli offered by Foucault's research are of enormous significance. His analysis of the obsolescence of the old figure of the 'universal intellectual' and the new role of 'specialised intellectuals' crosses paths both with Weber's problematic of formal rationality and (as De Giovanni has noted in a recent essay)[9] with Gramsci's problematic of the synthesis of specialisms and politics.[10] I believe,

---

7   Cf. G. Carli, 'I pensieri di un liberista', *La Repubblica*, 8 July 1978.
8   'Intellectuals and Power', in Foucault 1977, p. 213 [translation modified – editor's note].
9   De Giovanni 1977, pp. 11–35.
10 It is no chance thing, moreover, that the late Foucault expressly spoke of the 'political function of the intellectuals' [cf. Foucault 1977: https://www.radicalphilosophy.com/article/the-political-function-of-the-intellectual– editor's note].

however, that Foucault followed Gramsci's lead not only in his *merits*, but also in his *limits*. For both, indeed, power tends to be reduced to a *relation of forces*; but just as it is not enough to say that the state is the parallelogram of the relation of class forces (Gramsci), it is also necessary to establish what *form* this field of forces takes. Neither does it suffice to say that power is the terrain of conflict and thus alone possesses 'the intelligibilty of struggles, of strategies, of tactics';[11] it is also necessary to establish, within what *specific modalities* of the dissemination of Power-Knowledge, the contradictions internal to specialisms are produced (on this point, Massimo Cacciari's contributions to me seem fundamentally important).

We can only give a response to these questions – which are at the same time both theoretical and stategic – if we do not lose sight of the close interdependence between the two crucial transition processes that I have tried to bring out in this intervention: the *segmentation of the 'social brain'* and the *political morphology of the crisis*. Only by setting out from here is it possible to convert analysis of the contradictions internal to specialisms into a 'problematic of the constitution' of the new subjects emerging from the various sectors of divided knowledge. It is not enough to register the existence of the 'plurality of languages' and of cognitive 'networks' – and the irreversible crisis of grand syntheses that this entails. Nor is it enough to bring out (as is being done today in what I hold to be the most advanced level of Italian Marxist discussion) the fact that the contradiction has penetrated into specialised spheres. It is necessary to establish, rather, *what* relation exists between the specific forms in which the contradiction appears in the various segments of the 'social brain', and the particular modalities in which political intentionalities are constituted within them.

This, then, is a 'Problematic of the constitution' – but not in the sense of a ('young-Lukácsian' type) programme of philosophical foundation of class consciousness within the perspective of a new 'totality' (even if overturning the terms of the traditional idealistic one); and neither in the sense of restoring the myth of a 'constitutive subjectivity'. In this connection, Foucault has the target well in his sights when he invites us to analyse 'the mechanics of power' outside of the hypostasising metaphysics of the 'constituent subject' and of 'the role of economics in the last instance' (meaning, the doctrine of ideology and of how base and superstructure 'condition' one another). It is necessary, instead, to start out from an analysis of specific contradictions (and modalities of consti-

---

11   Foucault 1980, p. 114.

tution), avoiding falling back under the 'spell' of attributing miraculous virtues of recomposition to Need or Desire – as if these were constituted in a different world to the one defined by the *actual* political form of crisis. (By that I do not at all mean to deny the importance of certain practices that take place 'across-the-board'; but even in this case, it is necessary to establish a rigorous distinction between profound and permanent movements – for example, women's struggle – and impetuous and passing ones, not to say mere 'bubbles' ...).

At the same time, we should fundamentally criticise the illusion that sees the 'micro-physical' dissemination of power answered by the absolute centralisation of the state, an 'administrative' homogenisation of the political system under the auspices of 'authoritarian planning'. As against this 'negative apology' for the state-form, we must carry out a major effort to disaggregate what we have in recent years called the 'single mechanism' of late capitalism. We must vivisect the body and reconstruct its 'anatomy' in order to retrace the broken lines and multiple segmentations through which the contradiction operates: from production to the state, from 'civil society' to the 'political system'. In order to carry out this task, it is necessary to abandon any 'classic' linear vision of the contradiction and find new categories to designate the new objects of this discourse.[12]

This 'problematic of constitution' must first clear the terrain of any ambiguities – if, that is, we want to avoid running the risks that nestle in that weak and linear vision of the spread of politics that, having chased evolutionism out the door (rightly stressing the historic shift resulting from the extension and change-in-form of the state), lets it back in again through the window; as if politics were to be 'socialised' (and the constitution of specific subjectivities constituted into political subjects take place), without passing through the ruptures and 'disarticulations' that now characterise this 'process's' general form – from the factory to society and the state.

Althusser aptly grasps that the twin of this evolutionism – which ends up placing the accent only on the moment of participation – is the inefficacy of 'a "participation" which runs up against the wall of state power (since it can even organize it!)'.[13] But precisely for *this* reason, it is fundamentally import-

---

12 The category of 'state-process' introduced by Giuseppe Vacca can be accepted for now, on one specific condition: that we are clear that when we employ the term 'process' we are using it to allude, with an old and noble metaphor, to a new complex of phenomena that we have not yet managed to define.

13 Althusser 1977.

ant that the workers' movement does not recoil from the institutional terrain, and addressses the crucial node of the relation between 'pluralism's' various democratic institutions (from Parliament to elected assemblies, from factory and neighbourhood councils to school boards, and so on) and the *formation processes of political decision*. Otherwise, the 'socialisation of politics' will just mean a multiplying number of debating chambers and 'microparliaments' that will never manage to insinuate themselves into the actual mechanisms of political decision. Against the ideologies of participationism and decisionism (which between the two wars tragically divided the workers' movement's front), we need to pose the problem of the interweaving – the progressive convergence – of *participation* and *political decision*.

In order to arrive at this objective, it is necessary not only to theorise and analyse, but also to *practise* and *experiment* with the tangle of 'power/knowledge effects' (to take up again Foucault's concepts) that link the moment of state decision to the fragments of decision disseminated amongst the various specialisms. But to what point are the form and organisational structure of the working-class parties adequate to carrying out this difficult task of analytico-practical reconnaissance with the necessary flexibility and elasticity?

Does the degree of interweaving we have arrived at today – between the 'stratigraphic' complexity of the social and the political morphology of the development-crisis nexus – not perhaps urgently pose the question of *reforming the party itself*?

If these are the problems posed, and if it is true that they originate from the context of the transformations we have here outlined, then it follows that the 'fate' of Marxist theory and of its relation with politics, depend upon our capacity to analyse *this* context. Without this, we will not have *theories*, but only tired re-postulation or predictable reworkings of the old – and politically fruitless – scripts of a scholarship that was once (in its own way) great, but today is irreversibly defunct.

Bibliography

No Author/Editor Provided

Illustrierte Geschichte der deutschen Revolution, Berlin: Internationaler Arbeiter-Verlag, 1929

I congressi dell'Internazionale comunista. Testi, manifesti e risoluzioni, Rome: Samonà e Savelli 1970

Protokoll über die Verhandlungen des Parteitages der Spd 1912, Berlin 1912 – available at http://library.fes.de/parteitage/pdf/pt-jahr/pt-1912.pdf – accessed 3 January 2019

Il marxismo italiano degli anni sessanta e la formazione teorico-politica delle nuove generazioni, Proceedings of the Istituto Gramsci, Rome: Editori Riuniti 1972

Abendroth, Wolfgang 1969, *Aufstieg und Krise der deutschen Sozialdemokratie*, Frankfurt am Main: Stimme-Verlag

Abendroth, Wolfgang 1955, *Die deutschen Gewerkschaften. Ihre Geschichte und politische Funktion*, Heidelberg: Rothe and

Accornero, Aris 1975, 'Dove cercare le origini del taylorismo e del fordismo', *Il Mulino*, 241, September–October

Adler, Max 1919, *Demokratie und Rätesystem*, Vienna: I. Brand

Adler, Max 1922, *Die Staatsauffassung des Marxismus*, Vienna: Verlag Weiner Volksbuchhandlung.

Adler, Max 1924, 'Wladimir Ilyitsch Lenin,' in *Der Kampf*, XVII (1924), 81–89.

Adler, Max 1932, 'Zur Diskussion über Sowjetrussland,' in *Der Kampf*, XXV (1932), 215–224, 301–311.

Adler, Max 1970 (1933), 'Linkssozialismus. Notwendige Betrachtungen über Reformismus und revolutionären Sozialismus' reprinted in *Austromarxismus*, ed. Hans-Jürgen Sandkühler and Rafael de la Vega, Frankfurt am Main and Vienna: Europa Verlag, 206–260.

Adler, Max 1974, *Il socialism e gli intellettuali*, edited by L. Paggi, Bari: De Donato.

Adler, Max 1976, *Causalità e teleologia nella disputa sulla scienza*, edited by R. Racinaro, Bari: De Donato.

Adorno, Theodore W. 1973, *Negative Dialectics*, New York: Continuum Publishing Company.

Adorno, Theodore 1974, *Minima Moralia*, London: New Left Books.

Adorno, Theodore 1976, *The Positivist Dispute in German Sociology*, London: Heineman.

Adorno, Theodore 2005, 'The Meaning of Working Through the Past', in T.W. Adorno, *Critical Models*, New York: Colombia University Press.

Agosti, Aldo 1969, 'Le matrici revisioniste della "pianificazione democratica": il planismo' in *Classe*, 1, 241–60.
Albrecht, Gerhardt 1931, *Wörterbuch der Volkswirtchaft*, Vol. I, Jena: Fischer.
Althusser, Louis 1977, 'Marxism as Finite Theory'. https://www.viewpointmag.com/2017/12/14/marxism-finite-theory-1978/
Arndt, Heinz Wolfgang 2015, *The Economic Lessons of the 1930s: A Report*, London: Routledge.
Asor Rosa, Alberto 1978, 'Il Potere e la critica', *Rinascita*, 41: 31–2.
Backhaus, Hans Georg 1980, 'On the Dialectics of the Value-Form' *Thesis Eleven*, 1: 1, 99–120.
Backhaus, Hans Georg 1974, 'Materialen zur Rekonstruktion der Marxschen Werttheorie', in *Gesellschaft. Beiträge zur Marxschen Theorie 1*, Frankfurt, 52–77.
Badaloni, Nicola 1972, *Per il comunismo. Questioni di teoria*, Turin: Einaudi.
Badaloni, Nicola 1973, 'Il "meccanismo unico" nel tardo capitalismo', in *Rinascita* XXX: 20, May 18, 23–5.
Badaloni, Nicola 1975, 'Le matrici economiche e sociali del politico' in *Rinascita – Il Contemporaneo*, 32, 30, 25 July.
Badaloni, Nicola, 1975, *Il marxismo di Gramsci*. Turin: Einaudi
Barcellona, Pietro 1976, *Stato e mercato: fra monopolio e democrazia*, Bari: De Donato.
Basso, Lelio 1967, 'Introduzione' to R. Luxemburg, *Scritti politici*, edited by L. Basso, Rome: Editori Riuniti.
Bauer, Otto 1912–13, 'Die Akkumulation des Kapitals', *Die Neue Zeit* XXXI, 831–8, 862–74
Baumann, Erich 1936, 'Keynes Revision der liberalistischen Nationalökonomie', *Zeitschrift für Sozialforschung*, V, 384–405.
Bedeschi, Giuseppe 1969, 'Introduzione' to Karl Korsch, *Karl Marx* Bari: Laterza.
Berkenkopf, Paul 1928, *Die Neuorganisation der deutschen Großeisenindustrie seit der Währungsstabilisierung*, Essen: Baedeker.
Bettelheim, Charles *L'Économie Allemande sous le Nazisme. Un Aspect de la Décadence du Capitalisme*, Paris: F. Maspero.
Bloch, Ernst 1991, *The Heritage of Our Times*, Cambridge: Polity Press.
Bock, H.M. 1969, *Syndikalismus und Linkskommunismus von 1918–1923*, Meisenheim am Glan: Anton Hain.
Bodei, Remo (1975) 2014, *La civetta e la talpa. Sistema ed epoca in Hegel*, Bologna: Il Mulino.
Böhm-Bawerk, Eugen von 1896, 'Zum Abschluss des Marxschen Systems', in *Festgaben für Karl Knies*, Berlin: O. Hearing.
Böhm-Bawerk, Eugen von 1949, *Karl Marx and the Close of His System*, edited by Paul M. Sweezy, New York: Augustus M. Kelley.
Available online with Rudolph Hilferding's response: https://mises-media.s3.amazona

ws.com/Karl%20Marx%20and%20the%20Close%20of%20His%20System.pdf?file=1&type=document – accessed 27 December 2018

Bollmus, Reinhard 2006, *Das Amt Rosenberg und seine Gegner*, Munich: Oldenbourg.

Bologna, Sergio 1972, 'Class Composition and the Theory of the Origin of the Workers' Councils Movement', *Telos*, 13, Fall, 4–27.

Bonacchi, Gabriella M. 1976, 'The Council Communists Between the New Deal and Fascism', *Telos*, 30, 43–72.

Bonacchi, Gabriella M. and Claudio Pozzoli (ed.) 1976, *Capitalismo e fascismo verso la guerra. Antologia dai 'New Essays'*, Firenze: La Nuova Italia.

Borkenau, F. 1934, *Der Uebergang vom feudalen zum bürgerlichen Weltbild*, Paris: Librairie Félix Alcan and reprinted as *Wissenschaftliche Buchgesellschaft*, Dramstadt 1971.

Borkenau, F. 1987, 'The Sociology of the Mechanistic World-Picture', in *Science in Context*, 1, 1987, 109–27.

Böse, Franz 1939, *Geschichte des Vereins für Sozialpolitik 1872–1932*, Berlin: Duncker & Humblot.

Brady, Robert Alexander 1933, *The Rationalization Movement in German Industry: A Study in the Evolution of Economic Planning*, Berkeley: University of California Press.

Braunthal, Alfred 1929, 'Der Zusammenbruch der Zusammenbruchstheorie', *Die Gesellschaft*, VI, 10.

Braunthal, Alfred 1972 *Die Entwicklungstendenzen der kapitalistischen Wirtschaft*, Frankfurt a. M.: Makol Verlag.

Brendel, Cajo 1974, preface to Anton Pannekoek, *Neubestimmung des Marxismus*, Bd. 1, West Berlin: Karin Kramer Verlag.

Brooks, Sidney 1925, *America and Germany 1918–1925*, New York: The MacMillan Company.

Broszat, Martin 1981, *The Hitler State: The Foundation and Development of the Internal Structure of the Third Reich*, London: Longman.

Bukharin, Nicholai/Rosa Luxemburg 1972, *The Accumulation of Capital. An Anti-Critique and Imperialism and the Accumulation of Capital*, New York: Monthly Review Press.

Buckmiller, Michael 1973, 'Marxismus als Realität, Zur Rekonstruktion der theoretischen und politischen Entwicklung Karl Korsch', in *Uber Karl Korsch*, Jahrbuch Arbeiterbewegung, Vol. 1, edited by Claudio Pozzoli, Frankfurt am Main: Fischer, 15–85.

Cacciari, Massimo 1972, 'Sul problema dell'organizzazione. Germania 1917–1921' in *György Lukács, Kommunismus 1920–1921*, Padua: Marsilio Editore.

Cacciari, Massimo 1976, *Krisis: saggio sulla crisi del pensiero negativo da Nietzsche a Wittgenstein*, Milan: Feltrinelli.

Cacciari, Massimo 1977, *Pensiero negativo e razionalizzazione*, Venice: Marsilio.

Cacciari, Massimo 1978a, *Dialettica e critica del politico: saggio su Hegel*, Milan: Feltrinelli.
Cacciari, Massimo 1978b, 'Le forze critiche che minano il rapporto capitalistico', *Rinascita–Il Contemporaneo*, 44, 30–1.
Cacciari, Massimo 1978c, 'Trasformazione dello Stato e progetto politico', *Critica marxista*, 5.
Cacciari, Massimo 1978d, 'Alcune riflessioni sul nuovo modello' in Anna Duso, *Keynes in Italia: teoria economica e politica economica in Italia negli anni Sessanta e Settanta*, Bari: De Donato.
Cacciari, Massimo 1979, *Walter Rathenau e il suo ambiente*, Bari: De Donato.
Carandini, Guido 1978, 'Introversione del imperialismo', *Rinascita–Il Contemporaneo*, 48, November.
Cassano, Franco 1973, 'Note d'analisi sullo sviluppo capitalistico', in *Critica Marxista*, XI: 6, November–December.
Cassese, Sabino 1974, *La formazione dello stato amministrativo*, Milan: Giuffrè.
Cavazutti, F. 1978, 'Categoria negoziale e istituzioni del capitalismo monopolistico', in *Categorie giuridiche e rapporti sociali. Il problema del negozio giuridico*, edited by Cesare Salvi, Milan: Feltrinelli.
Ceppa, Leonardo 1974, 'La concezione del marxismo in Karl Korsch', in *Storia del marxismo contemporaneo*, vol. XV *Annali Feltrinelli*, Milan, 1231–59.
Cerroni, Umberto 1973, *Teoria politica e socialism*, Rome: Editori Riuniti.
Cerruti, Furio, Detlev Claussen, Hans-Jürgen. Krahl, Oskar Negt and Alfred Schmidt 1971, *Geschichte und Klassenbewusstein heute*, Amsterdam: Verlag der Munter.
Claudin, Fernando 1974, *La crisi del movimento comunista. Dal Comintern al Cominform*, Milan: Feltrinelli.
Ciliberto, Michele 1977, *Intellettuali e fascismo. Saggio su Delio Cantimori*, Bari: De Donato.
Cogoy, Mario 1987, 'Neo-Marxist Theory, Marx and the Accumulation of Capital' in *International Journal of Political Economy*, 17: 2, Summer, 11–37.
Colletti, Lucio 1966, review of *Marxismo e filosofia* in the journal, *Problemi del socialismo* 10.
Colletti, Lucio 1972, 'Bernstein and the Marxism of the Second International' in *From Rousseau to Lenin: Studies in Ideology and Society*, New York, Monthly Review Press.
Colletti, Lucio 1973, *Marxism and Hegel*, London: New Left Books
Colletti, Lucio 1975, 'Marxism and the Dialectic', in *New Left Review*, I, 93, September–October
Colletti, Lucio and Claudio Napoleoni 1970, *Il futuro del capitalismo, crollo o sviluppo?*, Bari: Laterza.
Collotti, Enzo 1978, 'Tendenze recenti della storiografia sulla repubblica di weimar' in

Lotte sociali e sistema democratico nella Germania degli anni Venti, edited by Lucio Villari, Bologna: Il Mulino.

Cunow, Heinrich 1898–99, 'Zur Zusammenbruchstheorie' in *Die Neue Zeit*, XVIII, Bd. 1, p. 430

Curi, Umberto 1978, *La razionalità scientifica*, Abano Terme: Francisci.

Czichon, Eberhard 1968, 'Der Primat den Industrie im Kartell der nationalsozialistischen Macht', *Das Argument*, 47: 168–82.

Daghini, Giairo 1971, 'Lukács' Theory of the Offensive' in *Telos*, 10, Winter, 147–54.

D'Antonio, Mariano 1978, 'Kalecki e il marxismo', *Studi storici*, XIX, 1: 17–45

Däumig, Ernst 1969 (1919), 'Die Rätesystem' in *Theorie und Praxis der Arbeiterräte*, Berlin.

Dawson, William Harbutt 1890, *Bismarck and State Socialism*, London: S. Sonnenschein & co.

De Brunhoff, Suzanne 1978, *The State, Capital and Economic Policy*, London: Pluto Press.

De Felice, Franco 1978, 'Introduzione' to Antonio Gramsci, *Quaderno 22: Americanismo e fordismo*, Turin: Einaudi.

De Giovanni, Biagio 1970, *Hegel e il tempo storico della società borghese*, Bari: Laterza.

De Giovanni, Biagio 1973, 'Marx e lo Stato', *Democrazia e diritto*, 3.

De Giovanni, Biagio 1976, *La teoria politica delle classi nel "Capitale"*, Bari: Laterza.

De Giovanni, Biagio 1977, 'Intellettuali e potere', *Critica marxista*, 6.

De Giovanni, Biagio 1978a, 'Teoria marxista e Stato', *Critica marxista*, 3.

De Giovanni, Biagio 1978b, 'Stato e movimento operaio nel marxismo contemporaneo', paper to the conference held by the Veneto Section of the Istituto Gramsci on 16–17 December 1978 in Verona, 'Movimento operaio e mondo cattolico tra società civile e Stato'.

De Giovanni, Biagio 1978c, 'Il partito: laicità e critica della "doppiezza"', *Critica marxista*, 6.

De Man, Henri 1933, *Pour un plan d'action*, Brussels: L'Eglantine.

Detlev Albers, Josef Hindels, and Lucio Lombardo Radice (eds.), 1979 *Otto Bauer und der "dritte" Weg. Die Wiederentdeckung des Austromarxismus durch Linkssozialisten und Eurokommunisten*, Frankfurt am Main: Campus.

Diehl-Thiele, Peter 1969, *Partei und Staat im Dritten Reich; untersuchungen zum Verhältnis von NSDAP und allgemeiner innerer Staatsverwaltung 1933–1945*, Munich: Beck.

Di Leo, Rita 1970, *Operai e sistema sovietico*, Rome: Laterza.

Dillard, Dudley 1942, 'Keynes and Proudhon', *Journal of Economic History*, May, 63–76.

Donolo, Carlo 1978, 'Le forme della politica nella crisi sociale', *Quaderni piacentini*, 67–8, 97–113.

Drechsler, Hano 1965, *Die sozialistische Arbeiterpartei Deutschlands*, Meisenheim am Glan: Anton Hain.

Dutschke, Rudi 1974, *Versuch, Lenin auf die Füsse zu Stellen*, Berlin: Wagenbach.

Eichholtz, Dietrich and Kurt Gossweiler 1968, 'Noch einmal: Politik und Wirtschaft 1933–1945', *Das Argument*, 47: 210–27.
Eisner, Kurt 1969, *Die Halbe macht den Räten*, Cologne: Hegener
Elben, Wolfgang 1965, *Das Problem der Kontinuität in der deutschen Revolution. Die Politik der Staatssekretàre und der militärischen Führung vom November 1918 bis Februar 1919*, Düsseldorf.
Erich Eyck, *A History of the Weimar Republic*, Vol. I, Cambridge: Harvard University Press.
Fano, Ester 1974, 'La "Restaurazione antifascista liberista". Ristagno e sviluppo economico durante il fascismo', in *Il regime fascista*, edited by Alberto Aquarone and Maurizio Vernassa, Bologna: Il Mulino.
Fano, Ester 1978, 'I paesi capitalistici dalla guerra mondiale alla crisi del '29', in *La crisi del capitalismo negli anni '20*, edited by Mario Teló, Bari: De Donato.
Farneti, Paolo 1966, *Theodor Geiger e la conscienza della società industriale*, Turin: Giappichelli.
Farneti, Paolo 1970, *Saggi sulla società industriale*, Turin: UTET.
Flechtheim, Osip. K 1969, *Die KPD in der Weimarer Republik*, Frankfurt am Main: Verlangsanstalt
Foa, Lisa (ed.) 1969, *L'Accumulazione Socialista*, Rome: Editori Riuniti.
Foucault, Michel, 1977 'The Political Function of the Intellectual', in *Radical Philosophy*, 17, summer (https://www.radicalphilosophy.com/article/the-political-function-of-the-intellectual).
Foucault, Michel 1977, 'Intellectuals and Power', in *Language, Counter-Memory, Practice*, edited by D.F. Bouchard, New York: Cornell University Press.
Foucault, Michel 1980, 'Truth and Power' in *Power/Knowledge*, edited by C. Gordon, New York: Pantheon Books.
Galli Della Loggia, Ernesto 1974, 'La III Internazionale e il destino del capitalism: l'analisi di Evghenij Varga', in *Storia del marxismo contemporaneo*, vol. XV *Annali Feltrinelli*, Milan.
Gargani, Aldo Giorgio 1975, *Il sapere senza fondamenti*, Turin: Einaudi.
Geiger, Theodor 1931 'Die Mittelschichten und die Sozialdemokratie', Die Arbeit, VIII: 617–35.
Geiger, Theodor 1932, *Die soziale Schichtung des deutschen Volkes*, Stuttgart: Enke.
Giaccaro, Giulio 1940, *Storia del Movimento Sindacale Europeo*, Florence: Sansoni.
Giairo, Daghini 1971, 'Lukács' Theory of the Offensive' in *Telos*, 10, Winter, 147–54.
Gillman, Joseph M. 1957, *The Falling Rate of Profit*, London: D. Dobson.
Giva, Denis 1977, 'Storia dell'analisi economica e teoria dello sviluppo. Note su Schumpeter', *Annali della Fondazione Luigi Einaudi*, 11: 31–98.
Giorello, Giulio 1976, 'Introduzione' in *Critica e crescita della conoscenza*, Milan: Feltrinelli.

Gorter, Herman 1918, *De Wereldrevolutie*, Amsterdam: J.J. Bos.
Gorter, Herman 1969, 'Offener Brief an den Genossen Lenin. Eine Antwort auf Lenins Broschüre: Der Radikalismus, eine Kinderkrankheit des Kommunismus', Berlin o. J., ma 1921, now in A. Pannekoek and H. Gorter, *Organisation und Taktik der ploterarischen Revolution*, hrsg. und eingelteit von Hans Manfred Bock, Frankfurt a.M.: Raubdruck.
Gossweiler, Kurt 1971, *Grossbanken, Industriemonopole, Staat; Ökonomie und Politik des staatsmonopolistischen Kapitalismus in Deutschland, 1914–1932*, Berlin: Deutscher Verlag der Wissenschaften.
Gramsci, Antonio 1992, *Prison Notebooks*, vol. I, edited and translated by J.A. Buttigieg and A. Callari, New York: Colombia University Press.
Graziani, Augusto 1977, 'Introduzione' in Joseph Schumpeter, *Il processo capitalistico. Cicli economici*, Turin: Boringhieri.
Grossman, Henryk 1929, *Das Akkumulation- und Zusammenbruchsgesetz des kapitalistischen Systems*, Leipzig: Verlag C.L. Hirschfeld.
Grossman, Henryk 1929, 'Die Aenderung des ursprünglichen Aufbauplans des Marxschen *Kapital* und ihre Ursachen', in *Archiv für die Geschichte des Sozialismus und der Arbeiterbewegung*, XIV, 305–38
Grossman, Henryk 1932, 'Die Wert-Preis-Transformation bei Marx und das Krisenproblem', *Zeitschrift für Sozialforschung*, I, 55–84.
Grossman, Henryk 1969, *Marx, die klassische Nationalökonomie und das Problem der Dynamik*, Frankfurt a.M.: Europäische Verlagsanstalt.
Grossman, Henryk 1987, 'The Social Foundations of Mechanistic Philosophy and Manufacture', in *Science in Context*, 1, 129–80.
Grossman, Henryk 1992, *The Law of Accumulation and the Breakdown of the Capitalist System*, London: Pluto Press.
Grossman, Henryk 2017, *Capitalism's Contradictions: Studies in Economic Theory before and after Marx*, edited by Rick Kuhn, Chicago: Haymarket.
Grossman, Henryk 2019, *Henryk Grossman Works, Volume 1: Essays and Letters on Economic Theory*, edited by Rick Kuhn, Leiden: Brill.
Grossman, Henryk 2021, *Henryk Grossman Works, Volume 3: The Law of Accumulation and Breakdown of the Capitalist System, Being also a Theory of Crises*, Leiden: Brill.
Grotkopp, Wilhelm 1954, *Die grosse Krise: Lehren aus der Überwindung der Wirtschaftskrise 1929/32*, Düsseldorf: Econ-Verlag.
Gurland, A. 1941, 'Technological trends and economic structure under National Socialism', *Studies in Philosophy and Social Science*, IX: 226–63.
Habermas, Jürgen 1971, *Knowledge & Human Interest*, Boston: Beacon Press.
Habermas, Jürgen 1970, 'Bedingungen für einen Revolutionierung, spätkapitalisticher Gesellschaftssysteme', in *Marx und die Revolution*, Frankfurt: Suhrkamp.

Habermas, Jürgen 1976, *Legitimation Crisis*, London: Heinemann.
Habermas, Jürgen 1988, 'Between Philosophy and Science: Marxism as Critique', *Theory and Practice*, Cambridge.
Habermas, Jürgen 1989, 'Technology and Science as "Ideology"', in *Jürgen Habermas on Society and Politics*, Boston: Beacon Press.
Habermas, Jürgen and Niklas Luhmann 1974, *Theorie der Gesellschaft oder Sozialtechnologie: was leistet die Systemforschung?*, Frankfurt: Suhrkamp.
Hajek, Milos 1972, *Storia dell'Internazionale Comunista (1921–1935)*, Rome: Editori Riuniti.
Hallgarten, George and Joachim Radkau 1974, *Deutsche Industrie und Politik von Bismarck bis heute*, Frankfurt: Europäische Verlagsanstalt.
Harms, Bernhard 1931, *Kapital und Kapitalismus*, Berlin: Hobbing.
Haupt, Georges 1986, *Aspects of international socialism, 1871–1914: essays*, Cambridge: Cambridge University Press.
Hermanin, Federico 1973, 'Ueber einige Aspekte der Akkumulations- und Krisentheorie bei Grossman und Mattick', in Federico Hermanin, Michael Lauer, Axel Schurmann, *Drei Beiträge zur Methode und Krisentheorie bei Marx*, Giessen: Achenbach, 85–111.
Hilferding, Rudolph 1927, 'Die Aufgaben der Sozialdemokratie in der Republik' in *Protokoll der Verhandlungen des sozialdemokratischen Parteitages 1927 in Kiel*, Berlin.
Hilferdin, Rudolf, 1981, *Finance Capital*, London: Routledge.
Höhne, Heinz 1969, *Der Orden unter dem Totenkopf; die Geschichte der SS*, Frankfurt: Fischer.
Hoffman, Walther Gustav et al. 1965, *Das Wachstum der deutschen Wirtschaft seit der Mitte des 19. Jahrhunderts*, Berlin: Springer Verlag.
Horkheimer, Max 1978, 'The Authoritarian State', in *The Essential Frankfurt School Reader*, edited by Andrew Arato and Eike Gebhardt. New York: Continuum.
Horkheimer, Max and Theodor W. Adorno 1962, *Sociologica*, II, Frankfurt a.M.: Europäische Verlagsanstalt.
Horkheimer, Max and Theodor W. Adorno 2002, *Dialectic of Enlightenment*, Stanford: Stanford University Press.
Ihlau, Olaf 1969, *Die roten Kämpfer. Ein Beitrag zur Geschichte der Arbeiterbewegung in der Weimarer Republik und im Dritten Reich*, Meisenheim am Glan: Politladen.
Iliardi, M. 1978, 'Società civile e mediazione politica. Una rilettura di Theodor Geiger', *Democrazia e diritto*, XVIII, 5–6: 774–82
Jacoby, Russell 1975, 'Politics of the Crisis Theory', in *Telos*, 23, Spring, 3–52.
Jay, Martin 1973, *The Dialectical Imagination*, Toronto: Little Brown.
Jenssen, Otto 1931, 'Von der Revolte zur Massenorganisationen,' in *Die Organisation* in *Klassenkampf. Die Probleme der politischen der Arbeiterklasse*, Berlin and Biaritz: Marxistische Verlagsgesellschaft.
Kalecki, Michal 1971, *Selected Essays in the Dynamics of the Capitalist Economy*, Cambridge: Cambridge University Press.

Kalecki, Michal 1996, 'Stimulating the business upswing in Nazi Germany', in *Collected Works of Michal Kalecki*, Vol. VI, Oxford: Oxford University Press.

Kauder, E. 1972, 'Austromarxism vs. Austromarginalism', *History of Political Economy*, IV, 4: 398–418.

Kautsky, Karl 1909, *The Road to Power*, available at https://www.marxists.org/archive/kautsky/1909/power/ – last accessed 3 January 2019

Kautsky, Karl 1909–1910, 'Was nun?' in *Die Neue Zeit*, XXVIII, Bd. 2.

Kautsky, Karl 1911–1912, 'Der erste Mai und der Kampf gegen den Militarismus' in *Die Neue Zeit*, XXX, Bd. 2.

Kautsky, Karl 1913–14, 'Der Imperialismus', Id., XXXII, 1913–14, Bd. 2.

Kautsky, Karl 1971, *The Class Struggle*, New York: Norton.

Kautsky, Karl 1983, *Karl Kautsky. Selected Political Writings*, P. Goode (ed.), London: MacMillan.

Keynes, John Maynard 1919, *The Economic Consequences of the Peace*, London: MacMillan

Keynes, John Maynard 2010 [1926], 'The End of Laissez-Faire', *Essays in Persuasion*, Basingstoke: Palgrave Macmillan.

Keynes, John Maynard 1936, *The General Theory of Employment, Interest, and Money*, London: MacMillan.

Kirchheimer, Otto 1941a, 'Changes in the Structure of Political Compromise', *Studies in Philosophy and Social Science*, IX: 264–89.

Kirchheimer, Otto 1941b, 'The Legal Order of National Socialism', *Studies in Philosophy and Social Science*, IX: 456–75.

Kirchheimer, Oskar 1964, 'Weimar und was dann?' in *Politik und Verfassung*, Frankfurt: Suhrkamp.

Kocka, Jürgen 1969, *Unternehmensverwaltung und Angestelltenschaft am Beispiel Siemens 1874–1914: Zum Vertialtnis von Kapitalismus und Burokratie in der deutschen Industrialisierung*, Stuttgart: Klett.

Kocka, Jürgen 1972, 'Theorieprobleme der Sozial- und Wirtschaftsgeschichte', in *Geschichte und Soziologie*, edited by Hans-Ulrich Wehler, Cologne: Kiepenheuer & Witsch.

Kocka, Jürgen 1977, *Angestellte zwischen Faschismus und Demokratie: zur politischen Sozialgeschichte der Angestellten, USA 1890–1940 im internationalen Vergleich*, Göttingen: Vandenhoeck und Ruprecht.

Korsch, Karl 1912, 'Die Fabian Society', in *Die Tat*, IV: 8, November, 422–7.

Korsch, Karl 1933, 'Uber einige grundsätzliche Voraussetzungen für eine materialistische Diskussion der Krisentheorie', *Proletarier*, I, no. 1, Feb., 20–5. Available: https://www.marxists.org/archive/korsch/1933/crisis-theory.htm – last accessed 7 January 2019.

Korsch, Karl 1938, 'Economics and Politics in Revolutionary Spain', *Living Marxism* IV, May 3.

Available: https://www.marxists.org/archive/korsch/1938/economics-politics-spain.ht m – last accessed 6 January 2019.
Korsch, Karl 1938, 'Collectivisation in Spain', ibid., IV (April 6, 1939). Available at: https://www.marxists.org/archive/korsch/1939/collectivization.htm – last accessed 6 January 2019
Korsch, Karl 1968, *Arbeitsrecht für Betriebsräte (1922)*, Frankfurt am Main and Vienna: Europäische Verlagsanstalt.
Korsch, Karl 1970, *Marxism and Philosophy*, London: New Left Books.
Korsch, Karl 1971, 'Krise des Marxismus' (1931), in K. Korsch, *Die materialistiche Geschichtsauffassung*, hrsg. von E. Gerlach, Frankfurt a.M.: Europäische Verlagsanstalt.
Korsch, Karl 1975, 'What Is Socialisation?' in *New German Critique*, 6 Fall, 60–81.
Korsch, Karl 1977, 'Some Fundamental Proposition for a Materialist Discussion of Crisis Theory' (1938) in *Karl Korsch: Revolutionary Theory*, edited by D. Kellner, Texas: University of Texas Press.
Korsch, Karl 2016, *Karl Marx*, Leiden: Brill.
K. Korsch, P. Mattick, A. Pannekoek 1974, *Zusammenbruchstheorie des Kapitalismus oder revolutionäres Subjekt* Berlin: Karin Kramer Verlag.
Krahl, Hans-Jürgen 1971, 'Produktion und Klassenkampf', in *Konstitution und Klassenkampf*, Frankfurt: Verlag Neue Kritik Okt.
Krahl, Hans-Jürgen 1974, 'The Political Contradictions in Adorno's Critical Theory', *Telos*, 21, Fall, 164–7.
Krämer-Badoni, Thomas 1978, 'Crisi e potenziale di crisi nel capitalismo avanzato', in *Stato e crisi delle istituzioni*, edited by Lelio Basso, Milan: Mazzotta.
Krüger, Walter 1927, *Die moderne Kartellorganisation der deutschen Stahlindustrie*, Leipzig: W. de Gruyter.
Kuhn, Rick 2007, *Henryk Grossman and the Recovery of Marxist Theory*, Urbana and Chicago: University of Illinois Press.
Labriola, Antonio 1975, *Lettere a Benedetto Croce, 1885–1904*, Naples: Istituto Italiano per gli Studi Storici.
Lademacher, Horst (ed.) 1967, *Die Zimmerwald Linke. Protokolle und Korrespondenz*, Den Haag-Paris.
Laufenberg, Heinrich 1914, *Der politische Streick*, Stuttgart: J.H.W. Dietz Nachf.
Lederer, Emil 1940, *State of the masses; the threat of the classless society*, New York: Norton.
Lenin, Vladimir Illich 1960a, "What the 'Friends of the People' are and How They Fight the Social-Democrats" (1894), *Collected Works 1*, Moscow: Progress Publishers.
Lenin, Vladimir Illich 1960b, 'Once More on the Theory of Realisation' (1899), *Collected Works 4*, Moscow: Progress Publishers.

Lenin, Vladimir Illich 1960c, 'Reply to Mr. P. Nezhdanov' (1899), *Collected Works* 4, Moscow: Progress Publishers.
Lenin, Vladimir Illich 1964a, 'The Draft Resolution Proposed by the Left Wing at Zimmerwald' (1915), *Collected Works 21*, London: Lawrence and Wishart.
Lenin, Vladimir Illich 1964b, 'Opportunism and the Collapse of the Second International' (1916), in *Collected Works 22*, Moscow: Progress Publishers
Lenin, Vladimir Illich 1964c, 'Imperialism, the Highest Stage of Capitalism' (1916) in *Collected Works 22*, Moscow: Progress Publishers
Lenin, Vladimir Illich 1971, *Che fare?*, Turin: Einaudi.
Leser, Norbert 1968, *Zwischen Reformismus und Bolschewismus. Der Austromarxismus als Theorie und Praxis* Vienna: Europa Verlag.
Levi, Paul 1920, 'Die politische Lage in Deutschland', in *Die kommunistische Internationale*, 14, November.
Levi, Paul 1969, 'Unser Weg. Wider den Putschismus', in *Zwischen Spartakus und Sozialdemokratie*, Frankfurt am Main: Schriften, Aufsätze, Reden und Briefe.
Lippe, Rudolf zur 1974, 'Objektiver Faktor Subjektivität', in *Kursbuch*, 35, April, 1–35.
Lippi, Marco 1979, *Value and Naturalism in Marx*, London: NLB.
Lorwin, Luis H. 1931, *The Problem of Economic Planning*, Amsterdam.
Lowy, Michael 2012, 'Rosa Luxemburg's Conception of "Socialism" or "Barbarism"' in *On Changing the World: Essays in Political Philsophy from Karl Marx to Walter Benjamin*, Chicago: Haymarket.
Ludwig, E. 1920, 'Die Entwicklung der Arbeiterräte,' speech delivered to the IV KPD Congress April 14–15, 1920, in *Die Internationale*, II, 23, June 1.
Ludz, Peter 1967, 'Der Begriff der "demokratischen Diktatur" in der politischen Philosophie von Georg Lukacs', in Georg Lukacs, *Schriften zur Ideologie und Politik*, Neuwied und Berlin.
Lukács, Georg 1971, *History and Class Consciousness*, London: Merlin.
Lukács, Georg 1972, in 'Opportunism and Putschism', *Political Writings, 1919–1929*, London: New Left Books.
Luporini, Cesare 1974, *Dialettica e materialismo*, Rome: Editori Riuniti.
Luxemburg, Rosa, 1916, *The Junius Pamphlet*, available at https://www.marxists.org/archive/luxemburg/1915/junius/index.htm – last accessed 3 January 2019
Luxemburg, Rosa 1919, *Rede zum Programm gehalten auf Gründungsparteitag der kommunistischen Partei Deutschlands [Spartakusbund] am 29–31 Dezember 1918*, Berlin: Rote 'Fahne'.
Luxemburg, Rosa 1972, Rosa Luxemburg/ Bukharin, Nicholai, *The Accumulation of Capital. An Anti-Critique and Imperialism and the Accumulation of Capital*, New York: Monthly Review Press.
Luxemburg, Rosa 2008, R. Luxemburg, 'The Mass Strike, the Political Party, and the Trade Unions', in *The Essential Rosa Luxemburg*, H. Scott ed., Chicago: Haymarket.

Maier, Charles S. 1974, 'Strukturen kapitalistischer Stabilität in den zwanziger Jahren', in Winkler (ed.) 1974.
Maier, Charles S. 1975, *Recasting Bourgeois Europe. Stabilization in France, Germany and Italy in the Decade after World War I*, Princeton: Princeton University Press.
Maldonado, Tomás 2002, *Tecnica y cultura: el debate alemán entre Bismark y Weimar*, Buenos Aires: Infinito.
Mandel, Ernest 1970, *Controle Ouvrier, Conseils Ouvriers, Autogestion*, Paris: François Maspero.
Mandelbaum, Kurt 1926, *Dia Erörterungen innerhalb der deutschen Sozialdemokratie über das Problem des Imperialismus (1895–2014)*, Frankfurt a.M.
Mandelbaum, Kurt and Gerhard Mayer 1934, 'Zur Theorie der Planwirtschaft', *Zeitschrift für Sozialforschung*, III, pp. 228–62.
Mandelbaum, Kurt and Friedrich Pollock (under pseudonym, 'Kurt Baumann') 1933, 'Autarkie und Planwirtschaft', *Zeitschrift für Sozialforschung*, II, 79–103.
Manganaro, P. 1969, 'La teoria dei consigli operai nel pensiero di Korsch', in *Giovane critica*, 20, 74–7.
Marcuse, Herbert 1941, 'Some Social Implications of Modern Technology', *Studies in Philosophy and Social Science*, IX: 414–39.
Marcuse, Herbert 1969, *Negations*, Boston: Beacon Press.
Marramao, Giacomo 1975, 'Ideologia e rapport sociali' in *Rinascita–Il Contemporaneo*, XXXII, n. 30, July, 23–5.
Marramao, Giacomo 1977, *Austromarxismo e socialismo di sinistra fra le due guerre*, Milan: La Pietra.
Marramao, Giacomo 1977 'Marx e il marxismo: il nesso economia-politica' in *Rinascita*, 2.
Marramao, Giacomo 1979, 'Zum problem der Democratie in der politischen Theorie Otto Bauers' in Detlev Albers, Josef Hindels, and Lucio Lombardo Radice (eds.), *Otto Bauer und der "dritte" Weg. Die Wiederentdeckung des Austromarxismus durch Linkssozialisten und Eurokommunisten* (Frankfurt/ Main: Campus, 1979).
Marx, Karl 1968, *Theories of Surplus Value*, Part II, Moscow: Progress Publishers.
Marx, Karl 1973, *Grundrisse*, London: Penguin.
Marx, Karl 1976a, *Capital*, Vol. I, Harmondsworth: Penguin.
Marx, Karl 1976b, *The Poverty of Philosophy*, in *Marx and Engels, Collected Works*, Vol. 6, London: Lawrence and Wishart.
Marx, Karl 1981, *Capital* Vol. III, Harmondsworth: Penguin.
Marx, Karl 1988 (1868), letter to Engels dated 30 April 1868, in *Marx and Engels, Collected Works*, vol. 43, London: Lawrence and Wishart.
Maschke, Erich 1964, *Grundzüge der deutschen Kartellgeschichte bis 1914*, Dortmund: Ardey Verlag.
Mason, Timothy 1968, 'Primat der Industrie? Eine Erwiderung', *Das Argument*, 47: 193–209.

Mason, Timothy 1972, 'The Primacy of Politics – Politics and Economics in National Socialist Germany' in *Nazism and the Third Reich*, edited by Henry Turner, New York: Quadrangle.

Mason, Timothy 1993, *Social Policy in the Third Reich: The Working Class and the 'National Community'*, Providence: Berg.

Matthias, Erich 1957, 'Kautsky und der Kautskyanismus. Die Funktion der Ideologie in der deutschen Sozialdemokratie vor dem ersten Weltkrieg,' in *Marxismusstudien*, II, Tübingen: J.C.B. Mohr.

Mattick, Paul 1959, 'Werttheorie und Kapitalakkumulation', in C. Rolshausen, *Kapitalismus und Krise. Eine Kontroverse um das Gesetz des tendentziellen Falls der Profitrate*, Frankfurt a.M. and Vienna: Europa Verlag 1970, 7–34 and available at: https://www.marxists.org/archive/mattick-paul/1959/value-theory.htm – last accessed 7 January 2019.

Mattick, Paul 1969, *Marx and Keynes: The Limits of the Mixed Economy*, Boston: Porter Sargent Publisher – also available at: https://www.marxists.org/archive/mattick-paul/1969/marx-keynes/index.htm – last accessed 4 January 2019.

Mattick, Paul 1972, *Intégration capitaliste et rupture ouvrière*, edited by Robert Paris, Paris: E.D.I.

Mattick, Paul 1973, 'Zur Marxschen Akkumulation- und Zusammenbruchstheorie', in *Rätekorrespondenz*, 4 (1934) now in K. Korsch, P. Mattick, A. Pannekoek, *Zusammenbruchstheorie des Kapitalismus oder revolutionäres Subjekt* Berlin: Karin Kramer Verlag.

Mattick, Paul 1973b, 'Marxismus und die Unzulänglichkeiten der Arbeiterbewegung', in *Jahrbuch Arbeiterbewegung – Theorie und Geschichte*, Bd. 1, *Über Karl Korsch*, edited by Claudio Pozzoli, Frankfurt a. M. 1973.

Mattick, Paul 1974, 'Krisen und Krisentheorien', in *Krisen und Krisentheorien*, Frankfurt a.M.: Fischer Taschenbuchverlag [in English: https://www.marxists.org/archive/mattick-paul/1974/crisis/index.htm – accessed 5 January 2019].

Mattick, Paul 1974, *Kritik der Neomarxisten*, Frankfurt a. M.: Fischer.

Merli, Stefano 1975, *Fronte antifascista e politica di classe. Socialisti e comunisti in Italia 1923–1939*, Bari: De Donato.

Mitchell, Wesley C. 1927, *Business Cycles: The Problem and its Setting*, New York: NBER.

Mommsen, Hans 1966, *Beamtentum in Dritten Reich*, Stuttgart: Deutsche Verlagsanstalt.

Mommsen, Hans, Dietmar Petzina and Bernd Weisbrod 1974, *Industrielles System und politische Entwicklung in der Weimarer Republik*, Düsseldorf: Droste Verlag.

Mommsen, Wolfgang J. 1984, *Max Weber and German Politics, 1890–1920*, Chicago: University of Chicago Press.

Mommsen, Wolfgang 1989, *The Political and Social Theory of Max Weber*, Chicago: University of Chicago Press.

Mondadori, Marco 1978, 'Struttura delle teorie scientifiche e progresso', *Quaderni della Fondazione Feltrinelli*, 2: 43–74.

Morf, Otto 1951, *Das Verhältnis von Wissenschaftstheorie und Wirtschaftsgeschichte bei Karl Marx*, Bern: A. Francke.

Morf, Otto 1970, *Geschichte und Dialektik in der politischen Oekonomie*, Frankfurt am. Main: Oelmuller.

Moszkowska, Natalie 1929, *Das Marxsche System. Ein Beitrag zu dessen Ausbau*, Berlin: Wilhelm Kromphardt.

Moszkowska, Natalie 1935, *Zur Kritik moderner Krisentheorien*, Prague: M. Kacha.

Moszkowska, Natalie 1974, *Per la critica delle teorie moderne delle crisi*, Turin: Musolini Editore.

Müller, Richard 1918, 'Das Rätesystem in Deutschland', *Theorie und Praxis der Arbeiterräte* Available at: https://www.sozialismus.info/2002/08/10026/ – last accessed 3 January 2019.

Negt, Oskar 1969, 'Marxismus als Legitimationswissenschaft. Zur Genese der stalinistischen Philosophie', in Abram Deborn and Nikolai Bukharin, *Kontroversen über dialektischen und mechanistischen Materialismus*, Frankfurt: Suhrkamp.

Negt, Oskar 1971, *Soziologische Phantasie und exemplarisches Lernen*, Frankfurt: Europäische Verlag.

Negt, Oskar 1975–6, 'Theory, Empiricism and Class Struggle: On the Problem of Constitution in Korsch,' *Telos*, 26, Winter, 120–42.

Negt, Oskar and Alexander 2016 (1972), *Public Sphere of Experience. Analysis of Bourgeois and Proletarian Public Space*, London: Verso.

Neuberg, A. 1970, *Armed Insurrection*, London New Left Books.

Neumann, Franz 1937, 'Der Funktionswandel des Gesetzes im Recht der bürgerlichen Gesellschaft', *Zeitschrift für Sozialforschung*, VI: 542–96.

Neumann, Franz 1943, *Behemoth: the Structure and Practice of National Socialism*, London: Victor Gollancz.

Neusüss, Christel 1972, *Imperialismus und Weltmarktbewegung des Kapitals*, Erlangen: Politladen.

Nolte, Ernst 1968, *Die Krise des liberalen Systems und die faschistischen Bewegungen*, Munich: Piper.

Offe, Claus 1972, *Strukturprobleme des kapitalistischen Staates*, Frankfurt: Suhrkamp.

Offe, Claus 1973, 'Krisen des Krisenmanagement. Elemente einer politischen Krisentheorie', in *Herrschaft und Krise*, edited by Martin Jänicke, Opladen: Westdeutscher Verlag.

Offe, Claus and Volke Ronge 1978, 'Tesi per una fondazione teorica della nozione di "Stato capitalistico" e per una metodologia materialistica della politologia', in *Stato e crisi delle istituzioni*, edited by Lelio Basso, Milan: Mazzotta.

Pannekoek, Anton 1911–12, 'Massenaktion und Revolution', in *Die Neue Zeit*, XXX, Bd. 2

Pannekoek, Anton 1912–13, 'Maxistische Theorie und revolutionäre Tatik', Id. XXXI, 1912–13, Bd. 1.
Pannekoek, Anton 1912–13, 'Dietzgen Werk' in *Die Neue Zeit*, XXXI, Bd. 2.
Pannekoek, Anton 1977, 'The Theory of the Collapse of Capitalism' (1934), *Capital and Class*, 1, 76, spring, 62–81.
Panzieri, Raniero 1964, 'Plusvalore e pianificazione. Appunti di lettura del *Capitale*', *Quaderni Rossi* 4.
Panzieri, Raniero 1972, *La ripresa del marxismo-leninismo in Italia*, edited by Danilo Lanzardo, Milan: Quaderni sapere.
Panzieri, Raniero 1972, Raniero Panzieri, 'Relazione sul neocapitalismo' (1961) in *La ripresa del marxismo-leninismo in Italia*, edited by Danilo Lanzardo, Milan: Quaderni sapere.
Pasquinelli, C. 1970, 'Ne Lukács, ne Korsch', in *Critica marxista* 4, 178–196.
Perulli, Paolo 1970, 'Note sui Delegati', *Contropiano*, 2.
Petzina, Dietmar 1968, *Autarkiepolitik im Dritten Reich*, Stuttgart: Deutsche Verlagsanstalt.
Pizzorno, Alessandro 1977, 'Scambio politico e identità collettiva nel conflitto di classe', in *Conflitti in Europa*, edited by. C. Crouch and A. Pizzorno, Milan: Etas Libri.
Plessen, Marie-Louise 1975, *Die Wirksamkeit des Vereins für Socialpolitik von 1872–1890: Studien zum Katheder- und Staatssozialismus*, Berlin: Duncker & Humblot.
Polanyi, Karl 1944, *The Great Transformation*, Boston: Beacon Press.
Pollock, Friedrich 1923, *Die Geldtheorie von Karl Marx*, Frankfurt a.M. – unpublished dissertation.
Pollock, Friedrich 1933, 'Bemerkungen zur Wirtschaftskrise', *Zeitschrift für sozialforschung*, II: 321–52.
Pollock, Friedrich 1938, 'Die gegenwärtige Lage des Kapitalismus und die Aussichten einer planwirtschaftlichen Neuordnung', *Zeitschrift für Sozialforschung*, I, 8–27.
Pollock, Friedrich 1941, 'Is National Socialism a New Order', *Studies in Philosophy and Social Science*, IX: 440–55.
Pollock, Friedrich 1957, *Automation: A Study of its Economic and Social Consequences*, New York: F.A. Praeger.
Pollock, Friedrich 1971, *Die planwirtschaftlichen Versuche in der Sowjetunion* (1929) reprinted Frankfurt a. M.: Verlag Neue Kritik.
Pollock, Friedrich 1973, *Teoria e prassi dell'economia di piano*, edited by Giacomo Marramao, Bari: De Donato.
Pozzoli, Claudio (ed.) 1973, *Über Karl Korsch*, Jahrbuch Arbeiterbewegung, Vol. 1, edited by Claudio Pozzoli, Frankfurt am Main: Fischer.
Pozzoli, Claudio 1976, 'Paul Mattick e il comunismo dei consigli' in *Il comunismo difficile. I comunisti dei consigli e la teoria marxiana dell'accumulazione e delle crisi*, Bari: Dedalo.

Preiser, Erich 1924, 'Das Wesen der Marxschen Krisentheorie', in *Wirtschaft und Gesellschaft. Festschrift für Franz Oppenheimer zu seinem 60. Geburtstag*, Frankfurt a. M.
Procacci, Giuliano 1960, 'Antonio Labriola e la revisione del marxismo attraverso l'epistolario con Bernstein e con Kautsky', in *Annali Feltrinelli*, vol. III, Milan: Feltrinelli.
Rabinach, A.G. 1974, 'Toward a Marxist theory of fascism and national socialism', *New German Critique*, 3.
Racinaro, Roberto 1978, 'Introduzione' in Hans Kelsen, *Socialismo e Stato. Una ricerca sulla teoria politica del marxismo*, Bari: De Donato.
Rathenau, Walter 1925 'Der neue Staat' in *Gesammelte Schriften*, Bd. V, Berlin: Fischer.
Reichelt, Helmut 1970, *Zur logischen Struktur des Kapitalbegriffs bei Karl Marx*, Frankfurt a. M.
Reinicke, H. 1971, 'Ware und Dialektik – Zur Konstitution des bürgerlichen Bewusstseins bei Sohn-Rethel', *Politikon* 36, April–May, 22–33
Reinicke, H. 1974, *Ware und Dialektik*, Darmstadt-Neuwied: Luchterhand.
Renner, Karl 1917, *Marxismus, Krieg und Internationale*, Stuttgart: Dietz.
Renner, Karl 1924, *Die wirtschaft als gesamtprozess und die sozialisierung*, Berlin: Dietz.
Ritter, Gerhard 1969–73, *The Sword and the Scepter: The Problem of Militarism in Germany*, Vol. III Coral Gables: University of Miami Press.
Ritter, Gerhard Albert and Susanne Miller 1975, *Die deutsche Revolution 1918–1919*, Hamburg: Hofmann und Campe.
Rolshausen, C. 1970, *Kapitalismus und Krise. Eine Kontroverse um das Gesetz des tendentziellen Falls der Profitrate*, Frankfurt a.M. and Vienna: Europa Verlag.
Rosdolsky, Roman 1973, *Studien über revolutionäre Taktik*, West Berlin: Verlag für das Studium der Arbeiterbewegung.
Rosdolsky, Roman 1980, *The Making of Marx's Capital*, London: Pluto Press.
Rosenberg, Arthur 1972, *Origini della Repubblica di Weimar*, Florence: Sansoni.
Rosenberg, Hans 1967, *Grosse Depression und Bismarckzeit: Wirtschaftsablauf, Gesellschaft und Politik in Mitteleuropa*, Frankfurt: Ullstein.
Rossi, Pietro 1958, 'Introduzione' in Max Weber, *Il metodo delle scienze storico sociali*, Turin: Einaudi.
Rossi, Pietro 1971, *Lo storicismo tedesco contemporaneo*, Turin: Einaudi.
Roth, Gunther 1971, *I Socialdemocratici nella Germania di Weimar*, Bologna: Il Mulino.
Roth, Karl Heinz 1974, *Die "andere" Arbeiterbewegung*, Munich: Trikont.
Ruffolo, G. 1978, 'Per un approccio scientifico alla democrazia socialista', *Mondoperaio*, XXXI, 10: 56–66.
Rühle, Otto (pseudonym of Carl Steuermann) 1931, *Weltkrise-Weltwende. Kurs auf Staatskapitalismus*, Berlin: Fischer Verlag.
Rusconi, Gian Enrico 1968, *La teoria critica della società*, Bologna: Il Mulino
Rusconi, Gian Enrico 1969, 'Karl Korsch e la strategia consigliare-sindicale,' in *Problemi del Socialismo*, XV, July–August, 767–77.

Rusconi, Gian Enrico 1971, 'Contro Kautsky, contro Lenin', introduction to Karl Korsch, *Il materialismo storico*, Bari Laterza.
Rusconi, Gian Enrico 1974, 'La problematica dei consigli in Karl Korsch,' *Annali Feltrinelli*, XV. Milan, 1197–1230.
Rusconi, Gian Enrico 1975, 'Tensione tra scienza e azione politica in Karl Korsch', introduction to K. Korsch, *Dialettica e scienza nel marxismo*, Bari: Laterza.
Rusconi, Gian Enrico 1975, 'Introduction to "What Is Socialisation?"' in *New German Critique*, 6, Fall, 48–59
Rusconi, Gian Enrico 1975, 'Introduzione', K. Korsch, *Scritti politici*, Bari: Laterza
Rusconi, Gian Enrico 1976, 'Korsch's Political Development,' *Telos*, 27, Spring, 61–78.
Rusconi, Gian Enrico 1977, *La crisi di Weimar*, Turin: Einaudi.
Rusconi, Gian Enrico and Alfred Schmidt 1972, *La Scuola di Francoforte. Origini e significato*, Bari: De Donato.
Rutigliano, Enzo 1974, *Linkskommunismus e rivoluzione in occidente*, Bari: Dedalo.
Ryder, A.J. 1967, *The German Revolution of 1918*, Cambridge: Cambridge University Press.
Salvadori, Massimo 1974, 'La concezione del processo rivoluzionario in Kautsky (1891–1922)' in *Storia del marxismo contemporaneo*, vol. XV *Annali Feltrinelli*, Milan, 26–80.
Salvadori, Massimo 1990, *Karl Kautsky and the Socialist Revolution (1880–1938)*, London: Verso.
Sandküler, H.J. and R. de la Vega 1970a, *Marxismus und Ethik*, Frankfurt am Main: Suhrkamp.
Hans-Jürgen Sandkühler and Rafael de la Vega (ed.) 1970b, *Austromarxismus*, Frankfurt am Main and Vienna: Europa Verlag, 206–60.
Santambrogio M. 1978, 'Sulla logica delle teorie scientifiche', *Quaderni della Fondazione Feltrinelli*, 2: 75–138.
Schacht, Hjalmar 1949, *Account Settled*, London: Weidenfeld and Nicolson.
Schmidt, Alfred 1968, 'Zum Erkenntnisbegriff der Kritik der politischen Oekonomie', in *Kritik der politischen Oekonomie heute. 100 Jahre Kapital*, edited by W. Euchner and A. Schmidt, Frankfurt a. M.: Europäischen Verlag.
Schmidt, Alfred 1970, 'Geschichte und gegenwärtige Bedeutung', *Zeitschrift für Sozialforschung*, Munich: Kösel Verlag.
Schmidt, Alfred 1971, *Geschichte und Struktur*, Munich: Hanser.
Schmitt, Carl 1999, 'The Further Development of the Total State in Germany', in *Four Articles 1931–1938*, Washington: Plutarch Press.
Schmitt, Carl 1988, *The Crisis of Parliamentary Democracy*, Boston, MA: MIT Press.
Schmitt, Carl 2004, *Legality and Legitimacy*, Durham: Duke University Press.
Schmitt, Carl 2008, 'The Age of Neutralisations and Depoliticizations' in *The Concept of the Political*, Chicago: University of Chicago Press.
Schneider, Dieter and Rudolf F. Kuda 1969, *Mitbestimmung*, Munich: Taschenbuch.

Schumpeter, Joseph 1908, Das Wesen und der Hauptinhalt der theoretischen Nationalökonomie, Leipzig, Duncker & Humblot.
Schumpeter, Joseph 1911, *Theorie der wirtschaftlichen Entwicklung*, Leipzig: Duncker & Humblot.
Schumpeter, Joseph 1928, 'The Instability of Capitalism', *The Economic Journal*, 38, 151: 361–86.
Schumpeter, Joseph 1939, *Business Cycles*, New York: MacGraw Hill.
Schumpeter, Joseph 1942, *Capitalism, socialism, and democracy*, London: Harper and Brothers.
Schumpeter, Joseph 1952, *Aufsätze zur ökonomischen Theorie*, Tübingen: JCB Mohr.
Schumpeter, Joseph 1954, Economic doctrine and method, an historical sketch, Oxford: Oxford University Press.
Schumpeter, Joseph 1974, *Capitalism, Socialism and Democracy*, London: Unwin University Books.
Schumpeter, Joseph 1991, *Imperialism and Social Classes*, Philadelphia: Orion.
Schweitzer, Arthur 1964, *Big business in the Third Reich*, Bloomington: Indiana University Press.
Shackle, George Lennox Sharman 1967, *The Years of High Theory*, Cambridge: Cambridge University Press.
Sohn-Rethel, Alfred 1971a, *Warenform und Denkform*, Frankfurt am. Main: Europa Verlag.
Sohn-Rethel, Alfred 1971b, *Geistige und körperliche Arbeit*, Frankfurt am. Main: Suhrkamp.
Sohn-Rethel, Alfred 1987, *The Economy and Class Structure of German Fascism*, London: Free Association.
Sontheimer, Kurt 1968, 'Der Tatkreis', in *Von Weimar zu Hitler, 1930–1933*, edited by Gotthard Jasper, Cologne: Kiepenheuer & Witsch.
Spinella, Mario 1966, 'Karl Korsch e gli sviluppi del marxismo', in Karl Korsch, *Marxismo e filosofia* Milan: Sugarco.
Stawar, André 1973, *Liberi saggi marxisti*, Florence: La nuova Italia.
Sternberg, Fritz 1926, *Der Imperialismus*, Berlin: Malik Verlag.
Sternberg, Fritz 1930, *Eine Umwälzung der Wissenschaft? Kritik des Buches von Henryk Grossman. Zugleich eine positive Analyse des Imperialismus*, Berlin: R.L. Prager.
Sultan, Herbert 1973 (1922), *Gesellschaft und Staat bei Karl Marx and Friedrich Engels*, Jena: Nachdruck Grießen.
Sweezy, Paul. M. 1968, *The Theory of Capitalist Development*, New York: Monthly Review Press.
Tafuri, Manfredo 1971, 'Austromarxismo e città. "Das Rote Wien"', in *Contropiano*, 2.
Tarantelli, Ezio 1978, *Il ruolo economico del sindacato e il caso italiano*, Bari: Laterza.
Therborn, Göran 1970, 'The Frankfurt School', *New Left Review*, 63, Sept.–Oct., 65–96.

Tjaden, Karl Hermann 1964, *Struktur und Funktion der KPD-Opposition*, Meisenheim am Glan: Anton Hain.
Tormin, Walter 1954, *Zwischen Rätediktatur und sozialer Demokratie. Die Geschichte der Rätebewegung in der deutschen Revolution 1918–1919*, Düsseldorf: Droste-Verlag.
Tronti, Mario 1972, 'Workers and Capital,' *Telos*, 14, Winter.
Tronti, Mario 1975, *Hegel politico*, Rome: Istituto della Enciclopedia Italiana.
Trottmann, Martin 1956, *Zur Interpretation und Kritik der Zusammenbruchstheorie von Henryk Grossman*, Zurich.
Tugan-Baranowski, M.J. 1901, *Studien zur Theorie und Geschichte der Handelskrisen in England*, Jena: Verlag von Gustav Fischer.
Tugan-Baranowski, M.J. 1966, *Modern Socialism in its Historical Development*, New York: Russell and Russell.
Vacatello, Marzio 1968, *Lukács: da 'Storia e coscienza di classe' al giudizio sulla cultura Borghese*, Florence: La Nuova Italia.
Vacca, Giuseppe 1976, *Quale democrazia*, Bari: De Donato.
Vacca, Giuseppe 1969, *Lukacs o Korsch*, Bari.
Vacca, Giuseppe 1976, 'Una figura della scissione tra tematica delle forme e analisi dei processi nel marxismo europeo fra le due guerre (Karl Korsch 1923–1938)', in *Problemi del socialism*, fourth series, XVII, April–June.
Varga, Evgenii 1930, 'Akkumulation und Zusammenbruch des Kapitalismus', *Unter dem Banner des Marxismus*, vol. IV.
Varga, Evgenii 1934, *ienri De Man et son Plan*, Paris: Bureau d'Éditions.
Varga, Evgenii 1969 *Die Krise des Kapitalismus und ihre politischen Folgen*, edited by Elmar Altvater, Frankfurt a.M.: Europäische Verlagsanstalt.
Veca, Salvatore 1977, *Saggio sul programma scientifico di Marx*, Milan: Il Saggiatore.
Vester, Michael 1970, *Die Entstehung des Proletariats als Lernprozess. Zur Soziologie und Geschichte dar Arbeiterbewegung*, Frankfurt am Main Europäische Verlagsanstalt.
Villari, Lucio 1975, 'Per una ricerca del taylorismo delle origini', *Il Mulino*, 239, May–June.
Von Beckerath, Herbert 1930, *Der moderne industrialismus*, Jena: Fischer.
von Oertzen, Peter 1954, *Betriebsräte in der Novemberrevolution*, Düsseldorf.
Warski, Adolf 1922, *Rosa Luxemburgs Stellung zu den taktischen Problemen der Revolution*, Hamburg: Verlag d. Kommunistischen Internationale.
Weber, Hermann 1963, *Der deutsche Kommunismus. Dokumente 1915–1945, und kommentiert von H. Weber*, Cologne: Kiepenheuer and Witsch.
Weber, Hermann 1969, *Die Wandlung des deutschen Kommunismus. Die Stalinisierung der KPD in der Weimarer Republik*, Frankfurt am Main: Europäische Verlagsanstalt.
Weber, Hermann (ed.) 1993, *Der Gründungsparteitag der KPD. Protokoll und Materialien*, Frankfurt am Main: Dietz.

Weber, Max 1978, *Economy and Society*, volumes 1 and 2, Berkeley: University Press of California Press.
Weber, Max 2009, 'Politics as Vocation', in *From Max Weber: Essays in Sociology*, London: Routledge.
Wehler, Hans-Ulrich 1970, *Krisenherde des Kaiserreichs, 1871–1918*, Göttingen: Vandenhoeck und Ruprecht.
Wehler, Hans-Ulbrich 1971, *Sozialdemokratie und Nationalstaat*, Göttingen: Vandenhoeck und Ruprecht.
Wehler, Hans-Ulbrich 1973a, *Bismarck und der Imperialismus*, Cologne: Kiepenheuer und Witsch.
Wehler, Hans-Uhlbrich 1973b, *Das deutsche Kaiserreich, 1871–1918*, Göttingen: Vandenhoeck und Ruprecht.
Wehler, Hans-Ulbrich 1974, 'Der Aufstieg des Organisierten Kapitalismus und Interventionstaates in Deutschland', in Winkler (ed.).
Winkler, Heinrich August 1964, *Preussischer Liberalismus und deutscher Nationalstaat*, Tübinger: Mohr.
Winkler, Heinrich August 1972, *Mittelstand, Demokratie und Nationalsozialismus*, Munich: Beck.
Winkler, Heinrich August 1974 (ed.) *Organisierter Kapitalismus. Voraussetzungen und Anfänge*, Göttingen: Vandenhoeck und Ruprecht.
Winschuh, Joseph 1941, *Costruzione della nuova Europa*, Florence: Cya Carlo.
Wittfogel, Karl 1924, *Geschichte der bürgerlichen Gesellschaft*, Berlin: Malik-Verlag.
Wittfogel, Karl 1935, 'The Foundations and Stages of Chinese Economic History', *Zetschrift für Socialforschung*, vol. IV, 26–58.
Wittfogel, Karl 1938, 'Die Theorie der orientalischen Gesellschaft', *Zetschrift für Socialforschung*, vol. VII, 90–120.
Wittfogel, Karl 1939, 'The Society of Prehistoric China', vol. VIII, 138–183.
Wittfogel, Karl 1931, *Wirtschaft und Gesellschaft Chinas*, Leipzig: C.L. Hirschfeld.
Woytinsky, Wladimir 1961, *Stormy Passage: A Personal History through two Russian Revolutions to Democracy and Freedom, 1905–1960*, New York: Vanguard.
Wygodski, Witali S. 1967, *Die Geschichte einer grossen Entdeckung*, Berlin: Verlag die Wirtscahft.
Zanardo, Aldo 1974, 'Aspetti del socialismo neo-kantiano in Germania', in *Filosofia e socialismo*, Rome: Editori Riuniti.
Zarone, Giuseppe 1978, 'Bernstein e Weber: revisionismo e democrazia', *Studi storici*, 2: 255–98.
Ziegler, Wilhelm 1932, *Die deutsche Nationalversammlung 1918–1920 und ihr Verfassungswerk*, Berlin: Zentral-Verlag.
Zolo, Danilo 1977, 'Introduzione' in Claus Offe, *Lo stato nel capitalismo maturo*, Turin: Einaudi.

Index

Abendroth   78–79, 82
accumulation   53–54, 117, 137, 143, 154, 159, 234–40, 246, 249, 252
Adler, Max   18, 19, 42, 85, 88–90, 169, 177
Adorno, Theodor   53, 115, 234, 256–61
Agosti, Aldo   153
agriculture   86, 139
alienation   35, 91, 193, 195, 261
allegory   165, 170
Althusser, Louis   35, 263, 269–70, 272
Altvater, Elmer   264
Americanisation   160
aporia   36, 51–52, 56, 71, 134, 141, 148, 176–77
Asor Rosa, Alberto   1–5, 7, 9, 12, 26, 76
Austria   6, 41, 63
Austro-Marxism   2, 5, 11, 16–17, 42, 51, 173, 217, 225
   neo-Kantian   92, 177
autonomies   15–16, 20–25, 46, 53, 63, 66, 71, 73–74, 200, 207, 224, 265–66, 268
autonomisation   22–23, 153, 178

Backhaus, Hans-Georg   180, 257
Badaloni, Nicola   206–14
Bakunin, Mikhail   188
banks   138–39, 158–59
   central   114–15
barbarism   119, 253
Bauer, Otto   5–6, 12, 27, 42, 50, 63, 226, 236, 239–41, 266
Baumann, Kurt   253
Bentham, Jeremy   7, 67
Bernstein, Eduard   37, 46, 129, 136, 146, 167, 170, 173, 176
Bettelheim, Charles   83
Bismarck, Otto von   64, 99, 220
Bobbio, Norberto   31, 264
Böhm-Bawerk, Eugen von   150, 238
Bologna, Sergio   4, 13, 26, 28, 84, 116, 159, 170–71
Bolshevism   6, 26, 92, 177
Bonacchi, Gabriella   6, 188, 207
Bonapartism   226
Borkenau, Franz   234
bourgeoisie   11–12, 44, 48, 82, 99, 124–26, 135–36, 141–42, 199, 203, 212

bourgeois revolution   99, 126, 188, 197
Brandler, Heinrich   98, 102
Braunthal, Julius   176, 178, 241
breakdown   38, 41, 52, 54, 116–17, 121–59, 162–63, 165–66, 172–75, 182–83, 234, 236, 239–41
Buckmiller, Michael   87, 170
Bukharin, Nikolai   172, 241, 252
bureaucracy   12, 24, 27, 82, 228

Cacciari, Massimo   4, 7, 10–19, 22, 24–26, 37, 40, 83–84, 90–91, 93, 170–71
Caesarism   45, 265
capital   3, 13, 15, 18, 20–25, 33–35, 106–7, 111–13, 138–40, 158–59, 161–65, 169–70, 172–73, 179–87, 193, 211–13, 235–38, 249–54
   organic composition of   183, 249
catastrophe   25, 53, 118, 147, 154, 167, 213
civil society   25, 44, 53, 87, 108–9, 188–89, 194, 263, 265, 269
class consciousness   89, 91–93, 119, 161, 177, 180, 187, 191, 193, 196, 199, 204–5, 242–43, 261
class struggle   20, 86, 89, 117–20, 122, 124, 126–27, 178, 181–82, 188–89, 195, 204, 207, 212–13, 241–42
Collotti, Enzo   12, 26, 64
Communist International (Comintern)   65, 106, 122, 131, 138, 140–41, 152–54, 157
consciousness   81, 87, 89–90, 128, 134, 178, 180, 187, 197–99, 204–5, 210, 212, 259–61
council communism   2, 5, 13, 16, 18, 29, 121, 142, 145, 173
councils   79–82, 85–88, 90, 93–98, 102–4, 106–8, 111, 118, 137, 141, 200, 202
crisis theories   129, 141, 143, 146, 151, 157, 162, 165–68, 173–74, 181, 186, 248–49, 251–52
Critical Theory   30, 33, 51, 61, 116, 173, 179–80, 233, 247, 255, 260–62
Croce, Benedetto   192, 196, 207–9, 211–12
Cunow, Heinrich   129–30

Däumig, Ernst   93, 98, 101–3, 106
Dawes Plan   14, 115, 220
democracy   17, 63, 67, 210, 222, 226

dialectic   10–11, 34–35, 37, 82, 85, 162, 164, 192, 194, 197, 199, 252, 254, 256–57, 261
Della Volpe, Galvano   4, 34, 192–93, 195
Dietzgen, Joseph   133
Dilthey, Wilhelm   46
Dobb, Maurice   239, 249
Dutschke, Rudi   92

Ebert, Friedrich   81
economics   40, 44, 46, 51, 86–87, 154, 159, 174–75, 228, 233
    the primacy of   62, 64, 219
Engels, Friedrich   143, 182, 188, 208, 238
Erfurt Programme   80, 130

factories   3, 20, 43, 83–84, 94, 102–4, 107–8, 159, 163–64, 258
fascism   69, 135, 143, 154, 157, 169, 216, 219, 226, 228, 230
fetishism   35, 109, 112, 133, 151, 193, 195, 200
First World War   2, 13, 251
Fischer, Gustav   109
Fordism   159, 217–18
Foucault, Michel   75, 270–71
Frankfurt School   1–2, 5, 32, 51–52, 155, 161, 219, 255

Gramsci, Antonio   4, 6, 135, 141, 159–60, 206–12, 214, 266, 270–71
Great Depression   37, 46, 61, 216, 218, 265
Grossman, Henryk   116–17, 143–47, 149, 151, 155–59, 171–75, 178–79, 181–83, 186–87, 207, 235–45, 248–49, 251, 256–57
Grünberg, Carl   115

Habermas, Jürgen   54–56, 59–61, 71, 176, 218, 232, 261
Hegel, G.W.F.   25, 40, 44, 193–97, 203–4
hegemony   24, 74, 99, 107, 159, 195, 210, 269
Heidegger, Martin   10, 19, 27, 260
Hilferding, Rudolf   41–42, 46, 50, 136–37, 146, 150–55, 157–58, 173, 176, 178, 221–24, 227, 250
History and Class Consciousness   191, 199, 205
Hölz, Max   103
Horkheimer, Max   52, 219, 228, 234, 247, 251, 257, 260

ideology   55, 66, 69, 83, 86, 91–92, 98, 197–99, 203–4, 259–60, 262, 268, 270–71, 273
ideology critique   45, 65, 203, 255, 260, 262, 264
immanence   20, 25, 92
imperialism   69, 124–25, 131–32, 135, 137, 140, 144, 152, 155, 159, 162, 171–72

Jacobinism   133, 203
Jay, Martin   51, 228
Junius Pamphlet   80
Junkers   99, 104

Kalecki, Michael   157, 160, 231
Kant, Immanuel   90
Kautsky, Karl   122, 124–29, 131–32, 135–36, 139, 163, 170, 173, 201–2
Kelsen, Hans   5, 50, 64–66, 70, 222–23, 264
Keynes, J.M.   62, 66–67, 72–73, 84, 100, 106, 187, 189
Kirchheimer, Otto   62–63, 226–28, 267
Korsch, Karl   85–89, 92, 107–9, 116–18, 129, 143, 146–49, 151, 166–71, 173–76, 184–85, 187–89, 191–205
KPD (German Communist Party)   93, 95, 97, 101–2, 110, 116, 137, 188
Krahl, Hans-Jürgen   176, 179, 187, 242, 260
Kun, Béla   102, 131

Labriola, Antonio   2, 27, 206–9, 212, 214
Lassalle, Ferdinand   251
Lauer, Michael   172
Lenin, V.I.   12, 20–21, 113–14, 124–26, 135, 138–40, 158–59, 163, 168–69, 171, 191–92, 209, 250, 252
Leninism   88, 92, 121–23, 135, 169, 192, 195–96, 200–202, 226
Levi, Paul   80, 99–104
Liebknecht, Karl   136
Lih, Lars   21, 27
Lukács, Georg   92–93, 103, 170–71, 187, 191–92, 195–96, 198–99, 204–5, 243, 258–61
Luporini, Cesare   119, 170, 179, 181, 186, 212–13, 268
Luxemburg, Rosa   80, 117, 126, 131–32, 166, 170–74, 236–37, 241, 252

INDEX

Malthus, Thomas   251
Mandelbaum, Kurt   166, 234–36, 245, 253, 256
Marcuse, Herbert   228, 234, 255–56
Marx, Karl   35–38, 40–41, 43–44, 53, 112, 142–43, 150–52, 156, 164–65, 169–70, 172–73, 176, 180–82, 185–86, 188–89, 193–99, 210–12, 236–40, 246–51
Mattick, Paul   117–19, 149–51, 156–57, 166, 172–75, 178, 181, 186–87, 235–37, 239–42, 249
money   84, 106, 111–12, 114–15, 155, 180, 248, 254

National Socialism   33, 62, 64, 69, 104, 217, 221, 224, 253
Negative Dialectics   92, 260
Negri, Antonio   3, 4, 57
Negt, Oskar   31, 87, 89, 180, 187, 204, 242
New Deal   106, 114–15, 143, 216, 228, 253, 269
Nietzsche, Friedrich   1, 7, 10, 20
Nolte, Ernst   82
Noske, Gustav   81, 99

October Revolution   92, 122, 137, 216, 251
organised capitalism   30, 33, 42, 46, 51, 54–55, 61–64, 68, 70, 121–59, 219, 221–22, 224–25

Pannekoek, Anton   117–18, 132–36, 138, 142, 145, 147, 149, 151, 166, 174–76, 178, 181–82
Panzieri, Raniero   162–64, 166, 183, 185, 258
parlamentarianism   253
Piazzi, Alessandro   2, 26
planner-state   57, 59, 65, 215, 230, 268
   authoritarian   227
planning   19, 30, 46, 75–77, 84, 93–94, 113, 154, 163, 184, 230
Polanyi, Karl   33, 68, 216
Pollock, Friedrich   155, 159, 217, 225, 228, 233–34, 244–48, 251–54, 256, 258–59
Popular Front   225
Pozzoli, Claudio   142, 170, 188
Proudhon, Pierre-Joseph.   95, 106, 188

Quaderni Rossi   3, 27, 162, 200

Rabinbach, Anton   219
Radek, Karl   102, 131

Rathenau, Walter   1, 10, 13–16, 66, 267
rationalisation   11, 13, 17–19, 41–44, 46–48, 53, 59, 62, 64–65, 68–69, 83, 217–19, 263–73
regulation   81, 115, 154, 167, 233, 251
Renner, Karl   42, 46, 50, 177, 222–23
reproduction   118, 121, 144, 149, 157, 159–60, 182, 186, 189, 233, 237, 265, 267
   expanded   156, 171–72, 236
   social   60, 70–71, 76, 181, 189, 267
revolutionary subjectivity   117, 132, 173, 195, 205, 213, 241, 261
revolutionary theory   180, 184, 202, 204
Ricardo, David   203–4, 238, 248
Rodbertus, Johann Karl   251
Roosevelt, Franklin D.   235, 269
Rosdolsky, Roman   174, 179–80, 237, 239–40, 250, 254
Rosenberg, Arthur   69, 78, 84, 101, 110–11, 115, 128, 218

Schacht, Hjalmar   111–14, 221
Schmidt, Alfred   52, 179–80, 186–87, 242–43
Schmitt, Carl   1, 20, 39, 65, 227
Schumpeter, Joseph   30, 37–38, 41–43, 47–48, 50, 53, 62, 65, 69, 72–73, 222
science   36–37, 40, 44, 130, 133–34, 186, 201, 206, 210, 247–48, 264–65
Second International   122–24, 128–29, 136, 139–41, 144–45, 159, 162, 166, 168, 176, 179, 202, 204, 207, 250–51
simple reproduction   37, 149, 151, 156, 173, 240
social democracy   6, 17–18, 41–42, 77, 79–80, 84–85, 90–92, 99, 109, 111, 136–37, 176–77, 222–24, 226
socialisation programme   78–79, 83, 93
social sciences   31, 41, 46, 51, 254, 257, 265
Sohn-Rethel, Alfred   55–56, 58, 62, 179, 218, 220
Sorel, Georges   148, 168, 170, 208–9, 212
Soviet Union   84, 88, 104, 115, 234, 246, 253, 260
SPD (German Socialist Party)   63, 79–83, 85, 91, 93, 102, 111, 116, 129, 136
Spengler, Oswald   1, 43
Sraffa, Piero   211
Stalin, Joseph   114
Stalinism   192, 195, 266

state apparatus   57, 89, 113, 226
state capitalism   131, 143, 146, 152–53, 155, 157, 160, 172, 234, 253–54
Sternberg, Fritz   144, 147–48, 166, 171–72, 241
subjectivity   19, 76, 87–89, 92–93, 106–7, 119, 132, 161, 176–77, 213, 272
surplus value   34, 96, 112, 140, 152, 154, 159, 165, 172, 236–37, 249
syndicalism   92

Tafuri, Manfredo   92
Thalheimer, August   98, 102, 226, 266
Third International   31, 90–91, 99–102, 120, 131, 141, 160, 163, 200, 204
totality   25, 40, 60, 91, 145, 150, 175, 179–82, 196–99, 209–10, 213
Tronti, Mario   3–4, 6, 12, 20–23, 25–27, 40, 73, 99, 200
Tugan-Baranowski, Mikhail   156, 236, 250

underconsumption   144, 153–54, 172, 250, 252

Vacca, Giuseppe   26, 148–49, 196–201, 203
Varga, Eugen   153–55, 157, 238
Villari, Lucio   12–14, 22, 28, 159

Wagemann, Ernst   156, 225
war communism   246
war credits   84, 136
Weber, Max   10–12, 41–47, 51, 54, 61, 92, 137, 219, 223, 228, 264–65, 270
Weimar Constitution   78, 81–82, 226–27, 267
Western Marxism   123, 130, 166, 177, 191–92, 196, 235
Wittfogel, Karl   234, 236
Wittgenstein, Ludwig   1, 10, 12
Workerism   2–4

Zetkin, Clara   98, 102
Zusammenbruchstheorie   122, 129–30, 143, 163, 165–66, 171

www.ingramcontent.com/pod-product-compliance
Lightning Source LLC
Chambersburg PA
CBHW071230070526
44583CB00017B/2127